THE
AMERICAN
EXPRESS
POCKET GUIDE TO

ENGLAND
& WALES

John Tomes

with a major contribution by
Michael Jackson

SIMON AND SCHUSTER
NEW YORK

The Author
John Tomes is the author of the Blue Guides to Belgium and
Luxembourg, Holland, Scotland, and Wales and the Marches
(Ernest Benn Ltd). He also contributed the chapters on
Scotland and on Wales and the Welsh Borders to *The National
Trust Atlas*, and has had a number of short stories published.

Contributors
Michael Jackson (Restaurants and a selection of hotels
including those in London, and Accommodations, food and
drink in Planning)
Catherine Jackson (compiled Basic information, the Calendar
of events in Planning, and, in the A–Z, London, Shopping and
Events)
Fiona Duncan (compiled Nightlife)

Acknowledgments
The author's thanks go to his wife who, notwithstanding the demands of
her own profession, still managed to combine the roles of navigator,
critic and marathon typist. The author and publishers would also like to
thank the countless people at information desks throughout England and
Wales who have been so generous with time, advice and documentation.

Few travel books are without errors, and no guidebook can ever be
completely up-to-date, for telephone numbers and opening hours change
without warning, and hotels and restaurants come under new
management, which can affect standards. While every effort has been
made to ensure that all information is accurate at the time of going to
press, the publishers will be glad to receive any corrections and
suggestions for improvements, which can be incorporated in the next
edition. Price information in this book is accurate at the time of going to
press, but prices and currency exchange rates do fluctuate. Dollar
amounts relate to exchange rates in effect in mid-1983.

Editor Gilly Abrahams
Executive Editor Hal Robinson
Chief Sub-Editor David
Townsend Jones
Researcher Catherine Jackson
Editorial Assistants Alison
Hancock, Sue McKinstry, Paddy
Seymour
Indexers Teamworkers

Art Editor Eric Drewery
Designer Nigel O'Gorman
Illustrators Jeremy Ford (David
Lewis Artists), Illustrated Arts,
Rodney Paull
Map Editor David Haslam

Executive Art Editor Douglas Wilson
Production Sarah Goodden
Consultant Editors Ila Stanger, Maria Shaw (*Travel & Leisure*)

Edited and designed by
Mitchell Beazley International Limited
87–89 Shaftesbury Avenue
London W1V 7AD
© Mitchell Beazley Publishers 1984
All rights reserved including the
right of reproduction in whole or
in part in any form
Published by Simon and Schuster, Inc.
Simon & Schuster Building
Rockefeller Center
1230 Avenue of the Americas
New York, New York 10020

Library of Congress Cataloging
in Publication Data
Tomes, John.
The American Express pocket guide
to England and Wales.
Includes index.
1. England – Description and travel –
1971-   – Guide-books.
2. Wales – Description and travel –
1981-   – Guide-books.
I. Jackson, Michael, 1942- .
II. American Express Company.
III. Title. IV. Title: Pocket guide
to England and Wales.
DA650.T62 1984 914.2'04858 83–17597
ISBN 0–671–50023–6

Maps in 4-color by Clyde Surveys Ltd, Maidenhead, England, based on
copyrighted material of John Bartholomew & Son Limited, Edinburgh, Scotland.
Typeset by Vantage Photosetting Co. Ltd, Eastleigh, England.
Printed and bound in Hong Kong by Mandarin Offset International Ltd.

Contents

How to use this book

The American Express Pocket Guide to England and Wales is an encyclopedia of travel information, organized in the sections listed on the previous page. There is also a comprehensive index and gazetteer (pages 260–272), and there are full-color maps at the end of the book.

For easy reference, the *England A–Z*, the *Wales A–Z* and other sections are, as far as possible, arranged alphabetically. For the organization of the book as a whole, see *Contents*. For places that do not have separate entries in the *A–Z*, see the *Index and gazetteer*.

Abbreviations
As far as possible only standard abbreviations have been used. These include days of the week, months, points of the compass, addresses (Rd., Sq., St.), Saint (St), C for century, and measurements. See introduction to *A–Z* for less common abbreviations.

Floors
To conform with European usage, 'first floor' is used throughout the book to refer to the floor above the ground floor, 'second floor' to the floor above that, and so on.

Cross-references
Whenever a place or section title is printed in *sans serif italics* (for example, *Basic information* or *Bath*) in the text, this indicates that you can turn to the appropriate heading in the book for further information. Cross-references in this typeface refer either to sections in the book – *Basic information* or *Planning*, for example – or to individual entries in one of the *A–Z* sections, such as *Bath* (in the *England A–Z*), or *Swansea* (in the *Wales A–Z*). For convenient reference, use the headings printed at the top corner of the page (see, for example, *Basic information* on pages 7–15, *Bath* on pages 52–56, or *Swansea* on page 246).

Bold italics are used to identify sub-sections. For instance: 'see **Calendar of Events** in *Planning*' will refer you to page 30;

How entries are organized

Carlisle
Map 14C6. Cumbria. 58 miles (93km) w of Newcastle-upon-Tyne. Population: 72,000 i Old Town Hall, Greenmarket ☎ (0228) 25517.

Starting as a Roman camp close to *Hadrian's Wall* and later sacked by the Norsemen, Carlisle then experienced centuries of assault by the Scots who finally wrecked much of the **cathedral**.

Ⓗ **Crown and Mitre**
English St., Carlisle, Cumbria CA3 8HZ ☎ (0228) 25491 ⓣ 64183
▯▯ ⌂ 94 ▭ 94 ▭ ▭ ▭ ⇌ AE ⓞ ⓞ VISA
Location: Overlooking Market Sq. Behind a Victorian facade this is a solid, spacious hotel with two cheerful bars, the pub-like **Railway Tavern** with appropriate decor and the more conventional **Peace and Plenty**.
‡ ▢ ▱ ☜ ☳

---

in the entry on the Assembly Rooms in *Bath* (on page 52) there is a reference to the **Museum of Costume**, which is described below.

Bold type is used in the text primarily for emphasis, to draw attention to something of special interest or importance. It is also used to pick out places – shops or museums, for example – that do not have separate descriptions of their own.

Map references
Each of the color maps at the end of the book is divided into a grid of squares, which are identified vertically by letters (A, B, C, D, etc.) and horizontally by numbers (1, 2, 3, 4, etc.). A map reference identifies the page and square in which the town or place of interest can be found – thus *Abbotsbury* is located in the square identified as Map **4M6**.

Price categories
Price categories are denoted by the symbols ☐ ☐☐ ☐☐☐ ☐☐☐☐ and ☐☐☐☐☐ which signify cheap, inexpensive, moderately priced, expensive and very expensive, respectively. In the cases of hotels and restaurants these correspond approximately with the following actual prices, which give a guideline at the time of printing. Although actual prices will inevitably increase, in most cases the relative price category – for example, expensive or cheap – will be likely to remain more or less the same.

Price categories	Corresponding to approximate prices	
	for **hotels**	for **restaurants**
	double room	*meal for one*
	(a single room is	*with service,*
	significantly	*tax and*
	cheaper)	*house wine*
☐ cheap	under $38	under $11
☐☐ inexpensive	$38–53	$11–15
☐☐☐ moderate	$53–68	$15–23
☐☐☐☐ expensive	$68–91	$23–38
☐☐☐☐☐ very expensive	over $91	over £38

––––– Bold blue type for entry headings.

––––– Blue italics for address, practical information and symbols, encapsulating standard information and special recommendations. For list of symbols see page 6.

––––– Black text for description.
––––– Sans serif italics used for cross-references to other entries.
––––– Bold type used for emphasis.

––––– Entries for hotels and restaurants follow the same organization.

––––– In hotels, symbols indicating special facilities appear at the end of the entry.

5

Key to symbols

☎	Telephone	✹	Garden
⑩	Telex	⇚	Outstanding views
★	Not to be missed	⇶	Swimming pool
☆	Worth a detour	⇗	Good beach nearby
♣	Good value (in its class)	✺	Tennis court(s)
i	Tourist information	✓	Golf course
⛟	Car parking	☝	Riding facilities
Ⓗ	Hotel	➤	Fishing facilities
⬛	Simple (hotel)	☖	Conference facilities
🏛	Luxury (hotel)	Ⓡ	Restaurant
▭	Cheap	▰	Simple (restaurant)
▱	Inexpensive	△	Luxury (restaurant)
▰	Moderately priced	▱	A la carte available
▰	Expensive	▬	Set (fixed price) menu available
▰	Very expensive		
✿	Number of rooms	▬	Good for wines
▭	Rooms with private bathroom	◢	Open-air dining available
▦	Air conditioning	🏛	Building of architectural interest
▱	Residential terms available	†	Church/cathedral
AE	American Express	💲	Entrance free
CB	Carte Blanche	💲	Entrance fee payable
ⓓ	Diners Club	💲	Entrance expensive
ⓜ	MasterCard/Access	✗	Photography not permitted
VISA	Visa/Barclaycard		
▱	Secure garage	X	Guided tour available
▬	Own restaurant	🚩	Guided tour compulsory
▱	Meal obligatory	▰	Cafeteria
▱	Quiet hotel	✱	Special interest for children
⇕	Elevator		
⚕	Facilities for the disabled	⚘	Cocktail bar
▭	TV in each room	●	Disco dancing
▱	Telephone in each room	✿	Casino/gambling
		♫	Live music
▰	Dogs not allowed	⋓	Dancing

Before you go

Documents required

A valid national passport is usually all that is necessary to visit Britain, since citizens of the USA, Commonwealth and most European and South American countries do not need visas. Visitors from EEC countries need only an identity card.

An International Certificate of Vaccination is not usually required. However, it is wise to check if one is needed for re-entry into your country of origin.

International drivers' licenses are not required. A full valid national license will suffice. If you are bringing your own car, carry the vehicle registration certificate, an insurance certificate or green card, and a national identity sticker.

Travel and medical insurance

It is advisable to take out an insurance policy covering loss of deposits paid to airlines, hotels, tour operators etc., and emergency costs, such as special tickets home.

Free treatment under the National Health Service is available in emergencies, and to visitors from countries with reciprocal health service agreements. Payment will be required for treatment of previously known conditions, and for dental and ophthalmic treatment, so check that you are suitably insured.

Money

There is no exchange control in Britain, and therefore no limit on the amount of any currency that can be imported or exported.

The unit of currency is the pound sterling (£), divided into 100 pence (p). There are coins for $\frac{1}{2}$p, 1p, 2p, 5p, 10p, 20p, 50p and £1; and notes for £1, £5, £10, £20 and £50.

Travelers cheques issued by American Express, Thomas Cook, Barclays and Citibank are widely recognized; make sure you read the instructions included with your travelers cheques. It is important to note separately the serial numbers of your cheques and the telephone number to call in case of loss. Specialist travelers cheque companies such as American Express provide extensive local refund facilities through their own offices or agents.

Readily accepted charge and credit cards are American Express, Diners Club, MasterCard (linked in Britain with Access) and Visa (linked with Barclaycard); Carte Blanche is less widely accepted.

Customs

If you are visiting the United Kingdom for less than six months, you are entitled to bring in, free of duty and tax, all personal effects that you intend to take with you when you leave, with the exception of tobacco products, alcoholic drinks, perfume and toilet water. Bring dated receipts for valuable items.

Duty-free allowances (correct at time of writing) for import into Britain are given below. The figures in parentheses are the increased allowances for goods obtained duty and tax paid in EEC countries. Travelers under 17 are not entitled to the allowances on tobacco products and alcoholic drinks.
Tobacco products 200(300) cigarettes *or* 100(150) cigarillos *or* 50(75) cigars *or* 250(400g) tobacco. *Or* if you live outside Europe, 400 cigarettes *or* 200 cigarillos *or* 100 cigars *or* 500g tobacco.

Basic information

Alcoholic drinks   1(1.5) liter spirits or strong liquor (over 22% alcohol by volume) *or* 2(3) liters of alcoholic drink under 22% alcohol, fortified wine or sparkling wine *plus* 2(4) liters of still table wine.

Perfume   50g/60cc/2 fl oz (75g/90cc/3 fl oz).

Toilet water   250cc/9 fl oz (375cc/13 fl oz).

Other goods   Goods to the value of £28 (£120).

Prohibited and restricted goods include controlled drugs, firearms, fireworks, ammunition, explosives, other weapons and obscene publications (books, magazines, films, video tapes, photographs, etc). Dogs, cats and most other mammals that are brought into the country must be put in quarantine for six months. The quarantine period for birds is 35 days. Bringing pets on a short vacation is therefore not possible.

Further details regarding prohibited and restricted goods can be obtained from **H.M. Customs and Excise** (*Kent House, Upper Ground, London SE1 9PS* ☎ *(01) 928–0533*).

For exemption from Value Added Tax (VAT) on goods bought in Britain, see **Shopping** in *Planning*.

Getting there

London's Heathrow Airport is one of the busiest in the world, with both international and domestic flights on a wide range of airlines. Other major international airports include Gatwick, Manchester, Birmingham, East Midlands, Luton and Stansted, the last two being mainly used for charter flights. Smaller airports operating only a few international flights include Bristol, Exeter, Leeds, Liverpool and Southampton. See *A–Z* entries for telephone numbers.

Only Cunard operates frequent transatlantic sailings but ships operated by other lines sail to English ports (usually Liverpool or Southampton) less regularly. A network of short-distance passenger and car ferries links Britain with French, Belgian, Dutch, West German, Irish and Scandinavian ports. The main English and Welsh ports of entry are Dover, Folkestone, Harwich, Felixstowe, Southampton, Plymouth and Fishguard.

Climate

British weather is rarely given to extremes, but it is unreliable, can change character quickly, and can vary enormously from place to place. Average daytime temperatures for London range from 6°C(43°F) in winter (Dec–Feb) to 21°C(70°F) in summer (June–Aug), only occasionally going below 0°C(32°F) or above 27°C(80°F). Northern England is generally colder than southern England, however, while southwest England and the west coast are warmer but also more rainy than inland and eastern England.

London's annual rainfall is 24ins (60cm). Most of it falls during the winter, but rain is not uncommon at any time of the year.

Clothes

In the summer light clothes are adequate, but remember to include some protection against showers, and a sweater or jacket for cool evenings. During the rest of the year, take warm clothes. It is always wise to take an umbrella.

On the whole the British have a fairly casual attitude to what you wear although some traditional hotels and restaurants will expect conventional dress.

General delivery

Letters marked *Poste restante* and addressed to specific post offices or the central post office of a town will be kept for one month. Identification will be needed when collecting mail. American Express and Thomas Cook offer the same service to their customers.

Getting around

Flying

There is a good domestic network, the principal carrier being British Airways (☎ *(01) 370–5411*), with flights to and from Heathrow, Gatwick, Birmingham, Leeds, Liverpool, Manchester, Newcastle and Penzance as well as to Scotland, Ireland, the Channel Islands, the Scilly Isles and the Isle of Man. Only seasonal routes operate from Cardiff, Swansea and some other cities. British Caledonian (☎ *(01) 668–4222*), British Midland Airways (☎ *(01) 581–0864*) and Dan-Air (☎ *(01) 638–1747*) are some of the other airlines operating internal services.

The British Airways shuttle service, whereby a seat is guaranteed and passengers check in only 10mins before departure, operates from Heathrow to Manchester as well as to airports in Scotland and Northern Ireland.

Railway services

British Rail operates a fast and efficient Inter-City service, with restaurant and/or buffet cars on most trains. The new high-speed trains are even faster and more comfortable. First-class tickets cost about 50 percent more than second-class, and in each class there are both smoking and no-smoking cars.

For long-distance overnight journeys, sleeping cars with two berths per cabin for second-class passengers and single berth for first-class are available. The Motorail service enables you to travel comfortably and quickly between certain cities with your car on the same train. It is wise to make a reservation.

British Rail offers several worthwhile deals including one-day, weekend and three-month round-trip tickets, and special family or group deals are available from time to time. Visitors from abroad are eligible for a BritRail Pass, which gives unlimited rail travel for specified lengths of time. This ticket must be bought outside the UK.

Buses

An impressive and inexpensive system of long-distance buses (called coaches, and referred to as such throughout this book) links major cities, and local buses link cities with towns and villages. National Express is the largest coach company.

Foreign visitors are entitled to a BritExpress Travelcard, which may be purchased at major reservations offices if you show your passport. This allows unlimited coach travel for either five or ten days.

Taxis

The black London taxi is easily recognized and hailed, but in other towns and cities the simplest way to find a taxi is to look in the telephone directory Yellow Pages under *Taxis* or *Minicabs*.

Alternatively, there is usually a taxi stand outside major railway stations. Traveling by taxi is one of the more expensive methods of transportation; extra costs may include a surcharge for night trips and for extra baggage. The taxi driver will expect a tip of 10–15% of the fare.

Getting around by car

If you are intending to drive a car in Britain, you must be over 17 years old. Remember to drive on the left, and pass only on the right. See also *Documents required* in **Before you go**.

Standard international road signs are used. A solid white line across the road at an intersection means that you must stop before crossing; a broken white line means that you must give way to traffic on the road you are crossing or joining. A solid white line down the center of the road means no passing, and the line must not be crossed at all. If there is a broken line you may pass if it is safe to do so.

Pedestrian crossings are marked by black and white zones across the road and are sometimes controlled by traffic lights. If there are no traffic lights, pedestrians have the right of way. If there are traffic lights, pedestrians and traffic are controlled by them.

Car horns must not be used from 11.30pm–7am in built-up areas (streets with lights) except in emergencies, and seat belts must be worn by those sitting in the front seats of the car.

The speed limit in built-up areas is 30mph (48kph); on four-lane highways and superhighways (motorways) it is 70mph (112kph) and on all other roads it is 60mph (96kph) unless otherwise specified.

Roads in Britain consist of motorways (usually three lanes of traffic each way) denoted by the letter M; A-roads (primary roads, often four-lanes); B-roads (secondary roads); and minor roads.

Parking can be extremely difficult in towns and it is often advisable to go to the nearest public parking lot, where you may have to pay. Many towns operate a system whereby you can park for a limited time in restricted areas, either free or on a meter. Some towns operate a disc system whereby you display a disc indicating your time of arrival and move the car again after a limited period (usually two hours). Discs can be obtained free from local newsdealers or other shops.

Curbside markings also control parking: one yellow line prohibits parking during the working day Mon–Sat, and two yellow lines prohibit parking at any time. Look for an explanatory sign in a restricted zone. Parking is always prohibited near pedestrian crossings and intersections. For violating parking regulations you will be fined (but not on the spot), and in major towns you may have your car towed away or immobilized by the police who will charge a large sum for its recovery. For more details see *The Highway Code*, an inexpensive publication available from most newsdealers.

If you belong to an FIA-affiliated motoring organization in your own country and are bringing your own car, you can use the services of the Automobile Association (AA) and the Royal Automobile Club (RAC) (see **Useful addresses**).

Renting a car

Larger towns have representatives of most major international car rental firms, and you may be able to arrange to pick up the car in one place, including airports and railway stations, and leave it in another. For those intending to return the car to the original departure point, local car rental firms may be cheaper. They are listed in the Yellow Pages under *Car Hire – Self drive*.

To rent a car you must be over 21 (or 25 in some cases) and hold a valid national license. You can opt for either a daily rate plus a mileage charge, or a weekly rate with unlimited mileage. Insurance is usually included, but check before you leave. You may be asked to leave a cash deposit larger than your likely eventual overall charge, from which the difference will be refunded when you return the car; this can usually be avoided if you pay with a credit card.

Getting around on foot
Britain's countryside is easily accessible by a vast number of public footpaths and bridlepaths over land that is both publicly and privately owned. An excellent book with suggested walks and maps is *Walker's Britain* (Pan/Ordnance Survey). Alternatively, contact the **Ramblers Association** (*1 – 5 Wandsworth Rd., London SW8 2LJ* ☎ *(01) 582 – 6826*).

On-the-spot information

Public holidays
New Year's Day, Jan 1; Good Friday; Easter Monday; May Day (first Mon in May); Spring Bank Holiday (last Mon in May); August Bank Holiday (last Mon in Aug); Christmas Day, Dec 25; Boxing Day, Dec 26. All banks and almost all shops, offices and restaurants are closed on these days.

Time zones
British time is Greenwich Mean Time (GMT) in winter and changes to European Summer Time (EST), 1hr ahead of GMT, from the end of Mar to late Oct.

Banks and currency exchange
All banks are open Mon – Fri 9.30am – 3.30pm and some open on Sat 9.30am – noon. Money can also be exchanged outside these hours at *bureaux de change*, often to be found in hotels, railway stations, travel agencies and airports. Travelers cheques are widely accepted; the exchange rate is about the same as for cash.

Shopping and business hours
Most shops and businesses open Mon – Sat 9am – 5.30pm, but small food shops often open earlier in the country and may stay open later in towns; many shops close for an hour at lunchtime, usually 1 – 2pm. The shops in many towns close for half or even the whole day once a week (often Wed or Thurs). Large towns often have one evening of late-night shopping.

Rush hours
Rush hours in major cities are best avoided and are at their worst between 8 – 9.30am and 5 – 6.30pm. Traffic leaving large cities on weekends can cause extra congestion.

Post and telephone services
Post offices are usually open Mon – Fri 9am – 5.30pm, Sat 9am – 12.30pm.

Stamps are obtainable at post offices and occasionally from machines. There are two classes of inland mail, but the second

class is only a little cheaper and can sometimes be a lot slower.
You will also have to specify which rate you want for
international mail, as mail does not automatically go air mail to
countries outside Europe. When sending a parcel out of the
country you will have to fill in a customs form declaring the
contents. Mail can be posted in red mailboxes as well as in the
mailboxes at post offices.

Public telephones are found in red kiosks and in booths in
post offices, hotels, pubs, railway stations and other public
places. Every place has an area code which may have up to six
numbers. The area code is not used for local calls but it must
always be used when telephoning from outside the area. Most
international calls can be dialed direct from public telephones;
if the codes are not displayed in the booth call the operator
(☎ *100*) and ask for International Directory Enquiries.

The majority of public telephones take 5p and 10p (rarely
50p) coins. Do not insert the coins until you have dialed and
heard the call answered (a series of rapid beeps). When these
beeps recur, you must put in another coin if you wish to
continue your call or you will be cut off a few seconds later. The
ringing tone is a repeated double trill, and an intermittent shrill
tone means that the line is busy.

See also *Telephone services* in **Useful addresses**.

Public rest rooms
Well-maintained rest rooms will be found in all large public
buildings, such as museums, art galleries, department stores
and railway stations.

The public rest rooms in most towns are often dirty and
vandalized, although there are exceptions. They are usually free
of charge, but you may need a small coin to gain access, or to pay
to use a proper bathroom.

Electric current
The electric current is 240V AC. Plugs have three rectangular
pins and take 13-amp fuses. Visitors from abroad will need
adapters for their appliances.

Laws and regulations
Pubs are open on weekdays 11am–3pm and 6–10.30pm, but
there are different hours on weekends and also in large towns
and cities, where longer hours may apply. Other regulations
worth noting: smoking in public places such as theaters and
cinemas is usually restricted to certain areas and may be
prohibited entirely; non-medicinal drugs, in any form, are
illegal; and hitchhiking is prohibited on superhighways.

Customs and etiquette
The British are a tolerant people, so visitors are unlikely to
offend by tripping up on some point of etiquette. In most
circumstances, however, loud and obtrusive behavior is
frowned upon. The most important custom is that of lining up;
the British line up for everything, and if you do not wait your
turn they will not be amused.

Tipping
A tip of 10–15% is usual in restaurants unless a service charge
has been added to the bill. In hotels a small tip should be given
to the porter and room maid. Taxi drivers also expect about
10–15% of the fare. You need only give small tips to
hairdressers, cloakroom attendants, porters and
doormen.

Disabled visitors
The British Tourist Authority publishes a leaflet, *Britain for the Disabled*, and further information can be obtained from the **Royal Association for Disability and Rehabilitation** (RADAR) (*25 Mortimer St., London W1N 8AB* ☎ *(01) 637–5400*).

Local and foreign publications
Local papers contain information on local events and entertainments. The national papers include *The Times, The Guardian, The Daily Telegraph* and several tabloids such as the *Daily Mirror, Daily Express* and *Daily Mail. The Sunday Times* and *The Observer* are among those published nationally on Sundays. Some national foreign papers are available in the larger towns and cities on the same day as publication; others take a day or two to reach Britain.

Useful addresses

Tourist information
American Express Travel Service 6 Haymarket, London SW1Y 4BS ☎ (01) 930–4411. A valuable source of information for any traveler in need of help, advice or emergency services.
British Tourist Authority 64–65 St James's St., London SW1A 1NF ☎ (01) 499–9325
British Waterways Board Melbury House, Melbury Terrace, London NW1 6JU ☎ (01) 262–6711
Department of the Environment (Directorate of Ancient Monuments & Historic Buildings) 23 Savile Row, London W1X 2HE ☎ (01) 734–6010; *Welsh Office (Ancient Monuments)* Cathays Park, Cardiff CF1 3NQ ☎ (0222) 824249
English Tourist Board ☎ (01) 730–3400
Historic Houses Association 38 Ebury St., London SW1W 0LU ☎ (01) 730–9419
National Gardens Scheme 57 Lower Belgrave St., London SW1W 0LR ☎ (01) 730–0359
National Trust 42 Queen Anne's Gate, London SW1H 9AS ☎ (01) 222–9251
Wales Tourist Board Brunel House, 2 Fitzalan Rd., Cardiff CF2 1UY ☎ (0222) 499909, or 2–4 Maddox St., London W1R 9PN ☎ (01) 409–0969
Y.M.C.A. (National Council) 640 Forest Rd., London E17 3EF ☎ (01) 520–5599
Youth Hostels Association (National Office) Trevelyan House, St Stephen's Hill, St Albans, Herts AL1 2DY ☎ (0727) 55215
 For airlines, see *Flying* in **Getting around**.

Telephone services
To contact the operator, dial 100. To find the number of other telephone services such as international telegrams, telemessage, tourist events, speaking clock, weather and motoring information look in the local telephone dialing code book.

Motoring organizations
Automobile Association Fanum House, 5 New Coventry St., London, W1V 8HT. Information ☎ (01) 954–7373
Royal Automobile Club 49 Pall Mall, London, SW1Y 5JG ☎ (01) 839–7050

Basic information

Major libraries
All major town libraries are free, centrally located and well stocked with books which may be read within the library. In order to take books out, you must join the library which often means having a permanent local address.

Major places of worship
For information contact the following:
American Church ☎ (01) 580–2791
Catholic Information Services ☎ (01) 406–6711
Church of England Information Office ☎ (01) 222–9011
London Central Mosque ☎ (01) 724–3363
Office of the Chief Rabbi ☎ (01) 387–1066

Embassies and consulates in London
Australia Australia House, Strand, WC2 ☎ (01) 438–8000
Belgium 103 Eaton Sq., SW1 ☎ (01) 235–5422
Canada Canada House, Trafalgar Sq., SW1 ☎ (01) 629–9492
Denmark 55 Sloane St., SW1 ☎ (01) 235–1255
Finland 38 Chesham Pl., SW1 ☎ (01) 235–9531
France 24 Rutland Gate, SW7 ☎ (01) 581–5292
Germany (West) 23 Belgrave Sq., SW1 ☎ (01) 235–5033
Ireland 17 Grosvenor Pl., SW1 ☎ (01) 235–2171
Italy 20 Savile Row, W1 ☎ (01) 439–0271
Netherlands 38 Hyde Park Gate, SW7 ☎ (01) 584–5040
New Zealand 80 Haymarket, SW1 ☎ (01) 930–8422
Norway 25 Belgrave Sq., SW1 ☎ (01) 235–7151
Spain 20 Draycott Pl., SW3 ☎ (01) 581–5921
Sweden 23 North Row, W1 ☎ (01) 499–9500
Switzerland 16 Montagu Pl., W1 ☎ (01) 723–0701
USA 24 Grosvenor Sq., W1 ☎ (01) 499–9000

Many countries are represented elsewhere in Britain; check with the London embassy or consulate.

Conversion tables

cm	0	5	10	15	20	25	30
in	0 1 2 3 4 5 6 7 8 9 10 11 12						

Length

meters	0	0.5	1.5	2
ft/yd	0	1ft 2ft 3ft(1yd)		2yd

Distance

km	0 1 2 3 4 5 6 7 8 9 10 11 12 13 14 15 16	
miles	0 1 2 3 4 5 6 7 8 9 10	

Weight

	(¼kg)	(½kg)	(¾kg)	(1kg)
grams	0 100 200 300 400 500 600 700 800 900 1,000			
ounces	0 4 8 12 16 20 24 28 32			
	(¼lb) (½lb) (¾lb) (1lb) (1½lb) (2lb)			

Fluid measures

liters	0 1 2 3 4 5	liters	0 5 10 20 30
imp.pints	0 1 2 3 4 5 6 7 8	imp. gallons	0 1 2 3 4 5 6
US pints	0 1 2 3 4 5 6 7 8	US gallons	0 1 2 3 4 5 6 7

Temperature chart

°C	–15 –10 –5	0 5 10 15 20 25 30 35 36.9 40	100
°F	0 10 20 30 32	40 50 60 70 80 90 98.4 105	212

Emergency information

Emergency services (call free from any telephone)

Police 〕 ☎ 999
Ambulance 〕 You will be asked which service
Fire 〕 you require.

Hospitals with casualty (emergency) departments
In a real emergency an ambulance will take you to the nearest
hospital with a casualty ward. All hospitals are listed in the
Yellow Pages of the telephone directory under *Hospitals* and
will give free out-patient treatment to emergency cases.

Other medical emergencies
If your complaint does not warrant an ambulance or
hospitalization, you will have to call a doctor or dentist and
ask for advice. Consult the Yellow Pages of the telephone
directory. Druggists will not advise or diagnose.

Late-night chemists/drugstores
Many drugstores display a list of late-night pharmacies in
their windows and some local papers publish this
information. The local tourist office, hotels and the police
will also be able to tell you where to find a late-night drugstore.

Help lines
The Samaritans are well represented throughout the
country and will help you talk out your problems. They are
listed in the telephone directory under *Samaritans*.

Automobile accidents
—Do not admit liability or incriminate yourself.
—Ask any witness to stay and give a statement, or at least to
  give his or her name and address.
—Contact the police.
—Exchange names, addresses, car details and insurance
  companies' names and addresses with other driver(s).
—Give a statement to the police who will compile a report
  which insurance companies will accept as authoritative.

Car breakdowns
Call one of the following from the nearest telephone.
—The nearest garage/repair service.
—The police who will put you in touch with the above.
—The number you have been given if you rented the car.
—The AA or RAC if you are a member of an FIA-affiliated
  motoring organization.

Lost passport
Contact the police immediately, then your consulate for
emergency travel documents.

Lost travelers cheques
Notify the local police at once, then follow the instructions
provided with your travelers cheques, or contact the
nearest office of the issuing company. Contact your
consulate or American Express if you are stranded with no
money.

Lost property
Report your loss to the police immediately (many insurance
companies will not recognize claims without a police
report). Special lost property offices include those at major
British Rail stations.

Introduction

The British live under an ancient constitutional monarchy which is probably the world's most stable and most loved. The sovereign reigns aloof from party politics and exercises strictly defined powers, while a historic parliamentary democracy, an independent judiciary and a free press complete the foundations of a structure which as much by tradition as formal procedure emphasizes the importance of the free individual.

London is of course the national capital, and even if in some ways it has traded dignity and elegance for a raffish contemporary conformity the true Londoner would still not dream of living anywhere else. Yet London is only one of England's many regions. The inhabitants of, for example, East Anglia, Merseyside, Yorkshire, Tyneside and the true West Country of Devon and Cornwall betray individual characteristics and attitudes, and even if they all speak the same language it is often with strong regional accents. To the southerner, the industrial North can sometimes seem a remote, incomprehensible and even hostile place; to the northerner, the South can represent a complacent, unproductive and favored land. Yet on the whole the English are a friendly race wherever they live, and visitors will soon discover that two cherished beliefs – that this is a class-ridden society and that the English hide behind an impenetrable reserve – are but myth.

The principality of Wales enjoys a personality very much its own. However diluted now, the people remain basically Celts, more volatile and more emotional than their Anglo-Saxon neighbors. They take pride in their own flag and widely spoken language, and national sentiment has increasingly placed tongue-twisting Welsh beside its English counterpart on signs and notices. Celtic legend, too, is never far away: that fey world of the *Mabinogion* (see ***England and Wales in literature***, below) which to the receptive visitor can endow a mountain, a lake or just a cairn with a magical quality. And music seems all around; to hear a Welshman speak is to hear music, while Welsh male-voice choirs are world-famous.

Who's who in the Royal Family

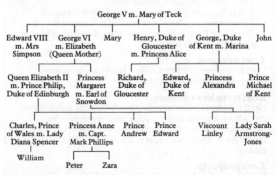

The following section does not presume to offer more than a skeleton of English and Welsh history, together with a glimpse of these countries' achievements in three selected areas: architecture, painting and literature.

Time chart

Prehistoric period

c.5000–	Immigration by Neolithic and Bronze Age peoples,
c.1000BC	the builders of Stonehenge and Avebury.
c.500–	Immigration by the Brythonic (British) Celts from
c.200BC	central Europe.

The Roman Occupation (AD43–c.early 5thC)

AD43	The Romans landed near Richborough.
AD60	Queen Boadicea led a revolt against the Romans.
c.AD78	Agricola exterminated the Druids in Anglesey.
122–30	The building of Hadrian's Wall.
Late 3rdC	Raiding by Angles, Saxons and Jutes forced the construction of the Saxon Shore forts such as Richborough, Pevensey and Portchester.
Late 4th– early 5thC	The Romans gradually withdrew, and Britain slid into the Dark Ages.

The Anglo-Saxon Conquest (5thC– late 8thC)

Angles and Saxons poured in to conquer and settle, partly absorbing the Romano-British inhabitants and partly pushing them westward. England split into several warring kingdoms and Wales into principalities.

663	The Synod of Whitby met to reconcile the conflicting Celtic and Roman strands of Christianity, the outcome being generally in favor of Rome.

The Viking years (793–1066)

865	The Danes overran Northumbria and Mercia.
886	Alfred the Great took London from the Danes.
973	Edgar was accepted by both English and Danes as ruler of all England and as suzerain of Wales and Scotland.
1066	Accession of Harold II who was later defeated at the Battle of Hastings.

The Normans (William I 1066–87, William II 1087–1100, Henry I 1100–35, Stephen 1135–54)

1066	William of Normandy crowned. He encouraged the earls of Chester, Shrewsbury and Hereford to subjugate as much of Wales as they could. By the 12thC virtually the whole of that country had been overrun except for Gwynedd and Powys.

The Plantagenets (Henry II 1154–89, Richard I 1189–99, John 1199–1216, Henry III 1216–72, Edward I 1272–1307, Edward II 1307–27, Edward III 1327–77, Richard II 1377–99)

1194– 1214	Llewelyn ap Iorwerth (the Great) became ruler of Wales.
1215	The barons forced John to sign Magna Carta.
1255	Llewelyn the Last styled himself Prince of Wales.
1264	Simon de Montfort defeated Henry III at Lewes and summoned the first representative national gathering, precursor of parliament.
1277–82	Edward I subjugated Wales.
1301	At Caernarfon Edward I presented his newborn son (later Edward II) as Prince of Wales.
1338	Start of the Hundred Years' War against France.
1348	The Black Death ravaged England and France.
1399	Death of John of Gaunt, Duke of Lancaster. Richard II seized all the Lancastrian estates, an act which quickly led to his deposition by Gaunt's son Henry Bolingbroke who was crowned Henry IV.

17

Culture, history and background

The Lancastrians *(Henry IV 1399–1413, Henry V 1413–22, Henry VI 1422–61)*

1415	Henry V renewed the war against the French whom he defeated at Agincourt.
1431	Henry VI was crowned King of France in Paris, but, inspired by Joan of Arc, the French gradually expelled the English; by 1453 Calais was all they held.
1455	The start of the Wars of the Roses between the houses of Lancaster (red rose) and York (white rose).

The Yorkists *(Edward IV 1461–83, Edward V 1483, Richard III 1483–85)*

1465–71	The Wars of the Roses continued with Edward IV's decisive victory at Tewkesbury in 1471 and the murder soon afterwards of Henry VI.
1483	The boy king, Edward V, murdered in the Tower of London, possibly at the instigation of his uncle, Richard of Gloucester, who assumed the crown as Richard III.
1485	Henry Tudor, the only surviving Lancastrian, defeated and killed Richard III at Bosworth Field; this marked the close of the Wars of the Roses and the integration of Wales with England.

The Tudors *(Henry VII 1485–1509, Henry VIII 1509–47, Edward VI 1547–53, Mary I 1553–58, Elizabeth I 1558–1603)*

1485–1509	Henry VII curbed the barons, favored the increasingly important landed gentry, repaired the country's economy and reformed the legal system.
1509–47	Reign of Henry VIII, a period popularly known for divorced and beheaded wives but historically more important for the removal of the Church from the jurisdiction of Rome, the Dissolution of the Monasteries and the advance of the Reformation in England and Wales.
1553	Accession of Mary I. A devout Catholic, she so diligently burned Protestants that she was branded 'Bloody Mary.'
1558	The accession of Elizabeth I ushered in the splendid Elizabethan Age of glittering royal favorites, daring seamen, and exploration (not only geographically but also in art and science).
1577–80	Francis Drake circumnavigated the world.
1588	Defeat of the Spanish Armada.

The Stuarts *(James I 1603–25, Charles I 1625–49, Charles II 1660–85, James II 1685–88, William III and Mary II 1688–1702, Anne 1702–14)*

1603	The accession of James I (James VI of Scotland) united the crowns of England and Scotland.
1620	The *Mayflower* sailed from Plymouth.
1629–40	Charles I governed without parliament.
1642–49	The Civil War, ending with the execution of Charles I.
1649–60	The Puritan Commonwealth under Oliver Cromwell.
1660	The Restoration of the Monarchy (Charles II).
1665–66	The Great Plague.
1666	The Great Fire of London.
1685	Accession of the Catholic James II. An invasion by the Duke of Monmouth was ruthlessly suppressed (Judge Jeffreys and the Bloody Assizes).

1688–	Under William and Mary a Bill of Rights established
1702	the supremacy of parliament.
1702	Outbreak of the War of the Spanish Succession, in which Blenheim (1704) was one of the many victories of John Churchill, Duke of Marlborough.
1707	The Treaty of Union united the parliaments of England and Scotland.

The Hanoverians *(George I 1714–27, George II 1727–60, George III 1760–1820, George IV 1820–30, William IV 1830–37)*

1756–63	During the Seven Years' War Britain won Canada from the French.
1757	Robert Clive's victory at Plassey assured the future of the British Indian Empire.
1773	The 'Boston Tea Party' signaled the start of the American War of Independence (concluded 1783).
1776–79	Captain James Cook explored the Pacific, claiming New Zealand and Australia (New South Wales) for Britain.
1789	Outbreak of the French Revolution, heralding the long Napoleonic Wars and in England and Wales giving great impetus to the Industrial Revolution.
1805	Nelson defeated the Franco-Spanish fleet at Trafalgar.
1808–14	The Peninsular War in which Wellington drove the French out of Portugal and Spain.
1811–20	The Regency Period, made necessary by George III's final lapse into madness.
1815	Wellington defeated Napoleon at Waterloo.
1825	The opening of the Stockton–Darlington railway heralded a revolution which within 50yrs covered the country in 14,000 miles (22,000km) of track.
1832	The Reform Bill became law, a first but significant step towards universal suffrage.

The Victorian and Edwardian eras *(Victoria 1837–1901, Edward VII 1901–10)*

These two reigns saw the continuation of the Industrial Revolution, the spread of the railways, the rapid urbanization of Britain, the splendors of Empire culminating in the elevation of the Queen to Empress in 1876, the birth of the trade unions, and, under Edward VII, the arrival in common use of, for example, the car and the telephone.

1851	The Great Exhibition, brainchild of Prince Albert.
1854–56	The Crimean War.
1899–	The second Boer (South African) War, which began
1902	with the siege of Mafeking.

The Windsors *(George V 1910–36, Edward VIII 1936, George VI 1936–52, Elizabeth II 1952–   )*

1914–18	World War I. USA involved from 1917.
1918	Women got the vote.
1936	Edward VIII abdicated.
1939–45	World War II. 1940: the evacuation from Dunkirk. 1941: USA took up arms. 1944: successful Allied invasion of northern France across the Normandy beaches.
1945	A Labour government was elected which introduced the Welfare State and started the process of dismantling the Empire.
1973	Britain joined the EEC.
1982	The Falklands War.

Architecture

Man has been building in England and Wales for more than 5,000yrs and, given the knowledge and tools of the time, monuments such as Stonehenge and Silbury Hill are achievements every bit as remarkable as anything produced during later centuries. The legacy of those ancient Stone and Bronze Age peoples is one of worship and burial; that of their Iron Age successors – for the most part hillforts – indicates an increasing need for enclosure and defense. The Romans, too, are represented by daunting defensive works – Hadrian's Wall is the most impressive – but by contrast they have also left rich evidence of a more gracious civilian life in the form of villas such as Lullingstone and Chedworth, of amphitheaters (Caerleon and Chester are among the best), and indeed whole towns such as Viroconium. However, after the Romans left Britain in the early 5thC, there was no more building in stone until the arrival of Christianity gave rise to simple Anglo-Saxon churches, today rare and much altered, although several towers and, more interestingly, some crypts (such as the one in Ripon Cathedral) survive untouched.

The Normans: strength through simplicity
In 1066 the Normans arrived. Determined to impress and over-awe, they were enthusiastic builders destined to give their name to a whole period and style of architecture, represented largely by great churches and castles, although the interesting shell of a 12thC merchant's home can still be seen at Southampton, while the Jew's House at Lincoln dates from the same period.

Strength through a crude simplicity is the keynote, with great square castle keeps and, in churches, massive pillars, rounded arches, arcading and buttresses. Yet at the same time, almost as if reacting against such simplicity, the Norman masons adorned their churches, and sometimes also their castles, with a rich, distinctive, geometric decoration. The Norman legacy is widespread. Rochester Castle still stands as one of the more impressive keeps, Durham Cathedral is perhaps the supreme ecclesiastical example, while several smaller places – Kilpeck and Barfreston churches, for example – encourage intimate study of Norman decoration.

Meanwhile, ordinary people continued to live in modest wattle-and-daub or fragile timber homes, and it was only the rich and powerful who enjoyed the protection of stone.

By about the 12thC the Normans' keeps had succeeded the timber, and later stone, motte-and-bailey castle design, and soon these keeps gave way to battlemented curtain walls linking powerful towers and entered only through heavily defended gatehouses – steps in a process which culminated in the great concentric castles built all over Wales by Edward I.

Uplifting Gothic styles
Largely through the influence of the proliferating religious houses, especially Cistercian, Norman church architecture also began to give way (the period of change is known as Transitional) to forms both more sophisticated and more in sympathy with contemporary aspirations. The pointed arch and ribbed vaulting opened up new structural horizons; whereas Norman churches had sat squat and anchored to the earth, the new style – light, airy and soaring, with slender lancets

and needle spires – carried men's spirits upward toward their God. Known today as Gothic, the style evolved from about the 12th–16thC and can be divided into three periods: Early English (1180–1260), when simplicity was the essence; Decorated (1250–1370), the richest years, during which windows became larger and masons let themselves go in their use of delicate and flowing tracery, corbels and bosses; and Perpendicular (1300–1540), a more severe period with an emphasis on straight lines but also famous for its use of glorious fan vaulting.

There are numerous examples of Gothic achievement throughout England and Wales – Salisbury Cathedral, for example, is pure Early English, Exeter Cathedral is Decorated, and King's College Chapel, Cambridge, is famous for its fan vaulting – but York Minster is perhaps the most impressive and satisfying, both for its size and for the way in which it integrates all three periods.

The principal medieval residential trend, one largely associated with the minor aristocracy and gentry, was the progression from primitive feudal hall to manor house, some built as such but many growing out of an original hall. Stokesay Castle is a particularly interesting and attractive fortified example, showing features ranging from a 12thC half-timbered gatehouse to a 13thC hall. Some surviving almshouses and pilgrims' hospices also reach back to medieval times. One such is Canterbury's Hospital of St Thomas, and at Winchester there are two others, the Pilgrims' Hall and the Hospital of St Cross.

With the accession of Henry VII (1485), the first of the Tudors, England and Wales finally emerged from the Middle Ages. Free at last of the Wars of the Roses, and under Tudor law and order enjoying an unwonted prosperity, men became aware of new horizons of comfort and elegance and started to build accordingly. The aristocracy began to convert their castles into splendid mansions, a process much boosted when the monasteries were dissolved and their lands acquired by men wealthy and powerful enough either to convert the existing buildings or, as was more often the case, to raise new great houses. Often built in brick (the craft had recently been revived), these incorporated the newly fashionable Long

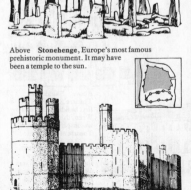

Above **Stonehenge**, Europe's most famous prehistoric monument. It may have been a temple to the sun.

Above **Kilpeck Church**. The elaborate Norman stone carving ranks among the richest examples in England.

Left **Caernarfon Castle**. Integral with the walled town (see diagram), this is a good example of Edward I's concept of combined castle and borough.

21

Galleries, and sprouted forests of chimneys to serve the new insistence on warmth. Burghley House, Hampton Court, Longleat and Wilton House are just a few of the names belonging at least in part to this brilliant Tudor-Elizabethan period.

Also at this time (16th–17thC), a new race of prosperous merchants filled both town and countryside with the black and white half-timbered houses, so many of which have survived to delight succeeding centuries.

The new classicism

Hitherto building had been left to (usually nameless) masons and carpenters, but during the 17thC architects made their appearance. One of the first was Inigo Jones (1573–1652), a revolutionary who, deeply influenced by the Italian Renaissance and in particular by Andrea Palladio, introduced classicism with its symmetry and clean exteriors. An excellent example is the Banqueting Hall in London's Whitehall. Inigo Jones was followed by Christopher Wren (1632–1723), the master architect of the Restoration period and beyond. A classicist at heart (Oxford's Sheldonian Theatre is an early witness to this), he was also a genius of infinite versatility, well able to overcome the problems posed by the rebuilding of more than 50 of London's churches after the Great Fire. St Paul's Cathedral, combining Gothic, classical and Baroque features, remains his supreme memorial.

The long and architecturally rich period known as Georgian (for convenience the years of William and Mary and Queen Anne may be included) embraces many styles and a long list of distinguished names. John Vanbrugh (1664–1726), one of the first on the scene, is associated with buildings of breathtaking size and grandeur such as Castle Howard and Blenheim; the style of these buildings is known as English Baroque. Vanbrugh's contemporary and collaborator, Nicholas Hawksmoor (1661–1736), was another individualist and one willing and able to adapt from any set style; Oxford's severely classical Clarendon Building, Gothic All Souls' College and

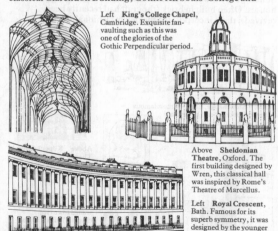

Left **King's College Chapel**, Cambridge. Exquisite fan-vaulting such as this was one of the glories of the Gothic Perpendicular period.

Above **Sheldonian Theatre**, Oxford. The first building designed by Wren, this classical hall was inspired by Rome's Theatre of Marcellus.

Left **Royal Crescent**, Bath. Famous for its superb symmetry, it was designed by the younger John Wood in the mid-18thC.

Baroque Queen's College are proof enough of this. Thomas Archer (1668–1743) is a third early Georgian name, known best for Birmingham's neat little cathedral (St Philip's) with its Baroque tower.

But Vanbrugh and his contemporaries represent no more than a brief and tentative flirtation with Baroque. The underlying preference of the 18thC was for the classical in one form or another (Palladian at the start but more severe toward the close). During this century churches, public buildings and, above all, great country houses sprang up. Carefully set within their landscaped grounds, these houses achieved individuality while at the same time generally conforming to the pattern of a restrained, symmetrical exterior, often with a classical portico, behind which the emphasis was on a noble and superbly decorated first floor.

From a throng of distinguished architects, some names stand out: James Gibbs (1682–1754), who designed London's St Martin-in-the-Fields; Lord Burlington (1695–1753), who was both patron and architect (Chiswick House); the two John Woods, father (1704–54) and son (1728–81), men whose vision was more of urban layout than of individual buildings and who devoted their genius to Bath; and, most importantly, William Kent (1684–1748), architect (Holkham Hall), furniture designer and landscape-gardener.

In the latter part of the 18thC Robert Adam (1728–92) was the most important influence. An architect and an interior decorator of elegant genius, Adam designed every detail from the strictly architectural down to fireplaces and ornaments. Much of his best work is in his native Scotland. In England, Harewood House, Kedleston Hall, Nostell Priory and (around London) Kenwood, Osterley Park House and Syon House are just some of the places where his work can be enjoyed.

The late-Georgian and Regency period is represented by three men in particular. Henry Holland (1746–1806) remained loyal to the external classical values while his interiors were rich with decoration; Berrington Hall is typical. However, James Wyatt (1746–1813) and John Nash (1752–1835) broke away,

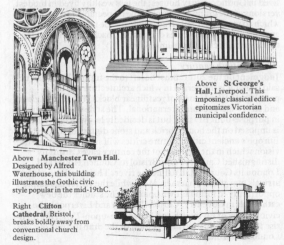

Above **St George's Hall**, Liverpool. This imposing classical edifice epitomizes Victorian municipal confidence.

Above **Manchester Town Hall**. Designed by Alfred Waterhouse, this building illustrates the Gothic civic style popular in the mid-19thC.

Right **Clifton Cathedral**, Bristol, breaks boldly away from conventional church design.

refusing to be shackled by any one style. The contrast between Wyatt's Neo-Gothic Strawberry Hill at Twickenham, battlemented Belvoir Castle, and his essentially Greek Radcliffe Observatory in Oxford is proof enough of this. John Nash transformed the Royal Pavilion in Brighton into an Oriental palace, and also gave London the great swath of Regent St. and Portland Place, which links the dignified terrace of Carlton House with his terraces in Regent's Park.

On a more modest level the Georgian and Regency periods live on through the elegant homes of the new middle class; charming, bow-fronted, brick houses which successfully achieve individuality within their terraces.

Victorian exuberance

The architecture of the Victorian era faithfully reflects the social upheavals that accompanied the Industrial Revolution, as well as the fact that exciting new materials – iron, glass and steel – were rapidly coming into use, especially in the design of bridges and of the vast stations that marked this heyday of the railways. The country aristocracy went into decline as industry drew millions of workers off the land and into the sprawling cities. At the same time, patronage shifted to these cities, where town halls, museums, libraries and churches proclaimed a civic rather than a personal pride and confidence. At the start of the era the preference remained classical; Liverpool's monumental St George's Hall (H.L. Elmes, 1813–47) and London's British Museum (Robert Smirke, 1781–1867) are two notable examples. But before the middle of the century Neo-Gothic became the preferred style. Alfred Waterhouse (1830–1905) gave Manchester its magnificent town hall; Charles Barry (1795–1860) gave the nation the Houses of Parliament; and that most prolific Gothic revivalist, George Gilbert Scott (1811–78) gave Queen Victoria the Albert Memorial (sited in London's Kensington Gardens).

During the Victorian era the population not only moved into the towns, it also increased fourfold, posing daunting problems for the builders of residential property. In the end, the rich lived in Gothic country houses; the less wealthy lived in modest versions of the grand homes or in the respectable row houses of which so many have survived; while for the masses the speculators provided miles of cramped, back-to-back housing that so soon became appalling slums.

The twentieth century

Judgment on the 20thC must be left to the future. What can be said is that it is the period in which architecture – in its post-World War II form of rectilinear blocks in concrete, glass and steel – has become international. The style works excitingly in purpose-built Brasilia, but is decidedly less welcome when it is imposed on the homey brick and stone dignity of some of Europe's ancient cities. Future critics will surely commend the vision which in the first part of the century gave Cardiff its distinguished Cathays Park, Bristol its Council House and London its County Hall to line the river. Their verdict on later arrivals may well be harsher. Meanwhile the visitor has ample opportunity to form his own opinion as he studies the new cathedrals in Coventry, Clifton (Bristol) and Liverpool, the civic centers of Plymouth and Newcastle-upon-Tyne, the high-rise towers typical of so many cities, or the drab fortress of London's Barbican.

Painting

Murals, altarpieces and illuminated manuscripts survive from medieval times, but painting as an attributed art dates only from the reign of Henry VIII who, in freeing England from papal authority, at the same time freed art from its obsession with religion. In the 16thC the portrait painters George Gower and Nicholas Hilliard, together with the German Hans Holbein, are among the first individually identifiable artists, but it is not until the Stuart era that familiar names begin to appear. Although William Dobson (1610–46) and Robert Walker (*c*.1607–*c*.57), respectively portrayers of Cavaliers and Roundheads, are not all that widely known, Van Dyck (1599–1641), Peter Lely (1618–80) and Godfrey Kneller (1646–1723), all foreign born, certainly are. Through these men the leading characters of their day live on.

James Thornhill (1675–1734) was an artist in an altogether different mold: a Baroque painter-decorator in the heroic manner. By contrast, William Hogarth (1697–1764) was an earthy realist whose conversation pieces and social engravings give startling and even disturbing glimpses of contemporary life.

The 18thC can boast four fashionable portraitists of distinction, their doyen being Joshua Reynolds (1723–92). The others were Thomas Gainsborough (1727–88), George Romney (1734–1802) and German-born Johann Zoffany (1733–1810), famous for his conversation pieces. Over the same period the Welshman Richard Wilson (1714–82) was one of the first great landscapists, bequeathing views of a tranquil countryside, while Samuel Scott (1702–72) captured contemporary London and George Stubbs (1724–1806) immortalized the horse-racing scene.

Genius crowds the 19thC. The two giants portraying nature were John Constable (1776–1837), whose landscapes convey the very essence of rural peace, and J.M.W. Turner (1775–1851), who painted, as Constable put it, in 'tinted steam.' In portraiture, the era's undisputed genius was Thomas Lawrence (1769–1830); his work glows with color and life, nowhere more sumptuously than in his victory over Napoleon series, assembled in Windsor Castle.

The undisputed Romantics of the century were that master of melodrama, John Martin (1789–1854), and Edwin Landseer (1802–73), who achieved immense popularity as much for his engravings of untamed nature as for the charming animal studies that touched every Victorian heart, while William Blake (1757–1827), the poet and mystic, painted religious subjects in a unique style.

But it is the Pre-Raphaelites who dominate the latter part of the century. Led by D.G. Rossetti (1828–82), W. Holman Hunt (1827–1910) and J.E. Millais (1829–96), they turned their backs on Victorian materialism and by clothing sentiment in color, light and precision of natural detail achieved effects often enchantingly fey.

The 20thC abounds in artists, trends and movements. Names that stand out include the idiosyncratic L.S. Lowry (known for his paintings of the industrial North), Graham Sutherland, Francis Bacon, and war artists such as Paul Nash and John Piper, while Yorkshire-born David Hockney, perhaps best known for his paintings of California swimming pools, will surely gain a niche in art history.

England and Wales in literature

The *Anglo-Saxon Chronicle*, initiated by Alfred the Great in the 9thC, represents the first attempt at English history in the native language, and in Wales at about the same time the bards were spinning the Celtic tales which in their modern form are generally known as the *Mabinogion*. Some three centuries later, William of Malmesbury (*died* 1143), writing in Latin, brought the English story up to 1142, while Gerald of Wales (*c.*1146–*c.*1223) in his *Itinerarium Cambrense* introduced his readers to the Wales of those days.

The 14thC brought two great names: those of William Langland (*c.*1332–*c.*1400), whose *The Vision of William concerning Piers Plowman* revealed the brutish side of medieval life, and of Geoffrey Chaucer (*c.*1345–1400), who through his *Canterbury Tales* offered lighter and more entertaining glimpses of the contemporary scene. From the Tudor years, England's greatest writer William Shakespeare (1564–1616) and Christopher Marlowe (1564–93) have left their dramatic if historically dubious pictures of a royal past, but it is the chroniclers writing in this period who claim more serious attention as witnesses; Raphael Holinshed (*died c.*1580), the chronicler of English history from whom Shakespeare drew many of his plots, and Richard Hakluyt (*c.*1553–1616), whose themes were adventure and exploration.

The 17thC was that of the Civil War, and it is in itself revealing that in such troubled times it should have been possible for an amiable spirit such as Izaak Walton (1593–1683) to have wandered little hindered about the countryside, fishing its 'silver streams' and enjoying the company at the various inns to which he repaired. The result, his gentle *The Compleat Angler*, portrays an England largely indifferent to the passions of the day and far removed from the polemical tracts of John Milton (1608–74).

The Restoration – to Milton the 'evil days' – is marked by two great diarists, Samuel Pepys (1633–1703) and John Evelyn (1620–1706). The former, a competent and conscientious civil servant yet a bon vivant who savored life to the full, has bequeathed lively pictures of his times, whether of the Great Plague and Fire of London, of his professional worries about the administration of the navy, or of the intimacies of his personal life. John Evelyn – another who described the Plague and the Fire – was a cultured gentleman of leisure, whose writings allow glimpses of such issues as London's smoke and the excessive influence of foreign fashion.

During the 18thC, writers increasingly portrayed the life around them, notably in the novel which now began to evolve towards its modern form. Early on, Samuel Richardson (1689–1761), in *Pamela, or Virtue Rewarded* and *Clarissa, or the History of a Young Lady*, gave his readers a rare mixture of romance and realism and future generations an oblique glance into early Georgian middle-class moral attitudes, while Henry Fielding (1707–54) presented a whole world of picaresque characters in his *The History of Tom Jones, A Foundling*. Tobias Smollett (1721–71), writing at about the same time and allying the picaresque with a new realism, made his name through his description of the brutalizing life in the navy. At the end of his life he published *The Expedition of Humphrey Clinker*, an altogether gentler work in which the modern reader can absorb much of the middle-class 18thC scene. Later in the century, and spilling over into the next, the breathless Fanny Burney (1752–1840) parades a gallery of the élite of her acquaintance in her enchanting diary, while Jane Austen (1775–1817) creates a different, fictional élite, little touched by a harsher world outside its privileged orbit. But it is Samuel Johnson (1709–84) who bestrides the century, as much through his personality and wit as through his literary output which included his scholarly and seminal *Dictionary of the English Language* and his *Lives of the Poets.*

In the middle years of the 19thC George Borrow (1803–81) toured Wales, and his *Wild Wales* remains a classic among idiosyncratic travel books. But it is the novel which more than any other form records the immensely varied life of that explosive century. Charles Dickens (1812–70) led the field. A deeply sincere social crusader pressing his theme through popular fiction, he is best known for the light he cast on the darker side of Victorian life, notably in *Oliver Twist*, yet at the same time in *The Pickwick Papers* he created a cheerful world which affords unique if caricatured glimpses of many contemporary attitudes and places. Among numerous others writing at about the same time were William Thackeray (1811–63) and Anthony Trollope (1815–82), both concerned with higher levels of society than Dickens; Mrs Gaskell (1810–65), like Dickens known for her novels of social protest (her scene was Manchester, as in, for example, *Mary Barton*), yet in *Cranford* painting a charming picture of provincial society; and the Brontë sisters, Charlotte (1816–55), Emily (1818–48) and Anne (1820–49), who often chose their native Yorkshire moors for their settings, as, a generation later and in much the same way, Thomas Hardy (1840–1928) used Dorset, which, with other West Country counties, he called Wessex.

From a crowd of 20thC names, some stand out for the way they capture the years of war and galloping social change. The many stories of H.G. Wells (1866–1946) reflect equally the social problems and the tantalizing scientific promise of the age, while Rudyard Kipling (1865–1936) immortalizes the spirit of Imperial India in both prose and verse. John Galsworthy (1867–1933), of *Forsyte Saga* fame, worked a perceptive and critical view of the society of the late 19th to early 20thC into a series of gripping novels and plays, and his contemporary, Arnold Bennett (1867–1931), achieved something similar through making social analysis the thread of a series of still very readable novels set within the Staffordshire Potteries. Poets such as Rupert Brooke (1887–1915) and Siegfried Sassoon (1886–1967) recall both the innocent patriotism as well as the harsh reality of war, while D.H. Lawrence (1885–1930), Aldous Huxley (1894–1963) and J.B. Priestley (*born* 1894) are three more writers concerned with the individual in society. Lawrence set his novels in and around mining towns; Huxley loved clever, fashionable London; Priestley brilliantly interpreted a solid middle-of-the-road England.

The years following World War II were, for some authors, the years of uncertainty, disillusion and revolt, epitomized by the writings of what came to be known as the 'angry young men.' John Braine (*Room at the Top*), Kingsley Amis (*Lucky Jim*) and John Wain (*Hurry on Down*) are among the better-known names. Then, in total contrast and almost as if to restore perspective, 1956 saw the publication of the splendid *History of the English Speaking Peoples*, by Winston Churchill (1874–1965).

PLANNING

Orientation map

SCOTLAND

NORTHERN
IRELAND

Belfast

Carlisle

CUMBRIA

Lake District NP

Isle of Man

Barrow

Lancaster

IRISH SEA

Blackpool
Preston
LANCS

MERSEYSIDE

GREATER

Dublin

Liverpool

EIRE

Holyhead   Anglesey   Llandudno

CHESHIRE

Chester

Snowdonia NP

CLWYD

Crewe

GWYNEDD

Cardigan Bay

Shrewsbury

POWYS

SHROPSHIRE

Aberystwyth

WALES

Worcester

ST GEORGE'S CHANNEL

DYFED

H AND W

Fishguard

Brecon Beacons NP

GWENT

Pembroke Coast NP

WEST GLAM

MID GLAM

Swansea

SOUTH GLAM   Cardiff

Bristol
AVON   Bath

BRISTOL CHANNEL

SOMERSET

✈	**International airports**
1	Birmingham
2	East Midlands
3	Gatwick
4	Heathrow
5	Luton
6	Manchester
7	Stansted

Exmoor NP

Taunton

DEVON

DORSET

Exeter

Dartmoor NP

Weymouth

CORNWALL

Plymouth

Truro

Penzance

Land's End

Isles of Scilly

ENGLISH

28

Berwick-upon-Tweed

Northumberland NP

ORTHUMB

Newcastle-upon-Tyne
T AND W

Durham

CO. DURHAM

Darlington ● Middlesborough
CLEVELAND

orkshire
ales NP
N Yorks
Moors NP

NORTH YORKS

Harrogate
York

Bradford Leeds HUMBERSIDE
Hull

WEST YORKS
MAN.
SOUTH YORKS
Doncaster
Grimsby

Sheffield M180 A18

Peak District NP

DERBY

STAFFS NOTTS LINCS

Lincoln

Derby Nottingham

Stafford

The Wash

E N G L A N D King's Lynn
Norwich A47
WEST
Birmingham NORTHANTS NORFOLK Gt Yarmouth

Coventry
Rugby
LEICS

WARWICKS

CAMBS SUFFOLK

Cambridge
Ipswich

OXON BUCKS BEDS
HERTS ESSEX Colchester

Cheltenham GLOS Oxford

Swindon
GREATER
LONDON

WILTS BERKS Reading

Salisbury
HANTS SURREY KENT

Canterbury

Southampton WEST Dover
SUSSEX EAST SUSSEX Folkestone
Chichester
Brighton

Bournemouth Portsmouth ● Calais
FRANCE
I OF W ● Boulogne

CHANNEL

Cherbourg

County abbreviations
ENGLAND
BEDS	Bedfordshire
BERKS	Berkshire
BUCKS	Buckinghamshire
CAMBS	Cambridgeshire
CO. DURHAM	County Durham
DERBY	Derbyshire
GLOS	Gloucestershire
GREATER MAN.	Greater Manchester
HANTS	Hampshire
H AND W	Hereford and Worcester
HERTS	Hertfordshire
I OF W	Isle of Wight
LANCS	Lancashire
LEICS	Leicestershire
LINCS	Lincolnshire
NORTHANTS	Northamptonshire
NORTHUMB	Northumberland
NORTH YORKS	North Yorkshire
NOTTS	Nottinghamshire
OXON	Oxfordshire
SOUTH YORKS	South Yorkshire
STAFFS	Staffordshire
T AND W	Tyne and Wear
WARWICKS	Warwickshire
WEST MIDS	West Midlands
WEST YORKS	West Yorkshire
WILTS	Wiltshire

WALES
MID GLAM	Mid Glamorgan
SOUTH GLAM	South Glamorgan
WEST GLAM	West Glamorgan

Inter-City rail network
Motorways
Primary or A road

CHANNEL ISLANDS

Alderney

Guernsey
St Peter Port
◇ Herm
◇ Sark

Jersey
St Helier

Cherbourg

0   20   40   60   80 miles
0   40   80   120 km

Calendar of events

See also *Sports and activities* and *Public holidays* in *Basic information*.

January
Early Jan. Winter sales. Most stores offer good reductions.

International Boat Show. See *London*.

February
Shrove Tuesday. Pancake races in various parts of the country.

March
Late Mar or early Apr. Grand National. See *Horse racing* in *Sports and activities*.

Mar or Apr. Boat Race. See *Rowing* in *Sports and activities*.

April
Maundy Thursday (Thurs before Easter). The Queen distributes Maundy money at the location of her choice (different place each year).

May
May or June. Bath International Festival of Music. See *Bath*.

Brighton Festival. See *Brighton*.

Hobby Horse Parade at Minehead. See *Exmoor*.

Spalding Flower Parade. See *The Fen District*.

Glyndebourne Festival Opera, until mid-Aug. See *Lewes*.

Chelsea Flower Show. See *London*.

Gillette London Marathon. See *London*.

Royal Academy Summer Exhibition, until Sept. See *London Sights*.

Malvern Festival, until early June. See *Malvern Hills*.

May Day celebrations. See *Oxford*.

Well dressing, until Sept. See *Peak District National Park*.

Helston Furry Dance. See *Truro*.

Royal Windsor Horse Show. See *Windsor*.

June
Aldeburgh Festival. See *Aldeburgh*.

Trooping the Colour. See *London*.

Royal Norfolk Show. See *Norwich*.

Dickens Festival. See *Rochester*.

The Derby. See *Horse racing* in *Sports and activities*.

Royal Ascot. See *Horse racing* in *Sports and activities*.

Henley Royal Regatta. See *Rowing* in *Sports and activities*.

June–July. Wimbledon Lawn Tennis Championships. See *Tennis* in *Sports and activities*.

Royal Bath and West Agricultural Show. See *Wells*.

July
World Wine Fair and Festival. See *Bristol*.

Cambridge Festival and Folk Festival. See *Cambridge*.

Miners' Gala. See *Durham*.

Great Yorkshire Show. See *Harrogate*.

Royal Tournament. See *London*.

Royal International Horse Show. See *Equestrian events* in *Sports and activities*.

August
Folk Festival and City Carnival. See *Durham*.

Three Choirs Festival. See *Gloucester*, *Hereford* and *Worcester*.

Harrogate Festival. See *Harrogate*.

Cowes Week. See *Isle of Wight*.

Grasmere Sports. See *Lake District National Park*.

Manchester Show. See *Manchester*.

Royal National Eisteddfod. Held alternate years in N and S Wales.

September
International Boat Show. See *Southampton*.

Windsor Festival, until Oct. See *Windsor*.

October
International Motor Show. See *Birmingham*.

Oct or Nov. State opening of Parliament. See *London*.

Goose Fair. See *Nottingham*.

November
London to Brighton Veteran Car Run. See *Brighton*.

Lord Mayor's Show. See *London*.

Nov 5. Guy Fawkes' Day. Nationwide. Bonfires, 'guys' and fireworks recall an unsuccessful attempt to blow up Parliament in 1605.

December
International Show Jumping Championships. See *Equestrian events* in *Sports and activities*.

Carol services in cathedrals and churches throughout England and Wales.

When and where to go

Personal considerations apart, two factors affect when you should choose to travel in England and Wales: the weather, and what is open when.

Weatherwise, England and Wales are not afflicted by extremes. This does not mean that there is no difference between summer and winter. Most certainly there is: the temperature over the year can range from below freezing up to around 23°C (73°F), but nevertheless mild or briskly cold sunny days can just as likely bless midwinter as weeks of rain and chill can wreck a summer. Indeed, the essential fact to grasp about England's weather is simply that it is totally unreliable. Nor, even if statistically the south is milder, is there necessarily any significant difference between north and south or east and west, other, of course, than that the high ground with its increased likelihood of cold and snow is to be found towards the north. Nevertheless one generalization may perhaps be made with reasonable confidence: more often than not, November to March is a dark and dismal span ready at any moment to strike with fog, storm or paralyzing snow.

Many if not most major places of interest are open throughout the year, and the winter visitor should suffer no disappointment at, for example, Stratford-upon-Avon, nor at Dept. of the Environment (DOE) or Welsh Office (WO) sites or at any cathedral. However, a great many other places, especially stately homes, close in winter (usually October to Easter).

To sum up, any period between Easter and October is worth considering, not forgetting that July and August are the popular vacation months.

When it comes to where to go, everybody – whether disinterested official or involved trader – is generous with advice. The tourist boards offer fat booklets listing specialized vacations which range from conventional pursuits such as walking, sailing, riding or bird watching, to more eccentric breaks studying witchcraft or playing the flute. Enthusiasts of this kind of vacation will probably already know where to go, but the booklets are useful for those considering sampling such activities. But the majority of travelers, including most coming from abroad, will have less defined aims, although it is likely that these will fall within the quartet of sightseeing (opportunities exist almost everywhere), sea, scenery, or a little of everything.

Shrugging off capricious weather and foreign competition, English and Welsh seaside resorts still attract the visitor, although more for the bracing, salt-laden air than for the indolent basking associated with more exotic climes. Invigoration, not sloth, rules. Entertainment, too, is a draw, for although most resorts have their shabby corners the majority are stylish places with distinguished hotels and restaurants, elegant promenades as inviting to the strider as the stroller, and programs of entertainment to suit all tastes.

The scenery of England and Wales ranges from what might be termed the parklike to the spectacular. For the latter the national parks are probably the best although certainly not the only bet. The former, though, is nearly always close; whether on London's doorstep in Kent, Sussex, Surrey and Buckinghamshire, or farther afield on the way to Stratford and beyond, or through the Marches and central Wales tracing the courses of the Wye and the Severn.

Area planners and tours

The essential attraction of England and Wales is their unequaled richness in places of interest, with scarcely a square mile
in which there is not something worth seeing. Any attempt to
identify specific touring areas, therefore, must inevitably be
arbitrary. Nevertheless certain regions do seem to have
achieved a particular repute and it is these, together with tours
out of London, that provide the pattern of areas suggested here.
Bear in mind, however, that for every tour outlined below there
are a dozen others that the traveler will enjoy finding for
himself, and that it is for those who venture along the by-roads
that the real rewards are reserved.

Area: One- or two-day excursions out of London
Although London is tucked away in the SE corner of England,
many places of prime tourist interest are within the reach of, for
example, a single day's coach excursion. Among those offered
are trips to Canterbury and Dover; Cambridge; Stonehenge,
Salisbury and Bath; Oxford and the Shakespeare country.
While nobody would pretend that such tours are
comprehensive, they do provide a convenient way of covering a
lot of ground in a short time. Visitors enjoying the
independence of a car can of course dawdle or roam farther
afield, and it is for their benefit that the following tours are
suggested.

Cambridge and some Suffolk and Essex villages
To Cambridge by A10 or M11. A1307 then A604 to just SE of
Haverhill; E on A1092 to Long Melford; then NE along a minor
road to Lavenham. A1141 SE via Kersey (short side trip) to
Hadleigh. S on B1070 to intersection with A12; A12 to
Colchester and London. 165 miles (264km).

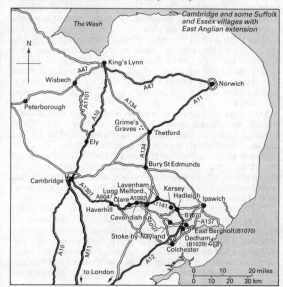

Even a superficial look at *Cambridge* will eat up an hour or two; to see the place in greater depth will take a whole day, so an overnight stop here makes sense. Around 20 miles (32km) SE are some of Suffolk's loveliest villages, places rich in warmth and character with their huge churches, spacious greens and half-timbered, crazily structured houses and cottages. Here are the attractive small town of Clare; Cavendish where pink-washed thatched cottages edge the green below the church; and aptly named Long Melford stretching away southwards from the National Trust's turreted Melford Hall, mellow and little changed since it was built in 1578. Nearby, medieval and Tudor Lavenham is close to perfection while, approaching Hadleigh and almost too picturesque to be true, Kersey drops timeless to its waterfall. Farther S, along the placid river Stour, connoisseurs of John Constable can turn off the road to visit familiar places such as Dedham, Flatford Mill, Stoke-by-Nayland and the artist's birthplace village of East Bergholt. Not far away, historic *Colchester* is a good overnight stop.

An East Anglian extension
From Cambridge to Ely and King's Lynn by A10. E along A47 to Norwich; then SW along A11 to Thetford and A134 to Bury St Edmunds. 127 miles (205km).

For those tempted to venture deeper into East Anglia, the cathedral at *Ely* beckons across the fens, Georgian Wisbech awaits beyond (via A47), and quaint *King's Lynn* surprises as a port on The Wash. To the E, historic *Norwich* offers so much that a stopover seems the only course, while, old-fashioned and respectable, Thetford (for Grime's Graves, see *King's Lynn*) sits at the center of the flatlands.

A taste of Kent and Sussex
Leave London by A20, at Farningham (beyond Swanley bypass) bearing S on A225 to Sevenoaks. Then either A21 and A26 to Tunbridge Wells and A264, A21, A262 and A28 to Canterbury, *or* A25 and A20 to Maidstone, continuing NE on A249 then A2 to Canterbury. A2 to Dover, then along the coast to Chichester on A20, A259 and A27. Return to London on A285, A272, A29 and A24. 279 miles (449km) via Tunbridge Wells, 262 miles (420km) via Maidstone.

Kent is called the Garden of England, but 'orchard' would be more appropriate, the acres of blossom making a fair show in

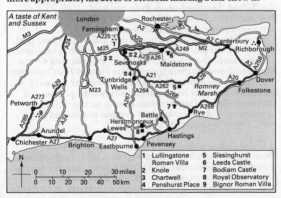

1	Lullingstone Roman Villa	5	Sissinghurst
2	Knole	6	Leeds Castle
3	Chartwell	7	Bodiam Castle
4	Penshurst Place	8	Royal Observatory
		9	Bignor Roman Villa

spring and early summer. Hops too are a feature, festooned around their distinctive enclosures and drying within the cowled oasthouses. Scenically Kent and Sussex are very similar; undulating pastoral, sometimes wooded landscape rises to open downs which lie back from the coast with its string of smart resorts. These are gentle, elegant, sophisticated counties which offer much.

A Roman villa, Lullingstone (see *Rochester*) comes first, followed by a cluster of stately homes: Knole, Chartwell, Penshurst Place and, to the E, Sissinghurst (see *Tunbridge Wells* for all four). For those who choose the Maidstone route, splendid *Leeds Castle* waits a short way SE, and a diversion W to *Rochester* is worth a thought. From *Canterbury*, travel on to Roman Richborough, 13 miles (21km) to the E, then on to *Dover* and Folkestone before crossing Romney Marsh to *Rye* and *Hastings*. Here a decision must be made: whether to move inland for *Bodiam Castle*, *Battle* and the Royal Observatory at Herstmonceux (see *Eastbourne*), or whether to follow the coast past Pevensey into Eastbourne. There follow *Lewes*, *Brighton*, *Arundel* and *Chichester*, before course is set for London by way of Bignor Roman Villa (see *Arundel*) and Petworth (see *Chichester*).

Winchester, Southampton, Salisbury and Stonehenge
From London by M3 and A33 to Winchester and Southampton. A27 and A36 to Salisbury. A345 to Amesbury (2 miles/3km W for Stonehenge) and A303 and M3 back to London. 195 miles (312km).

The tour's prime objectives are stated above, but there are also some worthwhile side trips for those with time to spare; from M3's exit 5, for instance, it is only 12 miles (19km) S to Jane Austen's house at Chawton (see *Winchester*). Close to Southampton there are the many and varied attractions of *The New Forest*, not to mention those of the *Isle of Wight*, while *Romsey*, with the late Lord Louis Mountbatten's Broadlands, lies on the suggested road to Salisbury. Just W of *Salisbury*, Wilton House is hard to resist.

Anyone with a particular interest in archeological sites may prefer to go from Winchester to Salisbury (on A272 and A30), then N on A338 and A346 to *Marlborough*; bear W on A4, then N on A361 to *Avebury Circle*. Return to London on A4 or M4.

To Oxford, Stratford-upon-Avon and back
M40 and A40 to Oxford. A34 to Stratford-upon-Avon. Return along same route. 200 miles (320km).

Once clear of London and across the Chilterns (beyond High Wycombe), the drive is through the rolling mixed agricultural and wooded land often cited as typically English, even if from Woodstock onward there is also always a hint of *The Cotswolds*.

As much time as possible should be allowed for the tour's two main objectives, but *Beaconsfield* is a rewarding detour and *Blenheim Palace* is beside the main road. If, after *Stratford-upon-Avon*, it proves possible to continue to *Warwick* (on A46), return to Oxford on A41 and A423.

A Cotswolds detour: Oxford to Stratford-upon-Avon
From Oxford W on A40 to Burford; S on A361 to Lechlade and W on A417 to Cirencester. A433 NE to Bibury, then a minor road briefly NW to intersection with A429 for Bourton-on-the-Water, Stow-on-the-Wold and Moreton-in-Marsh. W on A44 to

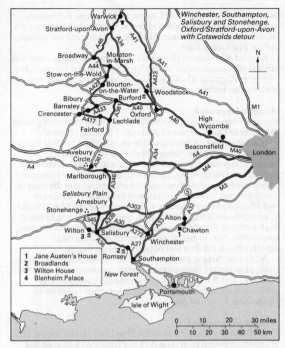

Winchester, Southampton, Salisbury and Stonehenge. Oxford/Stratford-upon-Avon with Cotswolds detour

1 Jane Austen's House
2 Broadlands
3 Wilton House
4 Blenheim Palace

Broadway; A46 to Stratford-upon-Avon. 91 miles (146km).

This meandering tour of *The Cotswolds* threads a cross-section of the region's lovely small towns and villages, each an individual gem.

Burford comes first, dropping steeply to its little river; Fairford next, famous for the 16thC glass of its substantial 'wool' church; beyond *Cirencester*, Barnsley cannot fail to charm, while Bibury seems almost too good to be true. Stow-on-the-Wold and Moreton-in-Marsh are typical market towns on the way to Broadway which, for all its manicured conservation, is still the star of the Cotswolds.

Area: The West Country
The tours outlined below offer a choice of three routes to Cornwall, followed by a tour of the Cornish coast.

A northern approach
From Bristol by A38, or from Bath on A39, to Bridgwater. Then by A39 to Minehead, Barnstaple, Bude and Camelford and B3266 to Bodmin. 162 miles (260km) from Bristol, 170 miles (272km) from Bath.

Both seafaring *Bristol* and elegant, Georgian *Bath* have much to offer at the start of this tour. The route from Bath goes through the charming cathedral city of *Wells*, and *Glastonbury* with its ruined abbey. Between the two routes lie the caves at Cheddar Gorge and Wookey Hole (see *The Mendip Hills*).

At Dunster a decision must be made between coast or inland. Choose the former and it is Porlock, snug below its notorious hill, and the twin resorts of Lynton and Lynmouth, wooded, romantic and the inspiration of poets. Choose the latter and it is minor roads across the heart of *Exmoor National Park* to rejoin A39 at Blackmoor Gate.

Beyond Barnstaple the road rides stubbornly inland, and side trips to the coast become 'musts'; to *Clovelly* and *Tintagel*, for instance; to spectacular Crackington Haven; or to Boscastle with its tiny harbor below the slate cliffs.

A central approach
From Stonehenge to Exeter by A303 and A30, continuing along the latter to Launceston and Bodmin. 156 miles (250km).

Stonehenge gets this tour off to an exciting start, but then a choice has to be made. Some will elect to carry on along A303, perhaps lingering across Salisbury Plain to explore prehistoric mounds and earthworks, perhaps diverting at Mere to see the famed gardens at Stourhead (see *Shaftesbury*) and the lions of *Longleat*, not far away. Others with tastes attuned more to cathedrals and stately homes will choose the parallel A30 to the s, a road that will tempt them with *Salisbury*, Wilton House, high-perched *Shaftesbury*, and *Sherborne* with its abbey and two castles. Not-to-be-missed Montacute House (see *Sherborne*) is sandwiched between the two routes.

At *Exeter* there is another choice: to stay on A30, the quicker road, or to plunge through the heart of *Dartmoor National Park* on B3212 and B3357. Connoisseurs of wild moorland and prehistory will certainly opt for the latter, then travel on to Bodmin on A390 and A38.

A southern approach
From Salisbury along A354 and A35 to Dorchester; then A35 to Honiton, A30 to Exeter, and A38 to Plymouth, Liskeard and Bodmin. 171 miles (274km).

Villages of character, such as Rockbourne with a large Roman villa and 16th–18thC houses and cottages, Milton Abbas, the 18thC creation of the local landowner (he had razed

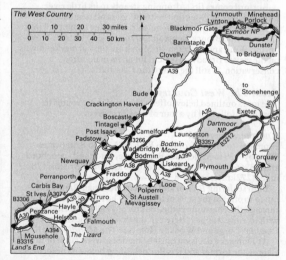

the earlier village because it blocked his view), and Tolpuddle, famed for its martyrs, lie to either side of the road before this tour's first key place, *Dorchester*, is reached. Between here and Honiton, A35 climbs and falls through some of the finest scenery in Dorset – high chalk downs, deep wooded valleys explored by narrow, sunken lanes, long seaward vistas – while smaller roads lead off to lost *Abbotsbury* and to *Lyme Regis*.

Between Exeter and Plymouth the motorist has only to escape w to find the deep lanes that lead to *Dartmoor National Park*, or E for the sophisticated delights of *Torquay*.

Around Cornwall's coast

Counterclockwise, starting along A39 from Camelford through Wadebridge, then inland to Fraddon. A30 to Hayle on Carbis Bay, then NW on A3074 to St Ives. The Land's End circuit is made by B3306, A30 and B3315 to Penzance. From here A30 and A394 to Helston and Falmouth; A39 to Truro; A390 to St Austell and Liskeard and A38 to Plymouth. 171 miles (274km).

A tempting maze of roads, mostly minor, approach or flank the coast and there is nothing to stop the dedicated potterer from plotting a course which is never far from the water.

Along the N coast, with its cliffs, golden sands and tireless surf, all below a harsh, windblown hinterland, lie legendary *Tintagel* and artist-haunted *St Ives*. But there is plenty in between: Padstow, for instance, snug and family oriented; Newquay, this coast's largest resort, a place for rocks, cliffs and beaches whether sheltered or wide open to a constant surf; little Perranporth, favorite with surfers; and Port Isaac, quaint certainly, yet with more than a touch of slate-gravity severity.

Land's End is stern; a barren, granite platform, unflinching before the giant Atlantic swells.

Sheltered, wooded, mild of climate and altogether gentler than the N, the S coast abounds in popular vacation places such as fashionable Penzance, *The Lizard*, famed for serpentine and coves, and Falmouth which seems to have everything. Above all, this is the coast for picture-postcard fishing ports: Mousehole, Mevagissey, Polperro, Looe – magical names which capture the total essence of seafaring Cornwall.

Area: The Pennines National Parks

The *Peak District National Park*, the *Yorkshire Dales National Park* and the *Northumberland National Park* straddle the Pennines between Derby to the S and the Scottish border. Although there are plenty of roads the problem is that except on the flanks of the parks those of any significance run E to W. The choice of tours is almost limitless, but of the two suggested here the route that progresses comfortably along the E flank of the parks might be called the easy way, while the route through the middle is more adventurous.

If time allows, continue on into the *Lake District National Park*, or return via *York* and *Lincoln*.

Along the E flank

From London, M1 to Leeds, then A61 to Ripon. A61, A1 and A1(M) to Darlington, then A68 to Carter Bar. 337 miles (540km).

All that has to be decided is at what points to divert. For the *Peak District National Park* leave the M1 at exit 28, 29, or 30, although 29 is best for most places: *Chatsworth House*, for example, as well as Matlock, Haddon Hall and the caves along A625 between Hathersage and Chapel-en-le-Frith.

A61 passes Harewood House (see *Leeds*) and *Harrogate* (divert here for the S part of *Yorkshire Dales National Park*) to reach *Ripon* and *Fountains Abbey*. But it is the N that boasts the two most famous dales, Wensleydale and Swaledale, reached either by A6108 out of Ripon or by speeding up A1 to the *Richmond* exit. The splendid Bowes Museum is only a short distance to the N at *Barnard Castle*.

Before exploring the lonely sweeps of *Northumberland National Park*, another detour can be made along *Hadrian's Wall*, the finest parts of which lie to the W along B6318.

Through the middle

From Derby, A6 to Rowsley; B6012 to Chatsworth House. Briefly NW along A623 before bearing right to follow B6001 to Hathersage. W on A625, then follow A6013 and A57 across the

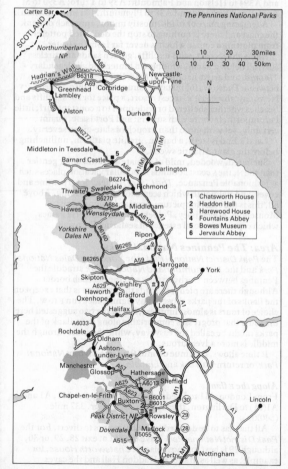

The Pennines National Parks

1	Chatsworth House
2	Haddon Hall
3	Harewood House
4	Fountains Abbey
5	Bowes Museum
6	Jervaulx Abbey

High Peak to Glossop. Urban roads through Ashton-under-Lyne, Oldham and Rochdale, then by A6033 to Keighley, and A629 NW to Skipton. B6265, B6160 and minor roads to Hawes and Thwaite. Down Swaledale by B6270 and A6108 to Richmond. From here B6274 across to A66 which is followed NW to Barnard Castle. Up Teesdale on B6277 to Alston, then A689 as far as Lambley, and minor roads to Greenhead on Hadrian's Wall at the base of Northumberland National Park. 220 miles (352km).

An alternative start to this tour would be to leave Derby by A52, which leads to Dovedale, one of the most scenic parts of the *Peak District National Park*, returning to A6 along A515 and B5055, to see medieval Haddon Hall, a clutch of famous caves, and *Chatsworth House*, the 'Palace of the Peak.'

A57 climbs across high wild country leading to the great urban complex whose heart is *Manchester*. Brontë fans will hasten on to Haworth (see *Brontë Parsonage*) or will bear left at Oxenhope from where the Pennine Way and other paths lead to the ruined farm believed to have inspired *Wuthering Heights*.

Skipton with its 13thC castle marks the border of *Yorkshire Dales National Park*, then at Hawes a choice has to be made: straight ahead to Thwaite, then down Swaledale, or E down Wensleydale. The former is scenically the more spectacular (Buttertubs Pass seems like the roof of the world), while Wensleydale is gentler and offers detours to Aysgarth Falls and Jervaulx Abbey.

The Bowes Museum at *Barnard Castle* provides rich cultural stimulus before the long drive to Greenhead on *Hadrian's Wall* at the southern limit of *Northumberland National Park*.

Area: South Wales

For a general view of the region see *The Valleys*, *Brecon Beacons National Park*, the *Preseli Hills* and *Pembrokeshire Coast National Park*.

The aim is to drive from the Severn Bridge to Carmarthen and then on to St David's, but *The Valleys* almost immediately block the way, forcing a decision between N or S. The southern road (the highway) will be the choice of those impatient for faraway places; it often goes above ugly industrial sores, but even these can hardly fail to make their impact, be it awe, revulsion or even sorrow for giants now helpless in decline. Those preferring countryside will break away to the N, making Abergavenny their starting point and there deciding how best to tackle *Brecon Beacons National Park*. But whichever route is chosen it would be a pity not to take at least a peek into the once notorious Valleys, for, transformed though they now are, they still insistently represent something uniquely Welsh.

The straight line

From the Severn Bridge M4 virtually all the way to Carmarthen. 95 miles (152km).

This is the easy way to take in a large number of important places described in the *Wales A–Z*: *Chepstow*, with Tintern Abbey just to its N up the lush Wye Valley; Romano-British Caerwent and Roman Caerleon (see *Newport*); *Cardiff*, the national capital and starting point for exploring the Rhondda, Cynon, Taff and Rhymney valleys, this last with awesome Caerphilly Castle; the steel town of Port Talbot below the Cwm Afan Scenic Route; *Swansea* and *The Gower Peninsula*; and *Kidwelly Castle* near the sea.

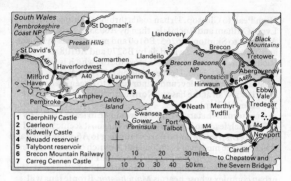

Between The Valleys and the National Park

From Abergavenny by A465 to Merthyr Tydfil, Neath and Swansea. 45 miles (72km).

Admittedly the A465 can be bleak, scarred and in places industrialized, but here it is not so much the road that matters as that it separates *The Valleys* and *Brecon Beacons National Park*, thus affording a choice of entry points into both. Ebbw Vale, Tredegar, Merthyr Tydfil and Hirwaun are all gateways to the Valleys, the bare pass high above Hirwaun being especially spectacular. Should the park be the objective, however, then any road N will speedily reach open country. If indecisive, then try the minor road from Merthyr Tydfil through Pontsticill to the Neuadd and Talybont reservoirs, a tranquil and lovely region in which forest, water and moorland mountain combine in rare perfection. What is more, for anyone who does not feel like driving, or maybe just to amuse the children, there is (at least for some of the way) the quaint Brecon Mountain Railway.

The northern route around Brecon Beacons National Park

From Abergavenny, A40 through Brecon to Llandovery and Carmarthen. 69 miles (110km).

Bustling yet dignified, Abergavenny sits between the two hard-to-resist heights of Blorenge and Sugar Loaf, both accessible most of the way by car although the approaches, especially to Sugar Loaf, are steep and narrow. The A40, if never spectacular, is pleasantly scenic, at Tretower cutting between the Beacons proper and the Black Mountains to reach *Brecon*, from where the interesting Mountain Centre on Mynydd Illtyd is only a short way sw. Farther on, the dramatically perched ruins of Carreg Cennen Castle are close to Llandeilo.

Into the southwest

A40 from Carmarthen to Haverfordwest, then A487 to St David's. 48 miles (77km).

The *Wales A–Z* entries for *Preseli Hills* and *Pembrokeshire Coast National Park* cover much of a region which is second to none in the richness and variety of what it has to offer, and there can surely be few visitors who fail to satisfy one or several personal interests. For prehistory there is Preseli; for admirers of Dylan Thomas there is *Laugharne*; for themes ecclesiastical, *St David's*, Lamphey, Caldey, St Dogmael's; for oil tankers, Milford Haven; for scenery, virtually the whole coast; and as for castles, they abound.

Area: Snowdonia National Park

This tour combines much of the best of Snowdonia with nearly all the sights and places of interest listed under *Snowdonia National Park* in the *Wales A–Z*.

From Conwy to Dolgellau and Machynlleth

From Conwy on A470 through Betws-y-Coed and Ffestiniog to Dolgellau, then A487 to Machynlleth. 64 miles (102km).

Betws-y-Coed in the N and Dolgellau to the S offer themselves as admirable bases from which to discover the park in more depth. From the former, famed for its forest walks, Snowdon proper is only a short drive to the W. The triangle formed by A4085, A498 and A4086 is a magnificent tour in itself. Nant Gwynant (A498) forms the base of the triangle and is by far the loveliest side: at first a gentle green ascent past woods and lakes, but breaking soon into the open as a cut along a mountainside high above a valley, the other wall of which is Snowdon's massif.

Dolgellau urges a clamber up Cader Idris or a taste of the coast, N for example to Harlech or S to Tywyn and a ride on the Talyllyn Railway.

There is plenty in between, too: along the Vale of Conwy, Bodnant Gardens (see *Conwy*) and the interesting Trefriw Woollen Mills (for these the river must be crossed near Bodnant or at Llanrwst); between Betws-y-Coed and Ffestiniog, the Gloddfa Ganol Slate Mine, the Llechwedd Slate Caverns, the Ffestiniog Hydro-electric Centre or a trip on the scenic Festiniog Railway; and between Dolgellau and Machynlleth, the instructive Centre for Alternative Technology, sited in a disused slate quarry.

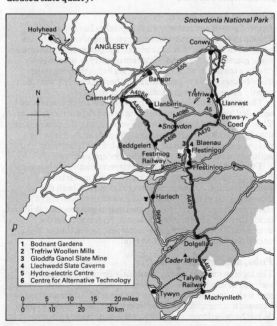

Snowdonia National Park

1 Bodnant Gardens
2 Trefriw Woollen Mills
3 Gloddfa Ganol Slate Mine
4 Llechwedd Slate Caverns
5 Hydro-electric Centre
6 Centre for Alternative Technology

| 0 | 5 | 10 | 15 | 20 miles |
| 0 | 10 | 20 | 30 km |

Accommodations, food and drink

The true glory of the British kitchen has always been its fine materials and simple methods of preparation. Every corner of Britain has its own specialties: oysters from Colchester, shrimps from Morecambe Bay, crab from Cornwall, cod and herring (the latter often kippered) from the North Sea, Dover Sole; beef from Scotland or Herefordshire; lamb from Wales or Sussex; pork and ham from Wiltshire; sausages from Oxford and Cumberland; prepared meats, and raised pies and tarts (both savory and sweet), from Leicestershire, Derbyshire, Yorkshire and Lancashire; a savory pudding from Yorkshire and several sweet ones from Sussex; fruits from Worcestershire and Kent; Cheddar cheese from the west of England and Stilton from the East Midlands; pastries and cakes from Lancashire; and laverbread, made from seaweed, from south Wales. A revival of interest in local specialties means that it is increasingly common to find these delights in local restaurants.

There has been a revival, too, in the alcoholic accompaniments: cider from the West Country and occasionally East Anglia; the English styles of ale, from Newcastle, Yorkshire, Burton (most important of all), London, Kent, and just about everywhere else; and English wines, from the south and west. No visitor to Britain should miss the single malt whiskies of Scotland, although the spirit of England is gin, from either London or Plymouth. Nor should it be forgotten that the British are largely responsible for the renown enjoyed by the red wines of Bordeaux, and that they helped create just about every fortified wine from Marsala to Madeira and, most notably, the great sherries and port.

Country house hotels

A new dawn of gastronomy and hospitality has appeared in Britain in recent years with the burgeoning of country house hotels. The ill wind that has reduced the old wealth has allowed some grand Georgian and Victorian country houses to enjoy new lives as hotels and restaurants. As befits their heritage, these houses strive to perpetuate the best of stately living, and greatly exceed that in gastronomic sophistication.

The grandest of the country house hotels are characterized by secluded locations, magnificent views and expansive grounds. They are reached by tree-lined driveways, and their owners or managers are apt to greet guests at the door and arrange for a welcoming cup of tea to be served in a lounge filled with antiques or on a terrace overlooking the croquet lawn.

Two or three country house hotels were pioneers of classical French cooking in provincial England, and much later of *nouvelle cuisine*. An even more recent trend has been the increasing use of fresh, local produce and the featuring of traditional regional recipes. In a setting of gastronomic skill and innovation, this has created dishes far removed from the overcooked meats and soggy, uninteresting vegetables which once passed for classical British food.

Pubs, inns and urban hotels

The foreign visitor seeking a uniquely British experience is inclined to like the idea of staying in a pub. The British traveler may well favor the same kind of place but for a different reason – because it is inexpensive. The snag is that the majority of pubs do not have bedrooms. A pub's role is to provide a place in which to meet, talk and drink. There are still a good many pubs which do not serve food, although more are doing so. A pub which serves English ale in the traditional fashion (conditioned in the cask and served at a natural temperature) may well be listed in the *Good Beer Guide* (published by CAMRA), and display a window-sticker announcing this. Although the guide's prime purpose is to identify sources of good ale, it does also indicate which pubs offer accommodation.

A pub that is seriously in the business of accommodation is likely to describe itself as an inn, and many places so designated offer all the services of a full-scale hotel. The more pub-like type of inn often offers very good value; but the imposing inn on the town square does not always live up to its outward appearances, either in food or service.

The same is true of many city-center hotels, which tend to favor the type of Franco-international menu that owes more to predictability and prefabrication than to culinary skill. This is notably the case in some industrial and business cities in the north of England and the Midlands and in Wales, where good restaurants are least common. This is not at all the case in London, however, where almost all the best-known hotels have outstanding kitchens.

Restaurants with rooms
The most recent trend, and a very welcome one, is the notion of the restaurant with rooms. Typically, a restaurant finds a little space in which to convert a few rooms for diners who want to stay overnight. This is helpful for those who do not wish to drive after having a couple of bottles of wine; it affords the opportunity to make a good dinner the focus of a country weekend; and it makes a gastronomic touring vacation easier.

Hotels and guesthouses
It is expensive to eat well in Britain, and hotel accommodations are not cheap. Price and availability aside, the decision must also depend upon the style of accommodations required. Perhaps the biggest distinction is between privately managed hotels and those owned by groups. Critics of the older type of privately managed hotel in Britain are inclined to point to draftiness and shabbiness, while there are travelers perverse enough to evince affection for such faults. Unperverse travelers will, of course, have fewer surprises – bad or good – in a chain hotel, especially if it is a modern one. Between the extremes, Britain has as varied and distinctive a range of hotels as can be found anywhere in the world. Guest rooms may sometimes be small, but the beds themselves, and the lounge areas, are usually very comfortable. Central heating is almost universal, and almost all British hotels these days have at least some *en suite* bathrooms, while increasingly televisions are provided in bedrooms. Business guests would be well advised, however, to check whether there are telephones in the rooms. As elsewhere in the world, service has declined recently. Tea-making apparatus is often provided in rooms, and some of the larger city-center hotels have switched to an unconvincing impersonation of the country house-party buffet breakfast. Apart from breakfast waiters, porters can also be in short supply.

Groups and chains
The grandest of the country house hotels and some of the most ambitious restaurants belong (although they are privately

43

owned) to the French organization *Relais et Châteaux*.
Membership is an accolade, in that they have to be elected.
Relais et Châteaux does not have a central reservation office in
Britain, and its headquarters are in Paris, at the Hotel Crillon
(*10 Place de la Concorde* ☎ *Paris 742–0020*).

A substantial number of privately owned hotels belong to
various marketing groups, among which the most useful from a
reservation viewpoint is **Prestige** (*13–14 Golden Sq., London
W1R 3AJ* ☎ *(01) 734–4267*). There are several national chains
owned by brewers, and there are three big groups: **Trust
House Forte** (*71–75 Uxbridge Rd., London W5 5SL* ☎ *(01)
567–3444*), **Grand Metropolitan** (*14–16 Dorland House,
Lower Regent St., London SW1Y 4PH* ☎ *(01) 930–7722*), and
Mount Charlotte (*2 The Calls, Leeds LS2 7JU* ☎ *(0532)
39111*).

Mount Charlotte's hotels tend to be the most idiosyncratic.
Although Trust House Forte owns many old hotels, members
of this chain show most strongly the mark of corporate control.
In style, the hotels belonging to Grand Metropolitan tend to fall
between the two.

Reservations

At vacation times and in tourist areas, a hotel reservation may
be essential. Many hotels will ask for a letter of confirmation, and
some for a small deposit. The English and the Welsh Tourist
Boards, and their Tourist Information Centres, can often help
with hotel bookings. Reservations are also essential in almost all
good-quality restaurants.

Hours

Pub hours   These vary slightly in different towns. See *On-
the-spot information* in *Basic information*.
Meals in hotels   Cooked breakfasts usually end at 9am,
although some hotels are more flexible. Lunch is normally
served from 12.30–2.30pm. Hotels which serve afternoon tea,
with sandwiches, scones and cakes, usually do so from
3.30–5.30pm. In the north of England and sometimes in
Wales, a high tea of cold meats or cooked fish may be served at
about 6pm instead of dinner, and the last serving of the evening
meal may be as early as 8pm, a time at which London
restaurants are just beginning to get into their stride.
Checking-out   Times vary between 11am and 1pm, although
most hotels will agree to an extension if they can.

Shopping

There are very few English or Welsh towns of any size that do
not have at least one modern shopping center. Some have real
character, most are stereotypes, all are well stocked. In most,
also, will be found at least three shops which in their way rank as
British institutions: **Marks & Spencer**, **Boots the Chemists**,
and **W.H. Smith** for magazines, books, stationery and much
else.

Although just about anything can be bought nearly anywhere, it is much more enjoyable, and sometimes cheaper, to
find specialty articles in their district of origin. Woolens and

textiles are a good example, and for price, choice and design nobody is likely to be disappointed in Wales, along the road between Carmarthen and Aberaeron for instance, or at Trefriw in the Conwy valley.

Antiques and chinaware can be found in most parts, yet there are also special districts. For antiques, East Anglia is a rich hunting ground, while on a more concentrated scale there is the small Wiltshire town of Hungerford in which antique shops line the main road. As for ceramics, potters abound, but the discerning buyer is likely to have his eye on one of the distinguished names: Wedgwood, perhaps, or Royal Worcester. Both these firms have their own retail outlets (see *Stoke-on-Trent* and *Worcester*). Stoke-on-Trent is, of course, the heart of the chinaware industry, and the tourist office will provide a list of china shops on request. Glassware ranks close to china, the elegant Dartington glass, for instance, being sold in an attractive retail shop beside Devon's river Dart, near Totnes (see *Dartmoor National Park*).

For sheepskin goods, two districts stand out: Glastonbury in Somerset, and the Lake District. Semi-precious and other stones are the target of many visitors. The choice here is wide and the hunt can lead to Cornwall's Lizard for the veined red and green serpentine, to the Peak District for the now rare Blue John, or to Whitby in Yorkshire for jet. Delicate Nottingham lace, esteemed since medieval times, can still be bought at the Lace Centre below the castle. And if you are still chasing that elusive out-of-print book, try Hay-on-Wye (Powys), accepted center of the second-hand book trade.

Through the Retail Export Scheme, certain visitors qualify for exemption from Value Added Tax. The scheme – which involves production of passport, the completion of a form, and the collection of the goods at the point of departure from Britain – is not operated by all shops.

Clothing sizes
When shops give clothing sizes in inches or centimeters, use the following conversion scale to determine the correct size

12 in	16	20	24	28	32	36	40	44	48
30 cm	40	50	60	70	80	90	100	110	120

When standardized codes are used, although these may be found to vary considerably, the following provides a useful guide.

Women's clothing sizes

UK/US sizes	8/6	10/8	12/10	14/12	16/14	18/16
Bust in/cm	31/80	32/81	34/86	36/91	38/97	40/102
Hips in/cm	33/85	34/86	36/91	38/97	40/102	42/107

Men's clothing sizes

European code (suits)	44	46	48	50	52	54	56
Chest in/cm	34/86	36/91	38/97	40/102	42/107	44/112	46/117
Collar in/cm	13½/34	14/36	14½/37	15/38	15½/39	16/41	16½/42
Waist in/cm	28/71	30/76	32/81	34/86	36/91	38/97	40/102
Inside leg in/cm	28/71	29/74	30/76	31/79	32/81	33/84	34/86

Shoe sizes	Women's					Men's				
UK/US sizes	3/4½	4/5½	5/6½	6/7½	7/8½	8/8½	9/9½	10/10½	11/11½
European	36	37	38	39	40	42	43	44	46

England and Wales A – Z

The A – Z section lists the best-known and most accessible sights and places of interest in England and Wales. Times and entry details are accurate at the time of printing, but last entry is often ½ hr before closing time and sights may be closed on public holidays; telephone to check. Photography is usually allowed, but flash, tripods or other equipment may be forbidden.

Department of the Environment (DOE), Welsh Office (WO) and National Trust (NT) properties have been indicated. The DOE and WO care for a cross-section of ancient monuments all of which are closed on Christmas Eve, Christmas Day, Boxing Day and New Year's Day; some of their smaller properties may close 1–2pm.

Inexpensive season tickets, valid for one year and entitling the holder to free entry to all DOE and WO sites, can be bought at virtually all sites at which there is a custodian.

The NT (*42 Queen Anne's Gate, London SW1H 9AS*) is the largest conservation society in Britain and its members are entitled to free entry to all NT properties. There is no overall policy on public holiday opening hours, so it is wise to check.

Open to View tickets, valid for one month, are available to non-British visitors and entitle the holder to free entry to the many sights participating in the plan. Tickets can be obtained from tourist offices (*for details, write to BTA, 64 St James's St., London SW1A 1NF*).

Sights and places of interest

A selection of major sights with cross-references to the *A–Z*: (W) denotes sights in *Wales A–Z*; *NP* denotes National Park.

Stately homes and occupied castles
Alnwick Castle
　See *Alnwick*
Blenheim Palace
Castle Howard
Chatsworth House
Erddig
　See *Wrexham* (W)
Hampton Court
　See *London*
Harewood House
　See *Leeds*
Hatfield House
　See *St Albans*
Leeds Castle
Longleat
Osborne House
　See *Isle of Wight*
Plas Newydd
　See *Anglesey* (W)
Warwick Castle
　See *Warwick*
Windsor Castle
　See *Windsor*
Woburn Abbey

Cathedrals and minsters
Beverley Minster
　See *Hull*
Canterbury
Coventry
Durham

Ely
Gloucester
Lichfield
Lincoln
St Albans
St David's (W)
St Paul's Cathedral
　See *London*
Salisbury
Wells
Winchester
York

Museums and art galleries
American Museum
　See *Bath*
Ashmolean Museum
　See *Oxford*
Beamish North of England Open
　Air Museum
　See *Newcastle-upon-Tyne*
Birmingham Museum and Art
　Gallery
　See *Birmingham*
Bowes Museum
　See *Barnard Castle*
British Museum
　See *London*
Castle Museum
　See *York*
Fitzwilliam Museum
　See *Cambridge*
Ironbridge Gorge Museum

England A-Z

Abbotsbury
Map 4M6. Dorset. On the coast, 7 miles (11km) NW of Weymouth. Population: 500.

Orc, a courtier of King Canute, founded a Benedictine monastery here in the 11thC, and the monks, with an eye to fresh meat, introduced a colony of mute swans. The birds have long outlived the monks, and most of the visitors who today flock into this charming village of stone and thatched cottages head straight for the swannery, casting only a passing glance at what little of the monastery survived the Reformation.

Sights and places of interest
Abbey Tithe Barn ▥
Between the village and the swannery. No admittance, but well seen from outside.
By the 15thC the monastery at Abbotsbury had become prosperous enough to justify the building of this huge barn for the storage of its wealth. Being both massive and useful, it survived the Dissolution. Today it still serves as a store, mainly for the local reed used for thatching.

Abbotsbury Swannery
s of the village, near the shore ▤ ✳ ➡ *Open mid-May to mid-Sept 9.30am–4.30pm.*
Each April hundreds of swans congregate here to nest in the reeds. Only when the nests are built and the eggs laid is the public admitted, the visitors showing an interest in the swans which is almost insultingly unreciprocated by the birds.

St Catherine's Chapel ✝
On Chapel Hill, immediately s of the village. DOE ▤ ◁≋ *Open mid-Mar to mid-Oct Mon–Sat 9.30am–6.30pm, Sun 2–6.30pm; mid-Oct to mid-Mar Mon–Sat 9.30am–4pm, Sun 2–4pm.*
Built for the monastery in the mid-15thC, this stone-roofed chapel survived the destruction of the Reformation probably because no one could be bothered to demolish anything so substantial and so inconveniently sited as a source of building material. It now stands as a conspicuous objective for all who feel a compulsion to climb hills.

Sub-tropical Gardens
Beyond the w end of the village ☎ *(030587) 387* ▤ ▣ ➡ *Open mid-Mar to mid-Oct 10am–6pm.*
A restful, sheltered place where peacocks display among exotic trees and plants. Shrubs and plants not easily found elsewhere are on sale.

Aldeburgh

Map 7J12. Suffolk. 20 miles (32km) NE of Ipswich.
Population: 2,800.

This small, quiet and unassuming coastal resort, with a long main street of some character behind a rather bleak shingle beach, is the home of one of England's leading music festivals, founded in 1948 by the composer Benjamin Britten, the singer Peter Pears and several other enthusiasts.

Events In June, Aldeburgh Festival. (*Festival Office, High St., Aldeburgh* ☎ *(072885) 3637.*) The program includes opera, orchestral concerts, chamber music, recitals, ballet and lectures at the Snape Maltings, 5 miles (8km) W, and at various locations in Aldeburgh.

Ⓗ **Brudenell**

The Parade, Aldeburgh, Suffolk IP15 5BU ☎ *(072885) 2071* ▮▮
🗪 47 ▭ 47 ▬ ▱ ▱ AE CB Ⓞ Ⓞ VISA
Location: Seafront, at s end of town. A modern hotel in a Victorian frame, with uninterrupted views across the North Sea which in stormy weather can surge thrillingly close. The hotel caters well to families.
‡ ☐ ⬚ ≪ ⌂ ⛵

Ⓗ **Wentworth**

Wentworth Rd., Aldeburgh, Suffolk IP15 5BU ☎ *(072885) 2312*
▮▮ 🗪 33 ▭ 20 ▬ ▱ ▱ Ⓞ *Closed Jan.*
Location: By the sea, at N end of town. Overlooking the beach, this family-run hotel has a relaxed style and something of the feeling of a small country house. The restaurant specializes in seafood.
⌂ ⅏ ☐ ⬚ ≪ ⌂ ⛵

Alnwick

Map 15B8. Northumb. 32 miles (50km) N of Newcastle-upon-Tyne. Population: 7,200 ℹ *The Shambles* ☎ *(0665) 603120.*

With its narrow streets and cobbled sloping center, below the evocatively named **Hotspur Tower** (a survival of the ancient walls), this small town still has a medieval feel about it. The great ducal castle that sprawls across its northern edge and to which it owes its birth, its history and to some extent its present-day prosperity, is the main attraction.

Alnwick Castle Ⅲ ☆

N edge of the town ☎ *(0665) 602722* 🄼 ▬ *Open May–Sept 1–5pm. Closed Sat.*

A Norman wooden motte-and-bailey fortress gave way in the 12thC to a stone successor, which was soon in its turn superseded by the great gray fortress of the Percys, earls of Northumberland and lords of the North. In the 18thC the first duke employed Robert Adam to restore the castle, and this work, followed by further restoration during the next century, resulted in today's sumptuous ducal residence.

The **gatehouses** are the main survivors from medieval times. Beyond, the **State Apartments** are notable in particular for paintings by such masters as Titian, Tintoretto, Canaletto and Van Dyck, while a museum of British and Roman antiquities and a state coach of 1825 are among much else of interest.

Sights nearby

Bamburgh Castle ☆

Bamburgh, on the coast, 16 miles (26km) N of Alnwick ☎ *(06684) 208* 🄼 ▬ *Open Easter–Oct from 1pm. Telephone for closing times.*

Only the most sluggish imagination will fail to quicken before this huge red-sandstone pile, standing almost arrogantly on its rocky basalt outcrop above the sea. Bamburgh's long and violent history goes back to AD547 when the first, wooden fortress was built. Wrecked by Vikings some 450yrs later, the fortress was rebuilt in stone by Henry II, only to be destroyed again by the bombards of Edward IV. Although much of the castle was restored in the 19thC, the keep dates from the 12thC.

Cragside ▥

9 miles (14.5km) sw of Alnwick. Entry from B6341 ☎ (0669) 20333. NT ▣▤ ▦ ➤ House open Apr−Sept 1−6pm (closed Mon except bank holidays); Oct Wed, Sat, Sun 2−5pm. Country park open Apr−Sept 10.30am−6pm, Oct 10.30am−5pm, Nov−Mar Sat, Sun 10.30am−4pm.

The Victorian industrialist Lord Armstrong bought the estate in 1864 and commissioned Richard Norman Shaw to convert the relatively modest house into a palatial mansion. Armstrong's and Shaw's progress was essentially additive, and the house is made up of a bewildering maze of rooms with a remarkable variety of styles, some riotously ornate.

Armstrong's bold thinking extended to the grounds, where he dammed streams to create lakes and planted 7 million trees. Much of this now ranks as a country park.

Dunstanburgh Castle

On the coast, 6 miles (9.5km) N of Alnwick ☎ (066576) 231. NT/DOE ▣▤ Open mid-Mar to mid-Oct Mon−Sat 9.30am−6.30pm, Sun 2.30−6.30pm; mid-Oct to mid-Mar Mon−Sat 9.30am−4pm, Sun 2−4pm.

Cars must be left either at **Craster**, 1 mile (1.5km) s or **Embleton**, 1½ miles (2.5km) N. Those reluctant to walk the whole distance will find that the extensive if rather skeletal ruins on their isolated headland soon come into view. Begun in 1316 by the Earl of Lancaster, the castle was much modified by John of Gaunt but failed to survive the Wars of the Roses.

Warkworth Castle

On the coast, 6 miles (9.5km) SE of Alnwick ☎ (0665) 711423. DOE ▣▤ ➤ Open Apr−Sept 9.30am−6.30pm.

Sprawled over its great motte high above a hook of the little river Coquet, Warkworth's still defiant stones represent some four centuries of defensive building. Something of the E curtain wall survives from Robert de Mowbray's stronghold of the 11thC; the gatehouse, the s wall and some other features illustrate enlargement during the early 13thC; and the massive cruciform **keep** (the view from the top makes the climb worthwhile) rose during the 14thC.

When approaching the village across the Coquet, do not miss the 14thC bridge with its most unusual fortified gate.

Ⓗ **The White Swan**
Bondgate Within, Alnwick, Northumb NE66 1TB ☎ (0665) 602109 ❾ 53168 ▯ ➪ 40 ▭ 40 ➤ ▭ ⇥ AE Ⓕ Ⓒ VISA

Location: *In town center, just below Hotspur Tower.* There is still something of the atmosphere of the old coaching inn here, especially in the dining room which is decorated with interesting period pictures and silhouettes. Try to look into the ballroom, the carved panelling of which came from the liner *Olympic*, sister ship of the *Titanic*.
▢ ▨ ▟

Arundel

Map 6M9. West Sussex. 18 miles (29km) w of Brighton. Population: 2,400 ℹ 61 High St. ☎ (0903) 882268.

Tradition rather than evidence insists that the pretty name of this ancient place derives from the French *hirondelle*, a swallow, but it is a fact that 'Harundell' was mentioned as early as AD877. When approaching the town from the N, do not fail to go down to the coastal plain and then look back, for it is the ensemble of the castle and adjacent Roman Catholic cathedral (1873) poised above the small town that is the visual essence of Arundel.

Arundel Castle ▥ ☆

Above the town on Mill Road ☎ (0903) 883136 ▣▤ ➤ Open Apr−May, Sept−Oct 1−5pm; June−Aug and bank holidays noon−5pm. Closed Sat.

For all its Norman effect, the present edifice (home of the dukes of

Norfolk) is largely a rebuilding of the 18th–19thC following the
wrecking by Cromwell of the late 11thC castle, which was known to have
been successor to an earlier fortification on this commanding site. The
castle contains portraits by, among others, Van Dyck, Gainsborough,
Reynolds and Lawrence.

Sight nearby
Roman Villa
Bignor, 5 miles (8km) N of Arundel ☎ *(07987) 259* ▨ ⇌ *Open
Apr–Sept 10am–6.30pm, Oct–Mar 10am–5.30pm. Closed Mon
except in Aug and on bank holidays.*
Romans lived in this pleasant spot below the South Downs from about
the 2nd–4thC AD. The occupants of the 4thC were of sufficient wealth
and good taste to be able to afford what are now regarded as some of the
finest mosaic floors in Britain, depicting a variety of subjects from
dolphins to dancing girls. A museum shows a plan of the original villa.

Ⓗ **Norfolk Arms**
High St., Arundel, West Sussex BN18 9AD ☎ *(0903) 882101* Ⅲ▢
⇋ 35 ▭ 26 ⇌ ▣▣▣ ⇌ AE ⏀ © VISA
Location: Town center, where the High St. runs through the Square. The
tenth Duke of Norfolk built this coaching inn in 1787 and touches of this
past live on in the wrought-iron staircase and the carefully arranged
antiques which give character to the public rooms. Log fires cheer the
two bars, the dining room (offering some local specialities) has brass
rubbings and carved panels, and there is a choice between modern and a
rather older although just as comfortable style of bedroom.
▢ ▨ ⚓

Hotel/restaurant nearby
Climping (*4 miles/6.5km S of Arundel*).

Ⓗ Ⓡ **Bailiffscourt** ⌂ Ⅲ
Climping, Littlehampton, West Sussex BN1Y 5RW ☎ *(09064)
23511* Ⅲ ⇋ 19 ▭ 19 ⇌ ▣▣ ⇌ AE ⏀ © VISA
Ⓡ Ⅲ▢ ▬ ▬ ⇌ *Last orders 9pm.*
*Location: Around a square courtyard, in a 1,000 acre estate near the sea, S of
Arundel Castle.* What looks like a superbly English eccentricity turns out
to be Irish whimsy. Lord Moyne (then the Honorable Walter Guinness)
had Britain searched for medieval stone arches, doorways and windows
so that he could re-create a monks' courthouse which had once stood on
this site. The result, architecturally correct in every detail, was
completed less than 50yrs ago. The bedrooms have log fires and oak
furniture, and seven have four-poster beds. The kitchen is appropriately
hearty, serving such specialties as its venison, orange and chestnut pie.
▨ ▢ ▨ ⚓ ⇌ ⚓ ℘ ⩗ ⚓ ⚓

Avebury Circle ★
*Map **4K7**. Avebury, Wilts. 10 miles (16km) S of Swindon*
i The Great Barn, Avebury ☎ *(06723) 425. NT* ▣ ⇌ *Always
open.*
This is one of the world's most extensive and exciting
prehistoric circle sites, made up of an outer earthwork belt
enclosing an area of over 28 acres, an inner trench which may
originally have been 40ft (12m) wide and 30ft (9m) deep, and a
ring of mysterious unhewn sarsen megaliths within which are
remains of two smaller circles. From the complex the remains of
an avenue of stones leads away to the SE. Although it is generally
agreed that it was built *c.*2300BC, there is no agreement as to the
monument's purpose.

  Avebury stands in a downland district rich in lesser
prehistoric sites such as **Windmill Hill**, **Silbury Hill** and **West
Kennet Long Barrow**. Information on these sites can be
obtained from the Avebury tourist office or the nearby
Alexander Keiller Museum (☎*(06723) 250; DOE* ▨ ⇌ *open
mid-Mar to mid-Oct Mon–Sat 9.30am–6.30pm, Sun 2–6.30pm*

except Apr–Sept 9.30am–6.30pm; mid-Oct to mid-Mar Mon–Sat 9.30am–4pm, Sun 2–4pm).

Aylesbury

Map 6J9. Bucks. 41 miles (65km) NW of London.
Population: 40,600 **i** *County Hall, Walton St.* ☎ *(0296) 5000.*
In spite of encroaching new developments, visitors to Aylesbury can still catch a glimpse of what the old town was like. **Market Square** contains the 18thC **County Hall** and the old **Bull's Head** inn. Nearby, the 15thC **King's Head**, owned by the National Trust, has a medieval gateway and windows, and a chair said to have been used by Oliver Cromwell. Good 17th–18thC houses can be seen in **Temple St.** and **Church St.**, and **St Mary's Church** is worth a visit for its fine Norman font.

Sights nearby

Claydon House 🏛
13 miles (21km) NW of Aylesbury ☎ *(029673) 349. NT* 🚻 🅿 ➡
Open Apr–Oct 2–6pm, bank holidays 12.30–6pm. Closed Thurs, Fri.
Wildly flamboyant Rococo decoration (including in one room what might almost be called Chinese Rococo) and Florence Nightingale memorabilia are offered here – a strange association of the frivolous and the serious explained by the fact that this 18thC mansion was once the home of the Verney family, and Florence often visited her sister Parthenhope, wife of the second baronet.

Waddesdon Manor
On A41, 6 miles (9.5km) NE of Aylesbury ☎ *(0296) 651211. NT* 🚻
🅿 *in house* 🅿 ➡ *Open late Mar–Oct: house 2–6pm; grounds Wed–Sat 1–6pm, Sun 11.30am–6pm. Good Fri and bank holiday Mon house and grounds open 11am–6pm. Closed Mon–Wed following bank holiday.*
When Baron Ferdinand de Rothschild built this ostentatious château (the name Manor is singularly inappropriate) in 1874–89, a bare hilltop had first to be leveled and any space not required for the house was then planted with literally hundreds of fully grown trees. The house contains Baron Ferdinand's art collection (notably French, Dutch and Flemish paintings and English portraits), the Sèvres collection and more general acquisitions. Priceless though these collections are, Waddesdon is almost suffocatingly furnished and decorated, and it is something of a relief to escape into the splendid grounds.

Hotel/restaurant nearby

Aston Clinton *(3 miles/5km SE of Aylesbury).*

🅷 🅡 **The Bell** 🏨 ⌂
Aston Clinton, Bucks HP22 5HP ☎ *(0296) 630252* ☎ *826715* 📟 *to*
📶 ⋟ *21* 🛏 *21* ➡ ⇌ *VISA*
🅡 📶 ⊡ ▬ ⚊ *Last orders 9.45pm.*
Location: In center, on A41. Once a coaching inn, this renowned old establishment with its own wine shop to serve every need of the oenophile, and with many of the bedrooms in a converted brewery, reaches close to being a Chiltern Hills heaven for the bibulous. Only cask-conditioned beer is missing. Elsewhere, all is arranged with great thought, from the sandwiches in the bar to the balance and proportion of the menu in the classical French/English restaurant.

Bell Inn Smokies head a list of fish starters, and there are about a dozen meatier selections for the main course, plus a roast which changes daily. There is also a good selection of English cheeses and traditional English and French desserts.
□ 🖾 ❧ ⚘

Barnard Castle

Map 15D7. Co. Durham. 15 miles (24km) W of Darlington.
Population: 5,300 **i** *43 Galgate* ☎ *(0833) 38481.*
A small country town, best known for its amazing **Bowes**

Museum. It also has a curious **market house** dating from 1747 and a ruined Norman **castle**.

Bowes Museum ★
At the E of the town ☎ *(0833) 37139* 🎫 🅿 🚗 *Open May–Sept Mon–Sat 10am–5.30pm, Sun 2–5pm; Mar–Apr, Oct Mon–Sat 10am–5pm, Sun 2–4pm; Nov–Feb Mon–Sat 10am–4pm, Sun 2–4pm. Closed one week at Christmas.*

A fantastic, French-style château built by John Bowes and his French wife Josephine, not as a residence but simply to house the paintings, furniture, ceramics, textiles and antiquities they collected from 1852–74. If, out of the museum's many main departments, a choice has to be made, then priority might be given to the lofty picture galleries, and, within these, to the Spanish school of which the museum has the largest collection in England, including El Greco's *The Tears of St Peter* and Goya's *Interior of a Prison* ★ – a work of haunting despair.

Bath ★
Map 4K7. Avon. 107 miles (170km) w of London. Population: 84,700 ℹ *Abbey Churchyard* ☎ *(0225) 62831.*

Romans below ground, Georgians above: that, in a nutshell, is Bath. It all started, or so we are told, in about 800BC when King Lear's leprous father, emulating his diseased swine, rolled in some mysteriously warm mud, found himself cured and built a city. Be that as it may, it was certainly comfort-seeking Romans who developed the baths in about AD55, calling their settlement Aquae Sulis, Sul being a local Celtic god.

Aquae Sulis lasted some 400yrs, but Bath then had to wait at least another 1,200yrs before once again becoming host to a wealthy society set on elegance, ease and pleasure. One woman and three men orchestrated this 18thC Bath: Queen Anne, who simply visited the town and liked it; Richard ('Beau') Nash who had the will and charisma to become the Master of Ceremonies; and the two John Woods, father and son, who, together with others close on their heels, created the honey-colored stone buildings that have ever since been the glory of Bath.

Event   In May or June, Bath International Festival of Music. Concerts are given in a variety of splendid settings such as the Assembly Rooms, the Banqueting Room of the Guildhall, the Theatre Royal and the abbey.

Sights and places of interest
Assembly Rooms
Alfred St. ☎ *(0225) 61111. NT* 🎫 🚗 *Open Apr–Oct Mon–Sat 9.30am–6pm, Sun 10am–6pm; Nov–Mar Mon–Sat 10am–5pm, Sun 11am–5pm.*

The younger John Wood built these elegant rooms in 1771, a German bomb gutted them in 1942, and they were later rebuilt with interior decoration in the original late 18thC style. As in the past, they are used for functions. The Assembly Rooms also house the *Museum of Costume* (see below).

Bath Abbey † ☆
Abbey Churchyard, at s end of High St. ☎ *(0225) 330289.*

A Saxon abbey of 791 was followed by a Norman cathedral in 1107, this in turn giving way to today's abbey, dating from 1499. On the turrets that

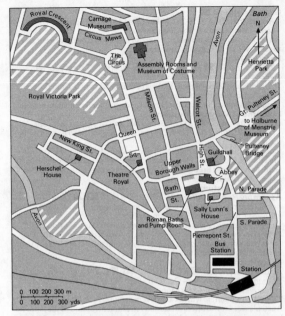

rise on either side of the w front, carved angels, some climbing, some descending, are said to represent a dream which inspired the decision to rebuild. Inside, all is height (the nave is nearly three times as high as it is wide) and the superb fan vaulting can be well seen, thanks to the high clerestory windows.

Carriage Museum

Circus Mews ☎ *(0225) 25175* ➤ *Open May to mid-Sept Mon–Sat 9.30am–6pm, Sun 10am–6pm, mid-Sept to Apr Mon–Sat 10am–5pm, Sun 11am–5pm. Carriage rides* *in summer only.*
In a building designed by the younger John Wood in 1759 to serve as stables and coach house for the wealthy residents of the Circus, this is one of the country's largest collections of carriages and coaching equipment.

Georgian Bath �🏛 ☆
Bath Street, known for its colonnades, includes the Cross Bath which, although medieval in origin, was redesigned by Thomas Baldwin in 1787. The bath, fed by one of the hot springs, can be seen through a grille.

The **Circus**, designed by the elder Wood, has three approaches each of which is faced by a perfect crescent of 11 houses.

The **Guildhall**, although built by Baldwin in 1766, was given its Baroque wings over a century later. The Banqueting Room, with magnificent 18thC chandeliers, is the principal internal feature (*open during normal working hours unless in use*).

Milsom Street, a high-class shopping street, includes the Octagon (Thomas Lightoler, 1767) which was once a chapel.

The spacious and dignified **Parades** (N and S and including Pierrepont St.), a short way SE of the abbey, stand as a marvelous memorial to the Palladian vision of the elder Wood.

Pulteney Bridge, graceful and wholly charming, was designed by Robert Adam. It is still a street of small shops.

Queen Square, intended to represent a palatial forecourt, stands as the elder Wood's first great achievement in Bath (begun 1729).

Royal Crescent ★ is Bath's most spectacular and graceful Georgian feature, begun in 1767. Designed by the younger Wood, it comprises 30 houses and 114 Ionic columns. Cobbles, ironwork and lawns add to the attraction and period atmosphere.

53

Georgian House ▥
1 Royal Cres. ☎ *(0225) 28126* 🅿 *Open Mar–Oct Tues–Sat
11am–5pm, Sun 2–5pm. Closed Mon.*

An opportunity to penetrate the superior dignity of Royal Crescent and
to see how its wealthy 18thC owners lived.

Herschel House
19 New King St. ☎ *(0225) 858106* 🅿 *Open Mar–Oct Wed, Sat
2–5pm.*

William Herschel lived here: his love of musical theory led him through
mathematics to astronomy and the discovery in 1781 of the planet
Uranus. Exhibits illustrate his musical and astronomical achievements.

Holburne of Menstrie Museum
Great Pulteney St. ☎ *(0225) 66669* 🅿 🍴 ⌦ *Open Tues–Sat
11am–5pm, Sun 2.30–6pm. Closed Dec–Jan and Mon except bank
holidays.*

Paintings, miniatures and decorative art acquired during the 19thC by
Sir Thomas Holburne. The emphasis is on English masters, including
Gainsborough and Stubbs, while the display of silver ranks among the
richest in Britain.

Museum of Costume
Assembly Rooms, Alfred St. ☎ *(0225) 61111* 🅿 🍴 *Open
Apr–Oct Mon–Sat 9.30am–6pm, Sun 10am–6pm; Nov–Mar
Mon–Sat 10am–5pm, Sun 11am–5pm.*

Designer and writer Doris Langley Moore started this collection of
authentic costumes that date from 1580 (the oldest complete outfit is a
1660s court dress) to the present day. Some light relief if not hilarity may
be derived from some astonishing underwear.

Pump Room
Abbey Churchyard ☎ *(0225) 61111* 🅿 🅿 *Combined entry with
Roman Baths. Open Apr–Oct 9am–6pm but may be open until 7pm
in July and Aug; Nov–Mar Mon–Sat 9am–5pm, Sun 11am–5pm.*

This elegant room, to which came 'every creature in Bath' in Jane
Austen's words, still offers music and refreshment, although the latter no
longer includes the water which, research has proved, does more harm
than good. Note the statue of Beau Nash and a clock made by Thomas
Tompion in 1709.

Roman Baths and Museum
Abbey Churchyard ☎ *(0225) 61111* 𝑋 *See Pump Room for entry
details.*

Public baths, pub, club, health farm, café, temple annex, even tourist
lure – all these purposes were served by Aquae Sulis, whose privileged
patrons enjoyed not only all the standard facilities of such establishments
but also water that was both naturally heated and (although today this is
disputed) medicinal.

With the departure of the Romans, Aquae Sulis went into decline,
finally sinking beneath mud and marsh. In the 18thC, portions
reappeared but it was not until 1878 that the baths were really
rediscovered. Visitors can wander through the adjacent areas of the
continuing excavations and the museum before reaching the gently
steaming baths.

Sally Lunn's House
4 North Parade Passage ☎ *(0225) 61634* ⌦ *open Mon–Sat
9.30am–5.30pm, also Sun Easter–Dec 10am–5.30pm.*

A place with several claims to the visitor's attention: as the oldest house
in Bath (*c.*1482); as the coffee house made famous in around 1680 by the
pastry cook Sally Lunn (the modern version of her tea-cakes can still be
enjoyed here); and later as a favorite haunt of Beau Nash and his coterie.
The tradition continues and the house is still a restaurant.

Sights nearby
American Museum ☆
Claverton Manor, Claverton, 3 miles (5km) SE *of Bath* ☎ *(0225)
60503* 🅿 🅿 ⌦ *Open late Mar–Oct 2–5pm, bank holiday Mon and
preceding Sun 11am–5pm.*

Americans have been overheard to observe that only by coming all the
way to Claverton could they learn so much about their own forebears.
For here, in a mansion of 1820 perched high above a glorious bend of the
river Avon, two Americans, Dr Dallas Pratt and John Judkyn, in 1961
opened this museum which so admirably interprets their ancestors'
domestic life of the 17th–19thC.

This is largely achieved through a series of displays and period rooms showing, in both homey and vivid form, lifestyles as far removed from one another as those of the native Indians, the colonists of New England, the western pioneers, and the Spanish in New Mexico. But the museum goes far beyond this, covering the achievements of craftsmen and women (for instance, woodwork, glass and textiles), mounting many special exhibitions, and also offering attractions as varied as a Conestoga wagon, an Indian tepee, a New England country store, a train observation platform which evokes the 'whistle stop' political tours of the turn of the century, and a tea room providing American cookies.

Dyrham Park
8 miles (13km) N of Bath ☎ *(027582) 2501. NT* 🔲 🔲 💭 🚶 *House and garden open 2–6pm or sunset if earlier: Apr–May, Oct (closed Thurs, Fri); June–Sept (closed Fri). Park open all year around noon–6pm or sunset if earlier.*

This was the site of one of the most decisive battles of early British history, for it was here in 577 that the Saxons defeated the Britons, next advancing to the Severn and finally dividing the Celtic inhabitants of these islands.

More than a thousand years later, in the late 17thC, William Blathwayt built his fine home here, a fitting place for a man who was secretary of state to William III and one in which he delighted to indulge in the Dutch styles that came over with his new sovereign – leather wall hangings, tapestry, delftware and pictures by notable Dutch artists.

Lacock Abbey 🎢
12 miles (19km) E of Bath ☎ *(024973) 227. NT* 🔲 🚶 *House and grounds open Apr–Oct 2–6pm. Closed Tues. Fox Talbot Museum open Mar–Oct 11am–6pm.*

Many a country mansion has its roots in a dissolved religious house, but where Lacock differs is in the way it has preserved the medieval cloisters and much of the conventual buildings of the early 13thC nunnery whose site it usurped. The 18thC brought Neo-Gothic alterations, including a great hall built by the great-grandfather of W.H. Fox Talbot (1800–77), creator of the first photographic negative, commemorated at the abbey entrance by the **Fox Talbot Museum** of early photography.

Lacock Village, unspoiled and enchanting, is also owned by the National Trust.

Hotels and restaurants

Ⓗ Pratt's ✿
South Parade, Bath, Avon BA2 4AB ☎ *(0225) 60441* ❚❚ ☎ 47 🔲 42 🔲 ⇌ 𝔸𝔼 ⊙ ⊙ 𝚅𝙸𝚂𝙰
Location: 220yds (180m) SE of the abbey. This hotel provides the opportunity to stay in one of the dignified buildings designed in 1743 by the elder John Wood. The provision of all modern facilities has been achieved without detriment to his design's essential character.
‡ 🔲 🖼 ♣

Ⓗ Ⓡ The Priory 🏨 △
Weston Rd., Bath, Avon BA1 2XT ☎ *(0225) 331922* ☎ *44612* ❚❚❚❚ ☎ 15 🔲 15 🚶 🔲 ⇌ 𝔸𝔼 ℂ𝔹 ⊙ ⊙ 𝚅𝙸𝚂𝙰 *Closed first two weeks in Jan.*
Ⓡ ❚❚❚❚ 🔲 🔲 🍴 🔲 *Last orders 9.30pm.*
Location: To the NW, a short walk from the city center. This lovely little Strawberry Hill Gothic house has the style of a country home, although its gardens overlook the elegant city of Bath. The same elegance is found in the hotel, which sets a high standard of comfort.

The restaurant serves French classical and provincial dishes with much use of game. Diners who enjoy vegetables, served with the respect they deserve, will particularly appreciate the Priory.
🔲 🖼 ✿ ⚓ ◁ ⇌

Ⓗ Ⓡ Royal Crescent 🏨 △
16 Royal Crescent, Bath, Avon BA1 2LS ☎ *(0225) 319090* ☎ *444251* ❚❚❚❚ *to* ❚❚❚❚ ☎ 29 🔲 29 🚶 ⇌ 𝔸𝔼 ⊙ ⊙ 𝚅𝙸𝚂𝙰
Ⓡ ❚❚❚❚ 🔲 🍴 🔲 *Last orders 10pm.*
Location: In the heart of Regency Bath. This hotel is linked through an international booking organization with London establishments such as

the Savoy, Claridges and the Connaught, and on a less grand scale has some of the club atmosphere of the last. Its kitchen is French and English, and specializes in game and fish dishes.

R **Hole in the Wall** ⌂
16 George St. ☎ *(0225) 25242*
Last orders 10pm. Closed Sun, Mon, Christmas, bank holidays.
It really is a hole in the wall – a former coal cellar beneath the pavement of a Georgian street – but there is an element of self-mockery in the name. George Perry-Smith's protégés and successors Tim and Sue Cumming did not underestimate the challenge he left them, and recently it has been recognized that their restaurant is going from strength to strength. Despite its cuisine having been from the start firmly based in French provincial cooking, this restaurant has always accommodated a variety of cosmopolitan classics, together with the creations of its owners. It is also famous for its cold hors d'oeuvres. Like several other fine restaurants near Bristol, it takes advantage of that city's excellent wine-shippers.

The Cummings have recently opened eight bedrooms (▮▮).

Hotels and restaurants nearby
Near **Freshford** *(5 miles/8km s of Bath).*

H R **Homewood Park** ⌂
Hinton Charterhouse, Bath, Avon BA3 6BB ☎ *(022122) 2643*
⌂ *8* ⌷ *8* ⌷ *Closed Christmas to mid-Jan.*
R ▮▮ ⌷ *Last orders 9.30pm.*
Location: Between A36 and Freshford. A new gastronomic star emerged when Stephen and Penny Ross opened Homewood Park in 1981. After their previous success as owners of Popjoy's restaurant in Bath (now in new hands), their move to Homewood established Stephen in the forefront of British cooking. The kitchen is English and French and has won particular acclaim for its masterly fish dishes, although carnivores will find plenty with which to sample the extensive list of Bordeaux. Specialties include *matelote* of carp, pike and trout; calf's liver, kidneys and sweetbreads with oranges and rosemary; hot chocolate soufflé.

Homewood is said to have been the home of the Abbot of Hinton, and the present building (18th and 19thC) is set in ten acres of gardens and woodland adjoining the 13thC ruin of the priory.

Hunstrete *(8 miles/13km w of Bath).*

H R **Hunstrete House Hotel** 🏰 ⌂
Chelwood, Bath, Avon BS18 4NS ☎ *(07618) 578* ☎ *449540* ▮▮ *to*
▮▮ ⌷ *20* ⌷ *20* ⌷ *Closed first week in Jan.*
R ▮▮ ⌷ *Last orders 9.30pm.*
Location: Set in valley, between A368 and Hunstrete. It was only a small move, both in miles and scale, when Thea and John Dupays left their celebrated hotel, The Priory, to move to the hamlet of Hunstrete in 1978. Its reputation may be grand, but the Georgian manor house of Hunstrete is friendly, almost intimate, in its proportions. It is a friendly place in its style of service, too, with that brisk British insouciance which can mask solicitous attention to detail. The light, summery bar, decorated with posters for art exhibitions, is just one of many individualistic touches. The two small, cottagey dining rooms are comfortable and welcoming. The kitchen uses lots of produce from the West of England – lobster and crab from Devon, perhaps in a *croustade*; Wye salmon poached with sorrel; fruits from the garden made into puddings and jams – but Norman chef Alain Dubois also offers much that is French provincial. Other specialties include terrine of venison, roast wood-pigeon, game pie, and summer pudding.

Tranquillity, which is one of the prerequisites for membership of *Relais et Château*, is provided by a location in the foothills of the Mendips. There is a tennis court and a heated swimming pool in summer, and riding and hunting by prior arrangement.

Ston Easton (*14 miles/24km* SW *of Bath*).

H R ● Ston Easton Park 🏰 △ 🏛
Ston Easton, Bath, Somerset BA3 4DF ☎ *(076121) 631* ❼ *444738*
▥ ☜ *14* 🛏 *14* 🍽 ➡ ⚿ AE ① ◉ *Closed Jan.*
R ▥ ▭ 🍽 ☰ *Last orders 9pm.*
Location: In the village, on A37. Ston Easton, with its 27 acres of
parkland, opened as a country house hotel in 1982. Its collection of
Georgian furniture is unequaled in any other hotel, and possibly
unmatched anywhere, while the *trompe l'oeil* paintings and the
Humphrey Repton cascade in the stream are flourishes which establish
the mood of this Palladian mansion, surely the most palatial of all the
country house hotels.

The kitchen is in the hands of Robert Jones, formerly at the Savoy.
Specialties include *quenelles* of pike and charcoal-grilled duckling.
⌂ ▭ 🖼 🦞 ⚓ ⚔ 🏋

Nightlife
Bath has a thriving cultural nightlife, with plenty of concerts at different
locations. The **Bach Choir** and the **Bath Choral and Orchestral Society**
are particularly worth looking out for.

The **Theatre Royal** (*Sawclose* ☎ *(0225) 65065*) reopened in late 1982
after restoration. It is the provincial headquarters of the National
Theatre, and also stages Royal Shakespeare Company productions as
well as many repertory productions destined for London's West End.

Shopping
Milsom St., in the center, has some of the best shops, while nearby
Northumberland Passage has expensive boutiques. Antiques can be
found at the **Great Western Antique Centre** (*Bartlett St.*) and at the
market in **Guinea Lane** (*Wed*). The **Guildhall** market (*Mon–Sat*) has
general goods; the **Bath market** (*Twerton Park, Thurs*) has secondhand
clothes; and the **antique/flea market** (*Sat*) is held at the cattle market.

Battle
Map 7M11. East Sussex. 6 miles (9.5km) NW *of Hastings.*
Population: 5,000 ℹ *88 High St.* ☎ *(04246) 3721.*
This agreeable little town was the site of the battle of 1066 which
paradoxically is always known as the Battle of Hastings. After
the contest William the Conqueror founded an abbey here, and
soon the inevitable settlement clustered around it. The center of
today's town is **Abbey Green**, an open area at the S end of the
High St.

Battle Abbey and Battlefield
Just off Abbey Green ☎ *(04246) 3792. DOE* 🖼 🚻 🍽 *Open
mid-Mar to mid-Oct Mon–Sat 9.30am–6.30pm, Sun 2–6.30pm
except Apr–Sept 9.30am–6.30pm; mid-Oct to mid-Mar Mon–Sat
9.30am–4pm, Sun 2–4pm.*
The abbey ruins, only fragments of which date from William's time, are
clearly identified. Of principal interest are the guesthouse, reredorter
(monks' privy), dormitory and, in the ruined church, the spot where
Harold fell – either victim of a sword thrust or of an arrow through his
eye.

Visitors interested in the battle have a choice between a 1-mile (1.5km)
walk (🚶) with explanatory displays at intervals or, for the less energetic,
a more detached view using the plan on the terrace of the abbey ruins.

Sight nearby
Bateman's
Burwash, 12 miles (19km) NW *of Battle* ☎ *(0435) 882302. NT* 🖼
🍽 *Open Mar–May, Oct 2–6pm; June–Sept Mon–Thurs
11am–6pm, Sat, Sun 2–6pm. Closed Fri except Good Fri.*
Puck of Pook's Hill (1906), *Rewards and Fairies* (1910) and many other of
Rudyard Kipling's works were written in this 17thC house, which was
the author's home from 1902 until his death in 1936. Kipling's rooms,
and most importantly his study, have been left as he knew them.

Beaconsfield
Map 6K9. Bucks. 25 miles (40km) NW of London.
Population: 12,600.

In 1876 Benjamin Disraeli (1804–81) assumed the title of Earl of Beaconsfield, and today's small town along the A40 (there is a newer section just to the N), with its spacious wide street flanked by dignified Georgian houses, still seems to reflect much of the great statesman's High Tory character.

Bekonscot Model Village
Warwick Rd., in the new town 1 mile (1.5km) N of old Beaconsfield
☎ *(04946) 2919* 🖾 🖾 ✻ *Open Mar 10am–4.30pm; Apr–Oct 10am–5pm, but in Aug Sat, Sun, bank holidays 10am–5.30pm; Nov–Feb 10am–sunset.*

The rock garden in the world's oldest model village provides the perfect setting for the miniature half-timbered or Georgian houses. The principal attraction is a model railway with five stations, which winds around the scattered village with its school, hospital, lake with lighthouse and pier, airport and, of course, cricket ground.

Sights nearby
Hughenden Manor
7 miles (11km) NW of Beaconsfield ☎ *(0494) 32580. NT* 🖾 🖾
Open Apr–Oct Wed–Sat 2–6pm, Sun, bank holiday Mon 12.30–6pm or sunset if earlier (closed Mon, Tues); Mar and Nov Sat, Sun 2–5pm or sunset if earlier (closed Mon–Fri).

Benjamin Disraeli, politician, novelist and favorite of Queen Victoria, bought this house in 1847, rebuilt it and made it his home until he died. On his deathbed, it is said that he declined a visit by the queen on the grounds that she would only ask him to take a message to her beloved Albert. The queen had to content herself with erecting a memorial in the nearby church where he was buried. The house contains political and personal relics of the period.

Jordans
2 miles (3km) E of Beaconsfield 🖾 🖾.

The three buildings, close together, all have strong Quaker connections. **Old Jordans**, in the 17thC a farm at which William Penn, founder of Pennsylvania, and his Quaker friends held meetings, is now run as a guesthouse by the Society of Friends. (*Teas served 3–5pm; reservations may be made for lunch and dinner* ☎ *(02407) 4586*).

Nearby is the **Mayflower Barn** 🏛 (*open 9am–5pm*), believed to have been built from timbers of the *Mayflower* four years after the ship had carried the Pilgrim Fathers to North America.

The **Meeting House** (*open 10am–6pm, closed Mon, Tues*), in the valley below the barn, dates from 1688 and is still in use. William Penn, his two wives, and several of their 16 children are buried in the graveyard.

Bedford
Map 6J9. Beds. 52 miles (83km) N of London. Population: 73,200 i 7 St Paul's Sq. ☎ *(0234) 215226.*

That strange Puritan mystic and writer John Bunyan (1628–88), author of *The Pilgrim's Progress*, spent most of his life here and in adjacent Elstow. Armed with an admirable leaflet provided by the local tourist office, the enthusiast can follow Bunyan trails in both Bedford and Elstow. Stand on the 'Hill Difficulty' or visit the 'House Beautiful.'

Sight nearby
Shuttleworth Collection
Old Warden Aerodrome, 6 miles (9.5km) SE of Bedford
☎ *(076727) 288* 🖾 🖾 ✻ 🚗 *Open 10.30am–5.30pm. Closed Mon except bank holidays. Flying displays May–Oct last Sun in each month.*

Not to be missed by aviation enthusiasts, this is a notable collection of historic aircraft which can sometimes be seen in flight. Other forms of transport, such as vintage cars and early motorcycles, are also exhibited.

Belvoir Castle 🏛
Map 12H9. Leics. 7 miles (11km) w of Grantham ☎ *(0476)*
870262 🚗 ♿ ⛵ *Open late Mar to Sept Tues–Thurs, Sat*
noon–6pm, Sun noon–7pm; Oct Sun 2–6pm; bank holiday
Mon 11am–7pm; Good Fri noon–6pm. There is an uphill
walk of some 10mins from the parking lot.

In spite of its French spelling, the name of this breathtaking
hilltop seat of the Dukes of Rutland is pronounced 'beever.'
The site is an old one – the first castle here was built by William
the Conqueror's standard bearer – but wars and fire have
broken the continuity. The present castle dates from the early
19thC, since when it has stood as a staggering monument to the
grandiose thinking of the fifth Duke and Duchess and their
architect, James Wyatt.

The richly decorated **state rooms** and **Gobelin tapestries** are
well worth seeing, but the real glory of Belvoir is its picture
gallery, offering works by such masters as Holbein, Teniers,
Steen, Poussin, Van Dyck and Gainsborough.

Berwick-upon-Tweed
Map 15A8. Northumb. 30 miles (48km) N of Alnwick.
Population: 11,700 i Castlegate Car Park ☎ *(0289) 307187.*
The northernmost town in England is a peaceful enough place
today, but for centuries it stood in the 'Debatable Lands'
between England and Scotland, changing hands time and time
again until a final settlement was reached in 1482.

If there is little that recalls the turbulent early years
(fragments of the castle do survive near the station), this is
certainly not true of the later centuries when Berwick was
fortified as a bastion against the Scots – so strongly that the
greater part of today's town still is sheltered by Tudor walls,
begun in 1555 and generally regarded as the best preserved of
their period in Europe.

Sight nearby
Norham Castle
On the Scottish border, 7 miles (11km) sw of Berwick-upon-
Tweed ☎ *(028982) 329. DOE* 🚗 *Open mid-Mar to mid-Oct Mon–*
Sat 9.30am–6.30pm, Sun 2–6.30pm; mid-Oct to mid-Mar Mon–Sat
9.30am–4pm, Sun 2–4pm.
One of the largest and most exciting of the Border strongholds, this great
keep and outworks, which belonged to the prince-bishops of Durham,
stands high on the rocks above the river Tweed.

⊞ King's Arms
Hidehill, Berwick-upon-Tweed, Northumb TD15 1EJ ☎ *(0289)*
307454 📞 🏨 ⇌ *37* 🛏 *20* ⇌ 🏧 ⇌ *AE CB ◑ ● VISA*
Location: Town center. A one-time Georgian coaching inn where Charles
Dickens stayed in 1858, apparently being satisfied enough to come again
three years later. Fresh local produce is a feature of the restaurant.
⬜ 🏷 🌱 ♿

Birmingham
Map 10I7. West Midlands. 118 miles (186km) NW of
London. Population: 1,000,000. Airport ☎ *(021) 743–4272;*
railway station – Birmingham New St. ☎ *(021) 643–2711;*
coach station ☎ *(021) 622–4373; bus station* ☎ *(021)*
622–4481 i 110 Colmore Row ☎ *(021) 235–3411 and*
National Exhibition Centre ☎ *(021) 780–4141.*
As the hub of the industrial Midlands, Birmingham does not
aspire to a high rating on the tourist circuit. But Britain's

second city is a vibrant, bustling place with a boldly rebuilt center, some imaginatively conceived shopping precincts (the **Bull Ring** and **New Street**, the latter confusingly also called the Birmingham), and at least two outstanding museums.

Event In Oct, International Motor Show at National Exhibition Centre.

Sights and places of interest
Barber Institute of Fine Arts ☆
The University, Edgbaston (to sw of city, at Edgbaston Park Rd. entrance to university) ☎ *(021) 472–9062* 🔲 *Open Mon–Fri 10am–5pm, Sat 10am–1pm. Closed Sun and when university closed.*

A fairly small connoisseur's gallery, some distance from the city center. Among artists ranging from the 13th–19thC are Veronese, Rubens, Frans Hals, Van Dyck, Watteau, Gauguin, Gainsborough and Turner. There is also applied art, and sculpture by such masters as Rodin and Degas.

Birmingham Cathedral (*St Philip's*) †
Colmore Row, in the city center ☎ *(021) 236–4333.*

Birmingham's surprisingly small cathedral, nicely set on a green rise and given some character by its Baroque tower, was even smaller when built as a parish church in 1715. It was given a chancel in 1884, and gained cathedral status in 1905. The stained-glass windows are by Sir Edward Burne-Jones.

Museum and Art Gallery ☆
Chamberlain Sq. ☎ *(021) 235–2834* 🔲 💭 *Open Mon–Sat 10am–5.30pm, Sun 2–5.30pm.*

For size and quality the collections here rank with those of the best museums in the country. They are arranged as five exhibition departments: Fine Art, Applied Art, Archeology and Ethnography, Local History, Natural History. The Fine Art department's collection of **Pre-Raphaelite paintings** ★ is generally accepted as being the world's finest. Time should also be allowed for the **Netherlandish Primitives**, the large number of important works spanning the 17th–19thC, and the distinguished collection of **English watercolors**.

Museum of Science and Industry
Newhall St. ☎ *(021) 236–1022* 🔲 *Open Mon–Fri 10am–5pm, Sat 10am–5.30pm, Sun 2–5.30pm.*

Exhibits as diverse as massive locomotives, old cars and motorcycles, a streetcar, mechanical musical instruments, typewriters and sewing machines are housed here. Especially intriguing are the ingenious devices developed for such varied purposes as folding envelopes, slicing and wrapping bread, making pins (1888) and bottle making (an extraordinary machine dating from 1928). Several exhibits can be operated by push-button, and engines are even run on true steam, usually on the first and third Wed in each month.

Sights nearby
Dudmaston Hall
Quatt, 20 miles (32km) w of Birmingham ☎ *(0746) 780866. NT* 🔲 💭 ⛟ *Open Apr–Sept Wed, Sun 2.30–6pm.*

A late 17thC house containing a small but excellent collection of botanical paintings by such artists as Jan van Huysum, Rachel Ruysch and Joseph Redouté. Other rooms show 20thC paintings and sculpture, including works by Barbara Hepworth and Henry Moore.

Hanbury Hall
Hanbury, 17 miles (27km) sw of Birmingham ☎ *(052784) 214. NT* 🔲 💭 ⛟ *Open Apr, Oct Sat, Sun, Easter Mon and following Tues 2–5pm or sunset if earlier; May–Sept Wed–Sun, bank holiday Mon and following Tues 2–6pm (closed Mon, Tues).*

From the outside this pleasingly symmetrical brick mansion of 1701 by an unknown architect may look rather sober, but the same cannot be said of the interior, which is positively flamboyant with James Thornhill's **painted staircase** ☆ of vivid classical scenes. Flemish, Dutch and French flower paintings and a notable collection of English porcelain figures are displayed in the **Long Room**, where the ceiling painting is also by Thornhill.

Hotels and restaurants

H Grand 🏨

Colmore Row, Birmingham, West Midlands B3 2DA ☎ *(021)*
236–7951 ☎338174 ⃫ ⮥ 190 ▭ 140 ⇔ ⥇ AE CB ⏀ ⊙ VISA
Closed Christmas.
Location: By the cathedral. As grand in style as its name promises, this
hotel offers all the spaciousness and much of the plush decoration of its
Victorian past. Look into the opulent **Grosvenor Suite**, a banquet hall
described by John Betjeman as 'unique and superbly beautiful.'
‡ □ ≛

H Midland

128 New St., Birmingham, West Midlands B2 4JT ☎ *(021)*
643–2601 ☎338419 ⃫ ⮥ 117 ▭ 107 ⇔ ⥇ AE ⏀ VISA
Location: Just N of New St. Station. A rather conservative hotel,
remarkable for having four bars one of which, the Real Ale Bar, has a
pub-like, Dickensian ambience. Of the two restaurants, the Castillane
(French cuisine) is the smarter, while Peel's Grill offers fast service.
‡ ⌖ □ ⮡ ≛

H R Plough and Harrow 🏨 ⌂

135 Hagley Rd., Edgbaston, Birmingham, West Midlands
B16 8LS ☎ *(021) 454–4111* ☎ 338074 ⃫ ⮥ 44 ▭ 44 ⇔ ⥇ AE
CB ⏀ ⊙ VISA *Closed Christmas and bank holidays.*
R ⃫ ⌷ ⮡ ⥇ *Last orders 10.30pm.*
Location: In Edgbaston, w of city center. This Queen Anne building has
long been something of a landmark in the suburb of Edgbaston but the
hotel has achieved new distinction since renovation by the Crest chain.
Its gilded splendor may have been aimed at visiting executives but its
classical French kitchen and its range of Bordeaux, with Médoc very
strongly represented, provides a welcome oasis for the gastronome who
has strayed accidentally into Birmingham. Specialties include *oeuf poché
au délice de saumon mariné, queue de lotte au poivre noir, tournedos à la
moëlle, soufflé chaud aux framboises.*
⌂ ‡ ⌖ □ ⮡ ⬥ ⬦ ≛

Hotels nearby

Solihull (*11 miles/17.5km s of Birmingham*).

H Barn Motel

Stratford Rd., Hockley Heath, Solihull, West Midlands B94 6NX
☎ *(05643) 2144* ⃫ ⮥ 51 ▭ 51 ⇔ ⥇ AE ⏀ ⊙ VISA
Location: On A34, 7 miles (11km) sw of the National Exhibition Centre.
Unlike many so-called motels, this one is genuine: cars are parked right
beside the rooms, which are in a quiet area behind the main building.
The bar and restaurant, which of its kind is good, scatter themselves
crazily but snugly on different levels around the converted ancient barn.
□ ⮡ ⬦

Near **Wishaw** (*8 miles/13km NE of Birmingham*).

H The Belfry

Lichfield Rd., Wishaw, Sutton Coldfield, West Midlands B76 8BR
☎ *(0675) 70301* ☎ 338848 ⃫ ⮥ 60 ▭ 60 ⇔ ⥇ AE ⏀ ⊙ VISA
Closed one week at Christmas.
Location: In 360 acre park between A46 and A4091. A golfers' paradise,
with two championship courses of its own. One of the hotel's bars has a
golf theme, and it also boasts an 'American-style diner.' A Best Western
hotel in an extended Victorian manor house notable for its conservatory.
⌂ □ ⮡ ⬦ ⸖ ⟋ ≛

Shopping

New St., **High St.**, **Corporation St.** and **Bull St.**, all in the central area
circled by Queensway, are the main shopping streets, while the **Bull Ring
Shopping Centre** and the **New Street Shopping Centre** contain air
conditioned arcades with a wide range of shops and department stores.
The **Rag Market** (*Edgbaston St.*) has a variety of goods at knockdown

prices, while the neighboring **Row Market** (*both on Tues, Fri, Sat*) specializes in clothes for young people. The **Antiques Market** (*Edgbaston St., Mon*) is the haunt of collectors.

Place nearby
National Exhibition Centre
9 miles (14.5km) E of the city center, within the angle of the M42 and A45 ☎ *(021) 780–4141* ⑩ *336635 for reservation service for over 150 local hotels* 🍽 ⇌ 🍸

A huge modern complex incorporating eight exhibition halls of varying size, each identified by a vast numeral on the outside of the building; innumerable restaurants and bars ranging from top class to buffets; **Birmingham International Arena**, seating up to 12,000; hotel accommodations for up to 1,200, including the Birmingham Metropole (see below); shops, banks and information desks.

Ⓗ **Birmingham Metropole**
National Exhibition Centre, Birmingham B40 1PP ☎ *(021) 780–4242* ⑩ *336129* ⅢⅢ ☜ *709* 🛏 *709* 🚗 🖾 ⇌ 🅰🅴 ⓐ ⓘ 🆅🆂🅰
Location: See above. A palatial hotel with spacious and efficient conference facilities and standards of comfort and service to match.
🛎 ᕫ □ 🖾 ᑔ ᖾ

Blackpool
Map 10F6. Lancs. 40 miles (64km) N of Liverpool. Population: 152,000 **i** *1 Clifton St.* ☎ *(0253) 21623 and 87a Coronation St.* ☎ *(0253) 21891.*

Britain's most popular vacation resort has 7 miles (11km) of golden sands (the 'Magnificent Seven'); three piers, all packed and flourishing; at least eight theater stage shows; Blackpool Tower, over 500ft (150m) high, with ballroom, aquarium, animal farmyard, circus in summer, restaurant and elevator to transport visitors to the top; six public ballrooms; along the front, the 'brash and breezy' Golden Mile (in fact, a third that length) and finally the Amazement Park ✱ where devotees of nerve-wracking trips can loop-the-loop, ride a tidal wave or cruise in the Starship Enterprise.

The world-famous **Illuminations** are in Sept and Oct.

Ⓗ **Clifton**
Talbot Sq., Blackpool, Lancs FY1 1ND ☎ *(0253) 21481* ⅠⅠ ☜ *77* 🛏 *67* 🚗 ⇌ 🅰🅴 ⓐ ⓘ 🆅🆂🅰
Location: Near the Tower. The lobby, staircase and most of the public rooms are splendid examples of Victorian grandeur, but the bedrooms have all been well modernized, some to deluxe standards.
🛎 ᕫ □ 🖾 ᖾ

Ⓗ **Warwick** ✿
603–9 New South Promenade, Blackpool, Lancs FY4 1NG ☎ *(0253) 42192* □ ☜ *68* 🛏 *38* 🚗 🖾 ⇌ 🅰🅴 *Closed two weeks in Jan, two weeks in Nov.*
Location: On the shore at the S end of the town. Forming a long, low terrace set a short way back from the main promenade, this is a relaxed and friendly hotel with some exceptionally large and comfortable bedrooms overlooking the sea. The restaurant can be recommended.
ᖯ ≈ ᖾ ⊙

Hotel/restaurant nearby
Little Thornton (*5 miles/8km NE of Blackpool*).

Ⓗ Ⓡ **The River House** ✿
Skippool Creek, Thornton-le-Fylde, Blackpool, Lancs FY5 5LF ☎ *(0253) 883497* □ ☜ *4* 🛏 *1* 🚗 🖾 ⇌ 🅰🅴
Ⓡ ⅢⅡ □ ᕫ ≈ 🚗 *Last orders 9.30pm. Closed Mon.*
Location: On the river, in Little Thornton, off A585. Originally the 19thC

home of a gentleman farmer, this peaceful riverside hotel is one of the smaller and more modest type of country house. The kitchen uses local produce to provide traditional English and soundly prepared French dishes – including salmon *angelique*, *noisettes* of lamb, beef Wellington and roast suckling pig.

It is a good spot in which to have Sunday lunch, but reservation is, of course, essential. The extensive and geographically eclectic wine list has sensible ideas such as a separate section for half-bottles and another for bin-ends of all prices. The restaurant also offers about 40 liqueurs.

Nightlife
The **Horseshoe Showbar** (*525 Promenade* ☎ *(0253) 45247*) stages spectacular cabarets from June–Nov. Meals are served during the show and there is also dancing. At the **Winter Gardens and Opera House** (*Church St.* ☎*(0253) 27787*) the summer season show (*July–Oct*) features top-level comedy or singing stars, and the **Grand Theatre** (*Church St.* ☎*(0253) 28372*) and the three **Pier Theatres** also have variety shows from June–Oct.

Among the best discotheques are **Trader Jack's** at the **Imperial Hotel** (*North Promenade* ☎*(0253) 23971*), the **Metro** at the **Pembroke Hotel** (*Pembroke Gardens, North Promenade* ☎*(0253) 23434*) and **Sands** (*Palatine Buildings, Promenade* ☎*(0253) 28800*).

Shopping
Situated behind the Tower, the **Hounds Hill Centre** for department stores and specialty shops has proved a successful mixture of 19thC and modern architecture.

Blenheim Palace 🏛 ☆
Map 5J8. Woodstock, Oxon. 8 miles (13km) NW of Oxford
☎ *(0993) 811325* 🚌 🚶 *about every 10mins, duration 1hr* 🅿
🚗 ⇌ *Open mid-Mar to Oct 11am–6pm.*

Among the gifts and honors showered on John Churchill, first Duke of Marlborough, after he defeated the French at Blenheim, Bavaria, in 1704, was the manor of Woodstock together with funds to build a palace. And here the palace now stands, a grandiose and ponderous achievement by the wildly extravagant Vanbrugh, which impresses more through its location and sheer size than through its architecture. The interior, with superb decorative work by artists such as Grinling Gibbons and Nicholas Hawksmoor, is to the same almost oppressive scale, culminating in the chapel with the ostentatious tomb of John and his duchess Sarah.

In 1874, Winston Churchill was born in this perhaps fitting setting, although in a room of startling simplicity. He is buried in the village churchyard at nearby **Bladon**.

For many, it is the park rather than the palace which is the real glory of Blenheim, the essence of this being the twisting, landscaped lake created in 1764 by Capability Brown. Military-minded visitors should note the groups of trees planted to form a plan of the Battle of Blenheim.

Hotel/restaurant nearby
Woodstock (*⅔ mile/1km NW of Blenheim Palace*).

Ⓗ Ⓡ **Bear** 🏨 ☆
Park St., Woodstock, Oxon OX7 1SZ ☎*(0993) 811511* Ⓥ*837921*
🏨 to 🏨 🛏 *45* ▭ *38* 🚗 ⊜ ⇌ AE CB ◑ ① VISA
Ⓡ 🍴 □ 🍽 ▤ *Last orders 10.30pm.*
Location: In the center. The Bear is part of a small, family-run group of hotels. It has some fine antiques in its drawing room, and sensitively furnished bedrooms.
♿ □ 🖉 ✔ ✓ 🐾 ⬮ 🏊

Bodiam Castle ☆
Map 7L11. East Sussex. 7 miles (11km) NE of Battle
☎ *(058083) 436. NT* ▣ ▤ ▰ *Open Apr–Oct 10am–7pm or sunset if earlier; Nov–Mar 10am–sunset (closed Sun).*

Although little more than a romantic shell, Bodiam still has its massive crenellated walls and corner drum towers, the whole surrounded by a wide moat. It was built in 1386 to deter the French who had already burned *Rye* and Winchelsea, and certainly succeeded in its purpose. In summer there is an audio-visual presentation about life in a medieval castle.

Ⓗ **Justins**
Sandhurst Rd., Bodiam, Robertsbridge, East Sussex TN32 5UJ
☎ *(058083) 372* ▮▯ ❧ *10* ▭ *8* ▰ ▱ ⇄ ▦ *VISA Closed Nov.*
Location: On the hill just N of Bodiam Castle. An unpretentious, fairly small, country house hotel in its own sylvan grounds. It is family owned and pride is taken in the personal service offered.
▱ ❦ ⊰

Bosworth Field
Map 11I8. Leics. Near Market Bosworth, 16 miles (26km) w of Leicester ☎ *(0455) 290429* ▣ ♣ ▰ *Battlefield Visitor Centre open Easter–Oct Mon–Sat 2–5.30pm, Sun, bank holidays 1–6pm. Battle Trail always open.*

The Battle of Bosworth Field (1485) marked the end of the Wars of the Roses and the confident arrival on the scene of the first Tudor, Henry VII. It was also, if Shakespeare is to be believed, the battle at which the doomed Richard III entreated 'A horse! a horse! my kingdom for a horse!'

A **Battle Trail** (refreshments halfway around) is generously provided with information boards and given a colorful touch of pageantry by the great pennants that flutter bravely over some of the command positions. Indoors there is a Visitor Centre where the story is told through armor, flags, models and audio-visual presentations.

Bournemouth
Map 4M7. Dorset. On the s coast, 106 miles (170km) sw of London. Population: 154,000. Railway station ☎ *(0202) 28216; coach station* ☎ *(0202) 21481; bus stations – Bournemouth Transport* ☎ *(0202) 522661, Hants & Dorset* ☎ *(0202) 23371* **i** *Westover Rd.* ☎ *(0202) 291715.*

Whereas other resorts tend to be beach and sea oriented, Bournemouth turns every bit as much inward, knowing that as many visitors come for its setting of landscaped parks and gardens, for shops, theaters and the symphony orchestra, as they do for sand and sea. Not, of course, that the sea is ignored. Bournemouth's beaches offer miles of soft, inviting sand, the Victorian pier thrives, and there is a good choice of boat rides.

Poole, to the w of Bournemouth, has a vast natural harbor that attracts waterfowl and yachting folk.

Sights and places of interest
Compton Acres Gardens ☆
Canford Cliffs Rd., near Sandbanks, Poole ☎ *(0202) 708036* ▣ ▤ ▰ ❧ *Open Apr (or Easter if earlier) to Oct, 10.30am–6.30pm except June–Aug Thurs 10.30am–sunset.*

Laid out soon after World War I, these lovely gardens above Poole Harbour comprise seven individual gardens, namely Japanese, Italian, Rock and Water, Heather, Roman, English and Palm Court. Plants and shrubs are on sale.

Poole Quay
4 miles (6.5km) w of central Bournemouth.

Poole is a working port, yet its old warehouses evoke the seafaring past.
There is plenty to do near the quay or close inland. The choice includes
Poole Pottery (*East Quay Rd.* ☎ *(0202) 672866* 🔊 ✗ *open Mon–Sat,
also Sun in Aug, 9am–5pm*), a **craft center**, **aquarium**, **model railway**
and **model museum** (*Poole Quay* ☎ *(0202) 686712* 🔊 *combined ticket;
open Easter–Oct 10am–10pm; Nov–Easter 10am–5pm*), as well as three
other **museums** (☎ *(0202) 675151* 🔊 *open Mon–Sat 10am–5pm, Sun
2–5pm*). These museums are the **Guildhall** in Market St., which tells the
story of Poole in the 18th–19thC; the **Maritime Museum** in late 15thC
cellars in Paradise St.; and **Scaplen's Court** in the High St., a
particularly fine example of a 15thC town house, now showing
archeological material and a typical sitting room, kitchen and scullery
from an Edwardian home.

Boat trips can be made to **Brownsea Island** nature reserve (☎ *(0202)
709445*).

Russell-Cotes Art Gallery and Museum
East Cliff, Bournemouth ☎ *(0202) 21009* 🔊 💷 *Open
10.30am–5pm. Closed Sun.*

Sir Merton and Lady Russell-Cotes presented their Victorian mansion,
with its Italianate interior and valuable contents, to the town. As well as
collections of fine and applied arts, there are theatrical relics (associated
with Henry Irving), period rooms and, outside, a geological display.

Hotels and restaurant

Ⓗ **Durley Dean**
Westcliff Rd., Bournemouth, Dorset BH2 5HE ☎ *(0202) 27711* 🏷
☎ *110* 🛏 *70* 🚗 🏠 ⬌
Location: About ¼ mile (1km) w of the pier. A solid, traditional style of
hotel which places some emphasis on entertainment including live music
in the restaurant, dancing and a games room.
‡ 🖂 ⇌ 🏆 ♫ ♥

Ⓗ **Royal Bath** 🏨
Bath Rd., Bournemouth, Dorset BH1 2EW ☎ *(0202) 25555*
☎ *41375* 🏷 ☎ *133* 🛏 *133* 🍴 🚗 🏠 ⬌ Ⓐ Ⓔ ⒸⒷ Ⓓ 🅥𝖨𝖲𝖠
Location: Near sE corner of Lower Central Gardens. A hotel that looks and
is something of a palace, and a very comfortable one too. There are ten
luxury suites, saunas, a hairdressing salon, four bars, and a superb
restaurant where dinner dances are held weekly.
‡ 🔥 🔲 💅 ☂ ❄ ⇌ 🏆 ♨ ♥

Ⓗ **Sun Court**
West Hill Rd., Bournemouth, Dorset BH2 5PH ☎ *(0202) 21343* 🏷
☎ *36* 🛏 *29* 🚗 🏠 ⬌ Ⓐ Ⓔ ⒸⒷ 🅥𝖨𝖲𝖠
Location: 300yds (270m) w of the Winter Gardens. Features of this hotel
include some roomy bedrooms (some with balconies), the plush
Victoriana bar and an air conditioned restaurant.
‡ 🔲 🏆

Ⓗ **Tralee** ♣
West Hill Rd., West Cliff, Bournemouth, Dorset BH2 5EQ ☎ *(0202)
26246* 🏷 ☎ *100* 🛏 *40* 🚗 🏠 ⬌ Ⓐ Ⓔ ⒸⒷ 🅥𝖨𝖲𝖠
Location: Just back from the clifftop, close to the elevator. A large hotel
sensibly geared to the needs of families. Among the facilities are a
solarium and sun-deck with a splendid coastal view; a heated indoor
pool, games room, guest laundry room and a beach chalet. Children are
particularly welcome – there is a wading pool and resident nanny, and
cots can be rented at a nominal charge.
‡ 🔥 ☂ ❄ ⇌ 🐾 🏆 ♫ ♥

Ⓡ **Crust**
Hampshire House, The Square ☎ *(0202) 21430* 🏷 🔲 🍴 Ⓐ Ⓔ Ⓓ
Ⓒ 🅥𝖨𝖲𝖠 *Last orders 11pm (Sat 11.30pm, Sun 10.30pm). Closed
Christmas, Sun lunch (Christmas–Easter).*
It is a curiosity that, after the more conventional restaurants at leading
hotels such as the Carlton and Royal Bath, Bournemouth's most

celebrated eating place is this modestly named and oddly located establishment near the bus station. Mundane it may sound, but Crust is an excellent, enthusiastic restaurant, with a well-chosen, good value wine list. The food is an inventive and well-prepared blend of bistro-style French and traditional English, with an emphasis on fish and game. Reservations are essential.

Nightlife
Concerts, operas, plays and ballets are staged at Bournemouth's **Pavilion** (*Westover Rd.* ☎ *(0202) 25861*) and **Winter Gardens** (*Exeter Rd.* ☎ *(0202) 296646*). The **Pier Theatre** (*Bournemouth Pier* ☎ *(0202) 20250*) is open in summer, usually starring well-known comics. The town has its own excellent orchestras, the **Bournemouth Symphony Orchestra** and the **Sinfonietta**. They hold concerts at the Winter Gardens every Sun, June–Sept, Thurs, Oct–May (*information on all programs from the tourist office*).

Bournemouth boasts four casinos, the pleasantest of which is the **Bournemouth Casino Club Royal** in the Royal Bath Hotel (see *Hotels*). There is a wide variety of nightclubs and discos in the town center.

Shopping
Bournemouth Sq. and the nearby streets form the principal shopping area while **Westover Rd.** is known for its jewelers, boutiques and furriers. The Victorian Arcades in **Old Christchurch Rd.**, and **Westbourne** and **Boscombe** on either side of the city center, are the places for *objets d'art*, antiques and Victoriana as well as boutiques.

Brighton
Map 6M10. East Sussex. 53 miles (85km) s of London. Population: 234,000. Railway station ☎ *(0273) 25476; coach and bus station* ☎ *(0273) 606600* **i** *Marlborough House, 54 Old Steine* ☎ *(0273) 23755.*

'London by the sea' is a title that Brighton has well merited since the 18thC when Society discovered the town, the accolade being the decision of the Prince of Wales to make his home here. From then on, what had for centuries been no more than a fishing village steadily developed into today's handsome and confident examplar of the best type of English coastal resort.

Events First two weeks in May, Brighton Festival.

First Sun in Nov, London to Brighton Veteran Car Run. Cars built before 1918 start at staggered intervals from Hyde Park in London and arrive throughout the day at Madeira Drive.

Sights and places of interest
Aquarium and Dolphinarium
w end of Marine Parade ☎ *(0273) 604234* ▨ ▣ ✴ *Open Apr–Oct 9am–6pm; Nov–Mar 9am–5pm. Dolphin shows about 6 times daily.*
Penguins, sea lions, turtles, dolphins and many kinds of fish share this part-Victorian, part-modern complex.

Attached to the complex is the **Brightonarium**, a Victorian environment containing shops, restaurants and an audio-visual theater which offers 'an entertaining historical trip through time.'

The Lanes
Just sw of the Royal Pavilion.
This small district of little houses, crowded along narrow streets and alleys, lures throngs of visitors to its antique shops, boutiques, pubs and restaurants.

Museum and Art Gallery
Church St. ☎ *(0273) 603005* ▣ ▣ *Open Tues–Sat 10am–5.45pm, Sun 2–5pm. Closed Mon.*
The high points of the museum are the **Willett Collection** of English Pottery and Porcelain, the 20thC **decorative arts collections**, and the **Fashion Gallery** (opened 1982), a display of clothes ranging from a child's 18thC costume through Twenties *haute couture* to Eighties punk.

The art gallery's collection of paintings ranges from Old Masters to the present day. Jan Lievens, Aert de Gelder and others represent the Netherlandish School while later artists include Lawrence (two striking portraits of George IV), Hogarth and William Blake. Names from even more recent times are Dali, Magritte and Picasso.

Royal Pavilion 🏛
Town center, just N of tourist office ☎ *(0273) 603005* 📷 *Open 10am–5pm (July–Sept to 6.30pm).*

An Arabian Nights fantasy. In 1811 the Prince Regent commissioned John Nash to rebuild his seaside villa, and this splendidly eccentric curiosity is the result. If the exterior with its onion-shaped domes and minarets is essentially Islamic or Indian, the interior may be called Regency Chinese. There are period rooms furnished in their original style, interesting pictures of old Brighton, and an annual Regency Exhibition (*July–Sept*).

Hotels

H Bedford
King's Rd., Brighton BN1 2JF ☎ *(0273) 29744* 📞 *877245* 🏨
🛏 *126* 🛏 *126* 🍽 ➡ 🆑 💳 📷 💳
Location: A short way w of West Pier. A modern hotel overlooking the sea and offering some large rooms with balconies. It is within the same chain as the nearby Brighton Metropole, all the facilities of which are available to guests of the Bedford.
🛎 ♿ ☐ 📷 🏊 🎿

H Brighton Metropole
King's Rd., Brighton BN1 2FU ☎ *(0273) 775432* 📞 *877245* 🏨
🛏 *333* 🛏 *333* 🍽 ➡ 🆑 💳 📷 💳
Location: Near the West Pier. A seafront hotel, architecturally of the grand Victorian vintage but in other respects thoroughly modern. It is much visited for its **Starlit Room** roof restaurant, where the cuisine is as outstanding as the view.
🛎 ♿ ☐ 📷 ◁€ 🎿

H Norfolk Continental
King's Rd., Brighton BN1 2PP ☎ *(0273) 738201* 📞 *877247* 🏨
🛏 *65* 🛏 *65* 🚗 🍽 ➡ 🆑 💳 📷 💳
Location: Seafront, at w end of the town. A large, cheerful bar overlooking the front makes a welcoming first impression. Built in 1865, and with something of the grandeur of that era preserved in its ground-floor rooms, the hotel has converted its two upper floors into a modern complex with restaurant, bars, roof garden and nightspot.
🛎 ☐ 📷 ◁€ 🎿 ●

H Old Ship
King's Rd., Brighton BN1 1NR ☎ *(0273) 29001* 📞 *877101* 🏨
🛏 *152* 🛏 *127* 🍽 🍴 ➡ 🆑 🆑 📷 💳 💳
Location: On the front s of The Lanes and between the piers. Brighton's oldest and most historic hotel started as a fishermen's inn, was later associated with the escape to France of Charles II, then became an important social center in Regency times. Today's visitor can enjoy all modern facilities but still savor something of a more spacious past, notably in the lovely ballroom of 1767, a place much favored by the Prince Regent. Good facilities for children.
🛎 ☐ 📷 🏊 ◁€ 🎿

Restaurants

Traditionalists perhaps go for the fish restaurants in The Lanes, such as **D'Arcy's** (*49 Market St.* ☎ *(0273) 25560* 🏨 to 🏨), **English's** (*29–31 East St.* ☎ *(0273) 27980* 🏨), or **Wheeler's** (*17 Market St.* ☎ *(0273) 25135* 🏨).

More determined gastronomes prefer Kemptown, for **Chez Moi** (*113 St George's Rd.* ☎ *(0273) 680317* ☐) or **Le Francais** (*1 Paston Pl.* ☎ *(0273) 680716* 🏨). In both price and style, Chez Moi is more like a bistro, while Le Francais raises the tricolor for classical dishes, using raw materials of a high standard, and with excellent service.

Nightlife

Brighton offers professional repertory companies at the **Theatre Royal**
(*New Rd.* ☎ *(0273) 28488*), rock and other concerts at the **Dome** (*29
New Rd.* ☎ *(0273) 682127*) and **Brighton Centre** (*Russell Rd.* ☎ *(0273)
202881*), and other cultural events at the **Gardner Centre** (*University of
Sussex* ☎ *(0273) 685861*). Details from the tourist office.

Shopping

The Lanes are famous for their antique shops, leather shops and
jewelers. Nearby **East St.** and **Regent Arcade** is another fashionable area
containing boutiques, jewelers and many restaurants. **Western Rd.** and
the pedestrian precinct at **Churchill Sq.** have major stores. A bric-à-brac
market is held in **Upper Gardner St.** (*Sat morning*).

Bristol

*Map 4K6. Avon. 120 miles (190km) w of London.
Population: 427,000. Lulsgate airport* ☎ *(027587) 4441;
railway station* ☎ *(0272) 276603; coach and bus station*
☎ *(0272) 553231 i Colston House, Colston St.* ☎ *(0272)
293891.*

Bristol looks back with pride and not a little nostalgia on
centuries of westward adventure. It must have been a
picturesque and bustling place when Cabot set sail for America
in 1497, and later even more so as the city grew rich on wine,
tobacco, sugar and slaves and the waterfront was crowded with
tall ships.

Much of the city was devastated by bombs in World War II
but elegant areas such as Georgian **Clifton** still stand. Although
today many of the ships have moved to Avonmouth, the
waterfront still claims attention: it is being redeveloped as an
exhibition, cultural and educational preserve.

Event In July, World Wine Fair and Festival at Bristol
Exhibition Complex.

Sights and places of interest

Arnolfini

Narrow Quay ☎ *(0272) 299191 or 299194 box office* 📖 � ☒
Open 11am–8pm. Closed Sun, Mon.

This early 19thC tea warehouse has been given new life as a go-ahead
center for the contemporary arts. There are exhibitions of many kinds,
live performances and film shows, while the bar and restaurant have
become a popular rendezvous.

Avon Gorge and Clifton Suspension Bridge ★

Clifton, 2 miles (3km) w of city center.

Barely outside the city center, the river Avon has carved itself a narrow
gorge through which it flows below precipitous cliffs. Across the gorge,
250ft (75m) above the water and much enhancing the scenic effect, hangs
the Clifton Suspension Bridge, designed by Isambard Kingdom Brunel
in 1831 but not completed until 1864, 5yrs after his death.

Bristol Cathedral †

College Green ☎ *(0272) 24879.*

Architecturally spanning the 12th–19thC (the nave and w towers belong
to the latter era), Bristol's Anglican cathedral sits remarkably well beside
College Green, the traditional meeting place in the 7thC of St Augustine
and the Celtic Christians and thus of special significance to the
Augustinians whose abbey was founded here five centuries later (1148).
The Norman **Chapter House** ★ with typical zigzag and ropework
decoration is the finest in England and all that survives of the original
foundation.

Bristol Industrial Museum

Prince's Wharf ☎ *(0272) 299771* ▣ *Open 10am–1pm, 2–5pm.
Closed Thurs, Fri.*

From horse-drawn vehicles to Concorde, from primitive machinery to jet
engines; within these brackets, ever-growing collections tell the
industrial story of the Bristol region.

City Museum and Art Gallery
Queen's Rd. ☎ *(0272) 299771* 🎫 💷 *Open 10am–5pm. Closed Sun.*

Admirably arranged, the museum covers, among other areas, technology, natural history, archeology and Egyptology, this last being of particular interest for the **Horemkenesi project**, the meticulously controlled unwrapping and scientific study of a mummy of *c.*1000BC.

The Art Gallery shows works spanning from the 14thC to modern times. L.S. Lowry is among several 20thC artists represented.

The interesting **Georgian House** and **Red Lodge** are branches of the museum.

Clifton Roman Catholic Cathedral 🏛 ✝
Clifton Park ☎ *(0272) 38411.*

A striking example of modern ecclesiastical architecture, unfortunately sited among streets of 18th and 19thC houses. The interior is worth visiting both for its highly original design and for its works of modern religious art.

Exchange and Nails
Corn St.

The expression 'to pay on the nail' is said to have originated from these four bronze tables (late Elizabethan to 1631) on which the merchants of Bristol once sealed their cash transactions. They stand in front of the Exchange, built in 1743 by the elder John Wood.

Harveys Wine Museum ☆
12 Denmark St. ☎ *(0272) 298011* 🎫 💷 *guided tours and wine tasting. Open Fri 10am–noon, 2–4.30pm* ✗ *at other times, by appointment only. Visitors must be 18 or over.*

As fascinating for its location as for what it shows and teaches, the museum is spread along the 13thC cellars of the Hospice of the Gaunts (see also *Lord Mayor's Chapel*). In the late 18thC the property was acquired by William Petty, who founded the wine firm that was to become famous as Harveys of Bristol. The cellars were used to store the barrels which could so easily be rolled along the few cobbled yards from the quay. The fine house above was destroyed by bombing in World War II, but the cellars continued in use until 1960 when they were converted into a museum and restaurant (see below).

The museum explains the whole wine process, illustrating each stage with exhibition material, including a priceless collection of 17th and 18thC glass. Be warned that the guided tour lasts 2½ hrs altogether – 1½ hrs of standing and walking, followed by 1hr spent sitting, first for a film, then for a generous but well-earned tasting.

John Wesley's The New Room
The Horsefair ☎ *(0272) 24740* 🎫 *but donation expected. Open 10am–4pm. Closed Wed, Sun.*

This sober chapel of 1739 was the first built for Methodist worship and it was here that Wesley commissioned his early preachers. Upstairs, the preachers' individual rooms lead off the common room.

Lord Mayor's Chapel (*St Mark's*) ✝
College Green 🎫 *but donation expected. Open 10am–noon, 2–4pm. Closed Sat.*

Originally the chapel of the Hospice of the Gaunts, founded 1220. Worth seeing for its 15thC ceiling.

St Mary Redcliffe 🏛 ✝
Redcliffe Way.

'The fairest, goodliest and most famous parish church in England.' Such was the judgment of Queen Elizabeth I on this famous example of 14thC Perpendicular architecture. The richly decorated great tower, unusual hexagonal N porch and soaring interior must have been among the features which so fired the queen's admiration.

St Nicholas Church Museum
St Nicholas St. ☎ *(0272) 299771* 🎫 *Open 10am–5pm. Closed Sun.*

Gutted by bombs, this part-medieval and part-18thC church has been converted to a most unusual museum, devoted to the early history of Bristol. The emphasis is on ecclesiastical material, superbly displayed.

SS Great Britain ☆
Great Western Dock, Gas Ferry Rd. ☎ *(0272) 20680* 🎫 💷 ⚓ 🚗
Open mid-Mar to mid-Oct 10am–6pm; mid-Oct to mid-Mar 10am–5pm.

Brunel's historic iron ship, the world's first ocean-going propeller-driven vessel, which in July 1845 crossed from Liverpool to New York in 15 days, is being restored in the yard from which she was launched. As work proceeds, visitors are free to pace the deck, explore the cavernous interior, or stand dwarfed beneath the mighty iron hull.

Zoological Gardens
Clifton Down ☎ *(0272) 738951* 🚗 💺 ♿ 🍴 *Open May–Aug Mon–Sat 9am–6pm, Sun 10am–6pm; Sept–Apr Mon–Sat 9am–5pm, Sun 10am–5pm.*
Spread around lovely gardens, this zoo is internationally known for its successful conservation work in the breeding of rare and endangered species. The penguins are fed at 12.30pm, the sea lions at 11.30am and 3.30pm, and the lions and tigers at 3pm.

Hotels and restaurant

Ⓗ **Avon Gorge**
Sion Hill, Clifton, Bristol, Avon BS8 4LD ☎ *(0272) 738955*
🖂 *444237* ▯▯ 🛏 *76* 🛏 *76* ▭ ⇌ AE CB ⓞ VISA
Location: Close to E approach to Clifton Suspension Bridge. Perched on the very rim of the Avon Gorge, but still less than 10mins by car from the city center, this hotel offers modern comfort and breathtaking views.
‡ ▯ 🖾 《←

Ⓗ **Ladbroke Dragonara**
Redcliffe Way, Bristol, Avon BS1 6NJ ☎ *(0272) 20044* 🖂 *449240*
▯▯▯ 🛏 *210* 🛏 *210* 🛏 ⇌ 🍴 ▭ AE CB ⓞ VISA
Location: Between St Mary Redcliffe and Temple Meads Station. A large, modern, hotel-casino complex. Many of the bedrooms – of reasonable size and fully appointed – command good views, notably of the famous 14thC church of St Mary Redcliffe. The hotel includes the highly original split-level **Kiln** restaurant, a fascinating conversion within a huge glass-kiln of 1780. The menu features West Country and Old English dishes.
‡ & ▯ ♿ 🖾 👥 🎯

Ⓗ **Unicorn**
Prince St., Bristol, Avon BS1 4QF ☎ *(0272) 294811* 🖂 *44315* ▯▯▯
🛏 *190* 🛏 *190* 🛏 ⇌ 🍴 ▭ AE CB ⓞ VISA
Location: E side of St Augustine's Reach. Consider the Unicorn if you have business at the nearby exhibition center, if you are a tourist intent on being within easy walking distance of the city's principal sights, or if you are a motorist thankful for an adjacent parking lot with direct access to each floor of the hotel. Features are a restaurant of growing repute, a popular waterfront bar, and bedrooms which, although small, enjoy views across the water.
‡ & ▯ 🖾 👥

Ⓡ **Harveys** 🍷
12 Denmark St. ☎ *(0272) 277665* ▯▯▯ 🞏 🍽 ⇌ 🍴 🎵 *Sat* 🍴 *Sat*
AE CB ⓞ ⓞ VISA *Last orders 11.15pm. Closed Sat lunch, Sun.*
Harveys restaurant offers a choice of 20 sherries, including four finos, a palo cortado and a manzanilla in its bar. Those who believe that only fino or champagne are serious aperitifs should not make their choice until they have consulted the list of wines from Rheims and Epernay. It is this happy dilemma, in such an appropriate location, that makes Harveys so special, although the appetites thus provoked will also be properly satisfied by the French cuisine of Andy Hunt. Oenophiles ought not to resist *tournedos* in madeira or *filet mignon* with port and Stilton sauce.

Hotel/restaurant nearby
Thornbury (*11 miles/17km N of Bristol*).

Ⓗ Ⓡ **Thornbury Castle** 🍷
Thornbury, Bristol, Avon BS12 1HH ☎ *(0454) 412647* ▯▯▯ 🛏 *10*
🛏 *10* 🛏 ⇌ 🍴 AE CB ⓞ VISA *Closed three weeks at Christmas.*
Ⓡ ▯▯▯ 🞏 ⇌ *Last orders 9.30pm.*
Location: Off Castle St. A 16thC castle restored with pre-Victorian pomp in 1830 sounds too grand to be a restaurant 'with rooms,' but that is what

it is. In a somewhat Gothic atmosphere, friendly staff welcome diners with hot savories. The menu sets out to be unpretentious, but has nonetheless caused chef-owner Kenneth Bell to be showered with gastronomic awards. The dishes responsible for this are probably such simple-but-excellent ones as his deviled crab or *pâté de foie de volaille*. A vineyard in the castle grounds produces riesling-sylvaner wines which, when available, highlight an eclectic list. The bedrooms are very comfortable and furnished mainly with antiques.

☐ ☑ ﹪ ⚲ ⁘ ☝ ⬤

Nightlife
The **Hippodrome** (*St Augustine's Parade* ☎ *(0272) 299444*) and **Colston Hall** (*Colston St.* ☎ *(0272) 291768*) are the main concert venues, and the Hippodrome also stages major plays and shows.

The **Bristol Old Vic** at the **Theatre Royal** and the **New Vic** (both *King St.* ☎ *(0272) 24388*) is one of the top theater companies in Britain.

Shopping
Queens Rd., **Park St.** and the roads running off them form the most central shopping area; **Broadmead**, farther E, is a large shopping center. The **St Nicholas Markets** (*open 9.30am–4pm*) incorporate the **Glass Arcade Flower Market** (*off High St.*) for flowers, fruit and vegetables; the **Fish Market** (*off Baldwin St., closed Sun*); the **Exchange Market** (*off Corn St.*) for antiques (*particularly on Thurs, Fri*), bric-à-brac and miscellaneous crafts; and the **Covered Market** (*off St Nicholas St.*) for groceries, craft materials and books, among other goods. The renowned **Clifton Antiques Market** (*26–28 The Mall, Clifton, open 10am–6pm, closed Sun, Mon*) has 60 antique stalls.

Brontë Parsonage
Map 10F7. West Yorks. Haworth, 20 miles (32km) w of Leeds ☎ *(0535) 42323* ▦ ➥ *Open Apr–Sept 11am–5.30pm; Oct–Mar 11am–4.30pm. Closed last three weeks in Dec.*

It was indeed a strange and almost theatrically tragic family that lived here from 1820–61: a recluse widower parson father (the only member to survive the whole period) and four children of individual and collective genius – Charlotte (*Jane Eyre*), Anne (*The Tenant of Wildfell Hall*), Emily (*Wuthering Heights*), and Branwell (unstable through drink and drugs yet a writer and artist of some talent). How did such a furnace of Gothick fantasy and boundless imagination ever blaze in surroundings as bleak and unpromising as these? A visit to the parsonage – not greatly changed and showing a wealth of Brontë detail – merely sharpens the question.

Except for its tower, the church has been rebuilt, but it is still very much Brontë territory, and (with the exception of Anne – see *Scarborough*) they all rest here in the family vault.

H **Old White Lion**
6 West Lane, Haworth, near Keighley, West Yorks BD22 8DU ☎ *(0535) 42313* ☐ ⬤ *12* ▤ *8* ➥ ⬤ ⬤ ▨
Location: *Upper town, close to the Parsonage.* By stopping at this unpretentious but comfortable, conveniently located hotel the visitor is treading where Branwell Brontë trod, for it was here that he came for bouts of fisticuffs with the local lads.
♣

Bury St Edmunds
Map 7I11. Suffolk. 79 miles (96km) NE of London. Population: 26,000 **i** *Abbey Gardens* ☎ *(0284) 64667.*

This pleasant and compact country town owes its name to the shrine of St Edmund, a king of East Anglia who was beheaded by the Danes *c.*870.

The **abbey ruins**, on the E side of the town, are of interest, although it is hard to accept that these scattered fragments beyond a handsome 14thC gateway represent an abbey that was founded in the 10thC and soon became one of the richest and most powerful in the land.

It was in the abbey church that the barons met to draw up the Magna Carta. What little is left of this church occupies the s part of the ruins, its front now incorporated into houses. On the s side of the cathedral (notable for its stained glass) stands the **Norman tower**, once the abbey's W gate.

Ⓗ **Angel**
Angel Hill, Bury St Edmunds, Suffolk IP33 1LT ☎ *(0284) 3926*
☎ *81630* ⅢⅢ ⟐ *43* ▭ *34* ⇔ ⇌ (AE) (◐) (○) (VISA)
Location: Opposite the abbey ruins. This ivy-clad hotel has been an inn since 1452. Rebuilt in the 18thC, it welcomed Charles Dickens in 1859 and 1861 and his room has been preserved more or less as it was. Guests with a yen for the past have a choice of rooms with four-poster beds. There are two attractive restaurants, one overlooking the abbey gateway and the other in the vaulted 13thC cellars.
◻ ⬚ ⛄

Cambridge ★
Map 6J10. Cambs. 60 miles (96km) N of London. Population: 99,000. Railway station ☎ *(0223) 311999; bus and coach station* ☎ *(0223) 353418* **i** *Wheeler St.* ☎ *(0223) 358977.*

One of the joys of Cambridge is that its plan is so straightforward. For all practical purposes only one street, or sequence of streets, needs to be kept in mind. Starting in the N at the **Church of the Holy Sepulchre** (a rare medieval round church, but much modernized), the sequence of St John's St. and Trinity St., King's Parade and Trumpington St. splits Cambridge into two. To the W, between this axis and the river, are most of the more interesting colleges, founded between the 13th–16thC and filling a strip only some 900yds (820m) long.

To the E of the road sequence – and hemmed in by an eastern line of 16thC colleges along Bridge St., Sidney St. and St Andrew's St. – crowds inner Cambridge, its marketplace filled with a colorful collection of stalls.

If this sightseeing convenience is one advantage that Cambridge enjoys over Oxford, another – and it is a superlative one – is that its small river, the Cam or Granta, flows gently beside some of the most beautiful of the colleges. Landscaped with lawns and trees and offering a dazzling architectural feast, these justly famous **Backs** are best enjoyed on foot or by boat.

In summer the river is crowded with punts, often making their way to **Grantchester** village ($2\frac{3}{4}$ miles/4.5km away), immortalized by the poet Rupert Brooke.
Event Last two weeks in July, Cambridge Festival and Folk Festival.

Sights and places of interest
Colleges
Six colleges generally accepted to be of principal tourist importance are described. Many others have some feature of interest and the visitor with time to spare is likely to be rewarded by looking into almost any college that is open to the public. For example, **Magdalene College** (*Magdalene St.*) has the famous **Pepys Library** (*open 2.30–3.30pm, closed Sun*), where the great diarist's books are kept in the cases he designed.

Colleges (although not necessarily their halls or libraries) are normally open mornings and afternoons. Many close during the examinations period (*mid-May to late June*), and some during the vacations.

Corpus Christi 🏛

Trumpington St. ☎ *(0223) 59418.*

This college is interesting on three counts. First, unlike so many colleges that are proud to claim royal, aristocratic or high ecclesiastical parenthood, Corpus Christi was founded, in 1352, by two modest church guilds. Secondly, the **Old Court** ☆ dating from 1377, is not only a place of mellow medieval charm but also the university's best example of a court of this early period. Finally, a portrait of 1585 in the hall is thought to be of the playwright Christopher Marlowe who studied here.

Jesus College

Jesus Lane ☎ *(0223) 68611. Open 9am–5.30pm.*

There was a convent here from 1135 to the late 15thC, but obviously not a very successful one since its occupants eventually dwindled to two. Reasonably enough, Bishop Alcock of Ely (note his cockerel motif over the gates and in the chapel) dissolved this pathetic remnant in about 1496 in order to make way for the college he wished to build.

The bishop based his plans on the original domestic buildings, adding a story to the **Cloister Court**, and an arch-braced roof to the nuns' refectory which became the **hall**. The **chapel** is known for its Pre-Raphaelite work, with ceilings by William Morris and windows by Morris, Burne-Jones and Madox Brown.

King's College Chapel ⬆ ★

King's Parade ☎ *(0223) 350411* 🅿 *Open in term: Mon–Sat 9am–3.45pm, Sun 2–3pm, 4.30–5.45pm. Open in vacation: Christmas, from Jan 1 9am–4pm; Easter, 9am–5pm; summer, mid-June to Aug 9am–5.45pm, Sept to early Oct 9am–5pm. Choral services in term: Tues–Sat 5.30pm, Sun 10.30am and 3.30pm. The chapel may be closed for rehearsals, especially on Sun.*

Unquestioned star of Cambridge, this chapel arose out of a decision by Henry VI to provide a worthy place for the further education of his scholars at Eton, which he had founded in 1440. His concept was a college around a vast court, flanked by a splendid chapel, but his vision far outstripped his ability to implement it and the work advanced only sluggishly, stopping altogether on Henry's deposition in 1461. However, to the great good fortune of future generations emphasis had been placed on the chapel, left sufficiently advanced to encourage Henry VII and Henry VIII to complete it.

Satisfying as it is from the outside, it is the chapel's interior that has earned it centuries of acclaim. Perhaps the w end is over-heavy in Tudor decorative motif, but beyond the screen, rows of slim stained-glass windows soar upward to meet a great honeycomb of exquisite fan-vaulting. Nor is this all, for the altarpiece is Rubens' *Adoration of the Magi*, given to the chapel in 1961.

Queens' College

Queens' Lane ☎ *(0223) 65511* 🅿 *Open 2–4.30pm, and also July–Sept 10.15am–12.45pm. Closed early May to mid-June.*

Two queens were patrons here: Henry VI's wife, Margaret of Anjou, and Edward IV's wife, Elizabeth Woodville.

The main features are the **hall**, dating from the 15thC but internally much altered with exuberant 19thC decoration by William Morris and Madox Brown, and the **Cloister Court**, an intimate 15thC gem in dark red brick.

St John's College

St John's St. ☎ *(0223) 61621. Open 9am–5.30pm.*

Benefactions from that compulsive patron of educational, charitable and religious institutions, Margaret of Beaufort, mother of Henry VII, founded this college in 1511. The richly decorated gateway with its rearing heraldic beasts leads into three courts (1516, 1602 and 1674). Beyond, the **Bridge of Sighs** (1831) is built in the style of its Venetian namesake.

Trinity College

Trinity St. ☎ *(0223) 358201.*

Henry VIII, the founder of Trinity (1546), sits on the outside of the great gateway to this, the largest of all the Cambridge colleges, known for its huge **Great Court** of c.1600. Although appropriately grandiose, the gateway dates in fact from 1518 and formed the entrance to King's Hall, one of two 14thC foundations (the other was Michaelhouse) absorbed by

Henry VIII's new college. The 16thC **chapel** contains statues of some of the college's distinguished members, including Francis Bacon, Isaac Newton and Tennyson. The **library** (*open noon–2pm; closed Sat, Sun*), built by Christopher Wren, with carvings by Grinling Gibbons, has manuscripts ranging from the 8thC to A. A. Milne's *Winnie-the-Pooh*.

Other sights

Botanic Gardens
Entrances in Hill's Rd., Trumpington Rd., or Bateman St.
☎ *(0223) 350101* 💷 ✇ *Open May–Sept Mon–Sat 8am–7.30pm or sunset if earlier, Sun 2.30–6.30pm; Oct–Apr 8am–sunset (closed Sun). Glasshouses 2–4.45pm or sunset.*
At nearly all times of the year there is something of interest to look at in these extensive gardens not far s from the center of the town.

Cambridge and County Folk Museum
Castle St. ☎ *(0223) 355159* 💷 *Open Tues–Fri 10.30am–5pm; Sat 10.30am–1pm, 2–5pm; Sun 2.30–4.30pm; bank holiday Mon 2–5pm. Closed Mon.*
Domestic, agricultural and other material recalling life as it has been lived in the town and county since medieval times.

Fitzwilliam Museum ☆
Trumpington St. ☎ *(0223) 69501* 💷 💷 *Opening times liable to change, but generally Tues–Sat 10am–2pm (lower galleries) and 2–5pm (upper galleries); Sun 2.15–5pm (both galleries). Closed Mon except bank holidays.*
The museum is based on the collections of fine and decorative art bequeathed to the university in 1816 by Viscount Fitzwilliam. Highlights include considerable Egyptian, Greek and Roman collections, Islamic art, European paintings from the Middle Ages to the present day (artists represented include Corot, Gainsborough, Hals, Rembrandt, Titian and Vuillard) and a collection of English porcelain.
   Due to the split opening times, a visit needs to be carefully planned and anybody wishing to see both the pictures (upper galleries) and the decorative art (lower galleries) should visit in the middle of the day.

Kettle's Yard
Northampton St. ☎ *(0223) 352124. Permanent collection open 2–4pm, gallery open Mon–Sat noon–6pm, Sun 2–6pm.*
Museum of 20thC art and sculpture, once a private house and still blessed with a unique atmosphere.

Sight nearby

Imperial War Museum (Air) ☆
Duxford Airfield, on A505 8 miles (13km) s of Cambridge
☎ *(0223) 833963* 💷 💷 ✇ ✇ *Open mid-Mar to Oct 11am–5.30pm or sunset if earlier.*
This famous Battle of Britain fighter airfield is now the home of historic aircraft, from a Blériot monoplane of 1910 to the Concorde prototype. Several of the aircraft fly, and throughout the season there are special events. An exhibition tells the story of the US 8th Air Force.

Hotels

🅷 **Blue Boar**
Trinity St., Cambridge CB2 1TG ☎ *(0223) 63121* 🔲 🔲 ✇ *48* 🛏 *11*
⇛ 🆎 🆑 ⊚ ⊚ 𝚅𝙸𝚂𝙰
Location: Opposite Trinity College. One of the few hotels really at the center, and only 3mins' walk from a multi-story, 24hr parking lot. Known to have been a hotel in the 17thC, the Blue Boar has a snug, intimate atmosphere, and makes a point of welcoming children, with special prices, cots and a children's menu.
🔲 🖼 ✇ ⚐

🅷 **Garden House**
Granta Place, Cambridge CB2 1RT ☎ *(0223) 63421* ☎ *81463* 🔲
✇ *117* 🛏 *117* ⇒ ⇛ 🆎 ⊚ ⊚ 𝚅𝙸𝚂𝙰 *Closed Christmas to New Year.*
Location: Beside the river, close to the Fitzwilliam Museum. This smart, modern hotel, extended and refurbished in 1982, will be the choice of those looking for a place near the river. Gardens lead down to the water, and guests can pass the time watching the punts go by.
✦ ♿ 🔲 🖼 ✇ ⚓ ⟨⟨ ⚐

⊞ **Gonville**
Gonville Place, Cambridge CB1 1LY ☎ *(0223) 66611* ⫼⫼ ☜❧ *62*
🛏 *62* 🚗 ⚎ AE ⊙ VISA *Closed Christmas.*
Location: *s point of Parker's Piece, about 15mins' walk from town center.*
With purpose-built extensions well grafted onto a Victorian core, this is a
solidly comfortable and well-managed hotel with attentive staff.
‡ ⅏ ▢ ☐ ☙

Nightlife
The **Arts Theatre** (*Peas Hill* ☎ *(0223) 352000*) puts on professional
productions and plays host to opera and ballet when they come to town.
The **ADC Theatre** (*Park St.* ☎ *(0223) 59547*) has amateur and student
productions. An excellent and fairly inexpensive cinema is the **Arts**
(*Market Passage* ☎ *(0223) 352001*), specializing in foreign films. A jazz
club which attracts big names is the **Modern Jazz Club**, every Fri, at
The Man on the Moon (*Norfolk St.* ☎ *(0223) 350610*).
  The best disco, also a restaurant, is **Ronelles** (*Heidelberg Gardens, Lion
Yard* ☎ *(0223) 64222*).

Shopping
**King's Parade, Trumpington St., Regent St., St Andrew's St., Sidney
St.** and **Lion Yard** are the main shopping areas while the smaller streets
running off them contain the more unusual boutiques and craft shops.
Cambridge is renowned for its bookshops, and a list of these (and of
antique shops) is available from the tourist office. The market (*Market
Hill, closed Sun*) sells fruit, vegetables and all sorts of other things.

Sports and activities
Boating Punts, canoes and rowboats may be rented (▨ *and deposit
needed*) from Quayside (*Bridge St.*) in the N of the town and Silver St. to
the S.

Canterbury
Map 7L12. Kent. 61 miles (98km) SE of London.
Population: 33,000 ℹ *22 St Peter's St.* ☎ *(0227) 66567.*
The Romans were here first but, not long after their departure,
Bertha, Christian queen of Ethelbert of Kent, invited St
Augustine to her court in 597. Ethelbert, a remarkably
indulgent husband, was soon converted and a year later
Augustine founded his abbey, followed by a church which soon
received cathedral status with Augustine as the first
archbishop. From here on the story of Canterbury is essentially
that of its **cathedral** and of the pilgrims (such as those in
Chaucer's *Canterbury Tales*) who flocked to it. The cathedral is
not all that this ancient city has to offer, however; there are
Roman remains, a Norman keep, picturesque medieval houses,
the **West Gate** and a splendid length of 14th–15thC walls.

Sights and places of interest
Canterbury Cathedral �🏛 † ★
Within the city walls, to the NE ☎ *(0227) 64212* ✗ *through the
Guides Office, 11b The Precincts* ☎ *(0227) 64212.*
The mother church of England stands on the site of St Augustine's
original church which was burned down in 1067. Rebuilding began three
years later but the cathedral was not completed until 1503.
  Historically, Canterbury's most important date is 1170, when the
'turbulent priest' Thomas à Becket was murdered in the cathedral, the
martyr's shrine in the **Trinity Chapel** becoming (and remaining until
destroyed at the Reformation) one of the most important places of
pilgrimage in Britain. The site of the murder, known as the Martyrdom,
is in the NW transept.
  Although from the outside the cathedral has neither the restful
simplicity of *Winchester* nor the soaring Gothic of *Salisbury*, its great
gray towers dominate the city. Inside there is a wealth of detail, and

several features which on no account should be missed: the way in which elaborate screens and canopied tombs separate the choir from its aisles; in the **Trinity Chapel**, the great tombs of Henry IV, the only monarch to rest in Canterbury, and of the Black Prince; the fan vaulting of the **Lady Chapel** just E of the NW transept; the **Great Cloister** (*c.*1400), with its painted bosses; the spacious and lofty **Chapter House**; the ingenious **Norman water tower** to the NE of the cloister; the medieval stained glass; and the **crypt**, where Becket's body was entombed until 1220.

Hospital of St Thomas the Martyr
At the junction of High St. and St Peter's St. ☎ *(0227) 62395* 🔟
*but donation expected. Open Mon–Sat 10am–1pm, 2–5pm, Sun
11am–1pm, 2–5pm. Subject to occasional closure.*
This ancient hospice for poor pilgrims, founded in 1180 (only ten years after Becket's murder) was carefully sited so that the guests could perform their ablutions (here a word of wide meaning) in the river Stour. Today's visitors see the chapel, Norman crypt, and refectory with an early 13thC mural.

Roman Pavement
Butchery Lane ☎ *(0227) 52747* 📷 *Open Apr–Sept 10am–1pm,
2–5pm; Oct–Mar 2–4pm. Closed Sun.*
Centuries before the arrival of St Augustine, and now almost within the shadow of the cathedral, a Roman family wealthy enough to enjoy expensive mosaic flooring and central heating had their home here.

Royal Museum and Art Gallery
The Beaney, High St. ☎ *(0227) 52747* 🔟 *Open 10am–5pm.
Closed Sun.*
Canterbury's principal museum with both permanent collections and temporary exhibitions also incorporates the museum of the Royal East Kent Regiment. The archeological material includes Roman and Saxon jewelry and glass.

Sight nearby
Richborough Castle ☆
9 miles (14.5km) E of Canterbury ☎ *(03046) 12013. DOE* 📷 🚗
*Open mid-Mar to mid-Oct Mon–Sat 9.30am–6.30pm, Sun
2–6.30pm except Apr–Sept 9.30am–6.30pm; mid-Oct to mid-Mar
Mon–Sat 9.30am–4pm, Sun 2–4pm.*
Richborough is generally accepted as the place where the Romans landed in AD43, but although there was soon a fort here these ruins mainly represent the strengthened defenses put up in the late 3rdC to deter the ever bolder Saxons. The site is an impressive one, a place which even today strikes as a daunting great square of earthworks and stone. It is also of interest for the fact that the W exit represents the start of **Watling St.** which ran through *St Albans* to Viroconium (see *Shrewsbury*).

Hotels

🇭 **County**
High St., Canterbury, Kent CT1 2RX ☎ *(0227) 66266* ☎*965076* ▥
🛏 *74* 🖃 *74* 🚗 🚗 🖃 ⚏ 🆎 ⓘ ⓘ 🆅
Location: City center, close to E river bridge. Beams, antiques, open fires and careful lighting all combine to continue the welcome which this hotel has extended to travelers since the 16thC. The County is as central and convenient today as its site was nearly 2,000yrs ago when the Roman forum stood here.
💲 ♿ ☐ 📷 🍴 ☺

🇭 **Falstaff**
St Dunstan's St., Canterbury, Kent CT2 8AF ☎ *(0227) 62138* ▥
🛏 *16* 🖃 *10* 🚗 ⚏ 🆎 ⓘ ⓘ 🆅
Location: West Gate. Picturesque both inside and out, and dating largely from the early 15thC, the Falstaff continues a centuries-long tradition of hospitality to pilgrims. This is an excellent choice for those who want modern amenities combined with a feel for the city's pilgrim past.
☐ 🍴

🇭 **Victoria**
59 London Rd., Canterbury, Kent CT2 7HG ☎ *(0227) 59333* ☐
🛏 *26* 🖃 *16* 🚗 🆎 ⓘ ⓘ 🆅
Location: On the first traffic circle on A2, just W of the city. A hotel for those

who would prefer to stay outside the city center and enjoy the pleasures of a garden. Buses to and from the center pass the door.
🖂 ♿ ☐ ☑ ⚓

Hotel/restaurant nearby
Boughton Aluph (*12 miles/19km sw of Canterbury*).

Ⓗ Ⓡ **Eastwell Manor** 🏠 △
Eastwell Park, Ashford, Kent TN25 4HR ☎ *(0233) 35751* ☎*966281*
▥▥ to ☐ ☜ 20 ▭ 20 ⏦ ▭ ◡ ▦ AE CB ⓓ ⓓ VISA
Ⓡ △ ▥▥ ☐ ☜ ▭ ☕ *Last orders 9.30pm.*
Location: On A251, in Boughton Aluph. An Elizabethan manor surrounded by a 3,000 acre estate, Eastwell Manor has very large bedrooms, an oak-panelled conference room and sprawling lawns.

Chef Ian McAndrew, former sous-chef at the Carlton Tower, has won a considerable reputation for his *nouvelle cuisine*, and such specialties as *sauté de foie gras*, *truite saumonée Languedocienne* and *piccata de veau aux mousserons*. The wine list is extensive.
🖂 ‡ ♿ ☐ ☑ 🐟 ⚓ ⟨⟨ ℘ 🐖 ☗

Shopping
The area beside the cathedral, particularly **Palace St.** and **Northgate**, is known for its antique shops. Antiques can also be found at the Saturday market in the **Sidney Cooper Centre** (*St Peter's St.*). The main shopping streets are the **High St.** and **St George's St.**

Carlisle
Map 14C6. Cumbria. 58 miles (93km) w of Newcastle-upon-Tyne. Population: 72,000 ⓘ *Old Town Hall, Greenmarket* ☎ *(0228) 25517.*

Starting as a Roman camp close to *Hadrian's Wall* and later sacked by the Norsemen, Carlisle then experienced centuries of assault by the Scots who finally wrecked much of the **cathedral**. Of this violent past the still-mutilated cathedral and the great **castle** are the obvious witnesses, but those who search around this now essentially modern city will also find stretches of the **city walls**, a 15thC **tithe barn**, the 17thC **Market Cross**, and some attractive 18th and 19thC houses, notably in **Abbey St.**

Sights and places of interest
Carlisle Castle
On the nw inner ring road (Castle Way) ☎ *(0228) 31777. DOE* 🖾
🐦 *Open mid-Mar to mid-Oct Mon–Sat 9.30am–6.30pm, Sun 2–6.30pm except Apr–Sept 9.30am–6.30pm; mid-Oct to mid-Mar Mon–Sat 9.30am–4pm, Sun 2–4pm.*

Begun in 1092, the castle is of interest not only for its great **Norman keep** but also because in 1568 it was the prison of that tragic figure, Mary, Queen of Scots.
Carlisle Cathedral ✝
Just w of Market Place ☎ *(0228) 35169.*

Many cathedrals have been damaged by war, but none can have suffered a fate such as this one. For nine months in 1644–45, the city withstood a siege by the Scots, who finally demolished all but two of the Norman bays of the cathedral's nave, using the stone to rebuild the city walls. It is worth going inside if only to wonder at the great **E window** and **Brougham Reredos** (or triptych), a splendid example of 16thC Antwerp carving in which every gilded figure is full of life and character. There are also carved **misericords** featuring birds, beasts and monsters.

The adjacent 13thC **Prior's Tower** offers a painted ceiling (1506) and a **museum** of the cathedral's history (🖾 🎟 *10am–4pm except Sun* 🍽).

Ⓗ **Crown and Mitre**
English St., Carlisle, Cumbria CA3 8HZ ☎ *(0228) 25491* ☎*64183*
▥▥ ☜ 94 ▭ ▭ 94 ⏦ ▭ ◡ ▦ AE ⓓ ⓓ VISA
Location: Overlooking Market Sq. Behind a Victorian facade this is a

solid, spacious hotel with two cheerful bars, the pub-like **Railway Tavern** with appropriate decor and the more conventional **Peace and Plenty**.

✓ □ ▱ ⚓ 🏭

Shopping

The specialty of the county, the Cumberland sausage – a long herb-flavored pork sausage – is made and sold by the traditional butchers in the **Covered Market** at the end of **Fisher St**. This fine building is also the home of stalls selling fruit, vegetables and general goods. **English St.** and **Botchergate** are the main shopping streets, and specialty shops can be found in the streets leading off them.

Castle Howard ☆

Map 16E9. North Yorks. 15 miles (24km) NE of York
☎ *(065384) 333* ▦ ▆ ☛ ⇌ *Open Easter–Oct: grounds 11am–5pm, house and costume gallery 11.30am–5pm.*

A breathtaking memorial to the grandiose thinking of two men, Charles Howard, third Earl of Carlisle, and his architect John Vanbrugh. Built over many years (1700–37) and to modern eyes ostentatious almost beyond measure, it must nevertheless have appeared to its creators as no more than the proper setting for a great aristocrat. A palace rather than a castle, its interior matches the exterior in scale and lavish decoration.

The house's valuable contents include Old Masters and fine furniture. Other attractions are a **Gallery of Costumes** (17thC to the present day) and, in the park, the family **mausoleum** (by Hawksmoor) and the **Temple of the Four Winds** (1725), Vanbrugh's last work.

Chatsworth House ▥ ☆

Map 11G8. Bakewell, Derby. 13 miles (21km) sw of Sheffield ☎ *(024688) 2204* ▦ ▆ ☛ *Open Apr–Oct, house 11.30am–4.30pm, garden 11.30am–5pm.*

The great classical seat of the dukes of Devonshire is one of England's most impressive country mansions. The creation (1687–1707) of William Talman and Thomas Archer, with later additions by Wyatville, the house and chapel contain many priceless treasures: painted ceilings by Laguerre and Verrio, 17thC Mortlake tapestries, Delft tulip vases, local Blue John ware, and paintings by a brilliant company of artists including Veronese, Van Dyck, Rembrandt and Frans Hals.

Chester ★

Map 10G6. Cheshire. 20 miles (32km) s of Liverpool. Population: 63,000 ℹ *Town Hall, Northgate St.* ☎ *(0244) 40144.*

Romans, **The Rows**, timbered houses and virtually intact city walls: Chester has a rich and varied heritage, and most places of interest are within or close to the walls. The modern inner town centers on The Cross and closely matches Deva, its Roman predecessor; there are corners where you can actually peep into the places where the Romans lived. In Northgate St., for instance, the basement of no.23 preserves remains of the **praetorium** (or headquarters) while just around the corner in **Hamilton Place** you can look through a window into a strongroom. Or cross over into **Bridge St.** where, at no.39, Lawleys Chinaware stands above the remains of a Roman bath.

The principal Roman site is the **amphitheater** which, although only the northern part has been excavated, is one of the largest discovered in Britain.

Sights and places of interest
British Heritage Exhibition
Vicar's Lane, opposite the Roman amphitheater ☎ *(0244) 42222*
🖃 *Open Apr–Sept Mon–Sat 9am–5pm, Sun 2–6pm.*

Audio-visual presentations, models of Chester at different periods, and a
life-size mock-up of a section of *The Rows* as they may have been in the
mid-19thC, combine to give a picture of the city's past.

Chester Cathedral †
350yds (320m) N of The Cross ☎ *(0244) 24756.*

Here for once a happy story springs from the Reformation. Although the
abbey of St Werburgh (a pious 7thC princess) was dissolved, the abbey
church was converted to a Protestant cathedral, and its redundant and
theologically broadminded abbot became the first dean.

The cathedral embodies something from almost every period between
Norman and 19thC, but it is the **choirstalls** ☆ which demand most
attention. Carved in the 14thC and splendidly canopied, their
misericords, depicting a glorious assortment of animals and figures,
alone are reward enough for going inside.

Chester Heritage Centre
St Michael's Church, Bridge St. Row ☎ *(0244) 317948* 🖃 *Open
Apr–Sept Mon, Tues, Thurs–Sat 10am–5pm, Sun 2–5pm; Oct–Mar
1.30–4.30pm; bank holidays 2–5pm. Closed Wed.*

Chester's architectural story and the future sought through conservation
are the themes of this instructive exhibition.

City walls ☆
*Several access points, but Eastgate (an 18thC replacement of a
medieval predecessor) is likely to be the most convenient for
visitors in the city center.*

Although the walls are essentially medieval, they were first erected by the
Romans, initially as earthworks but before long becoming a formidable
stone enceinte with 26 towers and entered only by four gates.

Enthusiasts can walk the full 2-mile (3km) circuit. Others with less
energy or time can enjoy the best of the walls by covering the 600yds
(550m) between **Eastgate** and **Northgate**, passing the tower where in
1645 Charles I watched the defeat of his army at nearby Rowton Moor,
and the 200yds (185m) between Eastgate and **Newgate**.

Grosvenor Museum
Grosvenor St. ☎ *(0244) 21616* 🖃 *Open Mon–Sat 10am–5pm,
Sun 2–5.30pm.*

Dioramas and models show what life was like for a Roman legionary
stationed here at Deva, and there is an important gallery of inscribed
Roman stones.

The Rows and old houses ☆
In the four streets leading away from The Cross.

The unique Rows – enhanced by half-timbered houses – are Chester's
most attractive feature. Thought to date from the 13thC, this strange
arrangement of an arcaded footway slicing through the first floors of
houses and shops may have developed because Chester's medieval
inhabitants refused to clear away the solid ruins bequeathed by the
Romans and instead built above and around.

Many of the best of Chester's older houses are on **Watergate** and
Bridge St., running respectively w and s from The Cross. On the s side of
the former are **God's Providence House**, bearing a text recording its
immunity from the plague; the 16thC **Leche House**; and **Bishop
Lloyd's House** (1615), known for its rich carving.

In **Bridge St.** the so-called **Dutch Houses**, although mainly 17thC, in
part go back another three centuries, but it is in **Lower Bridge St.** that
the most attractive houses will be found. Here are **The Falcon** (1626),
the 17thC **Ye Olde King's Head**, **Gamul House** in which Charles I
lodged, and the **Bear and Billet Inn** (1664).

Hotels and restaurant

Ⓗ **The Blossoms**
St John St., Chester, Cheshire CH1 1HL ☎ *(0244) 23186* ⓣ*61113*
▥ ⌖ *70* ▭ *70* ⌁ AE CB ⓓ ⓒ VISA *Closed late Dec.*
Location: Close to Eastgate. A smart and conveniently located hotel, last
in a succession reaching back to a 15thC inn.
⚷ ▢ ⌸ ⚌

H R **Chester Grosvenor** 🏨 ⌂
Eastgate St., Chester, Cheshire CH1 1LT ☎ *(0244) 24024* 🕭*61240*
▥▥ 🏨 *99* ▦▦ 🍴 *99* 🍴 ⬛ AE CB ◉ ⑩ VISA *Closed Christmas.*
R 🍷 🖵 ▬ 🛏 *Sat Oct–Apr* 🎿 *Sat Oct–Apr. Last orders 10pm.*
Location: Central, near The Rows. Against the small scale of Chester, the
grandeur of the Grosvenor comes as something of a surprise, especially in
its loftily chandeliered public rooms and well-stocked wine cellar rich in
first growths.

In the Grosvenor's French restaurant, chef Gilbert Schneider favors
classical cuisine, with specialties such as *l'oeuf poché en tartelettes*, *purée
de navets et saumon fumé*, and *l'émincé de volaille et scampi à l'oreille*.
⬍ ⅋ 🖵 🖾 ✓ 🛶 ♟

H **Ye Olde King's Head** 🏠
48 Lower Bridge St. ☎ *(0244) 24855* 🖵 🍷 *11* 🛶 🖾 🛏 ⇌ AE
⑩ VISA
Location: To the s of Chester Heritage Centre. An early 16thC building that
was a private house for 200yrs, until it became an inn in 1717. Low
ceilings, beams, twisting passages, cheerful bars and, so rumor has it,
even a ghost.

Shopping
The fascinating **Rows** (see *Sights*) contain some equally interesting
shops. The **Grosvenor Shopping Precinct** (*between Bridge St. and
Eastgate St.*) contains department stores and chain stores. Local produce
and other goods can be obtained at the **Forum** indoor market (*closed Wed
afternoon*). The renowned Cheshire cheese is made and sold by **W. Wild
& Son** (*Grange Farm, Parkroad Road, Mollington, 5 miles/8km N of
Chester, shop open Mon–Sat 9am–5pm*).

Chichester
*Map 6M9. West Sussex. 15 miles (24km) E of Portsmouth.
Population: 20,700 i Council House, North St.* ☎ *(0243)
775888.*
There is a satisfying mingling of the centuries here – an
essentially Georgian town with a street plan that is still Roman
sheltering within medieval walls, themselves supported by
Roman foundations. The Roman origin is clear from the
rectangular crossing of the four main streets (the actual Market
Cross dates from 1501, cupola 18thC). The most readily
accessible Georgian buildings are in North St. where the
Council House (1733) incorporates a Roman stone, found right
here and recording the dedication of a temple to Neptune and
Minerva.

Today Chichester is the haunt of yachtsmen and theatergoers; the former because of its winding, scenic harbor, the
latter because of the **Festival Theatre**, the focus of the annual
Chichester Festival (*about May–Sept* ☎ *(0243) 781312*).
The **District Museum** (*29 Little London* 📷 *open
10am–5.30pm, closed Sun, Mon*) and the **Guildhall Museum**
(*Priory Park* 📷 *open June–Sept 1–5pm, closed Sun, Mon* ☎ *for
both (0243) 784683*) are good sources for local history.

Sights and places of interest
Chichester Cathedral ✝
Immediately w of Market Cross ☎ *(0243) 784729.*
The high points of this essentially Norman cathedral (founded about
1091) are two brilliantly executed 12thC sculptured panels ☆ one
depicting the arrival of Christ at Bethany, the other the raising of
Lazarus; fine though they still are, they must have been superb when
brightly colored and with jewels set in the eyes. In contrast, several
modern features claim attention: a painting by **Graham Sutherland**, a
window designed by **Marc Chagall**, and an altar tapestry designed by
John Piper.

Sights nearby
Fishbourne Roman Palace and Museum ☆
Salthill Rd., Fishbourne, 1¼ miles (2.5km) w of Chichester.
☎ *(0243) 785859* 🔲 💷 *Open Mar–Apr, Oct 10am–5pm;*
May–Sept 10am–6pm; Nov 10am–4pm; Dec–Feb Sun only
10am–4pm.

The largest Roman residence found in Britain, built *c.*AD75 and
destroyed by fire in *c.*280. What is seen with its the N wing, with its
exceptionally fine mosaic floors, hypocaust (hot air) heating and bath
suite. There is also an admirable museum with an audio-visual program,
local finds, and several instructive plans and models.

The formal gardens, restored to their 1stC plan, are planted with what
might have been grown here at that time.

Petworth House ☆
14 miles (22km) NE of Chichester ☎ *(0798) 42207.* NT 🔲 *park* 🔲
house 💷 ⚘ *House open Apr–Oct 2–6pm. Closed Mon, Tues*
following bank holiday, and Fri. Deer park open all year 9am–sunset.

It is largely because of its Grinling Gibbons carving and paintings
spanning from Italian Primitives to Turner that visitors flock to
Petworth. The great house, successor to a medieval manor of which
traces survive, was built in 1696 by the 6th Duke of Somerset, and it was
he who commissioned Grinling Gibbons to carry out the exuberant
carving that still graces Petworth. Later, Turner often visited here and
painted the beautiful park, landscaped by Capability Brown. A
collection of Turner's works hangs in a special room.

Weald and Downland Open-Air Museum ☆
Singleton, 5 miles (8km) N of Chichester ☎ *(024363) 348* 🔲 💷
⚘ *Open Apr–May, Sept–Oct 11am–5pm (closed Mon); June–Aug*
11am–5pm; Nov–Mar Sun only 11am–4pm.

The gentle Sussex downland provides a fitting setting for the homely old
buildings 🏛 which now rest here safe from demolition. The purpose of
the museum is to rescue, study and show good examples of modest local
buildings, both domestic and commercial. Among those already here are
a 14thC house and a 19thC blacksmith's forge.

🏨 Ship
North St., Chichester, West Sussex PO19 1NH ☎ *(0243) 782028*
📞*957141* 🔲 ➡ *28* ⟡ *18* ⟡ ⟡ ⟡ ⟡ ⟷ AE CB ◎ 💳 VISA
Location: 300yds (275m) N of the Market Cross. Modern comfort within a
typical Georgian house built in 1790 for one of Nelson's admirals.

⬍ 📷 ⚞ ⚭

Cirencester
Map 4K7. Glos. 15 miles (24km) SE of Gloucester.
Population: 12,000 ℹ *Corn Hall, Market Place* ☎ *(0285) 4180.*

Now a pleasant, small Cotswolds town, Cirencester was once
the Roman Corinium, a town second only to London in size. In
the Middle Ages the town blossomed anew as a major wool
center, the prosperous merchants putting some of their profits
into enlarging the splendid Norman church.

Sights and places of interest
Corinium Museum
Park St. ☎ *(0285) 5611* 🔲 *Open May–Sept Mon–Sat 10am–6pm,*
Sun 2–6pm; Oct–Apr Tues–Sat 10am–5pm, Sun 2–5pm (closed
Mon).

A refreshingly selective and uncluttered museum which tells the local
story from prehistoric to modern times. Several mosaics have pride of
place and Roman life is vividly shown through reconstructions of a
workshop, a kitchen, a hypocaust, and even of a *triclinium* (dining
room), complete with a genuine mosaic floor.
St John Baptist †
Market Place.
Curiosities include the **three-storied south porch** especially built in 1490
so that secular business could be conducted without admitting the

king's representatives to the church itself; the **Bluecoat Boy**, a quaint figure who once begged for funds for local schools; the **Boleyn Cup**, made for Henry VIII's second wife two years before her execution; and the **pulpit**, one of the few to survive the Reformation and unique for its open tracery stonework.

Ⓗ **King's Head**

Market Pl., Cirencester, Glos GL7 2NR ☎ (0285) 3322 ⓣ 43470
▥◫ ❧ 70 ☒ 65 ⬤ ⬛ ⬰ AE CB ⬥ ⬤ VISA
Location: Center of the town, near the church of St John the Baptist. An old-world hotel which has served as the town's chief inn since the 14thC. In the Cocktail Bar, notice John Beecham's dramatic picture, depicting a Civil War incident when Charles I's recruiting commissioner, attacked by a mob, had to seek safety in the inn.
‡ ⬥ ⌂ ♣ ♈

Clovelly ☆

Map 3L4. Devon. On the N coast, 10 miles (16km) W of Bideford.

In peak vacation periods, the human throng threatens to swamp the charm of this outstandingly picturesque, cliffside village with its whitewashed cottages and little cove. Fortunately the cobbled road through Clovelly is too steep for cars and coaches, which are confined to a huge parking area at the clifftop.

Colchester

Map 7J11. Essex. 61 miles (98km) NE of London. Population: 77,000 **i** Town Hall, High St. ☎ (0206) 46379.

Walking around Colchester, one treads where Cunobelin (Shakespeare's Cymbeline), chief of the Trinobantes, held sway; where in AD50 the Romans established their first colony in these islands; where ten years later Queen Boadicea of the Iceni burned that colony; and where a thousand years later William the Conqueror erected one of the most formidable keeps in Europe. In addition, the town boasts fragments of two medieval abbeys and a wealth of Georgian and earlier houses.

Colchester is famed for its 'native' oysters, known to have been prized by the Romans and to have been developed commercially since the 12thC. Gourmets will find them at **Mussett's Oysters** (_Coast Rd., West Mersea_), or **Colchester Oyster Fishery Ltd.** (☎ _(0206) 384141_) where parties of 12 – 30 people can visit the beds and enjoy an oyster meal; individuals may visit on Friday.

Sights and places of interest
Colchester Castle and Castle Museum

Off High St., within NE angle of the walls ☎ (0206) 77475 ▨
✗ vaults in summer. Open Apr–Sept Mon–Sat 10am–5pm, Sun 2.30–5pm; Oct–Mar Mon–Fri 10am–5pm; Sat 10am–4pm (closed Sun).

First a Roman temple graced this site, then in 1080 William the Conqueror, making use of the temple's base and stonework, built this great keep, massive enough in its present form but until the 17thC even larger with an upper floor. Today it houses an imaginative museum devoted to archeology with emphasis on Roman Colchester.
St Botolph's Priory

SE of the town, near the station ⌕

The arcaded W front and part of the nave survive from the Augustinian priory which was built in 1100, mainly of Roman bricks.
The Walls ☆

Genuine Roman (not medieval) walls, which did of course undergo strengthening and repairs in later centuries. The best stretches are to the W beside Balkerne Hill, to the N of the castle, and to the SE on Priory St.

H Red Lion
High St., Colchester, Essex CO1 1DJ ☎ *(0206) 77986* ◫ ⌨ *70*
▭ *15* ⥬ AE CB ⊕ ⓘ VISA
Location: Across High St. from the town hall. An old-world ramble of
rooms behind a half-timbered frontage. There are grills, a coffee shop
and three bars of real character.
▢ ▨ ☷

H Rose and Crown
East St., Colchester, Essex CO1 2TZ ☎ *(0206) 866677* ◻ ⌨ *26*
▭ *16* ⥬ AE ⊕ ⓘ VISA
Location: At the E end of the town, beyond the river. This ancient place, an
inn since the 15thC, has a half-timbered exterior, rough and blackened
beams, crazily angled floors and open fires. The restaurant wine list
competes with mead and elderberry wine.
▢ ▨ ☷

Hotel and restaurants nearby
Near **Dedham** (*7 miles/11km NE of Colchester*).

H Maison Talbooth ▥
Stratford Rd., Dedham, Colchester, Essex CO7 6HN ☎ *(0206)*
322367 ▥ ⌨ *10* ▭ *10* ⊸ ⥬ AE CB ⊕ ⓘ VISA
R Le Talbooth
△ *Gun Hill* ▥ ◻ ▮ ➤ *Last orders 9pm.*
Location: Between A12 and Dedham, off B1029. Once a toll-booth for
river traffic on the Stour, this timbered 16thC cottage featured in a
Constable painting. Not surprisingly, considering the restaurant's
proximity to Colchester, oysters are foremost among its seafood
specialties, but in recent years Le Talbooth has gained a great reputation
for the whole of its English/French cuisine.

In an unusual arrangement, Le Talbooth has its bedrooms half a mile
away (1km) in a sturdy late-Victorian country house. Although this is
only a short walk, the hotel is treated as a separate establishment under
the name Maison Talbooth. The hotel has spacious, sumptuous rooms
and suites, and provides an atmosphere of relaxing luxury.
▭ ♿ ▢ ⬜ ▧ ⬥ ⟨⟨ ✓ ⬧ ➤ ☷

Manningtree (*on A157, 8 miles/13km NE of Colchester*).

R Old Coffee House ❦
3–5 South St. ☎ *(020639) 4102* ▥ ◻ ▮ ➤ ⊕ ⓘ VISA *Last*
orders 9.15pm. Closed Sun, Mon.
In spite of its name, this is a full-scale restaurant, and one of unassuming
merit. Manningtree is a small agricultural port on the Stour estuary,
about halfway between Colchester and Ipswich. The Old Coffee House is
run by Rhoda Dicks and her son, who does the cooking. Starters range
from home-made soups and smoked sprats to seafood pancakes, main
courses from steak and kidney pudding to pork Creole. There is an
excellent wine list.

Corfe Castle
Map 4M7. Dorset. 20 miles (32km) E of Weymouth
☎ *(0929) 480442* ▣ *Open Mar–Oct 10am–sunset;*
Nov–Feb Sat, Sun in fine weather 2–4pm.
The earlier Saxon castle on this mound was the scene of a dark
deed in 978 when King Edward the Martyr was murdered here
on the instigation of his stepmother, who wanted the throne for
her own son. Soon, however, a Norman castle was built, a place
of joy to King John who frequently came here, but one of
despair for Edward II, who was dragged here before being
removed to Berkeley Castle (see *Gloucester*) and death. The
ruins owe their tortured appearance to the castle's destruction
by Cromwell in 1646.

The Cotswolds ★
Map 4&5. Glos, H and W, Oxon **i** *22 New St., Chipping Norton, Oxon* **☎** *(0608) 41320; Corn Hall, Market Place, Cirencester, Glos* **☎** *(0285) 4180; Council Offices, High St., Moreton-in-Marsh, Glos* **☎** *(0608) 50881; The Library, St Edward's Hall, Stow-on-the-Wold, Glos* **☎** *(0451) 30352.*

This rolling land of broad hills, pasture and woods provides some of the gentlest yet loveliest countryside in England. The area is generally considered to be confined within lines linking (from the N, clockwise) Chipping Campden, Chipping Norton, Burford, *Cirencester*, Stroud, Cheltenham and Broadway.

The blessing which gives these hills their unique character is the warm Cotswold stone which over centuries has gone into the building of several wonderfully unspoiled small towns and villages. And if these places have another common feature, it is their great churches, memorials to the wealth that derived from the wool trade of the 13th–15thC.

For a tour of Cotswold towns and villages see *Planning*.

Sights and places of interest
Arlington Row ☆
Map 4J7. Bibury, Glos. NT. No admission. View from outside.
The whole essence of the old Cotswolds lives on in this homey row of early 17thC cottages in a green setting above the little river Coln.
Chedworth Roman Villa
Map 4J7. Glos. Near Yanworth, 8 miles (15km) SE of Cheltenham. **☎** *(024289) 256. NT* 🖾 🚗 *Open Mar–Oct 11am–6pm or sunset if earlier (closed Mon except bank holidays); Nov to mid-Dec, Feb 11am–4pm (closed Mon–Tues). Closed mid-Dec to Jan.*

This was not so much a villa as a large country house, the hub of an estate owned by prosperous Romans or Romano-Britons for some 200yrs from about AD180. Over 30 rooms have been identified, but what is of special interest here is that there are two sets of baths, the original damp heat type and also the later dry system.
Cotswold Countryside Collection
Map 4J7. Northleach, Glos **☎** *(04516) 715* 🖾 🚗 *Open May–Sept Mon–Sat 10am–6pm, Sun 2–6pm.*

Housed in a forbidding former house of correction, this is an imaginative and still developing museum. Attractions include a gallery illustrating the story of man in the Cotswolds, and exhibits explaining the skills of the shepherd, the carter, the wheelwright and others. The showpiece of the museum is a unique collection of Gloucestershire harvest wagons.
Cotswold Farm Park
Map 4J7. Temple Guiting, Glos (near Hailes Abbey) **☎** *(04515) 307* 🖾 🖾 ▯ ＊ 🚗 *Open May–Sept 10.30am–6pm.*

Soay sheep, known to have been domesticated even in Stone Age times, pigs with an ancient ancestry, and strange and rare poultry can be seen alongside other British farm animals of the past. A pets' corner, adventure playground and pony-trap rides will appeal to children.
Cotswold Wildlife Park
Map 5J8. Burford, Oxon **☎** *(099382) 3006* 🖾 ▯ ＊ 🚗 *Open 10am–6pm or sunset if earlier.*

The Cotswolds provide a glorious setting for, among larger animals, rhinos, camels and tigers and, among numerous smaller ones, chipmunks, monkeys and the strange little meerkats. Birds, butterflies and reptiles also find a home here. Additional attractions for children include an adventure playground, pony rides and a little railway.
Hailes Abbey
Map 4J7. Glos. Near Winchcombe, 8 miles (13km) NE of Cheltenham **☎** *(0242) 602398. NT/DOE* 🖾 🚗 *Open mid-Mar to mid-Oct Mon–Sat 9.30am–6.30pm, Sun 2–6.30pm except Apr–Sept 9.30am–6.30pm; mid-Oct to mid-Mar Mon–Sat 9.30am–4pm, Sun 2–4pm.*

Founded in 1246 by Richard, Earl of Cornwall, who was buried here in 1272, Hailes soon became famous for its relic of the Holy Blood, mentioned by Chaucer in his *Pardoner's Tale*. The extensive remains, in a peaceful pastoral setting, have 17 cloister arches as their principal feature, while a small museum recalls something of the place's rich past.

Hidcote Manor Garden
Map 5J8. Glos. 8 miles (13km) s of Stratford-upon-Avon
☎ *(038677) 333. NT* 🖼 💻 🚗 *Open Apr–Oct 11am–8pm, or 1hr before sunset if earlier. Closed Tues, Fri.*
Exquisite visual effects are created by a series of individual gardens, each specializing in plants of a particular type or color, separated by walls or unusual hedges. Famous for its rare shrubs, Hidcote draws large crowds on weekends in high season.

Snowshill Manor
Map 4J7. Snowshill, Glos ☎ *(0386) 852410. NT* 🖼 🚗 *Open Apr, Oct Sat, Sun, Easter Mon 1am–1pm, 2–5pm; May–Sept 11am–1pm, 2–6pm (closed Mon except bank holidays, Tues).*
This typically Cotswold, mainly Tudor manor house contains the astonishing possessions of its last owner, who could not resist collecting. Toys, bicycles, looms, clocks and Japanese armor are only a few of the things that took his eclectic fancy.

Sudeley Castle
Map 4J7. Winchcombe, Glos ☎ *(0242) 602308* ▓ 💻 ▮ 🚗 *Open Mar–Oct, castle noon–5.30pm, grounds 11am–6.30pm.*
Built in the 12thC, rebuilt in the 15thC, dismantled in 1644 and finally restored in the 19thC, Sudeley's main point of interest is that it became the home of Catherine Parr, sixth wife of Henry VIII, after the king's death. The castle contains paintings by Rubens, Van Dyck, Constable and Turner, Catherine Parr's tomb, and an enchanting collection of toys. Children will also enjoy the woodland play area with mock castle and tree-walk.

Hotels and restaurants
Bibury (*5 miles/8km NE of Cirencester*).

H **Swan Hotel**
Bibury, Cirencester, Glos GL7 5NW ☎ *(028574) 204* ▮▮▯ 🍽 24 🛏 24 🚗 🖼 🚗 🐟 🎨 *VISA*
Location: By the river Colne. This is an ivy-clad, mellow place in an idyllic riverside location. The good taste and standards inside the hotel fully meet the promise of the exterior.
🖼 🖼 🐟 🦢

Bourton-on-the-Water (*15 miles/24km E of Cheltenham*).

H **The Old Manse**
High St., Bourton-on-the-Water, Glos GL54 2BX ☎ *(0451) 20642* ▮▮▯ 🍽 8 🛏 8 🚗 🚗 🖼 *VISA Closed Dec–Jan.*
Location: Central, near the river Windrush. A small hotel, built in the 18thC as the home of a Baptist minister, today it welcomes visitors to one of the loveliest villages in the Cotswolds.
🖼 🖼 🍷 🦢

Broadway (*16 miles/26km NE of Cheltenham*).

H R **Lygon Arms** 🏨 🏛
High St., Broadway, H and W, WR12 7DU ☎ *(0386) 852255*
📠 *338260* ▮▮▯ 🍽 67 🛏 67 🚗 🖼 🚗 *AE* *CB* ① ① *VISA*
R 🖼 🖼 🖼 🍽 *Last orders 9pm.*
Location: On main road through Broadway. General Lygon fought with Wellington at Waterloo; today, what was once his family estate is inclined to be occupied by droves of tourists visiting the Cotswolds. Parts of the Lygon Arms are about 600yrs old, and it remains an unspoiled example of a typically mellow Cotswold-stone building.

The Lygon's gastronomic reputation is much more recent, however, and dates from the arrival of chef Shaun Hill, formerly of the Capital Hotel and Blakes, in 1980. Hill has won attention for his *nouvelle cuisine* while at the same time strengthening the Lygon's reputation for traditional English dishes – salmon, roasts, game – prepared from local ingredients. The wine list features some outstanding vintage ports.
♿ 🖼 🖼 🍷 🌙 🍴 🐟 🐎

Burford (_11 miles/17km s of Chipping Norton_).

Ⓗ **Golden Pheasant**
High St., Burford, Oxon OX8 4RJ ☎ (099382) 3223 ⅠⅠ 🕭 _12_ 🛏
_12_ 🚗 🖛 ⇶ ⒶⒺ ⒸⒷ ⓞ ⒸⒹ ⓋⒾⓈⒶ
Location: On the wide main street. Parts of the building date back to the
14thC, and a recent renovation has happily restored to view some large
beams and stone walls. Two rooms have four-poster beds, one a survivor
from the 17thC.
♿ ▢ ▱ 🖛 ▦

Chipping Campden (_23 miles/37km NE of Cheltenham_).

Ⓗ Ⓡ **King's Arms**
The Square, Chipping Campden, Glos GL55 6AW ☎ (0386)
_840256_ ⅠⅠⅠ _to_ ⅠⅠⅠⅠ 🕭 _14_ 🛏 _2_ 🚗 ⇶ ⒶⒺ ⓞ ⒸⒹ ⓋⒾⓈⒶ _Closed
Jan–Feb Mon–Fri._
Ⓡ ⅠⅠⅠ ▦ 🖛 🍴 _Last orders 9pm. Closed dinner Jan–Feb._
Location: On the market square. The husband-and-wife team who own
this inn describe it as 'cheerfully run,' and take pride in the profusion of
log fires and flowers. Their enthusiasm is shared by their patrons. The
rooms might be simple enough but it is a comfortable place, with an
excellent restaurant. Emphasis is placed on fresh local produce including
vegetables and fruit from the garden. The menu is English and French,
and there are some sound Bordeaux and Burgundies on the wine list.
There is also cask-conditioned Hook Norton ale.
🖂 🌽 🍸

Ⓡ **Caminetto**
High St. ☎ (0386) 840934 ⅠⅠ ▭ ▤▤ 🖛 ⓞ ⒸⒹ ⓋⒾⓈⒶ _Last orders
10.30pm. Closed lunch except Sun, Mon, three weeks in Jan and last
two weeks in Oct._
The name, meaning fireplace, was inspired by the restaurant's
inglenook. Even the most commonplace Italian dishes are prepared with
the skill and enthusiasm that characterize this warm, friendly restaurant
run by a Sardinian.

Lower Slaughter (_16 miles/25km E of Cheltenham_).

Ⓗ **Manor**
Lower Slaughter, Stow-on-the-Wold, Glos GL54 2HP ☎ (0451)
_20456_ ⅠⅠⅠⅠ 🕭 _8_ 🛏 _8_ 🖛 ⇶ ⒶⒺ ⓞ ⒸⒹ ⓋⒾⓈⒶ
Location: At the entrance to the village. A gracious country house offering
exceptionally large bedrooms, park-like grounds, heated swimming
pool, tennis court, private trout stream and, best of all, a wholly
undemanding ambience. In the restaurant, try home-made fish pâté at
dinner and Arbroath smokies for breakfast.
🖂 ▢ ▱ 🌽 ≋ 🖛 🍴

Lower Swell (_1 mile/1.5km W of Stow-on-the-Wold_).

Ⓡ **Old Farmhouse** ✿
☎ (0451) 30232 ⅠⅠ ▭ ⅠⅠⅠ 🚗 🖛 _Last orders 9pm. Closed Jan._
A 16thC farmhouse which has been turned into a comfortable, cottage-
style inn. There are bar meals at lunch and in the evening, and excellent
dinners in a small dining room, where simple dishes are prepared with
flair and imagination. There is a good wine list but, sadly, no cask-
conditioned beer, despite the proximity of Donnington, England's
prettiest brewery.
There are eight bedrooms attached to the restaurant (Ⅰ▭).

Shopping

Many Cotswold towns such as **Burford**, **Chipping Norton** and **Stow-on-
the-Wold** are renowned for their antique shops. Other specialties are
pottery, crafts and textiles. Notable shops include the **Campden Pottery**
(_High St., Chipping Campden_) and the **Cotswold Perfumery Ltd**
(_Victoria St., Bourton-on-the-Water_) which makes and blends its own
perfumes. A useful publication, _Crafts and Craftsmen in the Heart of
England_, is available from local tourist offices.

Coventry

*Map 11I8. West Midlands. 18 miles (29km) E of
Birmingham. Population: 335,000* ℹ *36 Broadgate*
☎ *(0203) 20084.*

Coventry means the motor industry, the appalling air raid of
November 1940 which at least provided Coventry with a
controversial new cathedral, and, of course, Lady Godiva,
11thC wife of Leofric, Earl of Mercia, who pleaded with her
husband to ease the taxes he was imposing. He agreed to do so if
she rode naked through the town, a feat she performed having
first enjoined all the people to remain indoors and then, as an
added precaution, suitably arranged her long hair. Legend
relates that only Peeping Tom looked, but adds that he was
struck blind before he saw anything worthwhile. A clock with
moving figures and a statue in **Broadgate** commemorate the
event.

Touches of Coventry's medieval past can be seen in the
Tudor almshouses (such as **Ford's Hospital** in Greyfriar's Lane
and **Bond's Hospital** in Hill St.), along **Spon St**. to the W of the
city and, most rewardingly, in **St Mary's Guildhall**.

Sights and places of interest

Coventry Cathedral † ☆
200yds (180m) E of Broadgate ☎ *(0203) 27597* ✗

On the night of November 14 1940, a German air raid destroyed much of
Coventry, including its 14thC cathedral. On May 25 1962, Basil Spence's
new cathedral, symbolically linked by a porch to the remains of the old,
was consecrated. The interior, with its striking angles, boldly conceived
windows and imaginative lighting, achieves some remarkably theatrical
effects. In addition, the cathedral has become something of a gallery of
modern art. The best known and most controversial furnishing is
Graham Sutherland's powerful tapestry depicting *Christ in Glory*, which
hangs above the altar. Outside, to the right of the porch, Jacob Epstein's
last great religious sculpture depicts *St Michael triumphing over the Devil.*

Museum of British Road Transport
Cook St. ☎ *(0203) 25555* 🅿 *Open Apr–Sept Mon–Fri 10am–4pm,
Sat, Sun 10am–5.30pm; Oct–Mar Fri 9.30am–4pm, Sat–Sun
10am–5pm (closed Mon–Thurs).*

Coventry has played a key part in the development of transportation,
especially road transportation, and this museum, opened in 1980,
illustrates much of what has been achieved. There are bicycles,
motorcycles, commercial vehicles, and a fine collection of British cars.

St Mary's Guildhall
Bayley Lane, near the cathedral ruins ☎ *(0203) 25555* 🖾 *Open
Easter, May–Oct Mon–Sat 10am–1pm, 2–5.30pm, Sun noon–5pm.
Closed when required for civic use.*

A magnificent example of a medieval guildhall, built for the Guild of
Merchants in 1342, handed over to the city in 1552 and still in use. The
Great Hall contains a remarkable 16thC tapestry.

Ⓗ **Leofric**

Broadgate, Coventry, West Midlands CV1 1LZ ☎ *(0203) 21371*
🖵*311193* ▥ 🕮 *90* 🛏 *90* ♠ ⇌ AE CB ⊕ ⊙ VISA *Closed
Christmas.*

Location: City center. A modern, purpose-built hotel with all facilities. It
overlooks the statue of Lady Godiva and, almost inevitably, has a
Peep-in-Tom coffee shop.

‡ ☐ 🎿

Shopping

The large pedestrian shopping center and the adjoining streets of **Trinity
St.**, **Hales St.** and **Corporation St.** form the central shopping area.
Many of the restored medieval buildings in **Spon St.** contain craft and
gift shops. A general market is held in **The Precinct** (*main days Wed, Fri,
Sat*).

Dartmoor National Park
Map 3M4–5. Devon. sw of Exeter **i** *Dartmoor National Park Authority, Parke, Haytor Rd., Bovey Tracey, Devon TQ13 9JQ* **☎** *(0626) 832093, open Mon–Fri 9am–5pm.*

This is wild, sometimes melancholy country, the place where Sherlock Holmes met the Hound of the Baskervilles and where in both fact and fiction desperate fugitives from the notorious prison have blundered around through fog and bog.

There is, of course, another side to Dartmoor, for this is country where many distinctive features mark what at first glance seems no more than miles of rock-spattered heath; the tors, for instance, where 300 million years of weathering have left exposed great piles of ancient bedrock; the bright streams that tumble their course to ports such as **Teignmouth** and **Dartmouth**; the rough ponies, semi-wild but each one individually owned; the relics left by Bronze Age man; and the medieval crosses and ancient bridges which marked the way to the once powerful abbeys that lay beyond the moor.

Several roads break up the E part of the moor, but only one (B3212) cuts across its heart. Leaving Moretonhampstead, this road climbs to the desolate **Shapley Common** and **Warren House Inn** (Bronze Age remains within easy walking distance), then drops to **Postbridge**, famous for its clapper bridge, continues to **Two Bridges** with, to the NW, a long crest of tors, and finally heads for the moor's edge at **Yelverton**, on the way passing the **prison**, opened in 1809 to house prisoners taken in the Napoleonic wars.

The essence of Dartmoor is the moor itself. In addition, there are a number of places of interest around the periphery and a selection of these is listed below.

Sights and places of interest
Castle Drogo ▥
Map 3M4. Drewsteignton, between A30 and A382 in the NE sector of the park **☎** *(06473) 3306. NT* ▨ ▣ ◚ *Open Apr–Oct 11am–6pm.*

It looks like a well-preserved Norman fortress perched above the gorge of the river Teign, but in fact it was built in 1910–30 and represents one of the most remarkable achievements of the architect Sir Edwin Lutyens.
Dart Valley Railway
Buckfastleigh, off A38 on the E edge of the moor **☎** *(03644) 2338* ▨ ▣ ✱ ◚ *Trains run 3–4 times daily at Easter, then Sun and bank holidays, then daily mid-June to mid-Sept. Telephone for exact times.*
For the steam train enthusiast there is a workshop, museum, models, a miniature railway, and 7 miles (11km) of working track along the wooded glades of the river Dart.
Finch Foundry Museum
Sticklepath, 4 miles (6.5km) E of Okehampton **☎** *(083784) 286* ▨ ◚ *Open 11am–6pm.*
In the early 19thC this village was known for its range of agricultural tools, all made with machines driven by waterwheels. Today some of this quite remarkable machinery is regularly demonstrated.
Lydford Gorge
Map 3M4. Lydford, in the NW sector of the park, between Tavistock and Okehampton **☎** *(082282) 320. NT* ▨ ▣ ◚ *Open 9am to 1hr before sunset. Nov–Mar access only as far as the waterfall.*
Here the little river Lyd has worn a deep gorge. The most dramatic features are the **White Lady Waterfall** and the **Devil's Cauldron**.
Museum of Dartmoor Life
Map 3M4. 3 West St., Okehampton ▨ *Open Mon–Sat 10.30am–4.30pm.*
Attractively housed in a 19thC mill, the museum has vintage farm vehicles, strange household utensils, material on the mining industry and many fascinating old photographs of life on Dartmoor.

Hotels and restaurants
Near **Chagford** (*10 miles/16km* SE *of Okehampton*).

H R **Gidleigh Park** 🏨 ⌂
Chagford, Devon TQ13 8HH ☎ *(06473) 2367* 🖭 *42551* ⚬ 12
🛏 *11* ⊟ ⊟
R ⚬ ⚬ ⚬ ⚬ *Last orders 9pm.*

Location: 1½ miles (2.5km) NE *of Chagford.* Many of the pilgrims who drive across Dartmoor to Gidleigh Park are aware that their hosts will be American. To those who don't know, the hint of Ivy League must seem even more incongruous than the huge mock-Tudor house suddenly rising from the isolation of the wooded hillside. There is a warm greeting in front of the log fire which perfumes the pleasantly airy, wood-panelled public rooms. The bedrooms are impeccably fitted and relaxing. In summer, tea is served on the terrace.

The slightly solemn *raison d'être* of Gidleigh is what the proprietors, Paul and Kay Henderson, dub *cuisine courante* rather than *nouvelle*; with a British flavor, too, in dishes like veal kidneys with juniper berry and brandy sauce, best end of English lamb on a bed of puréed leeks, or Scotch sirloin steak with Madeira sauce. Diners are also offered a choice of outstanding English cheeses (some local), and wines from one of Britain's most impressive cellars including, predictably, a remarkable collection from America. Keen, friendly young staff. No credit cards, but dollar checks accepted.
⌂ ▢ ☞ ⚬ ⚬ ⚬ ⚬ ⚬

Frenchbeer (*11 miles/18km* SE *of Okehampton*).

H R **Teignworthy** ❀
Frenchbeer, Chagford, Devon TQ13 8EX ☎ *(06473) 3355* ⚬ 9
🛏 *9* ⚬ ⚬ *Closed early to late Jan.*
R ⚬ ⚬ ⚬ ⚬ ⚬ *Last orders 9pm.*

Location: In village. The virtues of a good hotel – comfort, peace, service that is solicitous without being claustrophobic, and a hospitable dining room – have won Teignworthy an appreciative clientele. This small country house, in the archetectural style of Lutyens, has only six bedrooms, all well-equipped, with three more in the Hay Loft. Its 14 acres of grounds are sheltered, in spite of the hotel's position high on the moorlands. There are log fires in the public rooms and, for sybarites, a sauna, sunbed and spa bath. The kitchen makes good use of local ingredients to produce specialties such as spicy carrot soup, halibut steak with watercress sauce and quail roasted with coriander. There is an extensive wine list.
⌂ ▢ ☞ ⚬ ⚬ ⚬ ⚬ ⚬ ⚬

Moretonhampstead (*10 miles/16km* SE *of Okehampton*).

H **Manor House** 🏨
Moretonhampstead, Devon TQ13 8RE ☎ *(06474) 355* 🖭 *42794*
⚬ ⚬ 66 🛏 66 ⚬ ⚬ ⚬ AE CB ⊡ ⊡ VISA *Closed Christmas.*
Location: On E *side of B3212, 3 miles (5km)* SW *of Moretonhampstead.* Things are on the grand scale here, from the building itself, an immense stone mansion in acres of glorious park, down through its cathedral-like lounge to the bathrooms, some of which retain the huge baths of a more spacious past.
⌂ ⚬ ⚬ ▢ ☞ ⚬ ⚬ ⚬ ⚬ ⚬ ⚬

Postbridge (*17 miles/27km* S *of Okehampton*).

H **Lydgate House** ⌂
Postbridge, Yelverton, Devon PL20 6TJ ☎ *(0822) 88209* ▢ ⚬
10 🛏 *2* ⚬ ⚬ ⚬ AE ⊡ VISA
Location: Along a private drive leading SE *off B3212.* Nestling in its own grounds sprawled along a green and wooded slope above the Dart, this is a friendly and undemanding small country house hotel in which the personal touch is what counts.
⚬ ⚬

Shopping

Although the world-famous Dartington glass is actually made in
Torrington, north Devon, perfect specimens and seconds are sold at the
Dartington Cider Press Centre (*Shinners Bridge, Dartington*), just to the
E of the national park.

Sports and activities

Information on fishing, riding and guided walks (*1½–6hrs*) in the park is
listed in the *Dartmoor Visitor*, available free of charge from the tourist
office.

Derby

Map 11H8. Derby. 15 miles (24km) w of Nottingham.
Population: 220,000 i Reference Library, The Strand
☎ *(0332) 31111.*

Rolls-Royce aircraft engines and Royal Crown Derby porcelain
are what modern Derby is mainly about.

A large collection of Rolls-Royce engines can be seen in the
Derby Industrial Museum (*Full St.* ☎ *(0332) 31111* 🖾 *open
Tues–Fri 10am–5pm, Sat 10am–4.45pm, closed Sun, Mon*),
housed in a restored 18thC silk mill, the first to be established in
England.

Many fine examples of Crown Derby are on show at the
Museum and Art Gallery (*The Strand* ☎ *(0332) 31111* 🖾 *open
10am–5pm, closed Sun, Mon and bank holidays*), which also has
paintings by the local artist Joseph Wright (1734–97). The
Royal Crown Derby Porcelain Company (*Osmaston Rd.*
☎ *(0332) 47051*) may also be visited by appointment and its
museum (🖾 *open 10am–noon, 2–4pm, closed Sat, Sun*)
contains china dating from 1756.

Several 17th–18thC buildings have survived. A short way N
of Market Place, the **cathedral** with its high pinnacled tower
contains the monumental tomb of Bess of Hardwick. Dating
from 1527, the church was rebuilt in 1725 and became a
cathedral in 1927.

Sights nearby
Kedleston Hall
4 miles (6.5km) nw of Derby ☎ *(0332) 842191* 🖾 🖵 �"— *Open
Sun–Tues at Easter, last Sun in Apr to Sept Sun only plus bank holiday
Mon and following Tues: park, gardens and church 12.30–6pm,
house and museum 2–6pm. Hours liable to change.*

This masterpiece of symmetry was designed in the 18thC by a succession
of architects, most important of all Robert Adam who was responsible for
the domed s front and most of the interior with its marble hall and state
rooms. The 12thC church contains tombs of the Curzon family who have
lived at Kedleston for more than 800yrs. The museum shows Indian
works of art collected by Marquess Curzon when he was Viceroy
(1898–1905).
Sudbury Hall
Off A50, 12 miles (19km) w of Derby ☎ *(028378) 305. NT* 🖾 🖵 🏌
🖾 *Open Apr–Oct 1–5.30pm or sunset if earlier. Closed Mon except
bank holidays, Tues.*

This handsome 17thC house with carving by Grinling Gibbons and
decorative painting by Louis Laguerre has one of the most splendid
Restoration interiors in England. The **Museum of Childhood** illustrates
how children of the past lived, worked and played.

�H **Midland**
Midland Rd., Derby DE1 2SQ ☎ *(0332) 45894* 🛏 🍽 63 🖵 27 🚗
🚠 🖾 🖾 🖾 🖾 🖾

Location: At the railway station. The comfort and facilities are probably
the only things that are not old-fashioned about this magnificent and
spacious hotel.
🖾 🖾 🖾 🖾

Restaurant nearby
Belper (*On A6, 8 miles/13km N of Derby*).

R **Rémy's** ✿
84 Bridge St. ☎ *(077382) 2246* ‖‖‖ ▭ ▆ ▃ ▤ ◛ AE ① ◉
*Last orders 9.30pm. Closed Sun, Mon, 2 weeks Jan – Feb and
July – Aug.*
The splendidly-named Rémy Bopp has brought a touch of vintage
France, with hints of *nouvelle cuisine*, to this unlikely spot N of Derby. He
delights in his French service, remarkably speedy at busy lunchtimes,
and his specialties such as cream of quail soup, pike in pastry with a
Riesling sauce, steak Choron, and *vacherin glacé aux fruits*.

Shopping
The **Eagle Centre** to the SE of the city, **Iron Gate**, **Cornmarket**, **Victoria
St.** and **St Peter's St.** are the main shopping areas. Smaller and more
exclusive shops can be found in the attractive **Sadler Gate** pedestrian
area. The **market** (*Eagle Centre, Tues, Thurs – Sat*) sells general goods
and there is an adjacent **flea market**. **Royal Crown Derby Porcelain** can
be bought at the factory shop (*Osmaston Rd., open Mon – Fri*).

Dorchester
*Map 4M7. Dorset. 25 miles (40km) W of Bournemouth.
Population: 13,800* ℹ *Antelope Yard, South St.* ☎ *(0305)
67992.*

Today a busy market town, Dorchester was Durnovaria to the
Romans and Casterbridge in the novels of Thomas Hardy
(1840 – 1928). After the Monmouth Rebellion the infamous
Judge Jeffreys held his Bloody Assize here in 1685, sentencing
74 men to death and 175 to exile. The building where he lodged
is now a restaurant.
    Dorset County Museum (*High West St.* ☎ *(0305) 62735* ▨
open 10am – 5pm, closed Sun) has British and Roman antiquities
with finds from both the town and **Maiden Castle** (see below), a
reconstruction of Hardy's study and the manuscript of *The
Mayor of Casterbridge*.

Sights nearby
Clouds Hill
Near Wareham, 9 miles (14.5km) E of Dorchester. NT ▨ ⚔ ◛
*Open Apr – Sept Wed – Fri, Sun, bank holidays 2 – 5pm (closed Mon
except bank holidays, Tues, Sat); Oct – Mar Sun 1 – 4pm.*
T.E. Lawrence (of Arabia) bought this cottage in 1925 when, disgusted
at what he saw to be the Allies' failure to support his Arabs, he sought
anonymity in the RAF. In 1935 he was killed in a motorcycle accident at
nearby **Moreton** where he is buried.
Hardy's Cottage
Higher Bockhampton, 3 miles (5km) NE of Dorchester. NT ▨ ◛
*10mins' walk from parking lot. Garden open Apr – Oct 11am – 6pm.
Closed Tues, Thurs. Access to interior only by written application to
The Tenant, Hardy's Cottage, Higher Bockhampton, near Dorchester
DT2 8QJ.*
The novelist and poet was born in this thatched cottage built by his
great-grandfather. It was here that he wrote *Under the Greenwood Tree*
and *Far from the Madding Crowd*.
Hardy Monument ☆
Black Down, 6 miles (9.5km) SW of Dorchester. NT ◁ɛ *Viewpoint
always open.*
As a monument (to Admiral Hardy, flag-captain of the *Victory* at
Trafalgar and of 'Kiss me, Hardy' fame) this cylindrical tower lacks all
distinction. Its site, however, is unsurpassed in southern England, a bare
hilltop more than 750ft (230m) above the coast and offering breathtaking
views: westward all the way to the tors of *Dartmoor*; below, like a model,
Weymouth, **Portland** crowned by its castle, and **Chesil Bank**; eastward
to **St Alban's Head**; in the distance, there is a glimpse of the *Isle of
Wight*.

Maiden Castle ☆
2 miles (3km) sw of Dorchester. Always open.
This enormous and complex area of earthworks – probably the most important prehistoric hillfort in Britain – sprawls over 115 acres. It was in use for more than 2,000yrs, starting in about 2000BC as a Neolithic enclosure but seemingly only given its intricate defenses (with up to eight lines and an ingenious system of entrances) by the Iron Age occupants of the 1stC BC. The Romans took the place in AD43 (the skeleton of a warrior of this time, killed by a catapult bolt, can be seen in the ***Dorset County Museum***) and there is evidence that they built a temple near the top some 300yrs later.

Dover
Map 7L12. Kent. On the s coast, 78 miles (125km) SE of London. Population: 34,400. Railway station ☎ (0304) 202654; coach and bus information ☎ (0304) 206813
i Townwall St. ☎ (0304) 205108.
The closest port to the continent since at least Roman times when this was their naval base and township of Dubris, Dover essentially has seen few changes. Then as now people lived and worked and not infrequently fought in this pleasant valley below the White Cliffs; and then as now many more simply dashed through the place in search of or leaving their ships. Yet over the centuries marks have been left and it is worth pausing long enough to see some of the places that reflect Dover's history.

Sights and places of interest
Dover Castle
Above the town to the E ☎ (0304) 201628. DOE ☒ Grounds and Pharos ☒ Keep and Underground passages �... ◁€ Castle open mid-Mar to mid-Oct Mon – Sat 9.30am – 6.30pm, Sun 2 – 6.30pm except Apr – Sept 9.30am – 6.30pm; mid-Oct to mid-Mar Mon – Sat 9.30am – 4pm, Sun 2 – 4pm. Grounds open all year. Buses 594, 595 from center of Dover.
For well over 2,000yrs, since at least Iron Age times, a fortification on this clifftop has defied invaders or welcomed friends. There are four principal points of interest: the **Pharos**, the lighthouse which the Romans set up in the 1stC; the Saxon church of **St Mary-in-Castro**, dating from *c.*1000 but victim of many later alterations; the **keep**, built by Henry II in the late 12thC; and the mostly early 13thC **underground passages**.

The Roman Painted House ☆
New St. ☎ (0304) 203279 ☒ Open Apr, Sept – Oct 10am – 5pm; May – Aug 10am – 5pm. Closed Mon except bank holidays.
This exceptionally interesting site reveals an astonishing continuity of human use. Neolithic people dumped their flints here; Romans built over three centuries; then came a simple Saxon hut known to have been used for weaving, later followed by medieval and Victorian cesspits. The Roman house seems to have been built here in the 2ndC, but it was soon succeeded by a larger place with walls covered in painted plaster.

St Edmund's Chapel †
Priory Rd., near Town Hall ☒ Mass Sat 10am.
This humble little chapel of the 12th and 13thC was saved from demolition, reconsecrated in 1968 and could be the smallest church in England in regular use. Note the many little consecration crosses, and on the exterior wall the inserted fragments of Roman brickwork.

Sight nearby
Barfreston Church † ☆
Barfreston, 7 miles (11km) NW of Dover.
This small church in a small village has superb examples of Norman carving. Note especially the detail around the s door, where fourteen figures are set in ovals, and also the much carved E window. There are also two curiosities here: a blocked N entrance, the so-called **Devil's Door** which was always opened at baptisms to let the Devil out; and the church bell which hangs not in a belfry but in a yew tree.

H Holiday Inn

Townwall St., Dover, Kent CT16 1SZ ☎ *(0304) 203270* Ⓣ *96458*
IIII 🛏 *83* 🛏 *83* 🍽 ⬅ AE CB ⓓ VISA

Location: Just back from the seafront between the E and W docks. Very
conveniently located, and offering all that one expects of a Holiday Inn.
Children up to the age of 19 occupying the same room as their parents pay
no charge – no hardship when each twin room has two double beds.
‡ �& ☐ 🖼 ⇌ 👬

H White Cliffs

Sea Front, Dover, Kent CT17 9BW ☎ *(0304) 203633* Ⓣ *965422* II
🛏 *63* 🛏 *27* 🍽 ⬅ AE ⓓ VISA

Location: On the W sector of the front. This pleasantly older-style hotel
occupies part of an elegant seafront Regency terrace and provides some
usefully large bedrooms. In the restaurant, ask for a table on the narrow
terrace and watch the constant arrival and departure of the ferries.
‡ ☐ 🖼 ◁E 👬 ♫

Shopping

The central shopping area runs from **Market Sq.** to the **Town Hall**.
Market Sq. is the site of a fruit and vegetable market (*Sat*) and an indoor
market is held in **Bench St.** (*Tues, Thurs–Sat*).

Durham

*Map 15D8. Co. Durham. 15 miles (24km) s of Newcastle-
upon-Tyne. Population: 24,800* ℹ *13 Claypath* ☎ *(0385)
43720.*

The river Wear hairpins below an abrupt hill along the top of
which spread the **cathedral** and **castle**, two great Norman
edifices merging into one massive whole which allows Durham
to claim to be one of the most visually exciting cities in Britain.
The cathedral, one of Europe's greatest Norman achievements,
was built to house the remains of St Cuthbert; the monks
traveling with his coffin put it down here, then found they were
unable to shift it. It soon attracted pilgrims, and it was to satisfy
their needs that the settlement grew.
Events   In July, Miners' Gala; in Aug, Folk Festival and City
Carnival.

Sights and places of interest
Durham Castle
Just N of the cathedral ☎ *(0385) 65481* 🔲 🔲 *First three weeks in
Apr, July–Sept, tours every ½ hr, 10am–noon, 2–4.30pm; Jan–Mar,
late Apr, Oct–Dec Mon, Wed, Sat, tours on the hour, 2–4pm. May be
closed for university functions.*

Built in 1072, the castle soon became the palace of the prince-bishops and
although undergoing structural changes remained such until it was
handed over to Durham University in 1832. Visitors are shown the
Norman crypt chapel (the oldest surviving part of the castle) with its
beautifully carved pillar heads, the **Great Hall** of 1284, the **15thC
kitchens** with their enormous fireplaces, and the Renaissance **Black
Staircase** of 1662.
Durham Cathedral 🏛 ✝ ☆
s of castle and above Market Place ☎ *(0385) 64266.*

Dominating the city, Durham Cathedral is renowned for the grandeur of
its nave with its ribbed vaulting and alternating clustered and simple
pillars, 7ft (2m) in diameter and covered in a wealth of ornamentation.

Today's great church, virtually untouched since Norman times, was
begun in 1093, replacing the Saxon cathedral built to shelter the shrine of
St Cuthbert (*c*.634–687). That great theological scholar the Venerable
Bede (672–735) also rested here, after 1370 in a shrine in the **Galilee
Chapel**, at the opposite end from St Cuthbert's shrine behind the high
altar. Neither shrine survived the Reformation, but the remains of both
men lie below where their shrines once stood, while relics of both are in
the **Treasury**.

At the w end the marble boundary cross on the floor marks the point beyond which, in pre-Reformation days, women were not allowed.
Gulbenkian Museum of Oriental Art
Durham University, Elvet Hill ☎ *(0385) 66711* 🔁 *Open Mon–Fri 9.30am–1pm, 2.15–5pm, Sat 9.30am–noon, 2.15–5pm, Sun 2.15–5pm.*
Devoted entirely to Oriental archeology and art, and the only one of its kind in Britain, this very professionally arranged museum ranges geographically from Egypt to Japan. Highlights include pottery and porcelain from China, Tibetan paintings and Egyptian antiquities.

Hotel nearby
Chester-le-Street (*6 miles/9.5km N of Durham*).

Ⓗ **Lumley Castle**
Chester-le-Street, Co. Durham DH3 4NX ☎ *(0385) 885326* Ⅱ▢
🛏 *50* 🛏 *50* 🍽 ▭ ⇌ AE ⓐ ⓒ VISA
Location: On a hill immediately E of Chester-le-Street. Somewhat bogus, but enjoyable, a 13thC keep around a courtyard has been converted into a hotel in which Reception is approached across the dungeon, seen through a glass panel in the floor. The restaurant – which is good – is called the **Black Knight**, and there are rather grand bedrooms in the main keep although the majority are in the converted stables.
▢ ▨ ⚓ ⇟ 🏇

Shopping
The major shopping area comprises **North Rd., Silver St., Market Pl.** and the **Millburngate Shopping Centre**. An outdoor market is held in **Market Pl.** (*Sat*) and an indoor market in the **Town Hall** (*Fri, Sat*); both sell general goods.

See also **Beamish North of England Open Air Museum** under *Newcastle-upon-Tyne*.

Eastbourne
Map 7M11. East Sussex. 20 miles (32km) E of Brighton. Population: 71,000 𝒊 *3 Cornfield Terrace* ☎ *(0323) 27474.*
With the Downs inland and Beachy Head to the sw, this is a sunny, sheltered place, something the Victorians were not slow to profit by as soon as the railway arrived here in 1849. And they have left their mark, for this remains a resort with more than a touch of 19thC character. The beach is shingle (although there is some sand at low tide), and perhaps because of this the emphasis here is on entertainment, provided in generous measure by four theaters, a pier (1872) and a splendid bandstand. There are 200 acres of parks and gardens including the superb **Carpet Gardens** running along Grand Parade.

The most popular local excursion is to **Beachy Head**, some 3 miles (5km) sw, a headland with famous chalk cliffs dropping over 500ft (150m) to the sea. Boats leave in summer from the beach between the pier and the Wish Tower (☎ *(0323) 34701*).

Sights and places of interest
Redoubt Fortress and Museum
Royal Parade ☎ *(0323) 33952* 🔁 ✴ *Open Easter–Nov 10am–5.30pm.*
Built in 1804, at a time when Napoleon seemed likely to invade, the fort houses a combined services museum of local military history. There is also an **aquarium**, and **Treasure Island Play Centre** for children.
Royal National Lifeboat Institution Museum
Grand Parade ☎ *(0323) 30717* 🔲 *but donation expected. Open Easter–Oct 10am–1pm, 2–5.30pm.*
Exhibits include photographs and models of wrecks and former lifeboats, and lifeboat equipment.

Towner Art Gallery
9 Borough Lane ☎ (0323) 21635 ▣ Open Mon–Sat 10am–5pm,
2–5pm, Sun 2–5pm.

Housed in an 18thC manor, the permanent collections are mainly of
British 19th and 20thC fine and applied art, including works by John
Piper, Elizabeth Frink and Henry Moore. Some Georgian caricatures
and pictures of local scenes are of particular interest. There are also
frequent temporary exhibitions of many kinds.

Sights nearby
Herstmonceux Castle
11 miles (17km) NE of Eastbourne ☎ (032181) 3171 ▨ � Open Easter–Sept: grounds Mon–Fri noon–5.30pm; exhibition
Mon–Fri 2–5.30pm; grounds and exhibition Sat, Sun, bank holidays
10.30am–5.30pm.

Reflected in its wide moat, the red-brick, turreted castle (1441 in origin
but rebuilt from 1910 onward) has been the home of the **Royal
Greenwich Observatory** since 1948. Only the **Astronomical Exhibition**
rooms, containing a model of one of Europe's largest telescopes, are open
to the public; in July and Aug between 4–5pm an astronomer is on duty
to answer questions. The extensive grounds embrace formal gardens,
pastoral land, woods and a nature trail (booklet available).

Pevensey Castle
5 miles (8km) NE of Eastbourne ☎ (0323) 762604. DOE. Roman fort
always open. Norman keep ▨ ▬ Open mid-Mar to mid-Oct
Mon–Sat 9.30am–6.30pm, Sun 2–6.30pm except Apr–Sept
9.30am–6.30pm; mid-Oct to mid-Mar Mon–Sat 9.30am–4pm, Sun
2–4pm.

Casually glimpsed, this is just another ruined keep, but in fact Pevensey
is a site of exceptional interest, for both the Romans and the Normans
have left their mark here. In 340, hard pressed by marauding Saxons, the
Romans laid out a huge fortress protected at that time by the sea on three
sides. Some 700yrs later William of Normandy landed here and set up his
first defended camp within the Roman walls. Having established himself
as master of England, he handed Pevensey over to his half-brother
Robert who by 1080 had built the keep which, with a 13thC gatehouse, is
what can be seen today.

Restaurant nearby
Jevington (*off A22, 6 miles/9.5km NW of Eastbourne*).

▣ **Hungry Monk**
Jevington Rd. ☎ (03212) 2178 ▥▥ ▬ Last orders 10pm. Closed
lunch (except Sun), Christmas.

A flint cottage building, with exposed beams, log fires, enthusiastic
decoration and candlelight, housing a restaurant which has long been
popular. The cuisine is skillful and hearty with specialties such as
croustade of quails' eggs, beef Wellington and hot chocolate cake with
home-made ice cream. There is a selection of recommended house wines
in addition to the normal list.

Nightlife
The **Congress Theatre** (*Carlisle Rd.* ☎ (0323) 36363) stages concerts,
opera, ballet, summer shows, and celebrity concerts on Sun. The
Devonshire Park Theatre (*Compton St.* ☎ (0323) 21121) presents
plays, including pre-London runs. The **Royal Hippodrome** (*Seaside Rd.*
☎ (0323) 24336) is an Edwardian theater which has a Summer Holiday
Spectacular and celebrity concerts on Sun. The **Winter Garden**
(*Compton St.* ☎ (0323) 25252) is the home of ballroom dancing, family
evenings, fairs and exhibitions.

Shopping
Terminus Rd., running from the station through the large **Arndale
Shopping Centre** to the seafront, contains the major chain stores.
Smaller and more specialized shops, including those selling antiques, can
be found in **Grove Rd.** and **South St.** The bargains sold at the **Free
Enterprise Centre** near the station are a major attraction for visitors. The
adjacent **market** sells fruit and vegetables (*Tues, Sat*).

Place nearby
Alfriston (*8 miles/13km NW of Eastbourne*).
Alfriston Clergy House
☎ *(0323) 870001. NT* 🏞 *Open Apr–Oct 11am–6pm or sunset if earlier.*
Built around 1350, this charming, small, half-timbered and thatched house, forming part of an equally charming village, served first as home for a community of priests, then after the Reformation as the local vicarage, and finally (after 1790) as farm laborers' cottages. In 1896 the much decayed Clergy House became the first building to be acquired by the National Trust.

🏨 **Star Inn**
High St., Alfriston, East Sussex BN26 5TA ☎ *(0323) 870495* ▥
🛏 *34* 🛏 *34* 🟰 AE CB ⦿ ● VISA
Location: Village center. One of the oldest inns in England, founded in the 13thC and rebuilt *c.*1450. Half-timbering, blackened beams and Tudor fireplaces all contribute to the spirit of the place. There are bedrooms of this kind too, although most are in a modern wing.
♿ ▢ ☞ 🐾 🎣

🍽 **Moonrakers**
High St. ☎ *(0323) 870472* ▥ ▦ ▰ *Last orders 9.15pm (9.45pm Sat). Closed lunch, Sun, Mon, mid-Jan to mid-Feb.*
This old smuggling village about halfway between Brighton and Eastbourne is rich in history, and the Moonrakers restaurant is in a 400-year-old, oak-beamed house. Within that setting, its diligent new owners Elaine and Barry Wilkinson try to make each group of guests feel that they are at their own dinner party. The fixed-price English menu, with such dishes as Sussex haddock, South Downs mixed terrine, *noisettes* of lamb, rounded off with excellent home-made desserts, is similar to that which won Moonrakers a following before the Wilkinsons' arrival in 1981. The Wilkinsons make their own chocolate truffles, import their coffee from France, and are building up a collection of cognacs and whiskies.

Ely
Map 13l11. Cambs. 15 miles (24km) N of Cambridge. Population: 9,000 ℹ *24 St Mary's St.* ☎ *(0353) 3311.*
According to Bede, this quiet little fenland city, until the 17thC an island reached only by boat or causeway, owes its name to the eels which swarmed in the surrounding waters. According to another source, these came here as the result of a miracle performed by St Dunstan who, outraged at the moral laxity of the local monks, turned them all into eels.

Ely owes its origin to a decision in the 7thC by Queen Ethelreda of Northumbria that she had had enough of her husband and that a religious life would be preferable; she became abbess of the abbey she founded here.

Ely Cathedral ▥ ✝ ☆
City center ☎ *(0353) 2078.*
When St Ethelreda (also known as Audrey) founded her abbey here in 673, she could hardly have foreseen that four centuries later she would be enshrined in a great cathedral which, over yet another four centuries, would grow into a huge edifice beckoning the traveler for miles across the flat fenland. But this is what happened between 1083 when work started on the soaring Norman nave and about 1530 when the building of the Perpendicular chantries at the E end finally completed the cathedral. In 1322 the Norman tower collapsed and was replaced 6yrs later by the **Octagon ★** – an eight-sided tower and lantern widely accepted as one of the loveliest and most astonishing achievements of medieval church-building.

The cathedral's **Stained Glass Museum** (☎ *(0353) 5103* 🏞) includes exhibits ranging from the 14thC to the present day with notable panels by Burne-Jones.

H **Lamb**
Lynn Rd., Ely, Cambs CB7 4EJ ☎ *(0353) 3574* 🅟 *25971* ☐ 🍽 *32*
🛏 *32* 🍴 ⇌ AE CB ⊕ ● VISA
Location: Just N of the cathedral. A former coaching inn, unobtrusively
modernized and offering some rooms with views toward the cathedral.
☐ 📷 ♨

R **Old Fire Engine House** ♣
25 St Mary's St. ☎ *(0353) 2582* 🍴☐ ☐ 📷 🍽 ⇌ *Last orders 9pm.*
Closed Sun dinner, two weeks at Christmas, bank holidays.
There may be a tone of self-satisfaction about the Old Fire Engine
House, but there is also much about which to be pleased. The kitchen
concentrates on English cooking, using local recipes and ingredients
where possible. The size of helpings and the range of vegetables is greater
in the evening than at lunchtime but the excellent English cheeses and
splendid Adnams' beer from the cask are constant features. The wine list
reaches out to some of the less fashionable areas, with strong
representation from the Loire, Rhône and Midi, and even from Chile.

Exeter
Map 3M5. Devon. 172 miles (275km) sw of London.
Population: 95,900. Airport ☎ *(0392) 67433; railway station*
☎ *(0392) 33551; coach and bus station* ☎ *(0392) 56231* **i**
Civic Centre, Dix's Field ☎ *(0392) 72434.*
Air raids in 1942 destroyed whole districts of this once Roman
city, but in spite of this Exeter remains a historic place, still
surrounded by its ancient walls, with a **cathedral** and cathedral
close that can only delight, and a picturesque waterfront which
is home to the world-famous **Maritime Museum**.

Sights and places of interest
Exeter Cathedral †
City Centre, se of the Guildhall ☎ *(0392) 32189.*
Unique among English cathedrals because of its towers that arise from
the transepts, Exeter also differs in having an unusually secular close
with, on the N side, small shops, restaurants and a hotel; note the art
shop, once **Mol's Coffee House**, said to have been the haunt of sea
captains, including Drake and Raleigh.
　　The towers are the only significant survivals of the Norman edifice of
1112–1206. The **minstrels' gallery** with its carvings of heavenly
musicians, a 15thC mural and an ancient astrological clock in the N
transept, the 14thC carved **choir screen**, and the early 14thC **bishop's
throne** are some of the important features of the interior.
Guildhall
High St. ☎ *(0392) 56724* 🅿 *Open 10am–5.30pm unless required
for civic use. Closed Sun.*
The fascinating thing about this ancient hall is that it is still in use for
much the same purpose as when it was first built in the 14thC. There
have of course been structural changes: the ceiling with its gilded beams
resting on carved bears carrying staffs is 15thC, the panelled walls date
from 1594, and the portico is a Tudor addition.
Maritime Museum ☆
Town Quay and Canal Basin, 500yds (450m) s of the cathedral
☎ *(0392) 58075* 🅿 🖩 ✳ 🍽 *Open June–Sept 10am–6pm;
Oct–May 10am–5pm. The museum is on both sides of the river Exe
linked by a ferry, included in ticket.*
A lively, active place in old warehouses around an evocative waterfront
area. The museum boasts the world's largest collection of boats, ranging
from primitive reed craft to Arab dhows and Chinese junks and including
the world's oldest working steamboat. Children are encouraged to wear
themselves out at the pumps, the capstan or the windlass of a
windjammer.
Rougemont Gardens and Castle
Castle St., leading N off High St.
Following the line of the moat of William the Conqueror's castle (now a
ruin), these gardens are not only a restful oasis in the city center but also

provide a convenient pedestrian link between **Rougemont House** (*Castle St.* ☎ *(0392) 56724* 🔊 *open 10am–1pm, 2–5.15pm; closed Sun, Mon*), a museum of local archeology and history, and the **Royal Albert Memorial Museum and Art Gallery** (*Queen St.* ☎ *and entry details as above*), the most important general museum in the West Country.

St Nicholas Priory ☆
The Mint, Fore St. ☎ *(0392) 56724* 🔊 *Open 10am–1pm, 2–5.15pm. Closed Sun, Mon.*

In 1070 monks sent by William the Conqueror to care for Exeter's church of St Olave built themselves this priory. The domestic buildings survived the Reformation, and what can now be seen includes the wine cellar and larder (*c.*1100), the 15thC **Guest Hall**, the **kitchen** (13th and 15thC), and the **Prior's Chapel** with a notable medieval retable.

Sights nearby

Killerton House
Broadclyst, 5 miles (8km) NE of Exeter ☎ *(0392) 881345. NT* 🔊 ➡ 🔊 *Open Apr–Oct 11am–6pm. Garden open all year during daylight.*

The house (1778) contains the fine **Paulise de Bush Collection of Costumes** spanning the late 18thC to the present day, most attractively shown in a sequence of period rooms. The gardens comprise 15 acres of hillside with some lovely, typical Devon views and the opportunity for the energetic to climb higher to an Iron Age hillfort.

Ugbrooke ▥▥▥
Off A380, 10 miles (16km) s of Exeter ☎ *(0626) 852179* 🔊 💻 ➡ *House open 2–5pm, grounds 12.30–5.30pm: May Sun and bank holidays only, June–Sept Sun–Thurs (closed Fri, Sat).*

Remarkable for being Robert Adam's first castle-style house, this battlemented mansion is set in a fine park with two lakes landscaped by Capability Brown. The gracious rooms, owing much of their restrained and delicate style to Adam, show good portraits and other pictures (note the striking Restoration portraits by Lely), an outstanding collection of embroidery, 17thC Mortlake tapestries, and a collection of costume dolls.

Ⓗ **Royal Clarence**
Cathedral Yard, Exeter, Devon EX1 1HD ☎ *(0392) 58464* ☎ *23241* ▯▯ 🛏 62 ▭▭ 62 ➡▭ ▭➡ (AE) (CB) (◑) (◑) (VISA)
Location: Immediately N of the cathedral. A dignified Georgian place, as stylish inside as it is outside. The hotel forms a part of the cathedral close and provides just the right setting for a stay in this historic city.
🛢 ▭ 🗷 ▭

Hotel/restaurant nearby
Whimple (*7 miles/11km NE of Exeter*).

Ⓗ Ⓡ **Woodhayes** ❀
Whimple, Exeter, Devon EX5 2TD ☎ *(0404) 822237* ▯▯ ✿ 6 🛏 6 ➡▭ 🛢 ▭ (AE) (◑) (◑) (VISA) *Closed Jan.*
Ⓡ ▥/▥ ▬▬ ▭ *Closed lunch Sun and Mon to non-residents, and Jan.*
Location: In the village. A new, small country house hotel which has already won the respect of its peers. In the heart of cider-apple country, with an arboretum in its own 3 acres of grounds, Woodhayes is a pretty, Georgian house, with comfortable drawing rooms and an elegant dining room. Local products such as cider (in a sauce for pork tenderloin) are splendidly complemented by the liberal use of spices and herbs in a menu that is loosely *nouvelle.* Croissants, bread, ice cream and *petits-fours* are all home-made. An intelligent wine list offers excellent regional and stylistic variety at good prices.
🍴 ▭ 🗷 ▭ 🐾 ✿

Shopping
The **High St.**, and its extension, **Sidwell St.**, contain the major shops and department stores, while **Guildhall Precinct** has small, independent shops and cafes running within. **Fore St.** (*running into the High St.*) has many antique and bric-à-brac shops, and **Gandy St.** (*off the High St.*) has giftshops, bookshops and wine-bars.

Exmoor National Park and environs
*Map 3L4–5. Somerset and Devon. On the N coast, where
the counties meet* **i** *Exmoor National Park Centre, Exmoor
House, Dulverton, Somerset TA22 9HL* **☎** *(0398) 23665.*
The name is misleading, for only parts of the park are true
moor, the remainder being a mixture of farm land, woods
and half-hidden valleys down which crystal streams tumble and
slide to a dramatic coast along which runs the highly scenic
Somerset and North Devon Coast Path. The stretch from
Porlock to **Lynmouth** is breathtaking, both because of the
stunning views and the steepness of the gradient; nervous
drivers should take the toll road. Away from the coast the
land climbs high, too, to the broad hump of **Dunkery Beacon**
(1,705ft/520m) with many other hills spread not far below.
Minehead on the coast is the principal town, while villages such
as **Simonsbath** and **Exford** lie at the heart of the moor, with
R.D. Blackmore's *Lorna Doone* country to the N of the former.
Event On May Day, hobbyhorse parade at Minehead.

Sights and places of interest
Arlington Court
*Map 3L4. Off the W of the park on A39, between Blackmoor Gate
and Barnstaple* **☎** *(027182) 296. NT* 🏛 💻 🚻 *House and
carriage collection open Apr–Oct 11am–6pm, closed Sat. Garden
and park open Apr–Oct 11am–6pm, Nov–Mar during daylight.*
Jacob sheep and shetland ponies graze in the park, and there is a nature
trail through woods and beside a lake which is a wildfowl sanctuary; but
the main attraction is the large and well-known collection of horse-drawn
vehicles (*rides available*). The interior of the 19thC house is strictly for
the connoisseur of odds-and-ends; there are, for example, model ships,
shells, costumes, and small objets d'art.

Cleeve Abbey
Map 3L5. Near Washford on A39, 6 miles (9.5km) SE of Minehead
☎ *(09844) 377. DOE* 🏛 🚶 *Open mid-Mar to mid-Oct Mon–Sat
9.30am–6.30pm, Sun 2–6.30pm except Apr–Sept 9.30am–
6.30pm; mid-Oct to mid-Mar Mon–Sat 9.30am–4pm, Sun 2–4pm.*
Founded for Cistercians toward the end of the 12thC, this abbey has
survived rather better than some, enabling visitors to see the **gatehouse**,
the **dormitory** and the **15thC refectory** with its timbered ceiling.

Dunster Castle
Map 3L5. On A396, 2 miles (3km) SE of Minehead **☎** *(064382) 314.
NT* 🏛 🚶 *Open early Apr–Sept 11am–5pm (closed Fri, Sat), Oct
Tues, Wed, Sun 2–4pm.*
Splendidly castellated, Dunster Castle represents the culmination of
some six centuries of building; the final remodeling took place in the
19thC. Inside, there are a 17thC carved staircase, leather hangings
depicting scenes from the story of Anthony and Cleopatra, and notable
plasterwork, while on the grounds there is an 18thC working watermill.
    Below the castle lies Dunster's wide main street with its 17thC
octagonal **Yarn Market**.

Knightshayes Court
Map 3L5. Off A396, 2 miles (3km) N of Tiverton **☎** *(0884) 254665.
NT* 🏛 💻 🚶 *Open Apr–Oct: house 1.30–6pm, garden
11am–6pm.*
The Victorian Gothic house was built in 1869–74 by the architecturally
eccentric William Burges, and contains a collection of Old Masters. The
gardens, planned after World War II, aim at a constantly changing scene
and include woodland, rare shrubs, species trees, sweeps of spring bulbs,
summer beds, and topiary animals leaping over hedges.

West Somerset Railway
Map 3L5. Minehead Station **☎** *(0643) 4996* ✷ *Trains run
Easter–Oct. Telephone for exact times.*
With both steam and diesel trains, this is Britain's longest private
passenger railway. The route is between **Minehead** and **Taunton** (about
1½hrs), passing **Dunster** (for *Dunster Castle*) and **Washford** (for
Cleeve Abbey).

Hotels

Exford (*12 miles/19km sw of Minehead*).

Ⓗ **White Horse** 🏨
Exford, near Minehead, Somerset TA24 7PY ☎ *(064383) 229* ☐
🐾 *20* 🛏 *3* 🛬 🍴 ☲
Location: By the river bridge. This informal small hotel will suit those who
want a quiet stay in a typical Exmoor village.
🍽 🐴 🐟

Minehead (*31 miles/50km N of Tiverton*).

Ⓗ **Simonsbath House**
Simonsbath, near Minehead, Somerset TA24 7SH ☎ *(064383)*
259 ☐ 🐾 *9* 🛏 *6* 🛬 🍴 ☲ AE ● ⬤ VISA
Location: On B3223, to E of village. The building, with glorious views, is
long, low and 300yrs old. The hotel is a place of real individuality and
impeccable good taste; it has a restaurant of distinction and imagination
which emphasizes traditional (including local) dishes; there is also a
squash court.
☐ ⚡ 🐟 ⟨⟨

Farne Islands

Map 15B8. Northumb. 15 miles (24km) N of Alnwick
☎ *(0665) 720424. NT* 🔳 🍴 *at Seahouses. Open Apr–Sept*
daily in suitable weather. Restricted access during the
breeding season (mid-May to mid-July). Boats from
Seahouses to Inner Farne and Staple Islands.
Saints, seals and seabirds are the theme here. St Aidan and St
Cuthbert both used Inner Farne as a retreat, the latter dying
here in 687 (a tiny 14thC chapel may mark the site of his cell).
Today the islands are known for their gray seals (one of the
largest colonies in Britain), and about 20 species of seabirds
including puffins, kittiwakes, eider-ducks and guillemots
breed in this sanctuary.

The Fen District

Map 12&13. Lincs, Cambs, Norfolk. Around The Wash.
The Wash is all that remains of a great silted bay that once
covered much of what are now the flat lands of southern
Lincolnshire, Cambridgeshire and the western part of Norfolk.
The Romans made some attempt at drainage, but it was not
until the 19thC that reclamation was completed. In Saxon times
the local inhabitants strode through the area on stilts, or used
skates made out of bones when the water froze.

Today, this is a richly fertile region, broken by the dikes,
drains, canals and controlling sluices on which its survival
depends. It is a land of unbroken skies and distant horizons, a
place where boats seem to move across the fields, where sturdy
churches announce towns and villages, and across which in
spring and early summer the bulb fields splash their colors.

Among towns of interest are **Boston** in the N, in the 13thC a
port second only to London but today better known for its
namesake across the Atlantic (the court in which the Pilgrim
Fathers were tried in 1607 and the cells in which they were held
can be seen at the **Guildhall**); **Spalding**, a center of the bulb
industry; **Wisbech**, with Georgian frontages along the river
Nene; *King's Lynn*, the port on The Wash; and the cathedral
city of *Ely*.
Event In early May, Spalding Flower Parade. Millions of
tulips are used to decorate the floats taking part in the
parade.

Hotel
Spalding (*18 miles/29km N of Peterborough*).

Ⓗ **Cley Hall**
22 High St., Spalding, Lincs PE11 1TX ☎ (0775) 5157 ⅡⅡ ♙ 4
⬛━ 4 ━ 🛏 ⚏ AE ⬤ ⓞ VISA
Location: On the river, 4mins' walk from town center. The ambience is that
of a pleasant private house and the staff give the impression that nothing
is too much trouble. The restaurant is excellent with a red house wine
which is far above average. The hotel may be enlarged.
▢ ⬚ ☙ ⚓ ◔ ♟

Fountains Abbey ★
Map **15E8**. *North Yorks. 4 miles (6.5km) sw of Ripon*
☎ *(076586) 639. NT* ▨ ▭ ━ ⚏ *Open early Mar*
9.30am – 4pm; mid-Mar to May, Sept to mid-Oct
9.30am – 6.30pm; June – Aug 9.30am – 9pm; mid-Oct to Feb
Mon – Sat 9.30am – 4pm, Sun 9.30am – 4pm except
Nov – Feb 2 – 4pm. Opening hours subject to change.
Of the many abbey ruins scattered around England and Wales,
these are among the finest, in setting, in size and in preservation
of both church and domestic buildings. Cistercians settled here
in 1132 and the great Romanesque nave and transepts survive
from this early period. At the E end, the most unusual **Chapel of
the Nine Altars** was beautifully rebuilt in the 13thC, while the
tower was not erected until the first quarter of the 16thC.

Much can still be traced of the domestic buildings, the most
notable remains (between the sw corner of the cloister and the
river) being those of the undercroft of the lay brothers'
dormitory with its 19 pillars.

Glastonbury
Map **4L6**. *Somerset. 6 miles (9.5km) sw of Wells.*
Population: 6,600 **i** *7 Northload St.* ☎ *(0458) 32954.*
Legend and ancient sanctity pervade this pleasant town, once a
small settlement on the island of Avalon, one of many that
dotted what must have seemed a boundless swamp.

Early in the 1stC Joseph of Arimathea came here with his
staff and the Holy Grail. He stuck the staff into the ground
where it took life as a thorn, a miracle which prompted the
building of a tiny wattle-and-daub chapel that grew into a
powerful abbey claiming (almost certainly correctly) to be the
earliest Christian foundation in Britain. The Holy Grail he hid
below the waters of the **Chalice Well** (near the w foot of the
Tor), still treated as a sanctuary. Five hundred years later
Arthur and Guinevere joined the legend, for they are said to
have been buried on Avalon.

Glastonbury Tor (520ft/160m) is a small, steep hill that
offers a rewarding view. The tower, all that is left of the 14thC
St Michael's Church, stands on an ancient site; according to
tradition St Patrick came here in the early 5thC to rebuild a
chapel which even then was old enough to have fallen into ruins.

Two other places of interest are the **Somerset Rural Life
Museum** (*Abbey Farm, Chilkwell St.* ☎ *(0458) 32903* ▨ ▭ ━
*open Easter – Oct Mon – Fri 10am – 5pm, Sat – Sun 2 – 6.30pm;
Oct – Easter Mon – Fri 10am – 5pm, Sat – Sun 2.30 – 5pm*), housed
in a magnificent late 14thC barn; and **The Tribunal** (*High St.*
☎ *(0458) 32949; DOE* ▨ ━ *open mid-Mar to mid-Oct
Mon – Sat 9.30am – 6.30pm, Sun 2 – 6.30pm; mid-Oct to mid-Mar
Mon – Sat 9.30am – 4pm, Sun 2 – 4pm*), a charming old house
containing a small museum of local archeology.

.Glastonbury Abbey ★
Town center, just SE of Market Cross ☎ *(0458) 32267* 📷 *Open
9.30am. Closes Jan, Nov 5pm; Feb 5.30pm; Mar–Apr, Oct 6pm;
May, Sept 7pm; June–Aug 7.30pm; Dec 4.30pm.*
Whether or not Joseph of Arimathea first built here, there seems little
doubt that there were very early churches on this site; it is known that
steps were taken in 633 to preserve one of these and that new churches
were built in 708, 988 and again in early Norman times.

In 1184, however, fire destroyed virtually all this past, and what is seen
today are the remains of the great abbey built between 1184 and c.1303.
The **gatehouse** contains a museum, and within the area of the ruins there
are three principal points not to be missed: at the w end, the richly carved
Romanesque **St Mary's Chapel ★** or Lady Chapel, said to be on the
exact site of the very earliest church and thus perhaps the spot at which
Christianity was first preached in Britain; to the s, the strange-looking
Abbot's Kitchen, dating from the 14thC and a fine medieval survivor;
and in the choir the **Tomb of King Arthur and Queen Guinevere** (two
bodies exhumed in 1191 and accepted as being those of Arthur and
Guinevere were later interred on this spot).

Ⓗ **George and Pilgrims**
1 High St., Glastonbury, Somerset BA6 9DP ☎ *(0458) 31146*
🖅*45388* ⫴ 🍴 *14* 🛏 *7* 🛋 🖻 🖾 🍽 AE CB ✦ ⬤ VISA
Location: Market Cross. It would be hard to find a hotel more suited to the
spirit of its town. An inn since the 14thC, rebuilt in 1475 as an overflow
for abbey visitors, it has mullioned windows, heavy beams, four-poster
beds, and even a ghost. The restaurant serves several local specialties.
🐾

Hotels and restaurants nearby
Hatch Beauchamp *(22 miles/35km SW of Glastonbury).*

Ⓗ Ⓡ **Farthings** 🏠 ♣
Hatch Beauchamp, Taunton, Somerset TA3 6SG ☎ *(0823)
480664* ⫴⫴ 🍴 *6* 🛏 *6* 🛋 🖻 🍽 ⬤ VISA
Ⓡ ⫴⫴ 🍽 *Last orders 9.30pm.*
Location: In village, on A358. This pretty little Georgian house overlooks
the village soccer field. Mr and Mrs Cooper are extremely obliging
hosts, and run a small, agreeable dining room.
🖾 ▢ 🖻 🐾 ⚓ ⛵

Taunton *(22 miles/35km SW of Glastonbury).*

Ⓗ Ⓡ **Castle** 🏰 ⫴⫴⫴
Castle Green, Taunton, Somerset TA1 1NF ☎ *(0823) 72671*
🖅*46488* ⫴⫴ to ⫴⫴⫴ 🍴 *40* 🛏 *40* 🛋 🖻 🍽 AE ✦ ⬤ VISA
Ⓡ ⫴⫴⫴ ▢ 🍽 📷 *Last orders 9.30pm.*
Location: In town center. A shining example of the changing style in
British hotel-keeping and catering. The wisteria-clad, 18thC castellated
building, itself rich in history and adjoining Norman ruins, has always
been a comfortable, town-center hotel. Each of the bedrooms is now
individually decorated, with furniture and furnishings blending classical
English styles with imports from elsewhere in Europe and the USA. In
1981, the Castle recruited young John Hornsby, former sous-chef at the
Dorchester. After that, the Castle began to win a considerable
gastronomic reputation, with specialties such as chilled clear beetroot
soup with tomato and basil water-ice; watercress mousse; young river
eels in a shallot sauce; chicken breast filled with fresh tarragon and
spinach; and roast rack of lamb with local herbs. The Castle also runs
wine, music and theater weekends.
🛗 ♿ ▢ 🖻 🐾 ⚓ ⚲ 🏇 ← ⛵

Gloucester
*Map 4J7. Glos. 25 miles (40km) NE of Bristol. Population:
90,000* ℹ *6 College St.* ☎ *(0452) 421188.*
The Romans had to protect the lowest feasible crossing of the
river Severn, so in AD98 they built Glevum, a place which is still

present in the cross formed at the city center by the four main streets, each of which once led out to a gate. At **City East Gate** (*Eastgate St.* ☎ *(0452) 24131* 🚻 *open May–Sept Wed, Fri, 2–5pm, Sat 10am–noon, 2–5pm, closed Mon, Tues, Thurs, Sun*), a special exhibition room illustrates the city's Roman and medieval defenses, while the **Museum and Art Gallery** (*Brunswick Rd.* ☎ *(0452) 24131* 🚻 *open Mon–Sat 10am–5pm*) is best known for its Roman antiquities found locally.

Today, Gloucester is a lively commercial city and inland port, of interest to tourists mainly on account of the **cathedral**.

The **Severn Bore**, a tidal wave running up the river at very high tides, is a local curiosity.

Event In Aug, Three Choirs Festival takes place every 3yrs in the cathedral, alternating with Hereford and Worcester. In Gloucester in 1986.

Sights and places of interest
Folk Museum
99–103 Westgate St. ☎ *(0452) 26467* 🔲 *Open 10am–5pm. Closed Sun.*
A group of Tudor timber-framed houses, which in the 18thC served as a pin factory, now contains a well-arranged museum of local domestic, trade and agricultural life. Exhibits include a Double Gloucester cheese dairy, a wheelwright's shop and Severn river fishing tackle.
Gloucester Cathedral † ☆
Within the angle of Westgate St. and Northgate St. ☎ *(0452) 28095* ✗ *in summer: ask at bookstall.*
In 1327 the monks of Gloucester's abbey were shrewd and bold enough to accept into their church the body of the murdered Edward II, already refused elsewhere. As they doubtless foresaw, this soon attracted throngs of pilgrims who brought in such vast wealth that it became possible not only to rebuild much of the Norman church but also to indulge in the new Gothic Perpendicular style of which Gloucester became the first significant example (although still retaining its Norman nave).

The cathedral's major attractions are the elaborate canopied tomb of its unwitting benefactor Edward II in the N choir aisle; the **cloisters** with their fan vaulting (it even decorates the monks' lavatorium) – the earliest example in England of this style and perhaps the invention of the local masons; and the magnificent 14thC stained-glass E window.

There is also much detail of interest, including several tombs with delightful family groups or individual figures, for example the Machen family in the NE corner of the nave, the Bower family nearby in the N transept, and two Jacobean ladies ☆ in the **Lady Chapel**.
Sights nearby
Berkeley Castle
16 miles (26km) sw of Gloucester ☎ *(0453) 810332* 🚻 🏠 🚗
Open Apr and Sept 2–5pm (closed Mon); May–Aug Tues–Sat 11am–5pm, Sun 2–5pm (closed Mon); Oct Sun only 2–4.30pm; bank holiday Mon 11am–5pm.
It was to this feudal stronghold that the wretched Edward II was dragged in 1327 to suffer his horrific death. In external appearance little changed since those days – indeed since its building in 1153 – and still inhabited by the Berkeley family, the castle offers on the one hand moat, keep, dungeon, great hall and Edward's cell, and on the other, art treasures that include a famous collection of silver.
Slimbridge Wildfowl Trust
On the E shore of the Severn estuary, 9 miles (14.5km) s of Gloucester ☎ *(045389) 333* 🚻 🏠 ⚲ 🚗 *Open 9.30am–5pm or sunset if earlier.*
Home of the world's largest and most varied collection of wildfowl, Slimbridge is the headquarters of the Wildfowl Trust, founded by Peter Scott in 1946. Some of the birds, including flocks of all six of the world's species of flamingos, are permanent residents; others come to these bleak estuary flats just for the winter. The former are either free, or confined in special enclosures, while the latter can be seen from carefully sited hiding places. Other attractions are a **Tropical House**, a Visitor Centre, and an exceptionally tempting shop.

Restaurant nearby
Avening (*on B4014, 16 miles/26km S of Gloucester*).

R **Four Seasons**
High St. ☎ (045383) 3070 ⫽▯ ▭ ▱ AE ◉ ◐ VISA *Last orders
10pm. Closed Sat lunch, Sun, Mon, first three weeks in Jan.*
A high standard of cuisine in an elegant, small, family-run restaurant.
The short menu, which features English and classical French dishes,
changes every couple of weeks. The vegetables are excellent.

Shopping
Department and chain stores can be found in **Eastgate St.** and **King's
Sq.** The shops in **Westgate St.** are more individual. The **general market**
(*in the cattle market off St Oswald's Rd., Sat*) is the best place to buy
locally produced goods. The **Antique Centre** in the dock area comprises
several antique shops, and there is a collectors' market (*Sat*).

Guildford
*Map 6L9. Surrey. 32 miles (50km) SW of London.
Population: 57,000* **i** *Civic Hall, London Rd.* ☎ (0483) 67314.
The city of Guildford has a cobbled main street and several fine
old buildings such as the 17thC **Guildhall**, instantly
recognizable because of its bell tower and gilded clock.

The **cathedral** (*off A3 Guildford bypass* ☎ (0483) 65287), is a
complete contrast. Started in 1936 but not consecrated until
1961, the theme of Edward Maufe's building is simplicity, if not
austerity. The exterior of almost unrelieved red brick catches
the eye rather than the spirit, and the interior is equally
disciplined.

Sights nearby
Polesden Lacey
11 miles (17km) E of Guildford ☎ (0372) 57230. NT ▨ ▣ ▰ ▭
◁ *Open Mar and Nov Sat, Sun 2–5pm; Apr–Oct 2–6pm (closed
Mon except bank holidays, Fri). Garden open all year 11am–sunset.*
The playwright and politician Sheridan lived in a house on this site from
1797 until his death in 1816, and his wife planned part of the delightful
gardens. Today's 19thC mansion, designed by Thomas Cubitt, was
altered in 1906 by the Hon Mrs Greville, a star of Edwardian society but
also a connoisseur of fine and decorative art, and it is her dazzling
collection that is preserved here. There are woodland walks and superb
views across to Ranmore Woods.
Wisley Garden ☆
Near Ripley, off A3, 6 miles (9.5km) NE of Guildford ☎ (0483)
224234 ▨ ▣ ▰ ▭ *Open Mon–Sat 10am–7pm or sunset if
earlier; Sun 2–7pm or sunset if earlier. Sun 10am–2pm for Royal
Horticultural Society members only.*
The famous gardens of the Royal Horticultural Society offer massed
flowering shrubs, a pinetum, herbaceous borders, a rock garden, fruit
and vegetable gardens and greenhouses. There is also an information and
sales center.

Restaurant nearby
South Godstone (*on A22, 23 miles/37km E of Guildford*).

R **La Bonne Auberge**
Tilburston Hill ☎ (034285) 2318 ⫽▯ ▭ ▮▮ ▬ ⌂ ▰ ▾ ♫ *Fri,
Sat* ♥ *Fri, Sat* AE ◉ ◐ VISA *Last orders 10pm. Closed Sun, Mon
dinner.*
A French-owned restaurant in a modernized Victorian country house
with 14 acres of grounds and its own nightclub across the courtyard.
There is also a cocktail bar, in the larger of two dining rooms. In winter, a
wood fire is also used as a grill. Specialities include *feuilleté d'escargots à la
crème d'ail, quenelles de brochet Lyonnaise*, and *noisettes d'agneau à
l'estragon*.

Hadrian's Wall ☆
Map **14C6&7.** *Cumbria, Northumb, T and W. Bowness-on-Solway to Wallsend-on-Tyne* **i** *at Housesteads*
☎ *(04984) 363.*

Named after the emperor who ordered its construction around
AD122, this was not so much a bold defensive complex
in both length and depth, its purpose being to mark and control
this remote and savage imperial frontier. 74 miles (118km)
long, it comprised a wide ditch, a wall, a military road, and
another ditch called the Vallum. Along the wall itself there were
three main features: milecastles, which were small forts
occurring roughly every mile; towers, of which there were two
between milecastles; and 17 large garrison forts.

Much of this great complex can still be seen in varying forms
ranging from simple earthwork lines to reasonably intact
lengths of wall and remains of milecastles, towers and forts.
Visitors intent on study in depth walk much of the length of the
wall. For those with less time to spare the best advice is to drive
along B6318 between Greenhead to the w and Chollerford to the
E. This stretch covers the central and most interesting section of
the wall; numerous signs direct the traveler to points of interest,
nearly always with parking.

Access to most of the sites along the wall is unrestricted and
free. The three most important sites, however, have controlled
access and are described below.

Sights and places of interest
Chesters Fort and Museum (*Cilurnum*)
Off B6318, just w of Chollerford ☎ *(043481) 379. DOE* 🏛 🚶 *Open
mid-Mar to mid-Oct Mon–Sat 9.30am–6.30pm, Sun 2–6.30pm
except Apr–Sept 9.30am–6.30pm; mid-Oct to mid-Mar Mon–Sat
9.30am–4pm, Sun 2–4pm.*
Roman cavalry should be pictured clattering in and out of here, for this
was one of their forts, with its northern and southern sectors given over
to stables and barracks. The headquarters building (*principia*) with its
vaulted underground strongroom occupies the middle of the central
sector; immediately to its E lies the commander's house (*praetorium*),
complete with its private bath suite. The main bathhouse is by the river,
and the fort also preserves something of its four gates and of the turrets
along the s wall.

Housesteads Fort and Museum (*Vercovicium*) ☆
Off B6318, halfway between Greenhead and Chollerford **i**
☎ *(04984) 363. NT/DOE* 🏛 🚶 *but 20mins' uphill walk from parking
lot. Entry details as Chesters.*
Built for a garrison of 1,000 infantry, this is the most excitingly sited and
best preserved of the wall's forts, indeed the best preserved Roman fort
in Britain. Ramparts and gateways are clearly seen while most of the
other standard buildings can be identified.

In this area the National Trust also owns a considerable length of the
best part of the wall and several milecastles. On the slope up to the fort on
its ridge are various remains, such as terraces which the legionaries
attempted to cultivate, a bathhouse and three temples (to Mithras, Mars
Thingsus and Matres).

Corstopitum
Corbridge, 5 miles (8km) SE of Chollerford ☎ *(043471) 2349. DOE*
🏛 🚶 *Entry details as Chesters.*
Strictly, Corstopitum should not be regarded as part of Hadrian's Wall
since it is not only more than 2 miles (3km) to the s but was also built in
AD78, several years before the wall, its purpose being to protect the
crossing of the Tyne. In fact with the completion of the wall the place was
for a while abandoned. Reopened in 139 it became a supply base for the
forward garrisons and, as such, a small town. Ventilated granaries, a
large unfinished store, military compounds (their complicated shape due
to the need to build around temples already there) and the headquarters
with its cellar strongroom can all be seen.

⊞ **George** ♣
Chollerford, Hexham, Northumb NE46 4EW ☎ _(043481) 205_
℡ *53168* ☐ ⌕ *54* ▭ *54* ▬ ⌂ ⇌ Æ ⊙ ▣ VISA
Location: By the river bridge. A really excellent base from which to explore
Hadrian's Wall and the lovely country around it. A well-planned
extension has been added to the original simple inn, resulting in an
L-shape enclosing a private garden beside the North Tyne river. The
Fisherman's Bar preserves the atmosphere of the inn, and one of the
restaurants overlooks the garden and river.
& ☐ 🖻 ⚲ 《 🏌 🛶 🏌

See also **Hexham**.

Harrogate
Map **15E8.** _North Yorks. 17 miles (27km) w of York.
Population: 62,500_ _**i**_ _Royal Baths Assembly Rooms,
Crescent Rd._ ☎ _(0423) 65912._
Harrogate's many springs – there are at least 89 of them, of
which about 30 are in or around **Valley Gardens** – are of two
distinct types, sulfur and chalybeate. The fashionable world of
the 18th and 19thC flocked here to take the waters, but the spa
began to decline in popularity with the outbreak of World War
I. Nevertheless those leisured times left Harrogate a rich
endowment of all those things so cherished by Victorian and
Edwardian society: wide tree-lined streets and parks and
gardens in which to promenade, fine shops and, above all,
palatial hotels. That the Harrogate of today is no mere faded spa
is due to its own far-sightedness in realizing that this
endowment was just what was needed for a modern **Conference
and Exhibition Super Centre**.
Events In mid-July, The Great Yorkshire Show; in Aug,
Harrogate Festival.

Sights and places of interest
Harlow Car Gardens
Crag Lane, off Otley Rd. (B6162) ☎ _(0423) 65418_ 🖾 ⇌ _Open
Mar–Oct 9.30am–7.30pm; Nov–Apr 9.30am until sunset._
The Northern Horticultural Society's extensive trial grounds include a
variety of garden areas such as rockeries, woodlands and formal flower
beds containing a vast selection of species. Plants can be bought at the
shop.
Royal Pump Room Museum
Royal Parade ☎ _(0423) 503340_ ⊡ ♣ _Open Apr–Sept Tues–Sat
10.30am–5pm, Sun 2–5pm; Oct–Jan, Mar Tues–Sat 10am–4pm,
Sun 2–5pm. Closed Feb, Mon._
Since 1842 this building has housed the sulfur spring, one of the first to
be discovered in Harrogate and during the 19thC the mainstay of the
town's fashionable status; the water can be sampled by anyone able to
stomach its taste and smell. The **museum of local history** lays emphasis
on Victorian and Edwardian times, with a children's corner exhibiting
19thC games and a fine dollhouse.

⊞ **Crown**
Crown Place, Harrogate, North Yorks HG1 2RZ ☎ _(0423) 67755_
℡ *57652* ☐☐ ⌕ *120* ▭ *120* ▬ ⇌ Æ CB ⊙ ▣ VISA
Location: Just E of Valley Gardens. This is just one of Harrogate's several
palatial hotels, additionally interesting for having started as a simple
coaching inn. It was developed first when Harrogate took off in the
19thC, and again in recent times to meet the requirements of present-day
visitors.
‡ & ☐ 🍴 🏌

Hotel and restaurants nearby
Boroughbridge (_8 miles/13km NE of Harrogate_).

Ⓗ Ⓡ **Crown Hotel** ♣
Horsefair, Boroughbridge, North Yorks Y05 9LB ☎ *(09012) 2328*
Ⅲ ⬟ 43 🛏 43 🚗 🏠 🍽 AE ⊙ 🔵 VISA
Ⓡ Ⅲ 🖵 🍴 🚗 *Last orders 9.15pm.*

Location: In town center, on B6265. A large coaching inn, built in solid
Northern style in the little Dales town of Boroughbridge. The town itself
is old, with prehistoric and Roman remains, and the hotel dates back to
the 14thC, although its facade is Georgian in style. The Crown was
renovated and reopened as a town-center luxury hotel in 1980, under
private ownership. It has welcoming staff, comfortable and well-
appointed rooms, the best of which are furnished with antiques. The
excellent restaurant serves such specialties as halibut, chicken stuffed
with smoked salmon, and butterscotch mousse.
≡ & 🖵 🖾 ➡ 🚗 ● *sometimes.*

Pately Bridge (*on B6265, 10 miles/16km NW of Harrogate*).

Ⓡ **The Willow** ♣
Park Rd. ☎ *(0423) 711689* 🖵 *to* Ⅲ 🖵 🚗 AE VISA *Last orders*
9pm. Closed Nov–Easter.
Yorkshire pudding, with – of course – local beef, is among the specialties
at this 18thC Yorkshire stone cottage in Nidderdale. The emphasis has
been on local produce and English dishes, at competitive prices, since
The Willow was acquired in 1982 by chef Roger Moore, who trained at
the Grosvenor House in London. A limited wine list also aims at
moderate prices and features Paul Masson's California wines.

Shopping

Cambridge St. and **James St.** are the major shopping streets, while
Montpellier Parade and **Crescent Rd.** are renowned for their antique
shops. Food, clothes and general goods can be found at the **indoor
market** (*Cambridge St.*). Harrogate toffee can be bought from **John
Farrah and Harrogate Toffee Ltd** (*Royal Parade*).

Hastings and St Leonards

*Map 7M11. East Sussex. On the s coast, 64 miles (102km)
SE of London. Population: 74,000* i *4 Robertson Terrace,
Hastings* ☎ *(0424) 424242.*

To many people the name Hastings is synonymous with the
battle of 1066, a niche in history the town does little to
discourage although William of Normandy's defeat of Harold
took place 6 miles (9.5km) to the NW at what is now *Battle*. On
the seafront, the **Conqueror's Stone** is said to have been the
table used for William's first English meal, and up on the cliffs
there are the scanty ruins of the **castle** (*Castle Hill Rd., West
Hill* ☎ *(0424) 420942* 🔲 *open Easter–Sept 10am–12.30pm,
1.30–5pm*) built by the Conqueror.

Today, Hastings is a coastal resort with a long promenade, a
shingle and sand beach, and, at the E end, a touch of the past
surviving as the **Old Town**, a pleasant muddle of narrow
streets, timber-framed houses and, on the beach, the unique
tall, black wooden huts used for drying fishing nets.

By contrast, **St Leonards**, to the W, never forgets that it was
created in the 1830s as a stylish resort, and in spite of
amalgamation with Hastings in 1887 still stands aloof and very
conscious of its architectural elegance.

Sights and places of interest

Fishermen's Museum
Rock-a-Nore Rd. ☎ *(0424) 424787* 🔲 🚗 *Open Easter–Sept
10am–noon, 2–5pm.*
The former fishermen's church is now a museum of local fishing, the
principal exhibit being the last (early 20thC) of the locally-built sailing
luggers, boats with flattened bottoms to allow winching up the beach.

The Hastings Embroidery
Town Hall, Queens Rd. ☎ *(0424) 424182* 🚾 *Open June–Sept
Mon–Fri 10am–5pm, Sat 10am–1pm, 2–5pm (closed Sun);
Oct–May Mon–Fri 11.30am–3.30pm (closed Sat, Sun).*

To mark the 900th anniversary of the Battle of Hastings (1066), the
Royal School of Needlework made a 243ft-long (74m) tapestry depicting
not only the battle but also 81 major events in British history, such as the
Fire of London and the Industrial Revolution. Also in this hall are dolls
in 19th and 20thC costume, and a large model of the Battle of Hastings.

Museum and Art Gallery
Cambridge Rd. ☎ *(0424) 435952* 🎦 *Open Mon–Sat 10am–1pm,
2–5pm, Sun 3–5pm.*

The highlight of this general local museum is the **Durbar Hall**, an Indian
palace built for an exhibition in 1886 and now an appropriate setting for a
collection of Oriental art.

St Clement's Caves
West Hill ☎ *(0424) 422964* 🚾 🎬 *Open Easter–Sept
10.15am–12.15pm, 1.30–5.15pm; Oct–Easter Sat, Sun
10.15am–noon, 2.15–4.15pm. Guided tours leave regularly and last
20mins (summer), 45mins (winter).*

Although natural in origin, these caves have over the centuries been
enlarged by users of sand and even, it is said, by 18thC smugglers, while
during World War II they served as an air raid shelter. A tourist
attraction since 1827, they are now decorated with copies of prehistoric
murals and with figures of Sir Winston Churchill and Field Marshal
Montgomery.

Shopping

Queens Rd., **Castle St.** and **Robertson St.** in the center of Hastings
contain leading department stores and chain shops while streets in the
Old Town such as **George St.** and **High St.** are known for their antiques,
china and gift shops. There are general markets in Hastings in **George
St.** (*closed Sun*) and off **London Rd.** in St Leonards (*Wed, Sat*). **London
Rd.** and **Kings Rd.** are the central shopping streets in St Leonards.

Hereford

*Map 4J6. H and W. 25 miles (40km) sw of Worcester.
Population: 46,500* **i** *Shirehall, St Owen St.* ☎ *(0432)
268430.*

In Saxon times there was an army settlement here around a
ford, but by the 18thC Hereford had become notorious as a
place which still clung to much of its medieval squalor. A
ruthless program was put into effect to sweep away the past and
create a modern Hereford. Nevertheless, the **cathedral**, the
17thC **Old House** in High Town, the 15thC **Wye Bridge** and
traces of the Saxon defenses and medieval walls, now the route
of the inner-city beltway, have all survived to provide glimpses
of Hereford's past.

Event In Aug, Three Choirs Festival takes place every 3yrs in
the cathedral, alternating with Gloucester and Worcester. In
Hereford in 1985.

Sights and places of interest

All Saints Church ✝
High St.
The spire has a curious kink, the result of 19thC restoration to the 14thC
tower which had subsided. Inside, there are 14thC canopied stalls with
carved misericords, the font at which David Garrick was baptized and a
collection of 300 chained books (*by appointment only* ☎ *(0432) 272715*).

Churchill Gardens Museum
3 Venn's Lane ☎ *(0432) 267409* 🚾 🚶 *Open Apr–Oct 2–5pm,
(closed Mon); Nov–Mar 2–5pm (closed Sun, Mon).*
In a Regency house, exhibits include an important collection of
costumes, furniture, glass, porcelain, paintings by local artists, and
period rooms including a Victorian butler's pantry and a nursery.

City Museum and Art Gallery
Broad St. ☎ *(0432) 268121* 🖼 *Open Apr–Oct Tues, Wed, Fri
10am–6pm, Thurs, Sat 10am–5pm; Nov–Mar Tues, Wed, Fri
10am–6pm, Thurs 10am–5pm, Sat 10am–4pm. Closed Sun, Mon.*
The museum has, in its wide-ranging collection, Roman mosaics found
in the neighborhood, domestic bygones, and old equipment used for
cider-making – still a thriving local industry. The art gallery has
changing exhibitions of fine and applied art.

Hereford Cathedral ✝
Southern part of the city, toward the river ☎ *(0432) 59880.*
In 794 the ghost of Ethelbert of East Anglia (who had come to Hereford
to marry the daughter of Offa of Mercia, only to be murdered by the
latter) somewhat surprisingly insisted on burial here. Miracles soon
occurred, Ethelbert was canonized, and the pilgrims and revenue flowed
in on a scale sufficient to fund the building of a stone church in 825.

  The present cathedral spans the late 11thC–18thC, the oldest part being
the Norman nave with its great pillars and the s transept. The famous
Mappa Mundi ✿ in the N choir aisle is a fascinating example of medieval
educational cartography (*c.*1305) which richly rewards detailed study,
and the **Chained Library ✿** is probably the world's largest with around
1,450 manuscripts and books dating from the 7thC.

The Old House
High Town ☎ *(0432) 268121* 🖼 *Open 10am–1pm, 2–5.30pm.
Closed Sun; Apr–Sept Mon afternoon; Oct–Mar Mon and Sat
afternoon.*
Dating from 1621, this picturesque half-timbered house serves as a
Jacobean period museum furnished in contemporary style. There are
also pictures of three famous theatrical families – Garrick, Kemble and
Siddons – all associated with Hereford.

St John and Coningsby Museum
Widemarsh St. ☎ *(0432) 272837* 🖼 🚶 *Open Easter–Sept
2–5pm. Closed Mon, Fri.*
The 13thC hospice and chapel of the Knights of St John was expanded
into almshouses in the early 17thC by Sir Thomas Coningsby. Restored,
the place now shows material about the Order and illustrating the life of
the pensioners. The ruins of **Blackfriars Monastery** in the nearby
Blackfriars Gardens include a unique Friars' preaching cross.

Sight nearby
Kilpeck Church ✝ ★
6 miles (9.5km) sw of Hereford.
A small church in a small village, but one that is far-famed for the rich
12thC Norman carving which lavishly decorates both the exterior and
interior, and ranks among the best examples in the country. Although
Norman in period and execution, both Celtic and Scandinavian
influences have surfaced here, particularly around the s door where
beasts, warriors, flowers and fruit are part of an intricate design.

Ⓗ **Green Dragon**
Broad St., Hereford, H and W HR4 9BG ☎ *(0432) 272506* 🏩*35491*
💶 🐾 *88* 🛏 *88* 🖼 ⚌ Ⓐ🅔 🅲🅱 Ⓕ 🅞🅓 🆅🅸🆂🅰
Location: w side of Broad St. between All Saints and the cathedral. Behind
the 18thC facade this former coaching inn provides spacious public
rooms, some with old panelling, and bedrooms generally of good size.
Children are welcome and, given notice, baby-sitting can be arranged.
‡ ☐ ⚖ 👪

Shopping
The pedestrian precincts of **Eign Gate** and **High Town**, the **High St.** and
Commercial St. contain the major stores. In **Church St.**, a notable shop
is **The Society of Craftsmen** (*no.29*) in which local craftsmen sell their
wares. A large general market is held in **Newmarket St.** (*Wed, Sat*).

Hexham

*Map 15C7. Northumb. 20 miles (32km) w of Newcastle-
upon-Tyne. Population: 9,000 ℹ Manor Office, Hallgates*
☎ *(0434) 605225.*
The town seems peaceful enough today, but Hexham can look
back on a troubled past as victim first of marauding Danes and

then time and time again of the Scots who in 1290 even destroyed the nave of the **Priory Church**.

This imposing building, in turn Saxon cathedral and Augustinian priory, is fascinating for the construction span it embraces. The nave was rebuilt in 1908, but the walls of the crypt which were built by St Wilfrid in the 7thC incorporate Roman stones from Corstopitum (see *Hadrian's Wall*). Halfway between in time are the choir and transept, exquisite work of the 12th–13thC. The furnishings span much the same period, the Saxon **Bishop's Chair** which guaranteed sanctuary to anyone seated upon it, and a **cross** dating from about 740 being of particular interest.

Although the great church has always been the town's key feature, there are also other places to see such as the 14thC **Moot Hall**, the **Manor Office** of about the same date and once a prison, and the 18thC **Shambles**.

Holy Island (*Lindisfarne*)

Map 15A8. Northumb. Off the coast, 10 miles (16km) s of Berwick-upon-Tweed. Population: 200. The island is reached by a causeway which is impassable approximately 2hrs before and 3¼hrs following high tide **i** *NT office, Elm House, Marygate* ☎ *(0289) 89253.*

Implicit in its name and underscored by the abbey ruins there is an air of ancient sanctity about this isolated place. St Aidan and St Cuthbert both ruled here in the 7thC, the former spreading Christianity throughout Northumbria. The Lindisfarne Gospels, written in the priory in the early 8thC, are one of the treasures of the British Museum (see *Sights* in *London*), but there is a facsimile in **St Mary's Church**. Lindisfarne mead may be sampled at the factory near the priory, and dunes and a nature reserve to the N of the island invite exploration.

Sights and places of interest
Lindisfarne Castle
Near the village ☎ *(0289) 89244. NT* ◪ ◛ *Open Apr–Sept 11am–5pm (closed Fri except Good Fri); Oct Sat–Sun 11am–5pm.*

The castle, thrusting like some tailored volcanic core out of the surrounding flats, started out as a small 16thC fort built to deter the raiding Scots and was converted by Sir Edwin Lutyens in 1902 into a comfortable home of most distinctive style.

Lindisfarne Priory
At the edge of the village ☎ *(0289) 89200. DOE* ◪ *Open mid-Mar to mid-Oct Mon–Sat 9.30am–6.30pm; Sun 2–6.30pm except Apr–Sept 9.30am–6.30pm; mid-Oct to mid-Mar Mon–Sat 9.30am–4pm, Sun 2–4pm.*

This small but attractive sandstone ruin dates from the arrival here of Benedictine monks in 1082. The monks enjoyed nearly five centuries of peace, until their priory was dissolved by Henry VIII. The prior, clearly a man of elastic conscience, then became Bishop of Berwick although his priory was used as a source of stone with which to build **Lindisfarne Castle**. Later, in 1613, the Earl of Dunbar carried off the roof lead, the bells and much else, but failed to profit from his greed since the ship sank almost at once, taking its load of loot and looters with it. Various domestic buildings including the warming house, chapter house, brewhouse, kitchen, larder and cellar can all be identified.

Ⓗ **Manor House** ▥
Holy Island, Beal, Northumb TD15 2SQ ☎ *(0289) 89207* ▯ ♋ *11* ◛ ▥ ⇌

Location: Near the Priory. Small and unpretentious, the Manor House has a surprisingly imaginative menu.
♨ ⟠ ⬧ ⬩ ⬢ ⬚

Hull

*Map 12*F10. *Humberside. On the Humber, 35 miles
(56km)* SE *of York. Population: 286,000* i *Central Library,
Albion St.* ☎ *(0482) 223344.*

Businessmen or continental ferry travelers with a few hours to
spare in this major port and manufacturing center (officially
called Kingston-upon-Hull) should make a point of seeing the
Humber Bridge, to the W of the city. Opened in 1981, this is the
world's longest single-span suspension bridge.

In the center of the city, the **Ferens Art Gallery** (*Queen
Victoria Sq.* ☎ *(0482) 222750* 🖭 🖵 *open Mon – Sat 10am – 5pm,
Sun 2.30 – 4.30pm*) is an exceptionally good municipal gallery
with Dutch, Flemish and Italian Old Masters and several
attractive Humberside marine paintings. Modern art in its
various manifestations also has its place here.

Ⓗ **Centre** (*Paragon St., Hull, Humberside HU1 3PJ* ☎ *(0482) 26462*
☜ *52431* ⫼); **Royal Station** (*170 Ferensway, Hull, Humberside
HU1 3UF* ☎ *(0482) 25087* ☜ *52450* ⫼).

Place nearby

Beverley (*8 miles/13km* N *of Hull*).
Beverley Minster † ☆
At the SE end of town, the minster comes as a magnificent surprise.
Although the foundation goes back to a monastery built here by John of
Beverley in the 8thC, the building seen today grew between the
13th – 15thC and thus presents a sequence of styles – Early English
transepts and choir, Decorated nave and Perpendicular W end. Among
many interesting features, one above all demands attention, namely the
wealth of stone and wood carving. Small figures – many of them
astonishingly individual in character – abound, notably the medieval
musicians along the N aisle and on the **Percy tomb**. Many other carved
figures crowd the canopied choir stalls, famous for their 68 misericords.
St Mary's Church †
North Bar Within
It is worth dropping in here to look at the portrait panels of English kings
which form the chancel ceiling; they date from 1445, except of course for
that of George VI. And in the N choir aisle there is a carved rabbit, said to
have been the inspiration for Lewis Carroll's immortal character.

Ⓗ **Beverley Arms**
North Bar Within, Beverley, Humberside HU17 8DD ☎ *(0482)
869241* ⫼ ⇌ *61* 🛏 *61* ⇌ ⫧ ⒶⒺ ⒸⒷ ⓪ ⓒⒹ 🆅🆂🅰
Location: Just s *of North Bar.* Behind a dignified 18thC facade the hotel
extends through a pleasant ramble of public rooms. Above, some quiet
bedrooms at the back of the hotel overlook a parking lot, once the stables
of the Blue Bell Inn used by the notorious highwayman Dick Turpin.
‡ ❤ ▢ 🖼 ⚓ 🏌

Huntingdon

*Map 12*I10. *Cambs. 15 miles (24km)* NW *of Cambridge.
Population: 16,500* i *Reference Library, Prince's St.*
☎ *(0480) 52181.*

Huntingdon's main claim to fame is as the birthplace of Oliver
Cromwell (1599 – 1658). Memorabilia including several
portraits can be seen at the **Cromwell Museum** (*Market Sq.*
☎ *(0480) 52861* 🖭 ⇌ *open Tues – Fri 11am – 1pm, 2 – 5pm, Sat
11am – 1pm, 2 – 4pm, Sun 2 – 4pm, closed Mon*).

The town's most attractive feature is the 14thC bridge linking
it to **Godmanchester**. The two halves are different because the
bridge was built from both ends, Huntingdon apparently being
able to afford more decoration than its neighbor.

A few miles E at **St Ives**, which also has Cromwellian connections and a statue of the politician in the market square, the bridge has a tiny 15thC chapel in the middle.

Hotel nearby
Brampton (*3 miles/5km* w *of Huntingdon*).

Ⓗ **Brampton**
Brampton, near Huntingdon, Cambs PE18 8NH ☎ *(0480) 810434*
▮▮ ❧ *17* ▭ *17* ⇐ ⇋ AE ⊕ ⊙ VISA
Location: A1/A604 traffic circle. A new extension has been successfully grafted on to the old inn, giving modern bedrooms alongside, for example, the dark-beamed Shires Bar.
▢ ▥ ♨

Ipswich
Map 7J12. Suffolk. 79 miles (127km) NE of London.
Population: 123,000 **i** *Town Hall, Princes St.* ☎ *(0473) 58070.*
By Anglo-Saxon times, 'Gippeswic,' known to have been settled in Stone Age days, had become a thriving port and commercial community at the head of the Orwell estuary, a status which – with a pause in the 18thC when the Suffolk cloth market declined – the town has enjoyed until the present day.

Sights and places of interest
The Ancient House (*Sparrowe's*) ☆
Buttermarket ▣ *The house is a bookshop, open normal hours.*
Over 400yrs old and once a single hall, this house was acquired in 1603 by the Sparrowe family who in 1670 gave it the astonishingly pargeted facade which survives today as one of the country's best examples of decorative plasterwork.
Christchurch Mansion
s side of Christchurch Park ☎ *(0473) 53246* ▣ *Open Mon–Sat 10am–5pm or sunset if earlier, Sun 2.30–4.30pm or sunset if earlier.*
A 16thC mansion houses a distinguished museum and art gallery, a main feature of the former being a series of elegant period rooms, including the mansion's **Great Hall** and **State Bedroom**, illustrating household furnishings from Tudor to Victorian times. In the **Wolsey Art Gallery** Suffolk artists, including Gainsborough and Constable, are particularly well represented.
Sight nearby
Framlingham Castle
15 miles (24km) NE of Ipswich ☎ *(0728) 723330. DOE* ▣ ⇐ *Open mid-Mar to mid-Oct Mon–Sat 9.30am–6.30pm, Sun 2–6.30pm except Apr–Sept 9.30am–6.30pm; mid-Oct to mid-Mar Mon–Sat 9.30am–4pm, Sun 2–4pm.*
This moated 12th–13thC castle ruin has two strange features: its 13 towers are ornamented with Tudor chimneys, and within the ruin, occupying the site of the great hall, there stands a building erected in the 17thC as an almshouse by Pembroke College, Cambridge, to whom the castle had been bequeathed. It was here that Mary Tudor learned of the defeat of her rival Lady Jane Grey and of her proclamation as queen.

Ⓗ **Great White Horse**
Tavern St., Ipswich, Suffolk IP1 3AH ☎ *(0473) 56558* ▮▮ ❧ *55*
▭ *10* ⇌ AE CB ⊕ ⊙ VISA
Location: 300yds (275m) E of the Town Hall. One of the town's leading hostelries since 1518, it was here that Dickens lodged while working for the local paper. The hotel features in *The Pickwick Papers* (visitors wishing vicariously to relive the scene should reserve the Pickwick Room with its two four-poster beds – but also color TV). The courtyard lounge is a picturesque and pleasant spot in which to sit, and the Dickens theme is stressed in the restaurant.
▢ ▥ ⚉ ♨

Ⓗ **Marlborough** ✿
73 Henley Rd., Ipswich, Suffolk IP1 3SP ☎ *(0473) 57677* ▥ ☜ *21*
▭ *21* ☜ ⇄ Ⓐ︎Ⓔ︎ ⊕ ⓞ︎ Ⓥ︎Ⓘ︎Ⓢ︎Ⓐ︎
Location: Just NW of Christchurch Park. A cheerful welcome, a porter,
sherry brought to the bedroom, a canapé offered on sitting down to
dinner – these are just some of the touches which give this hotel style.
The imaginative à la carte dinner menu is as tempting to read as the
dishes are to taste; and this standard is repeated at breakfast.
& ▢ ☕ ⚓ ♨

Shopping
Westgate St., **Tavern St.** and **Carr St.** contain the major shops. More
exclusive shops can be found in **Buttermarket**. A market selling local
produce and general goods is held off **Tower Ramparts** (*Tues, Fri, Sat*).

Ironbridge Gorge Museum ☆
Map 10I7. Shropshire **i** *Ironbridge Gorge Museum Trust,
Ironbridge* ☎ *(095245) 3522* ▨ ☜ *All museum sites open
Apr–Oct 10am–6pm; Nov–Mar 10am–5pm.*
In 1709 the ironmaster Abraham Darby smelted iron ore with
coke in place of the charcoal used hitherto, and this led to a
whole succession of 'firsts' in and around this cleft cut by the
river Severn: the first iron steam engine, iron boat, iron rails,
iron wheels and, of course, iron bridge – achievements fully
justifying Ironbridge's claim to be the birthplace of the
Industrial Revolution. Much of this momentous past has
survived and can be seen at five main sites spread over some six
square miles (15sq.km). They are listed below in the most
practical order for visitors.
  The **Iron Bridge**, the world's first, was cast at Coalbrookdale,
erected in 1779 and finally closed to traffic in 1934. An
information center (*plan of sites available here*) and exhibition
occupy the tollhouse on the S side, while in Ironbridge to the N
there is an Ironbridge Gorge Museum Trust Shop.
  At the **Coalbrookdale Furnace Site and Museum of Iron** (*at
the NW of the complex, on Wellington Rd.*), Abraham Darby
achieved his historic breakthrough.
  The **Severn Warehouse** (*N river bank, a short way W of the
Iron Bridge*) was built by the Coalbrookdale Co. *c.*1840 and now
houses an interpretative center.
  In the 19thC the **Blists Hill Open Air Museum** (*E end of the
complex, on Coalport Rd.*) was a thriving industrial zone which
included an ironworks, a brick and tile factory and several coal
and clay pits, all served by a canal and a streetcar system. Much
has now been restored and rebuilt.
  At the **Coalport China Works Museum** (*E end of the
complex*), Coalport china was made from the 18thC until 1926,
when the company moved to Staffordshire. Some of the original
buildings have been restored to house today's instructive
museum. There is also a shop.

Hotel/restaurant nearby
Shifnal (*5 miles/8km NE of Ironbridge*).

Ⓗ Ⓡ **Park House**
Park St., Shifnal, Shropshire TF11 9BA ☎ *(0952) 460128*
▥ ☜ *25* ▭ *25* ☜ ⇐ ⇄ Ⓐ︎Ⓔ︎ ⊕ ⓞ︎ Ⓥ︎Ⓘ︎Ⓢ︎Ⓐ︎ *Closed Christmas.*
Ⓡ ▥ ▭ ☕ *Last orders 9.45pm. Closed Sun.*
Location: In town center. This hotel comprises two handsome buildings,
one 17thC and the other 18thC, which have been modernized. It is a
well-equipped, privately-owned hotel, with efficient and friendly staff.
It has a buffet and a more luxurious restaurant with cocktail bar.
▢ ☕ ⚓ ≈ ♨ ⚲

Isle of Wight

Map 5M8. I of W. Off s coast, s of Portsmouth. Population: 118,000 i 21 High St., Newport (the island's principal town) ☎ (0983) 524343. Also local offices in other towns. Getting there: Sealink (among other companies) operates passenger ferries between Portsmouth ☎ (0705) 827744 and Ryde, and car ferries between Lymington and Yarmouth and Portsmouth and Fishbourne; Hovertravel operates a passenger hovercraft between Southsea ☎ (0705) 829988 and Ryde ☎ (0983) 65241; Red Funnel operates a car and passenger ferry as well as a passenger hydrofoil between Southampton ☎ (0703) 26211 and Cowes ☎ (0983) 292704. Reservation is essential for car ferries during the summer. On the island there is an excellent bus service linking major towns, and a train service runs from Ryde to Shanklin.

Queen Victoria bought (and Prince Albert helped to redesign) **Osborne House**, near **Cowes**, as a quiet, seaside family retreat; her presence did much to establish the island as a vacation destination, ironically thus undermining the very tranquillity she so much enjoyed.

Scenically this is an island of contrasts: to the N of the central chalk downs the landscape is gentle, but to the S there is some spectacular country, especially along the coast between **Shanklin** and **Freshwater Bay**. At the island's w end the broken white teeth of the **Needles** lie not far from **Alum Bay**, famed for its multicolored strata and sands. Dotted here and there are photogenic old villages with thatched cottages.

For families seeking sandy beaches and safe swimming there is a choice of pleasant resorts, some, such as **Seaview**, retaining something of their Victorian charm, while **Ventnor** spills steeply down its terraces from clifftop to shore. Walkers can use the many marked paths that crisscross the island's 23 by 13¼-mile (37 by 21km) area, and there are no less than six nature trails, the most famous of which is at **Robin Hill Country and Zoological Park** (*Downend, Arreton*). Last but not least, the Isle of Wight is a mecca for sailing enthusiasts.

Event First week in Aug, Cowes Week. The famous yacht races culminate in a maritime fireworks display.

Sights and places of interest
Arreton Manor
Arreton, 3 miles (5km) SE of Newport ☎ (0983) 528134 🔲 ✶ 🚗 ➡ *Open Easter–Oct Mon–Sat 10am–6pm, Sun 2–6pm.*
Although the estate is mentioned in Alfred the Great's will, today's house, known for its Elizabethan and Jacobean carved oak panelling, dates from 1595. Other attractions are a folk museum, collections of toys and dolls, and a radio museum.

Blackgang Chine Theme Park
At the s tip of the island ☎ (0983) 730330 🔲 💷 ✶ 🚗 *Open Easter–May, late Sept–Oct 10am–5pm; June–late Sept 10am–10pm.*
Opened in 1843, the park changes constantly in its search for innovation. Today, for children, there are a smugglers' lugger, a cowboy town, a tank to drive, a rocket to launch and the fulfilment of many another dream; for adults there are some splendid water gardens with dancing fountains and, at **Blackgang Sawmill**, a World of Timber exhibition.

Brading Roman Villa
Brading, 7 miles (11km) E of Newport ☎ (0983) 406223 🔲 🚗 *Open Mar–Sept Mon–Sat 10am–5.30pm, Sun 10.30am–5.30pm.*
Dating from the 1st–3rdC, this villa is known in particular for its mosaic floors. Do not miss the **hypocaust** (Roman heating system) which is under a separate shelter adjacent to the main building.

Carisbrooke Castle
Just sw of Newport ☎ *(0983) 522107. DOE* 🏛 💻 ➾ *Open mid-Mar to mid-Oct Mon–Sat 9.30am–6.30pm, Sun 2–6.30pm except Apr–Sept 9.30am–6.30pm; mid-Oct to mid-Mar Mon–Sat 9.30am–4pm, Sun 2–4pm.*

There is a poignancy about this place where Charles I spent some of the last months of his life and in which his heartbroken daughter Elizabeth died of fever at the age of 15.

The **Isle of Wight County Museum** occupies the part of the castle in which father and daughter were held; it displays archeological material, some touching Stuart relics, and Tennyson exhibits (the poet acquired a house at **Farringford** in 1853), including his famous large hat and cloak and a striking photo-portrait by the brilliant Julia Margaret Cameron.

The oldest part of the castle is the early Norman keep, itself on Roman foundations, 71 steps to the top and worth it for the view, although much can be seen by walking around the ramparts. In the 16thC well-house a donkey treads a wheel to raise the water.

Gatcombe Park
3 miles (5km) s of Newport ☎ *(098370) 777* 🏛 💻 ☀ ➾ *Open Mar–Oct 10am–5pm; Nov–Feb Sun noon–4pm.*

Built in 1750, this mansion's stylish Georgian rooms contain a large costume collection, theatrical costumes from the Monte Carlo Opera, and engravings of island scenery. There is also an exhibition of bicycles and horse-drawn vehicles, while the large park offers a children's play area, tropical plant houses, a forest trail and a lakeside walk.

Isle of Wight Steam Railway
Havenstreet Railway Station, 3 miles (5km) sw of Ryde ☎ *(0983) 882204* 🏛 💻 ☀ ➾ *Trains run frequently 11am–4.45pm: Easter, May–June, Sept Sun, bank holidays; July–Aug Thurs, Sun, bank holidays; daily during week before Aug bank holiday. Station open daily July–Aug. Telephone for exact times.*

The main attraction is the 3-mile (5km) round trip on a steam train, but there are also displays of locomotives and coaches and a **museum** of old railway mementoes.

Osborne House ☆
Just se of Cowes ☎ *(0983) 292511. DOE* 🏛 💻 ➾ *Open Easter–June, Sept–early Oct 11am–5pm; July–Aug 10am–5pm. Closed Sun.*

Little has been changed in either the state or private apartments since Queen Victoria died here in 1901. Completed in 1851, Osborne soon became one of the queen's best-loved homes, especially after Albert's death. The Indian-style Durbar Room, designed by Rudyard Kipling's father, is remarkable. The **Swiss Cottage** on the grounds was shipped to Osborne in 1853 and became the refuge of the royal children. Its delightfully simple rooms are in marked contrast to the main house. Queen Victoria's bathing machine is on show near the cottage.

Hotels

Cowes (*on N coast, 5 miles/8km N of Newport*).
Holmwood (*Egypt Point, 65 Queens Rd., Cowes, I of W PO31 8BW* ☎ *(0983) 292508* □).
Freshwater Bay (*on s coast, 9 miles/14.5km w of Newport*).
Albion (*Freshwater Bay, I of W PO40 9RA* ☎ *(0983) 75361* ▮□).
Newport (*in center of island*).
Bugle (*High St., Newport, I of W PO30 1IP* ☎ *(0983) 522800* □).
Ryde (*on N coast, 7 miles/11km NE of Newport*).
Yelfs (*Union St., Ryde, I of W PO33 2LG* ☎ *(0983) 64062* ▮▮□).
Sandown (*on E coast, 8 miles/13km SE of Newport*).
St Catherine's (*Winchester Park Rd., Sandown, I of W PO36 8HJ* ☎ *(0983) 402392* □).
Shanklin (*on E coast, 10 miles/16km SE of Newport*).
Cliff Tops (*Park Rd., Shanklin, I of W PO37 6BB* ☎ *(0983) 863262* ☎ *86725* ▮□).
Ventnor (*on s coast, 14 miles/20km SE of Newport*).
Ventnor Towers (*Madeira Rd., Ventnor, I of W PO38 1QJ* ☎ *(0983) 852277* □).
Yarmouth (*on N coast, 10 miles/16km w of Newport*).
George (*Quay St., Yarmouth, I of W PO41 0PB* ☎ *(0983) 760331* □).

Nightlife
The **Ryde Pavilion Theatre** (*Esplanade* ☎ *(0983) 63465*), the **Sandown Pavilion Theatre** (*Esplanade* ☎ *(0983) 402295*) and the **Shanklin Theatre** (*Steep Hill* ☎ *(0983) 862739*) have a full program of events in the high season, often including a summer show with top names.

Shopping
The major towns on the Isle of Wight are small enough for the central shopping areas to be recognizable. However, there are a number of specialty shops and areas that are of particular interest. Cowes is renowned for its ships' chandlers and other shops associated with nautical life. **Curds and Whey** (*14 Park Rd., Cowes*) sells Isle of Wight cheeses as well as 60 others. Newport, the island's capital, has a good selection of nationally known shops, many in the High St. The **Cheese Shop** (*Pyle St.*) stocks several types of cheese as well as other local produce.

Interesting craft shops and studios on the island include the **Chessell Pottery** (*Shalcombe, between Newport and Freshwater*) for decorative handpainted porcelain; **Hasely Manor Craft and Pottery Centre** (*near Arreton*) for hand-thrown pottery; and **Isle of Wight Country Craft Workshops** (*Arreton Manor Farm*), a working center with shops. Local drinks include cider from Godshill Cider Barn and wine made at Adgestone, Barton Manor and Cranmore.

Jodrell Bank
*Map **10**G7. Cheshire. 17 miles (27km) s of central Manchester* ☎ *(0477) 71339* 🖼️ 💺 🚗 *Open mid-March to Oct 10.30am – 5.30pm; Oct to mid-Mar Sat, Sun 2 – 5pm (closed Mon – Fri). Planetarium presentations every 45mins from 10.45am.*
The exhibition **Concourse** tends to be technical and to be fully appreciated certainly demands some background knowledge. Nevertheless the colorful displays must surely attract the layman and, if nothing else, instill a sense of awe. The **Planetarium** will be enjoyed by all, and for those who want to come back to earth there are 30 acres of **Arboretum**.

Kendal
*Map **14**E6. Cumbria. 20 miles (32km) N of Lancaster. Population: 21,500* **i** *Town Hall* ☎ *(0539) 25758.*
With its gray limestone buildings set along a ridge above the little river Kent on the E edge of the Lake District, Kendal is associated with cloth, shoes, a strong-tasting local mintcake, and Katherine Parr, sixth and last wife of Henry VIII, who was born in 1512 in the small ruined castle to the E of the river.

Local history, archeology and natural history exhibits can be seen at **Kendal Museum** (*Station Rd.* ☎ *(0539) 21374* 🖼️ 💺 🚗 *open Mon – Fri 10.30am – 5pm, Sat 2 – 5pm, closed Sun*), while the **Abbot Hall Art Gallery and Museum** (*Kirkland* ☎ *(0539) 22464* 🖼️ 💺 🚗 *open Mon – Fri 10.30am – 5.30pm, Sat, Sun 2 – 5pm, closed two weeks at Christmas*) shows special exhibitions and permanent collections of porcelain, silver and glass and portraits by Romney in restored 18thC rooms. In the stables, a **Museum of Lakeland Life and Industry** includes reconstructions of a wheelwright's workshop, a blacksmith's forge and a 17thC farm parlor.

Ⓗ **Woolpack**
Stricklandgate, Kendal, Cumbria LA9 4ND ☎ *(0539) 23852*
☎53168 ▯ 🗝️ 58 ▭ 58 🚗 🍽️ AE ⊕ ⊙ VISA
Location: Opposite the post office and Market Place. A modernized 18thC inn which still retains much of its older character, notably in the Crown Bar which was once Kendal's wool auction room.
♿ ▯ 🖂 🏌️

King's Lynn

Map 13H11. Norfolk. At the SE corner of The Wash.
Population: 30,000 ℹ *Town Hall* ☎ *(0553) 63044.*

For King's Lynn, still a busy port on the Great Ouse river, the
really great years were those of the 12th–15thC. From S to N
Nelson St., **Queen St.** and **King St.** run parallel to and a short
way back from the river and it is between these streets and the
water that old Lynn can be found. Here, again from S to N, are
Hampton Court, a medieval warehouse; the 15thC **Hanseatic
Warehouse**, leaning crazily over the street; the **Guildhall of the
Holy Trinity** (Town Hall); **Clifton House**, of the 16th–17thC
but with a 14thC cellar (*open Mon–Fri*); the dockside **Custom
House** (1683); and **St George's Guildhall**. And at the S
approach to the town the 15thC gate still stands:

Sights and places of interest

Regalia Rooms

Town Hall ☎ *(0553) 77281* 🔲 *Open Apr–Oct Mon–Sat
10am–4pm. Closed Sun.*

The checkered **Guildhall of the Holy Trinity** ☆ – now the Town Hall –
dates from 1421 and in the 18thC incorporated the jail (note the chains
above the door). In the cellar there is some of the finest municipal plate
and regalia in the country, the outstanding piece being the elaborately
worked, 14thC **King John Cup** ☆ engraved with pictures of men and
women hunting and hawking.

St George's Guildhall

King St ☎ *(0553) 4725. NT* 🔲 *Open when not in use Mon–Fri
10am–1pm, 2–5pm, Sat 10am–12.30pm. Closed Sun.*

Built in the early 15thC and containing many original features, this is
both the largest and the earliest example in England of a medieval
guildhall. It is still in active use as a theater.

St Margaret's Church †

Saturday Market Place.

In the choir s aisle, two well-known brasses ranking among the most
elaborate in the country commemorate Adam de Walsoken (*died* 1349)
and Robert Braunche (*died* 1364), the former illustrating rural scenes,
the latter a feast at which Edward III was present.

Wedgwood Glass

Oldmedow Rd., Hardwick Estate ☎ *(0553) 65111* 🔲 ✗ *Open
Mon–Fri 9.30am–2.30pm. Closed Sat, Sun. Guided tours for five or
more people may be arranged in advance.*

An opportunity to see ancient skills being used to produce modern glass.
Casual visitors are admitted to a viewing gallery; parties on a guided tour
see a good deal more, but children under 10yrs are not allowed on the
factory floor. Wedgwood glass can be bought from the well-stocked gift
shop.

Sights nearby

Castle Rising ☆

4 miles (6.5km) N of King's Lynn ☎ *(055387) 330. DOE* 🔲 🚗
*Open mid-Mar to mid-Oct Mon–Sat 9.30am–6.30pm, Sun
2–6.30pm; mid-Oct to mid-Mar Mon–Wed, Sat 9.30am–4pm, Fri,
Sun 2–4pm (closed Thurs).*

With the gaunt shell of its 12thC keep standing atop a massive platform
of earthworks, this is a starkly striking example of a Norman fortress.

Grime's Graves

Near Weeting, 20 miles (32km) SE of King's Lynn ☎ *(0842)
810656. DOE* 🔲 🚗 *Open mid-Mar to mid-Oct Mon–Sat
9.30am–6.30pm; Sun 2–6.30pm except Apr–Sept
9.30am–6.30pm; mid-Oct to mid-Mar Mon–Sat 9.30am–4pm, Sun
2–4pm.*

Not in fact graves, but ancient mines and workshops where Stone Age
man using antler picks prized out the flint and fashioned his tools and
weapons. Within an area of about 30 acres there are more than 300 shafts
up to 30ft (9m) deep. Visitors can go down one of the shafts by ladder to
look at the radiating galleries; it is advisable to take a flashlight and to
wear sensible shoes.

Holkham Hall
22 miles (35km) NE of King's Lynn ☎ *(0328) 710227* 🚗 📇 ⬜
Open June, Sept Mon, Thurs, Sun 2–5pm; July–Aug Mon, Wed,
Thurs 11.30am–5pm, Sun 2–5pm.
A splendid example of Palladian architecture, Holkham was built by
William Kent in 1734 and contains priceless collections of fine and
decorative art. Visitors with a farming background will know that this
was the home of the pioneering farmer Coke of Norfolk (Thomas
William Coke, Earl of Leicester, 1752–1842).

Sandringham House
6 miles (9.5km) N of King's Lynn ☎ *(0553) 26751* 🚗 📇 ⬜ *Open
Easter–Sept: Mon–Thurs house 11am–4.45pm, grounds
10.30am–5pm; Sun house noon–4.45pm, grounds 11.30am–5pm.
Closed Fri, Sat. House closed mid-July to early Aug, and grounds
late-July to early Aug, and also when the Royal Family is in residence.*
The Royal Family has used Sandringham as an informal country retreat
ever since Queen Victoria bought the estate for the Prince of Wales in
1862. Royal portraits are of particular interest here; there is also a
museum containing such diverse exhibits as vintage cars and hunting
trophies, and a nature trail and gardens.

Ⓗ Duke's Head
Tuesday Market Pl., King's Lynn, Norfolk PE30 1JS ☎ *(0553)
4996* ☎*817349* 🏠 🅿 *72* ⬜ *72* 🚗 🚆 AE CB Ⓓ Ⓞ VISA
Location: On E side of Tuesday Market Pl. A hotel of some character with a
modestly imposing facade dating from 1685. The Duke's Head has all
the solid comfort of the typical market town hostelry, and the good
restaurant produces some local dishes.
‡ 🖃 📷 🎿 👬

Ⓡ Riverside Rooms
Fermoy Centre, King St. ☎ *(0553) 3134* 🏠 🍴 🚆 🍺 🚗 🎵 AE
Ⓓ VISA *Last orders 10pm. Closed Sun, bank holidays, last three
weeks in Feb.*
With its views over the river Ouse, this converted warehouse, built with
the help of ships' timbers, is now a National Trust property. It provides a
relaxing showcase for the work of its intensely proud owner-chef, Roger
Savage, whose eclectic menu rests firmly on fresh local produce
purchased daily. His light lunches and attractively priced dinners
embrace dishes ranging from steak and kidney pie or roast rack of
English lamb to *chile con tacos*. The wine list is equally cosmopolitan and
excellent, and there is cask-conditioned Greene King beer.

Shopping
In the center, **High St.**, **New Conduit St.**, **Norfolk St.**, **Broad St.** and
Tower St. form a modern shopping area, much of which is set aside for
pedestrians. A large market is held in **Tuesday Market Pl.** (*Tues*), and
there is a smaller market in **Saturday Market Pl.** (*Sat*). A wide range of
lavender products is available from the shop at **Norfolk Lavender Ltd**
(*Caley Mill, Heacham, 12 miles/19km N of King's Lynn*).

Kingston-upon-Hull See *Hull.*

Lake District National Park and environs ★
*Map **14D–E6**. Cumbria. Between the sea and the M6
motorway* ⓘ *Bank House, High St., Windermere* ☎ *(09662)
2498 or Lake District National Park Centre, Brockhole,
Windermere* ☎ *(09662) 2231.*
What the name does not reveal is that there are mountains here
too. Without these to frame and complement them the lakes
would count for little, but given their mountains these sheets of
water – there are around 17 of them and, to add to the magic,
they style themselves 'water' or 'mere' rather than the prosaic
'lake' – fashion a region of natural beauty the greater part of
which is also one of wild and solitary grandeur, climbing
through crags and fells to the three highest peaks in England,

Scafell, **Helvellyn** and **Skiddaw**, all above 3,000ft (914m).
Curiously, but possibly because it is England's largest,
Windermere seems to be the best known and is certainly the
most crowded of the lakes; curiously, because, although it can
be a sparkling delight within its sylvan and pastoral bowl,
Windermere is overhung by none of the dark mountain
outcrops that are such a feature around the other lakes.

The whole National Park measures only some 35sq. miles
(90sq.km) and for all its wildness is well served by roads,
narrow and twisting though they may be. Any selection of
sights must surely include (in the form of a hook northwards
from Windermere) **Ullswater**, with the finest scenery in all
Lakeland and reached across the steep **Kirkstone Pass**;
Castlerigg Stone Circle; **Derwent Water** where green fells,
brown crags and patterned woods combine with several islets to
produce what many consider to be the most harmonious of the
lakes; and, beyond, incomparable **Borrowdale**, from which the
western escape is the precipitous **Honister Pass** preceding the
drop to serene **Buttermere** and **Crummock Water**, one
following the other and together filling a long trench of a valley.
Nor should one other lake be forgotten, **Wastwater** to the sw, a
black and forbidding place below high screes and massed
mountains.

There are boat services or excursions on virtually all the
major lakes, and to get out onto the water is undoubtedly the
best and also the most tranquil way of becoming one with the
scenery. (See *Sports and activities*, *Steam Yacht Gondola*
and *Fell Foot Park*, below.)

Event In late Aug, Grasmere Sports. Wrestling, fell runs,
hound trials, on sports field in the village.

Sights and places of interest

Brantwood
Map 14D6. E side of Coniston Water ☎ *(09664) 396* 🖾 🚗 *Open
Easter–Oct 11am–5.30pm. Closed Sat.*
Writer, artist and art critic John Ruskin bought this house in 1871 and
lived here more or less permanently from 1884 until his death in 1900.
Brantwood offers Ruskiniana and several pictures (and a particularly
good nature trail), but more about his life and work may be discovered at
the **Ruskin Museum** (*Coniston Village* ☎ *(09664) 359* 🖾 *Open
Easter–Oct 10am–sunset*). He was buried in **Coniston churchyard**.

Brockhole Lake District National Park Visitor Centre ☆
Map 14D6. Just N of Windermere ☎ *(09662) 2231* 🖾 🖳 🚗 *Open
late Mar–early Nov from 10am. Closing times vary.*
An audio-visual presentation entitled *Living Lakeland*, theme
exhibitions and a program of talks on flora and fauna, geology or even the
Lakeland poets, explain what the Lake District is all about. This
beautifully sited estate also offers lakeside walks, a picnic area, boat
trips, a shop, and a program of special events.

Castlerigg Stone Circle ☆
Map 14D6. 2 miles (3km) E of Keswick. NT 🗔 ⟨⟨ *Always open.*
Even though no lake can be seen, this high, green downland plateau
encircled by mountains provides one of the most splendid yet easily
accessible viewpoints in the Lake District. Bronze Age man may or may
not have appreciated views, but nevertheless it can surely only have been
some sense of awe that drove him to choose this windswept platform as a
place of ritual.

Dove Cottage and Wordsworth Museum
Map 14D6. Grasmere ☎ *(09665) 464* 🖾 *Open Mar Mon–Sat
10am–4.30pm (closed Sun); Apr–Sept Mon–Sat 9.30am–5.30pm,
Sun 11am–5.30pm; Oct Mon–Sat 10am–4.30pm, Sun
1.30–5.30pm.*
The poet William Wordsworth wrote much of his best work during the
years he lived in this cottage (1799–1808). The adjacent museum, with

manuscripts, first editions and other memorabilia, has been much brightened by portraits of members of the Wordsworth coterie on loan from the National Portrait Gallery, London.

Fell Foot Park
Map 14E6. At s end of Windermere ☎ *(0448) 31273. NT* 🏛 🍴 🚗 *Park always open. Information Centre and boat rental Easter–Oct.*

A place for picnics, safe swimming, fishing and boating; both rowing and sailing craft can be rented here.

Furness Abbey
Map 14E6. 1½ miles (2.5km) NE of Barrow-in-Furness ☎ *(0229) 23420. DOE* 🏛 🚗 *Open mid-Mar to mid-Oct Mon–Sat 9.30am–6.30pm, Sun 2–6.30pm; mid-Oct to mid-Mar Mon–Sat 9.30am–4pm, Sun 2–4pm.*

Now a red-sandstone ruin, this Cistercian abbey, founded in 1124, was once one of the most powerful in the N of England, its abbot exercising wide secular powers. Although little survives from Norman times, the Early English work makes a visit worthwhile.

Holker Hall
Map 14E6. Cark-in-Cartmel, between Windermere and Grange-over-Sands ☎ *(044853) 328* 🏛 🍴 ✳ 🚗 *Open Easter–Sept 10am–6pm. Hall closed Sat.*

This rambling 16th and 19thC hall, justly renowned for its woodcarving, offers an exceptional range of attractions. Best known are the **Lakeland Motor Museum** and the hot-air ballooning demonstrations, but there are also, for example, a craft exhibition, a countryside museum, an aquarium, a model railway, a children's farm and adventure playground and, on most weekends, special events.

Lakeside and Haverthwaite Railway
Map 14E6. Haverthwaite, 3 miles (5km) s of s end of Windermere ☎ *(0448) 31594* 🏛 🍴 ✳ 🚗 *at both ends. Service operates Easter, May–Sept approximately 10.30am–6pm.*

The track-length is only 3½ miles (6km), but it is a scenic journey along the river Leven, usually on a steam train. Buy one-way or round-trip tickets, or take an excursion connecting with a Sealink Windermere steamer. At **Haverthwaite** there is an exhibition of locomotives.

Levens Hall 🏛
Map 14E6. 5 miles (8km) s of Kendal ☎ *(0448) 60321* 🏛 🍴 🚗 *House open Easter–Sept 11am–5pm (Steam Collection 2–5pm). Closed Mon except bank holidays, Fri, Sat. Topiary gardens open daily.*

The house, a 13thC pele-tower developed into a gracious home mainly in the 16th–17thC, has a truly sumptuous interior, but it is the gardens with their superb **topiary** ☆ that have drawn tourists ever since they were first laid out in 1690. The virtually untouched design incorporates yew and box hedges clipped into the shape of chess pieces, birds and even a coach and horses.

The **Steam Collection** of models and full-size engines (*rides available*) traces the growth of industrial steam power from around 1820–1920.

Ravenglass and Eskdale Railway
Map 14D5. Ravenglass, on the coast 17 miles (27km) s of Whitehaven ☎ *(06577) 226* 🏛 ✳ 🚗 *at both ends. Trains run Jan–Oct, most frequent service mid-July to early Sept 7.45am–6.40pm. Telephone for exact times.*

England's oldest narrow-gauge line was opened in 1875 to carry iron ore and now enables railway enthusiasts and those who simply enjoy a ride (usually on a steam train) to travel the 7 beautiful miles (11km) between Ravenglass and Eskdale. At the former, a small **museum** tells the story of the line.

Steam Yacht Gondola
Map 14D6. Jetties at Coniston and Park-a-Moor ☎ *(0448) 31539. NT/Sealink* 🏛 *Services Easter–Oct with frequent trips in high summer. No service on Sat.*

The steam-propelled *Gondola* was launched in 1859. Long derelict, she has now been restored so that once again Lake Coniston can be cruised in Victorian confidence and splendor.

Windermere Steamboat Museum
Map 14D6. Rayrigg Rd., Windermere ☎ *(09662) 5565* 🏛 🍴 ✳ 🚗 *Open Easter–Oct Mon–Sat 10am–5pm, Sun 2–5pm.*

Steamboats and other craft of the past, mostly associated with

Windermere and of stylish Victorian or Edwardian vintage, are shown here in a setting that is as lovely as it is appropriate. The oldest craft is the *Dolly, c.*1850; the *Esperance* (1869) claims to be the oldest boat on Lloyd's Register of Yachts; and a hydroplane speedboat represents modern times. Lake trips are usually available.

Wordsworth House

Map **14D6**. Main St., Cockermouth ☎ *(0900) 824805.* NT 🔲 💷
Open Apr–Oct Mon–Wed, Fri–Sat 11am–5pm, Sun 2–5pm.
William Wordsworth was born here in 1770. The house, furnished in 18thC style, has mementoes of the poet and his sister Dorothy, and there is an audio-visual display in the old stables.

Hotels and restaurants
Ambleside (*5 miles/8km* NW *of Windermere*).

H R **Rothay Manor** 🏰
Rothay Bridge, Ambleside, Cumbria LA22 0EH ☎ *(09663) 3605*
Ⓣ *65294* 🏷 🚐 12 🛏 12 🚗 🏠 🚉 AE Ⓥ *Closed last three weeks in Jan.*
R 🏷 🍽 🍴 🍽 Ⅲ *Last orders 9pm.*
Location: Just w *of Ambleside on A593.* A Regency house built on secluded grounds near Lake Windermere for a wealthy Liverpool merchant. Today it is a notably friendly, family-run hotel seeking to provide rather grand country house hospitality with a Georgian flavor. After taking one of the hotel's nature rambles, walking on the fells, riding, rowing or fishing, guests are no doubt ready for the traditional roasts or game dishes in which the Manor specializes. Rothay has Dickensian evenings, gourmet weekends and wine-tastings.
🖼 🔲 🗺 🌜 🎿

Grasmere (*3 miles/5km* NW *of Ambleside*).

H R **White Moss House**
Rydal Water, Grasmere, Cumbria LA22 9SE ☎ *(09665) 295* 🏷
🚐 7 🛏 7 🚗 🏠 🚉 🍽 *Closed early Nov to mid-Mar.*
R 🏷 🍽 🍴 *Last orders 8pm.*
Location: On Rydal Water, 1 mile (1.5km) s *of Grasmere on A591.* White Moss offers an unpretentious style of English country living. The genuinely English kitchen has won a widespread reputation for its roasts, its imaginative vegetable combinations and its puddings. Pride is taken in the English cheeses, and a good wine list emphasizes Bordeaux.
🖼 🍴 🌜 🎿 ✸ 🌂 🍾

On **Ullswater** (*7 miles/11km* SW *of Penrith*).

H R **Sharrow Bay** 🏰 ⛴
Ullswater, Penrith, Cumbria CA10 2LZ ☎ *(08536) 301* 🏷 🚐 29
🛏 21 🏠 🚉 🍽 *Closed early Dec to early Mar.*
R 🏷 🍽 🍴 *Last orders 8.30pm.*
Location: Overlooking Ullswater, 2 miles (3km) s *of Pooley Bridge.* The birthplace of the country house hotel movement at the beginning of the 1950s, Sharrow Bay remains under the same ownership and is still a leader. Having been pathfinders for French regional cuisine in Britain, Francis Coulson and Brian Sack are now among the leaders of a gentle move toward what might be termed the new English kitchen. The famous list of 20 starters at dinner still includes plenty of Gallic-sounding dishes but the rest of the five-course meal begins to sound progressively Franco-English, with river Eden salmon in sorrel sauce; English lamb on a bed of root vegetables, with rosemary, served with an onion sauce tartlet; or roast grouse on a bed of celery and apples; not to mention the celebrated syllabub. It all makes for a tightly-scheduled meal, in a cramped dining room, which is no doubt the price of popularity.
   The little house by the lake, with Italianate architecture to match a stunning view over the mountains, has long been too small to accommodate all of the guests, but other rooms are available in various buildings on the grounds.
🖼 🖻 🔲 🗺 🍴 🌜 🎿 🍾

Windermere (*9 miles/14.5km NW of Kendal*).

⬛Ⓗ ⬛Ⓡ **Miller Howe** 🏨 ⬒
Rayrigg Rd., Windermere, Cumbria LA23 1EY ☎ *(09662) 2536* ▐▌▐▌
🛏 *13* 🛏 *13* 🍽 ➡ 🛋 ➡🚗 ⒶⒺ Ⓒ *Closed mid-Dec to early Mar.*
⬛Ⓡ ▐▌▐▌ 🍽 ➡ *Dinner at 8.30pm (Sat 9.30pm). Closed lunch.*
Location: On A592 just w of Windermere. One-time actor John Tovey
brought a startling theatricality to serious English dining when he
opened Miller Howe in 1970 and in spite of many raised eyebrows in the
kitchens of the land, he has since earned a national reputation.

Tovey's creations are served in a five-course dinner, with no choice
except for the dazzling selection of desserts. The menu, which changes
daily, is presented on a strict schedule, with carefully chosen music and
dimmed lighting. Typical among the dishes offered are pea, pear and
watercress soup; roast sirloin of beef served with blackcurrant and
beetroot jelly and mustard pudding; kiwi and passion fruit mousse. The
personal tastes of the proprietor are further presented in an extensive
wine list.

The well-equipped, richly furnished rooms have spectacular views.
▨ 🌱 🍷

Witherslack (*5 miles/8km NE of Grange-over-Sands*).

⬛Ⓗ ⬛Ⓡ **The Old Vicarage**
Church Rd., Witherslack, Grange-over-Sands, Cumbria LA11 6RS
☎ *(044852) 381* ▢ 🛏 6 🛏 6 ➡ 🛋 ➡🚗 ⒶⒺ Ⓒ Ⓥ🅸🆂🅰 *Closed*
Christmas week.
⬛Ⓡ ▐▌▐▌ 🍽 *Last orders 8pm.*
Location: On edge of village. Set in 7 acres of woodland, The Old Vicarage
is quiet and secluded. The two families who jointly run the hotel provide
a friendly welcome and some enjoyable local touches such as
Cumberland sausage for breakfast. An even more esoteric specialty is
sometimes available at dinner, as a starter: a dish featuring fluke, the
small, tasty plaice-like fish which are caught in Morecambe Bay. Great
emphasis is placed on fresh foods.
▨ ▢ 🍴 🌱 🍷 ♫ ✓ 🐴 🍷

Shopping
Within the heart of the Lake District the three centres are **Windermere**,
Ambleside and **Keswick**, all of which offer opportunities for buying
locally made mintcake, knitwear and sheepskin goods.

Sports and activities
Boating   Rowboats, sailing dinghies and low-powered motorboats can
be rented on Lake Windermere, Ullswater, Coniston Water and
Derwent Water.
Camping   A useful and inexpensive publication, *Sites for Caravans and
Tents in Cumbria*, is available from information centers. The **Caravan
Advisory Service** (☎ *(09662) 5555*) operates Easter–Sept.
Fishing   A North West Water Authority License is needed for all
fishing and in many cases a permit is also needed; both are available from
tackle shops and information centers. A useful publication, *Fishing*, is
available from information centers.
Riding   *Riding and Pony Trekking*, available from information centers,
lists places offering reliable fell ponies.
Walking   Guided walks depart from Ambleside, Bowness Bay,
Buttermere, Coniston, Grasmere, Hawkshead, Keswick, Pooley Bridge,
Ravenglass, Seatoller, Skelwith Bridge and Ullswater; inexpensive
publications with maps are also available. Walkers are advised to wear
boots or thick shoes and windproof clothing (☎ *(09662) 5151 for
weather information for walkers*).

Lancaster
Map 14E6. Lancs. 50 miles (80km) N of Liverpool.
Population: 50,000 𝒊 *7 Dalton Sq.* ☎ *(0524) 32878.*
Although Lancaster is of Roman and Norman origin, little
survives of its early days, except some minor earthworks to the NW

of the castle and the castle's keep. The town's main attractions
are its 17th-19thC buildings, including Georgian houses in
Castle Park and **Castle Hill**, the **Old Customs House** (1764)
beside the river, and, near the post office, **Penny's Hospital**
almshouse (1720).

Sights and places of interest

Judges' Lodgings
Church St. ☎ *(0524) 32808* 🖼 *Open Apr, Oct Mon–Fri 2–5pm;*
May–June Mon–Sat 2–5pm; July–Sept Mon–Fri 10am–1pm,
2–5pm, Sat 2–5pm.

Built in 1662 as a private home and then from 1826 what its name
implies, this dignified house which claims to be the oldest in Lancaster
now contains a **Museum of Childhood** which includes a collection of
dolls. Furniture, notably that of Gillow of Lancaster, is also shown.

Lancaster Castle
Between the inner town and the station ☎ *(0524) 64998* 🖼 🗽
🚶 *Open Easter–Sept Mon–Sat 10.30am–4pm when courts are not*
in session, and sometimes when they are.

There are, it must be admitted, more cheerful places to visit. A Roman
fortification here was followed by an early Norman keep (much restored
in the late 16thC), but because today's complex is still used as law courts
and a prison, only parts are open to the public. The tour, which is
shortened if the courts are in session, includes the **dungeons**, virtually
without light or ventilation; the 18thC **Crown Court** which claims the
macabre distinction of having been the scene of more death sentences
than any other court in England; and, alongside **Hanging Corner**, the
Drop Room, in which the condemned wretch was finally bound. Also
shown are the splendid **Shire Hall** (1798) and **Hadrian's Tower**, built
*c.*1200 and with nothing whatsoever to do with Hadrian beyond the fact
that he was emperor when the Romans first settled here and that some of
their masonry is probably incorporated in the tower.

Sight nearby

Steamtown Railway Museum
Warton Rd., Carnforth, 5 miles (8km) N *of Lancaster* ☎ *(052473)*
4220 🖼 🍴 🚶 🚗 *Open 9am–5pm. Steam operations Easter–May,*
Sept–Oct Sun; June Sat, Sun; July and Aug daily. Also bank holidays.
The *Flying Scotsman* is indisputably the most distinguished of around 30
great locomotives which have a permanent home in this former railway
depot. There is much else to see too (workshops, coaling tower, signal
box) and on steam days there are rides in vintage coaches.

Shopping

Market St., **Penny St.** and **Cheapside** form the central shopping area.
Crafts made by local artists are available from **Down to Earth Galleries**
(*9a King St.*), and **Hornsea Pottery** (*Wyresdale Rd*) has a factory shop.

Leeds

*Map 11F8. West Yorks. Central England between Hull (*E*)*
*and Manchester (*w*). Population: 496,000. Airport* ☎ *(0532)*
508194; railway station ☎ *(0532) 448133; coach station*
☎ *(0532) 460011; bus station* ☎ *(0532) 451601* i *Central*
Library, Calverley St. ☎ *(0532) 462454.*

This large, lively, industrial and commercial center would
never claim to be a tourist magnet, yet it offers excellent
opportunities for shopping and entertainment, a renowned art
gallery, a superb ruined abbey, one of the country's most
imaginative folk museums and an imposing 19thC Town Hall.

Sights and places of interest

Abbey House Museum ☆
Abbey Rd., Kirkstall, w *of center* ☎ *(0532) 755821* 🖼 🍴 🚶 🚗
Open Apr–Sept Mon–Sat 10am–6pm, Sun 2–6pm; Oct–Mar
Mon–Sat 10am–5pm, Sun 2–5pm.

While the most popular feature of the museum is the rebuilt 18th and
19thC streets with their inn, shops and cottages, there is much else

including collections of costumes and toys (both spanning the mid-18thC to the present day) and the Folk Galleries, which vividly illustrate how 18th and 19thC families cooked, washed, lit their homes and kept warm.
City Art Gallery
1 The Headrow ☎ *(0532) 462495* 🔲 *Open Mon–Fri 10am–6pm, Sat 10am–4pm, Sun 2–5pm.*

Recently given major refurbishment, an important part of which was the **Moore Sculpture Gallery** (20thC sculpture, including works by Henry Moore), the Art Gallery shows distinguished collections spanning from Old Masters to modern works including one of the country's leading collections of English watercolors.
Kirkstall Abbey ☆
Abbey Rd., Kirkstall, w of center ☎ *(0532) 755821* 🔲 *Open 9am until sunset.*

Leeds owes much to the monks of this abbey (founded 1152), for it was their astute trade in wool that ensured the growth and prosperity of the surrounding district and settlements. After *Fountains Abbey*, the ruins are the finest preserved Cistercian example in Yorkshire, if not in England, and include the almost intact **chapter house**, the great **church**, the **cloisters**, and the **abbot's lodging**.
Leeds Industrial Museum
Armley Mills Canal Rd., Armley ☎ *(0532) 637861* 🚻 🅿 🚗 *Open Apr–Sept Tues–Sat 10am–6pm, Sun 2–6pm; Oct–Mar Tues–Sat 10am–5pm, Sun 2–5pm. Closed Mon.*

In what was once the world's largest woolen mill, exhibits bring to life the city's industrial past and include a working water wheel, engines, and textile, clothing and printing machinery.

Sights nearby
Harewood House
6 miles (9.5km) N of Leeds ☎ *(0532) 886225* 🚻 🅿 ⚱ 🚗 ⇌ *Open Apr–Oct; Feb–Mar, Nov Tues–Thurs, Sun (closed Mon, Fri, Sat): gates open 10am, house opens 11am. Closing times vary.*

Designed by John Carr and Robert Adam, this grand 18thC house with its sumptuous interior contains collections of porcelain, Chippendale furniture, many portraits, and English and Italian paintings.

The park was laid out by Capability Brown. Imaginatively set above the lake, the **Bird Garden** ☆ has nearly 200 exotic species, and now includes small mammals and even some reptiles. There is also an **adventure playground**.
Nostell Priory ☆
N side of A638, 12 miles (19km) SE of Leeds ☎ *(0924) 863892. NT* 🚻 🅵🅵 🅿 🚗 *Open Apr–June, Oct Thurs, Sat, Sun noon–6pm; July–Sept noon–6pm (closed Fri); bank holiday Sun, Mon, Tues 11am–6pm.*

Here is a connoisseur's gem, an 18thC house by James Paine and Robert Adam with an interior that combines the former's Rococo with the latter's calmer elegance. But the highlight of Nostell is its furniture, for here Chippendale, sometimes working to designs by Adam, can be seen at his best. A Palladian dollhouse may even be one of his earliest works.

There are also **museums of motorcycling and aviation** in the park.
Temple Newsam House and Park
5 miles (8km) E of Leeds ☎ *(0532) 647321* 🚻 🅿 🚗 *Open 10.30am–6.15pm or sunset (Wed July–Aug open until 8.30pm). Closed Mon except bank holidays.*

The historical interest of Temple Newsam is that this was the birthplace in 1545 of that sorry figure Lord Darnley, second husband of Mary, Queen of Scots; but not in this house, which was built nearly a century later and given its Georgian decoration in the 18thC. Now owned by the municipality of Leeds, the house shows good collections of furniture, applied art and pictures, while the park and gardens are much visited.

Hotels

🅷 **Ladbroke Dragonara** (*Neville St., Leeds, West Yorks LS1 4BX* ☎ *(0532) 442000* 🕿 *557143* 🏮); **Merrion** (*Merrion Centre, Leeds, West Yorks LS2 8NH* ☎ *(0532) 439191* 🕿 *55459* 🏮); **Metropole** (*King St., Leeds, West Yorks LS1 2HQ* ☎ *(0532) 450841* 🕿 *557755* 🏮); **Queen's** (*City Sq., Leeds, West Yorks LS1 1PL* ☎ *(0532) 431323* 🕿 *55161* 🏮).

Hotel and restaurants nearby
Halifax (*15 miles/24km SW of Leeds*).

Ⓗ Ⓡ **Holdsworth House**
Holmfield, Halifax, West Yorks HX2 9TQ ☎ *(0422) 244270* ▯▯ ⌖
30 ▭ 30 ⇔ ⇌ Ⓐ Ⓒ Ⓑ 🖰 🖰 ⅥⅤⅣ *Closed one week at Christmas.*
Ⓡ ▯▯▯▯ ⌷ ▅ ▬ *Last orders 10pm. Closed one week at Christmas,*
Sat lunch, Sun.
Location: Right off A629, 2 miles (3km) N of Halifax. At the point where
the outskirts of a Victorian industrial town billow up into the moorlands of
Brontë country, this is a delightful Elizabethan house in Yorkshire
stone, with lots of history, but with some hidden brusque extensions.
The hotel has an indifferent bar but a good wine list and a quietly
excellent kitchen. The food is French and the menu offers a good choice.
◻ ◩ ✈ ♨

Ripponden (*on A58, 21 miles/33km SW of Leeds*).

Ⓡ **Over the Bridge**
Millfold ☎ *(0422) 823722* ▯▯ ▬ ▬ ⇔ Ⓐ *Last orders 9.30pm.*
Closed Sun, bank holidays.
A good, sound restaurant offering a sensibly limited range of French
dishes. The kitchen has a light touch without being altogether *nouvelle*,
and the game is excellent – so are the sorbets and ices. Wines include a
good selection of Bordeaux from Loeb and an interesting range from
Germany, with further representation from Rioja.

Shopping
In the central area, **Briggate**, **The Headrow** and **Burton Arcade** leading
into the **Bond St. Centre** contain major department stores and chain
shops. In the **Victorian Arcades** (*on either side of Briggate*) there are small
shops such as jewelers and boutiques. Slightly N of the center is the
Merrion Centre which incorporates an attractive Georgian arcade and a
general market (*closed Sun*). **Kirkgate Market** (*off Kirkgate and New
Market St.; at its best on Tues, Fri, Sat*) has local produce, general goods
and new and secondhand clothes.

Nightlife
City Varieties (*The Headrow* ☎ *(0532) 430808*) is the oldest survivor of
that fast disappearing brand of entertainment, the English music hall.
The **Civic Theatre** (*Cookridge St.* ☎ *(0532) 453505*) presents amateur
productions by members of the Civic Arts Guild. The **Grand Theatre**
(*New Briggate* ☎ *(0532) 450891*) is the home of the Opera North
company. The **Leeds Playhouse** (*Calverley St.* ☎ *(0532) 442111*)
presents plays and musicals, and local repertory companies.

Leeds Castle ☆
Map 7L11. Kent. 5 miles (8km) SE of Maidstone ☎ *(0622)*
65400 ▦ �ⓟ ⇔ ⇌ *Open Apr–May noon–5pm (closed*
Mon); June–Sept noon–5pm; Oct–Mar Sat–Sun
noon–4pm.
A fairytale castle straddling two small islands in a beautifully
located lake, its story and name reach back some 1,100yrs to a
shadowy character called Led, chief adviser in 857 to the king of
Kent. Led's castle would have been a modest affair of wood, and
it was not until 1119 that a stone Norman castle arose here, soon
to become a royal residence and to remain such until the reign of
Henry VIII, the last royal owner and the one who transformed
an uncomfortable fortress into a sumptuous palace. Later Leeds
was owned by Lord Culpeper, governor of Virginia (1680–83).

There is much to enjoy here: inside the castle a Norman
cellar, Henry VIII's Banqueting Hall and, by contrast, a gallery
of Impressionist paintings; in the park peacocks, an exotic
aviary, a collection of rare waterbirds and a huge free picnic area.

An excellent way of seeing the castle is to go on a day trip from
London on the Orient Express (☎ *(01) 928-5837*).

Leicester

Map 11H9. Leics. 22 miles (35km) NE of Coventry.
Population: 284,000. Railway station ☎ (0533) 29811; bus
and coach station ☎ (0533) 29161 ⓘ 12 Bishop St. ☎ (0533)
556699.

A bustling, industrial city of Roman origin, Leicester offers a
quite remarkable choice of museums, all of unusual interest, all
free, and the majority in a compact group at the city center.

Sights and places of interest

Leicester Cathedral †
Just E of St Nicholas Circle ☎ (0533) 25294.
Although extensively rebuilt in the 19thC, this cathedral retains its
medieval core. The twin S aisles are the most interesting aspect of the
interior; note the grotesques in the roof of the outer aisle. The cathedral
stands on a site believed to have been occupied by a Roman temple.

Leicester's museums
🖭 *Open Mon–Thurs, Sat 10am–5.30pm, Sun 2–5.30pm. Closed*
Fri.

Belgrave Hall (*Church Rd., on N outskirts* ☎ *(0533) 666590*) offers
Georgian furnishings, coaches and agricultural implements in the
stables, and period gardens.

    City Museum and Art Gallery (*New Walk* ☎ *(0533) 554100*) has
extensive collections including displays of natural history and ancient
Egyptian material and a spectacular geological display, as well as English
Victorian paintings (George Morland, Frederic Leighton, G.F. Watts),
20thC English paintings (Laura Knight, Augustus John, Stanley
Spencer), and German Expressionism and Impressionism. Rodin,
Henry Moore and Epstein are among the sculptors represented.

    Guildhall Museum (*Guildhall Lane* ☎ *(0533) 554100*) has few
exhibits as such but should be visited as a fine old house. Dating in part
from the 14thC, it was Leicester's town hall from 1495–1876. The
principal rooms are the half-timbered **Great Hall**, the **library** (Leicester
was one of the first towns in England to provide a public library,
c.1633) and the 16thC **Refectory Hall**.

    Jewry Wall and Museum (*St Nicholas Circle* ☎ *(0533) 554100*) is the
most interesting corner in Leicester. The Roman wall, dating from
c.125–130, was possibly part of an exercise yard; there are also remains
of a bathhouse. Below ground both prehistoric and early Roman work
has been identified. Alongside, there is an outstanding museum of local
archeology spanning pre-Roman to medieval times. Murals and mosaics
are particularly well displayed together.

    Newarke Houses Museum (*The Newarke* ☎ *(0533) 554100*) records
the social history of the county. While the main feature is a mock-up of a
cobbled 19thC street, perhaps the most intriguing room displays
ingenious and colorful water-closets.

    Wygston's House Museum of Costume (*St Nicholas Circle* ☎ *(0533)*
554100) spans from the mid-18thC to 1925. There are also delightful
reconstructions of small shops of the 1920s, and the house itself is a
museum piece in its own right, with wattle and daub, late-medieval
construction exposed in an upstairs room.

🏨 **Holiday Inn** (*St Nicholas Circle, Leicester, Leics LE1 5LX* ☎ *(0533)*
531161 ☎ *341281* ▥) is convenient for the museums.

Nightlife
The **Haymarket Theatre** (*Belgrave Gate* ☎ *(0533) 539797*) presents
plays and musicals starring well-known names.

Shopping
Major stores can be found in the town center, in **High St.**, **Eastgates**,
Gallowtree Gate, **Humberstone Gate** and the adjacent **Haymarket
Centre**. Smaller and more specialized shops are in the streets and arcades
radiating from Market Pl. such as **Loseby Lane**, **St Martin's**, and **Silver
St.** which contains an attractive Victorian arcade with boutiques and gift
shops. General markets are held in **Market Pl.** (*main days Wed, Fri, Sat*)
and in the adjacent **Market Centre** (*closed Sun, Mon*).

Lewes

Map 6M10. East Sussex. 7 miles (11km) NE of Brighton.
Population: 14,000 **i** *32 High St.* ☎ *(07916) 71600.*

What is so pleasant about this attractive and conservative small
town clinging compactly to its spur of the Downs is that even
from the center several of the streets allow glimpses toward
open countryside. **Keere St.**, dropping s off High St., is the
most picturesque, with cobbles, flint houses and, at the foot,
something of the old walls.

The town's other attractions include the **castle** (*High St.,*
☎ *(07916) 4379* 🖼 *open Apr–Oct Mon–Sat 10am–5pm, Sun
2–5pm; Nov–Mar Mon–Sat 10am–5pm, closed Sun*), started in
1100 and built unusually on two mottes at either end of an oval
bailey; the **Barbican House Museum** (*entry details as castle*), its
well-arranged archeological displays and models spanning from
prehistoric to medieval times; the ruins of the **Priory of St
Pancras** (*s of the town, by the railway* 🖼 ⚓ *always open, access
from Mountfield Rd. s of the station*), once the most important
Cluniac house in Britain; and the **Anne of Cleves House
Museum** (*Southover High St.* ☎ *(07916) 4610* 🖼 *open mid-Feb
to Mar, Nov 10am–5pm, closed Sun; Apr–Oct Mon–Sat
10am–5pm, Sun 2–5pm; closed Dec to mid-Feb*) where exhibits
displayed in a charming, mainly late medieval and Elizabethan
building illustrate local history and custom.

Between 1768–74 Lewes was the home of Thomas Paine (he
lived at the Bull House in High St.) whose writings so
influenced the thinking behind the American Constitution.
Event Late May to mid-Aug, Glyndebourne Festival Opera.
(*For details* ☎ *(0273) 812321.*) International stars gather for a
short, prestigious season of operas held at the Glyndebourne
Opera House near the village of Glynde, 3 miles (5km) SE of
Lewes. Tickets sell out far in advance.

Sight nearby
Glynde Place
Glynde, 3 miles (5km) SE of Lewes ☎ *(079159) 337* 🖼 💺 ⚓
*Open 2.15–5.30pm : Easter Sun and Mon, bank holidays, mid-May to
mid-Oct Wed, Thurs.*

Dating from the 16thC, although with 18thC modifications, Glynde
Place is best known as the home of Rubens' original cartoon for the
ceiling of the Banqueting House in Whitehall (see *Sights* in *London*).
There are also portraits by such artists as Hoppner, Lely and Zoffany.

H **White Hart**
55 High St., Lewes, East Sussex BN7 1XE ☎ *(07916) 4676* ▯
🖚 *32* 🖾 *21* ⚓ ⇌ *AE* ⓘ ⓓ *VISA*
Location: Opposite the castle approach. Panelling and beams confirm the
age of this inn, built partly in the 16thC and licensed in the 18thC. It was
here that Thomas Paine expounded his views to the Headstrong Club.
♿ ▢ 🖾 🖾

R **Kenwards**
Pipe Passage, 151a High St. ☎ *(07916) 2343* ▯▯ ▭ 🖚 ⇌ 🖙
*Last orders 10.30pm. Closed Sun, Mon, late July, early Nov, for one
week at Christmas.*

Kenwards specializes in local produce: fish from the nearby coast; meat
from local farms; and Sussex game. Vegetables and herbs are bought
from nearby smallholders, and also come from the restaurant's own
garden. The Kenwards cook with a light touch, and use English drinks
such as cider in the sauces. They have a well-chosen wine list.

Shopping
The antique shops and antiquarian bookshops on **High St.** and the
antique market on **Cliffe High St.** are well known. **Clothkits** (*24 High
St.*) sells ready-to-sew garments for adults and children.

Lichfield

Map 11H8. Staffs. 16 miles (26km) N of Birmingham.
Population: 22,700 i 9 Breadmarket St. ☎ *(05432) 52109.*
Some come to Lichfield to admire its unique triple-spired
red-sandstone cathedral; others to absorb something of the aura
of the house in which the wit, biographer and highly
idiosyncratic lexicographer Samuel Johnson lived for most of
his first three decades.

Sights and places of interest
Lichfield Cathedral ▥ †
200yds (60m) NW of the Market ☎ *(05432) 56120.*
Modest in size but rich in decoration, this cathedral (built in the 13th and
14thC in Early English and Decorated styles) is last in a succession of
churches which have sanctified this site since *c.*700. Features of the
exterior are the **three spires** – the 'Ladies of the Vale' – and the carved W
front, a modern but admirable copy of its medieval predecessor.

Inside, Lichfield's most respected citizens, Johnson and the actor
David Garrick, are commemorated by busts by Westmacott. The real
glory of the cathedral, however, is its **Lady Chapel** ▨ of which the
windows include splendid 16thC glass from the Belgian Cistercian
convent of Herkenrode which was disestablished by Napoleon in 1797.

Samuel Johnson Birthplace Museum
Breadmarket St. ☎ *(05432) 24972* ▨ *Open May–Sept Mon–Sat*
10am–5pm, Sun 2.30–5pm; Oct–Apr Mon–Sat 10am–4pm (closed
Sun).

Johnson observed that every man had a 'lurking wish to appear
considerable in his native place,' and were he to return to Lichfield today
he would surely be pleased to find his bust in the cathedral, his statue in
the Market, and the house in which he was born in 1709 welcoming
visitors from all over the world. The museum contains a library of
Johnsonian books and manuscripts as well as many personal relics.

Ⓗ **Angel Croft**
Beacon St., Lichfield, Staffs WS13 7AA ☎ *(05432) 23147* ▯
▱ *12* ▭ *5* ▰ ⥈ ⓪ ⑩ ⱱⁱˢᵃ *Closed Christmas.*
Location: Just SW of the cathedral. A friendly, unassuming family-run
hotel, very convenient to the cathedral.
▰ ⤋

Ⓗ **Swan**
Bird St., Lichfield, Staffs WS13 6PW ☎ *(05432) 55851* ▯ ▱ *32*
▭ *32* ▰ ▱ ⥈ ⒶⒺ ⓪ ⑩ ⱱⁱˢᵃ
Location: On W side of main N–S through-road. This one-time coaching inn
dates back to the 16thC and is the oldest inn of its kind in the city.
▯ ▱ ▰ ⤋

Shopping
Market St. and **Bakers Lane** (both for pedestrians), **Bird St.** and **Bore**
St. contain the major, nationally-known shops as well as smaller shops.
The continuation of Bore St., **Tamworth St.**, contains several antique
shops. **Tudor Row**, an attractive precinct containing several small
boutiques, crafts and gift shops, backs on to the **Tudor Cafe**, known for
its chocolates. A general market is held in **Market Sq.** (*Fri, Sat*).

Lincoln

Map 12G9. Lincs. 35 miles (56km) NE of Nottingham.
Population: 74,000 i 9 Castle Hill ☎ *(0522) 29828.*
Massive, confident, superior physically and spiritually to the
lesser world below, the **cathedral** will always be Lincoln's
principal attraction. However, long before it was built,
Romans, Saxons, Danes and Normans had all forced their way
here and left their mark, and an excellent brochure, *Lincoln's*
Heritage – A Pictorial Guide (available from the tourist office),

outlines three walks which guide the visitor to the many fascinating places that reflect the city's history. From Roman times there are lengths of wall, the **West Gate** and the remains of the **East Gate**, and the **Newport Arch** of the 2ndC; from Saxon times the distinctive towers of churches such as **St Mary-le-Wigford** and **St Peter-at-Gowts**; from the Danes, street names rather than buildings, the suffix 'gate' being Scandinavian for 'street'; from the Normans the keep of the **castle** (now mainly appealing to those with an interest in the more unpleasant aspects of Victorian penology), and some ancient houses, notably the early 12thC **Jew's House**, a rare example of Norman domestic architecture; and from Lincoln's medieval inhabitants a rich legacy of timber-framed buildings.

To fill out the picture, the **City and County Museum** (*Broadgate* ☎ *(0522) 30401* ⬛ *open Mon–Sat 10am–5.30pm, Sun 2–5pm*) has displays on local archeology, history and natural history and also a notable oak-barrel roof in the upper room; the **Museum of Lincolnshire Life** (*Old Barracks, Burton Rd.* ☎ *(0522) 28448* ⬛ ▣ ⬛ *open Mon–Sat 10am–5.30pm, Sun 2–5pm*) covers late medieval to comparatively modern times; and the **Usher Gallery** (*Lindum Rd.* ☎ *(0522) 27980* ⬛ *open Mon–Sat 10am–5.30pm, Sun 2–5pm*) is best known for its collection of pictures by Peter de Wint (1784–1849), who specialized in English landscapes, especially those of the fenland around Lincoln. The gallery also has a **Tennyson Room** (the poet was born at nearby Somersby).

Lincoln Cathedral 🏛 ✝ ★
Upper city ☎ *(0522) 30320.*
Lincoln's cathedral with its three great towers, once graced with three daring needle spires, completes its hill, a landmark of reassurance to centuries of travelers.

From the outside it is the w front that demands particular attention, for its central portion represents the only significant survival of the original late 11thC cathedral, wrecked by an earth tremor in 1185 (rebuilding continued into the early 14thC).

Inside, the visitor is offered detail rather than vista. Architecturally the undoubted pride of the cathedral is the mid-13thC, Gothic Decorated **Angel Choir** (E end) with its 30 carved angels. Here perches the famous **Lincoln Imp**, a small devil who, trapped like a bird, made such a fuss that the exasperated angels turned him to stone when he alighted near the top of the last complete pier on the N side. In the main choir, the **misericords** on the 14thC canopied stalls are among the most varied and fascinating in England. Historically, though, it is the **Chapter House** – a striking decagonal building in which a single central column splays into vaulting – that has most to say, for in the reigns of the first two Edwards parliament frequently conferred here, the kings presiding from the throne which is still in situ.

The **Cathedral Library** (*by appointment*) contains medieval manuscripts, early printed books and a copy of the Magna Carta.

Ⓗ **Eastgate Post House**
Eastgate, Lincoln, Lincs LN2 1PN ☎ *(0522) 20341* ☏*56316* ▥▢
⬛ *71* ▭ *71* ⬛ ⇌ ⒶⒺ ⒸⒷ ⑥ ⓪ ⓋⒾⓈⒶ
Location: Just N of the cathedral. This comfortable hotel has a high-standard restaurant with views of the cathedral.
⬆ ⬡ ▢ ☑ ⬛ ⬛ ⬛

Ⓗ **Grand**
St Mary's St., Lincoln, Lincs LN5 7EP ☎ *(0522) 24211* ▥▢ ⬛ *50*
▭ *50* ⬛ ⬛ ⇌ ⑥ ⓪ ⓋⒾⓈⒶ
Location: A short way N of Central Station (lower city). A good, average hotel with rather small bedrooms. In addition to the restaurant there is a convenient coffee shop providing meals throughout most of the day.
▢ ▢ ⬛

129

H **White Hart**

Bailgate, Lincoln, Lincs LN1 3AR ☎ *(0522) 26222* ☏ *56304* ⅠⅠ▯
⇌ 68 ⊟ 56 ▯ ▭ ⇌ AE CB ◑ ◔ VISA

Location: Immediately w of the cathedral. Age and elegance are the
keywords here. Age because the hotel was first mentioned as an inn in
1460 (and it may well be nearly a century older); elegance because today's
hotel prides itself on its warmth engendered by antique furniture and
fine materials.
≬ ▢ ⊡ ⚲ ☷

R **Whites** ⅢⅠⅠ

Jew's House, 15 The Strait ☎ *(0522) 24851* ⅠⅠ▯ ▭ ▰ ⇌ ⇌ AE
*Last orders 10pm. Closed Sun, Mon lunch, two weeks in July or Aug,
one week at Christmas.*

An unusual location and some imaginative dishes. The Jew's House was
already of considerable historical interest but, since it ceased to be an
antique shop and became a restaurant in 1979, it has also achieved
gastronomic renown. Owner-chef Colin White has worked in some of
Britain's best kitchens – including that at Sharrow Bay – and their
influence, inevitably underpinned by that of Elizabeth David,
contributes to a highly personal repertoire, which includes specialties
such as carrot soup flavored with orange juice; turbot baked in dry cider
with a *coulis* of fresh tomatoes and Dijon mustard; wild rabbit cooked in
red wine; and lemon custard in a biscuitcase with jelly. A good,
interesting wine list offers some excellent value

The restaurant is tiny but there are two rooms available for bed and
breakfast at a very reasonable price (▯).

Shopping

The top end of the **High St.**, from St Mary's St. upward, and **Stonebow**
running off the High St., contain the larger, nationally known shops.
More unusual shops can be found in the **Bailgate** area N of the cathedral.
Steep Hill linking the two areas contains several antique shops and the
Jew's House (*closed Sun, Mon*) which is now a **Regional Craft Centre**
selling locally-made crafts. The open-air market in **Cornhill** (*closed Wed
afternoon*) sells general goods and local produce, including fresh fish
which is sold from a barge on the river.

Liverpool

*Map 10G6. Merseyside. On the NW coast, 30 miles (48km)
w of Manchester. Population: 610,000. Speke airport*
☎ *(051) 427–4101; railway station* ☎ *(051) 709–9696;
coach station ☎ *(051) 709–6481; bus station* ☎ *(051)
227–5181; ferries and river cruises* ☎ *(051) 630–1030* i *St
George's Hotel, Lime St.* ☎ *(051) 709–3631.*

This great city and port – vibrant, restless, intensely individual
and above all flaunting a solid-based self-confidence – is the
heart of the whole industrial complex of Merseyside. It is
renowned worldwide for soccer players, comedians and pop
stars; and if, by building a castle, King John put Liverpool on
the map in 1207, the Beatles and the 'Liverpool sound' certainly
kept it there in more recent times. But the city is also known for
its two controversial cathedrals, its imposing civic and
commercial buildings, such as the immense classical **St
George's Hall** ✩ built in 1854, and its distinguished art
galleries and orchestra.

For the tourist, the city may be said to have three centers:
Lime St. (for the tourist office, St George's, the County
Museums and Walker Art Gallery); **St James Mount** and
Mount Pleasant (linked by Hope St.) with **Brownlow Hill**
beyond (for the cathedrals and the university art gallery); and
the **waterfront** which, with its ferries and widely recognized
large buildings such as the Royal Liver (1910), is for many the
most typical and interesting quarter of the city.

Sights and places of interest

Cavern Mecca
18 Mathew St. ☎ *(051) 227–1026* 🔲 🖵 *Open 10am–5.30pm.
Closed Sun, Mon.*
In a reconstruction of the original Cavern Club, where the Beatles were
first discovered, a museum displays original memorabilia including such
diverse items as stockings, wallpaper and huge heads of the Beatles. Fans
come from all over the world to buy souvenirs.

County Museums
William Brown St. ☎ *(051) 207–0001* 🔲 🖵 *Open Mon–Sat
10am–5pm, Sun 2–5pm.*
A whole bemusing day could be spent in these widely instructive halls.
The fields covered include an aquarium and vivarium; Merseyside's
transportation, with some strange and nostalgic vehicles; the story of the
port of Liverpool told from its social, technical and commercial aspects;
antiquities – Egyptian, classical, African and local – including some
remarkable Anglo-Saxon jewelry and English silver; ethnography; the
history of ships; world natural history; and space and time, with a
planetarium (🔲 *closed Mon*).

Liverpool Anglican Cathedral †
St James Mount ☎ *(051) 709–6271.*
Started in 1904 but not completed until 1978, this Neo-Gothic red-
sandstone mass designed by Giles Gilbert Scott is the largest Anglican
cathedral in the world. Heavy and almost oppressive, the place conveys a
message of established wealth rather than one of soaring spiritual uplift.
Yet its sheer size is certainly impressive both from the outside and within
where it is impossible not to feel puny below the huge central tower.

Liverpool Roman Catholic Cathedral †
Mount Pleasant ☎ *(051) 709–9222.*
Linked by Hope St. to the Anglican Cathedral, this cone crowned by a
glass-panelled cylinder extended by a ring of spikes has an originality
which externally is challenging and internally provides a temple bathed
in ever-changing hues diffused through stained glass of daring color and
design. The central altar as the hub of a circular nave is a further and
successful escape from convention.

Designed by Frederick Gibberd, with stained glass by John Piper and
Patrick Reyntiens, the cathedral was built in 1962–67, an earlier design
by Lutyens having been abandoned when only the **crypt** had been built.

Merseyside Maritime Museum
Pier Head ☎ *(051) 236–1492* 🔲 🖵 🚢 *Open late May–Oct
10.30am–5.30pm.*
A new museum still being developed in the old Pilotage building and
around the restored 19thC quays. A quayside trail may be followed;
maritime skills are demonstrated; all sorts of craft are on view, some in
the **Boat Hall**, some afloat; displays explain modern activities along
today's river; and there is a program of demonstrations – for example,
cargo handling with steam machinery, sail making, coopering and even
chantey singing.

University of Liverpool Art Gallery
3 Abercromby Sq. ☎ *(051) 709–6022* 🔲 *Open Wed, Fri
noon–4pm.*
The university owns notable collections of fine and decorative art
including works by Turner and Audubon.

Walker Art Gallery ☆
William Brown St. ☎ *(051) 227–5234* 🔲 *Open Mon–Sat
10am–5pm, Sun 2–5pm.*
One of the country's most distinguished galleries outside London, the
Walker is internationally known for its collections of Italian and
Netherlandish Old Masters including Spinello Aretino, Simone Martini,
Michelangelo, Rembrandt and Rubens, and British paintings spanning
the 16th–19thC. Burne-Jones, Kneller, Lely, Rossetti and Watts are just
a few of the artists represented here.

Sights nearby

Lady Lever Art Gallery ☆
Port Sunlight, s of the Mersey ☎ *(051) 645–3623* 🔲 🚢 *Open
Mon–Sat 10am–5pm, Sun 2–5pm.*
Although dedicated to his wife, this gem of a gallery represents the wide
but discriminating personal taste of the first Lord Leverhulme
(1851–1925), more widely known for his concern for those who worked

in his soap factory for whom he created **Port Sunlight Village**, a concept decades ahead of its time and worth a visit on its own account.

Leverhulme's art-collecting interest was almost entirely confined to British fine and decorative arts, the exception being Chinese ceramics from about 200BC to the 18thC. From the riches which this gallery offers only highlights can be picked out: for example, the paintings by Georgian and Victorian artists (Constable, Millais, Turner, Pre-Raphaelites), the **Wedgwood Collection** which includes plaques by Stubbs, and the series of beautifully decorated and furnished period rooms.

Speke Hall ☆
The Walk, 8 miles (13km) SE of the city center ☎ (051) 427–7231. NT 🔄 💷 🚌 *Open Apr–Sept Mon–Sat 10am–5pm, Sun and bank holidays 2–7pm; Oct–Mar Mon–Sat 10am–5pm, Sun 2–7pm.*
One of the most perfect and unaltered half-timbered houses in the country, dating from the 16thC and a miracle of survival in its setting of industrial buildings alongside Liverpool's airport. The ornate internal panelling and plasterwork, notably in the **Great Hall** and **Great Parlour**, are roughly contemporary. Priest-holes indicate the religious outlook of the Norris family who lived here in the first part of the 17thC.

Sudley Art Gallery
Mossley Hill Rd., 4 miles (6.5km) SE of the city center ☎ (051) 724–3245 🔄 🚻 *Open Mon–Sat 10am–5pm, Sun 2–5pm.*
Among the many painters represented in this collection of 18th–19thC British art are Gainsborough, Holman Hunt, Millais and Turner. The gallery is also used by the County Museum for temporary exhibitions.

Hotels

ℍ **Adelphi** (*Ranelagh Pl., Liverpool, Merseyside L3 5UL* ☎ (051) 709–7200 📞629644 📖); **Holiday Inn International** (*Paradise St., Liverpool, Merseyside L1 8JD* ☎ (051) 709–0181 📞627270 📖); **Lord Nelson** (*Lord Nelson St., Liverpool, Merseyside L3 5PD* ☎ (051) 709–4362 📖); **St George's** (*St John's Precinct, Lime St., Liverpool, Merseyside L1 1NQ* ☎ (051) 709–7090 📞627630📖).

Nightlife
Liverpool's main theaters are the **Empire** (*Lime St.* ☎ (051) 709–1555); **Everyman** (*Hope St.* ☎ (051) 709–4776); **Neptune** (*Hanover St.* ☎ (051) 709–7844); and the **Playhouse** (*Williamson Sq.* ☎ (051) 709–8363). The Royal Liverpool Philharmonic Orchestra can be heard regularly at **Philharmonic Hall** (*Hope St.* ☎ (051) 709–3789) and rock concerts are put on at the **Royal Court Theatre** (*Roe St.* ☎ (051) 709–4321).

Shopping
Most of Liverpool's department stores and chain shops are concentrated in one pedestrian area – **Church St.** and the surrounding roads. The **St John's Shopping Centre** contains smaller chain stores and incorporates a general market (*closed Sun*). **Bold St.**, running E from Church St., contains a few antique shops and leads into the **Chinese quarter** (*Berry St. and Nelson St.*) which has Chinese supermarkets, shops and restaurants.

The Lizard
Map 2N–O2. Cornwall. On the s coast, 24 miles (39km) E of St Michael's Mount.
The southernmost point of England, the Lizard peninsula comprises a background of moorland and downs edged by fine cliff scenery much of which is under the care of the National Trust. **Mullion Cove** and **Kynance Cove** are the Trust's star beauty spots, the latter known for its weird rock formations, sands and mottled-green serpentine cliffs. Other features of the Lizard are a satellite communications station on **Goonhilly Downs**, caves and a beautiful coastal path.

London

Map **6K10**. *SE England. Population: 7,452,300. Airports:
Heathrow* ☎ *(01) 759–4321, Gatwick* ☎ *(01) 668–4211.
Railway stations:* ☎ *(01) 928–5100 for Charing Cross,
Waterloo and Victoria serving s and SE England* ☎ *(01)
283–7171 for Liverpool Street serving East Anglia* ☎ *(01)
262–6767 for Paddington serving SW and W England and s
Wales* ☎ *(01) 387–7070 for Euston and St Pancras serving
the Midlands, NW England, N Wales and W Scotland* ☎ *(01)
278–2477 for King's Cross serving NE England and E
Scotland. Bus station: Victoria Coach Station* ☎ *(01)
730–0202. London Transport Information Centre, 55
Broadway, SW1* ☎ *(01) 222–1234* **i** *London Tourist Board,
26 Grosvenor Gdns., SW1* ☎ *(01) 730–0791 (multilingual
service). There are also information centers at Victoria
Station, Heathrow Central Station, and at Harrods and
Selfridges department stores. For consulates, emergency
and medical services see Useful addresses in Basic
information. American Express Travel Service, 6 Haymarket,
SW1* ☎ *(01) 930–4411.*

Born of and sustained by the river Thames, London has grown
from two ancient townships: the 2,000yr-old Roman city of
Londinium, which occupied the area now known as 'The City,'
and Westminster, which was founded by Edward the Confessor
in the mid-11thC. Modern London adds to these a patchwork of
different 'villages,' each with its individual atmosphere,
covering a huge area from Greenwich in the E to Richmond in
the W. Home of the British government and the Royal Family, a
major financial center and an important center for the arts,
London is unquestionably the dominant city of the British
Isles. Its eventful history greets the visitor in an almost
overwhelming panoply of sights including several major
cathedrals and some of the world's greatest museums.

The following sights, with brief descriptions, are the most
important for anyone making only a short visit to London. For
those fortunate enough to enjoy a longer stay, *The American
Express Pocket Guide to London* provides a thorough guide to
every aspect of England's capital city.

Events In Jan, International Boat Show at Earl's Court.

In May, Chelsea Flower Show at Royal Hospital, Chelsea.

In mid-May, Gillette London Marathon. A 26-mile (42km)
race through the streets of London.

On nearest Sat to June 11, Trooping the Colour on Horse
Guards Parade. The Queen rides from Buckingham Palace to
receive the Colour from her Foot Guards.

In July, Royal Tournament at Earl's Court. Display by the
Army, Navy, Marines and Air Force.

In Oct/Nov, State Opening of Parliament by the Queen.
Procession from Buckingham Palace to Palace of Westminster.

On nearest Sat to Nov 12, Lord Mayor's Show. Procession of
coaches and floats from Guildhall to the Law Courts.

Sights and places of interest

Several areas of London are described individually. The
following are also well worth exploring.

Belgravia, centered around the massive, classically
decorated Belgrave Sq., has magnificent rowhouses, once the
homes of dukes; **Bloomsbury**, N of New Oxford St., is best
known for its literary connections; **Chiswick**, on the Thames to
the W of London, clings picturesquely to the river bank and still
contains noteworthy old houses (especially Chiswick House and

Hogarth's House); **Hampstead**, only 4 miles (6km) N of the
center of London, has retained much of its village atmosphere,
and offers a superb view over the City from Parliament Hill;
Knightsbridge, running from the Brompton Oratory to Apsley
House (at Hyde Park Corner), is best known as a smart
shopping center with the world-famous Harrods department
store as its major attraction; **Mayfair**, bordered by Oxford St.,
Park Lane, Piccadilly and Regent St., is London's most
exclusive area, synonymous with wealth and elegance;
Piccadilly, which runs from Hyde Park Corner to Piccadilly
Circus (rather drab but a famous meeting place) is lined with
imposing buildings such as the Royal Academy, the Ritz and
Wren's St James's Church; **Richmond**, S of the Thames to the
W of London, has a pleasant countrified atmosphere, some
lovely houses and a breathtaking view from Richmond Hill;
Soho, London's red-light area, is famous for its nightclubs,
restaurants, delicatessens, pubs and for its cosmopolitan
mixture of people and trades; and finally, **Westminster**,
dominated by the Palace of Westminster and Westminster
Abbey, but also containing the Roman Catholic Westminster
Cathedral, is devoted to the business of government.

British Museum ▥ ★
Great Russell St., WC1 ☎ *(01) 636–1555* ⊡ ▰ *Open Mon–Sat*
10am–5pm, Sun 2.30–6pm. Tube Russell Square, Tottenham Court
Road.
One of the world's great museums, founded in 1753 and housed in a
massive Neoclassical building. Greek and Roman exhibits include the
famous **Elgin Marbles**, which once adorned the Parthenon. Other
important reliefs and sculptures are from Assyria and Ancient Egypt, the
latter also being represented by a fascinating selection of **mummies**. The
Oriental art collection includes one of the world's finest displays of
Chinese ceramics. The **British Library Galleries** display a selection
from the library's incomparable wealth of literary treasures and
manuscripts. Other rooms are devoted to prehistoric and Romano-
British objects and post-Roman and later material, a notable example
being the **Sutton Hoo treasure**, from a 7thC Anglo-Saxon burial ship.

Buckingham Palace ✩
☎ *(01) 930–4832. Not open to the public. Tube Victoria, Hyde Park*
Corner.
The home of the British monarchy since 1837, Buckingham Palace is
architecturally disappointing (the 20thC facade hides John Nash's older
palace), but the splendor of **The Mall**, the **Queen Victoria Memorial**,
and the guards in their scarlet tunics and bearskins create a majestic
atmosphere.
   The ceremony of the **Changing of the Guard** takes place daily at
11.30am (*alternate days in winter*). Also of interest are the **Queen's**
Gallery (*open during exhibitions*) and the **Royal Mews** with its display of
the Queen's carriages.

Chelsea
This fashionable area combines elegant well-maintained houses in quiet
streets with the noisy, exuberant **King's Road**. Interesting building
include the magnificent **Royal Hospital** (*Royal Hospital Rd.* ☎ *(01)*
730–0161), built in 1682 by Sir Christopher Wren as a place of
retirement for old soldiers, and the fine old rowhouses of **Cheyne**
Walk.

The City
i St Paul's Churchyard, EC4 ☎ *(01) 606–3030.*
The City covers one square mile of London. Elements of the various
stages of its life that have survived such disasters as the Great Fire of 1666
and World War II provide an appealing muddle of old streets and Wren
churches behind a more evident facade of modern concrete and glass
banks and offices.
   The area E of **London Bridge** and Liverpool St. Station is dominated
by maritime-associated buildings such as the **Lloyd's** buildings. Other
landmarks include the *Tower of London* and **The Monument**, which

commemorates the Great Fire. The southern area, from Sir Christopher Wren's *St Paul's Cathedral* to London Bridge, contains the **Mansion House** (the Lord Mayor of London's official residence) with Wren's delightful church of **St Stephen Walbrook** behind. Most of the City's financial buildings, notably the **Bank of England**, **Royal Exchange** and **Stock Exchange**, are situated in the northern part of the City. Also in this area are the **Barbican Centre**, home of the Royal Shakespeare Company and London Symphony Orchestra, the **Guildhall** which is both parliament and palace for the Corporation of the City of London, and many Wren churches. The area w of **Ludgate Circus** includes **Fleet St.**, home of British journalism, and several buildings associated with the law, notably the **Royal Courts of Justice** and the **Old Bailey**.

Covent Garden
Recent development has skillfully transformed the original fruit and vegetable market buildings in the piazza designed in the early 17thC by Inigo Jones into an exciting center with lively shops, restaurants and market stalls. At the w end of the piazza stands Jones' **St Paul's**, London's first entirely classical parish church, while at the E end of the piazza is the **London Transport Museum** (☎ *(01) 379–6344*) with its display of historic public transportation vehicles. Nearby, in **Bow St.**, is the **Royal Opera House**, home of the Royal Opera and Royal Ballet.

Greenwich
Best approached by river. Boat trips available from Westminster pier ☎ *(01) 930–2074. Or train to Greenwich from Charing Cross.*
Originally the capital port of a great seafaring nation, Greenwich has a vast wealth of seafaring exhibits, of which the most spectacular is the *Cutty Sark*, an 1869 tea clipper. Dominating the river is the magnificent Baroque **Royal Naval College** with its outstanding Painted Hall and chapel by Sir Christopher Wren. Farther back is Inigo Jones' splendid **Queens House**, part of the **National Maritime Museum** with its extensive collection ranging from the finds of marine archeology to an entire paddle tug. In Greenwich Park are the **Royal Observatory** (see also *Herstmonceux Castle*, near *Eastbourne*) designed by Wren and now housing a museum of clocks and telescopes, and the **Meridian Building**, the location of the meridian upon which Greenwich Mean Time is based, where the world's time is standardized.

Hampton Court ▥ ★
Hampton, Middlesex ☎ *(01) 977–8441* ▨ ✗ *summer only* ▨
Open Mar–Apr, Oct Mon–Sat 9.30am–5pm, Sun 2–5pm;
May–Sept Mon–Sat 9.30am–6pm, Sun 11am–6pm; Nov–Feb
Mon–Sat 9.30am–4pm, Sun 2–4pm. Train to Hampton Court from Waterloo.
This riverside palace, w of London, is a mixture of Tudor and Baroque architectural styles. It was built by Cardinal Wolsey and added to by Henry VIII who lived here for many years in the 16thC. Baroque additions were superimposed a century later by Sir Christopher Wren. In the **State Apartments** the Tudor period is represented by **Wolsey's Closet** and by Henry VIII's **Great Hall** with its **hammerbeam roof**, while **William III's bedroom** is typically Baroque with its original gilded furniture and rich tapestries. The more elegant **Cumberland Suite** dates from the 18thC.

The palace contains a fine collection of paintings, mainly from the Italian High Renaissance. External features include **Base Court**, **Anne Boleyn's Gatehouse**, a fabulously complex **astronomical clock** of 1540 and Wren's magnificent **Fountain Court**. The grounds include a famous maze dating from 1714.

Kensington
Predominantly made up of 19thC rowhouses and villas, Kensington is best known for its important museums clustered in the area known as South Kensington: the **Natural History Museum** (*Cromwell Rd.* ☎ *(01) 589–6323*), the **Geological Museum** (*Exhibition Rd.* ☎ *(01) 589–3444*), the **Science Museum** (*Exhibition Rd.* ☎ *(01) 589–3456*), and the *Victoria and Albert Museum*. These were set up by Prince Albert who is commemorated by the **Albert Memorial** and **Royal Albert Hall**.

The eastern boundary runs into **Knightsbridge** and northward to include the extensive **Kensington Gardens** (adjacent to **Hyde Park**) and **Kensington Palace** (*Kensington Gdns.* ☎ *(01) 937–9561*), a royal residence with sumptuously decorated state apartments.

Madame Tussaud's ☆
Marylebone Rd., NW1 ☎ *(01) 935–6861* ▆▆ ▆ ✻ *Open Apr–Sept
10am–6pm, Oct–Mar 10am–5.30pm. Tube Baker Street.*
Madame Tussaud began her wax modeling in France and opened her
museum in London in 1835. Waxworks include **Sleeping Beauty**, with a
breathing mechanism cast from one of the museum's oldest molds, the
portraits of contemporary celebrities, and the grisly collection in the
Chamber of Horrors.

In the **Planetarium** next door (*lectures every 45mins from
11am–4.40pm*) visitors can tip back their seats and see the heavens
projected and explained on the dome above.

National Gallery ★
Trafalgar Sq., WC2 ☎ *(01) 839–3321* ▣ ✖ ▆ ⇥ *Open
Mon–Sat 10am–6pm, Sun 2–6pm. Tube Charing Cross.*
One of the world's greatest and most comprehensive art collections
including over 2,000 Western European works ranging from Duccio in
the 14thC to Cézanne in the 19thC.

Rooms 1–14 show early Italian paintings and icons, and the superb
Italian Renaissance collection including Michelangelo's unfinished
Entombment, Leonardo's mysterious *Virgin of the Rocks* and Titian's
Bacchus and Ariadne. Rooms 15–28 show a huge collection of Northern
European works including Jan van Eyck's *Arnolfini Marriage* and
Holbein's *Ambassadors*; the Dutch 17thC is strongly represented by
Rembrandt and Vermeer (*Woman Standing at a Virginal*) and the
Flemish 17thC by Rubens and Van Dyck. 17thC French art is
represented by Poussin, Claude and others in Rooms 32–33. Rooms
35–36 and 38–39 show English 18th–19thC works by Hogarth,
Gainsborough, Constable and Turner, among others. Rooms 41–42
exhibit works by Spanish painters, among them El Greco and Velàzquez.
The remaining rooms (43–46) chart the emergence of modern art with a
fine collection of Impressionist paintings.

National Portrait Gallery ☆
2 St Martin's Pl., WC2 ☎ *(01) 930–1552* ▣ ✖ *Open Mon–Fri
10am–5pm, Sat 10am–6pm, Sun 2–6pm. Tube Charing Cross.*
Opened in 1859, this gallery has always emphasized the subjects of the
pictures rather than the artists. The result is fascinating, with a collection
ranging from the Middle Ages through to the 20thC.

Royal Academy ▥
Burlington House, Piccadilly, W1 ☎ *(01) 734–9052* ▆▆ ✖ ▆
Hours vary with each exhibition. Tube Piccadilly Circus, Green Park.
The home of many large-scale temporary exhibitions and of the annual
Summer Exhibition (*May–Sept*) in which contemporary British artists
exhibit their works.

Royal Botanic Gardens, Kew
Kew ☎ *(01) 940–1171* ▨ *Gardens open 10am–sunset;
greenhouses, galleries and museums Mon–Sat 11am–5pm or
sunset if earlier; Sun 11am–6pm or sunset if earlier. Tube Kew
Gardens, or train to Kew Bridge from Waterloo.*
Primarily a scientific institution for the study, classification and
cultivation of a vast number of plants from all over the world, Kew
Gardens comprises 300 acres of outstandingly beautiful grounds
including orchards, deciduous and pine woods, the **rhododendron dell**,
and the azalea garden. The spectacular greenhouses are not to be missed.

St James's
The area between **St James's Park** and **Piccadilly** is traditionally the part
of London belonging to the English gentleman, and **Pall Mall** is indeed
famous for its exclusive gentlemen's clubs. The area originally grew
around **St James's Palace**, once the official residence of the monarch.
Clarence House, home of the Queen Mother, is attached to it, and it is
flanked by **Marlborough House** (*Pall Mall* ☎ *(01) 930–2100, tours by
appointment only*) designed by Sir Christopher Wren for the Duke of
Marlborough in 1709–11, and **Lancaster House** (*Stable House, The
Mall* ☎ *(01) 839–3488*) with its highly decorated Baroque interior.

St Paul's Cathedral ▥ ✝ ★
Entrance and movement restricted during services. Tube St Paul's.
Built after the Great Fire of 1666 had reduced London's medieval
cathedral to ruins, this is Sir Christopher Wren's masterpiece. The basic
Gothic plan incorporates a nave, aisles, a crossing, transepts and a
chancel forming a Latin cross. The crossing is covered by the first great

dome in England, following the example of St Peter's in Rome.

The interior is dramatically Baroque. The **crypt** (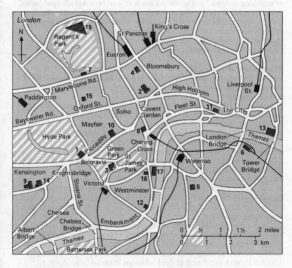) contains tombs of national figures, and artists buried in **Painters' Corner** include Van Dyck and Constable; Wren himself is buried nearby.

Stairs in the s transept lead to the **Whispering Gallery and Dome**. The acoustics inside the dome enable the slightest sound to be heard across its span. Winding steps lead even farther, to the **Golden Gallery** which provides a stunning view of the concourse below.

Tate Gallery ★
Millbank, SW1 ☎ *(01) 821–1313* 🏧 🚼 𝐾 🖳 ⇌ *Open Mon–Sat 10am–6pm, Sun 2–6pm. Tube Pimlico.*

Founded by sugar magnate Sir Henry Tate, this world-famous gallery has two distinct sections: the **British collection**, with its 16th–19thC paintings including works by Hogarth, Gainsborough, Constable and Turner, and the **modern collection** which covers the main currents in 20thC art, from the Impressionists to contemporary artists such as Hockney and Bacon.

The Thames
Running from beyond **Richmond** – with its superb park and many historical houses – to *Greenwich* (with its own unique attractions) and the sea, the river Thames flows sedately through London, passing several of its most important sights. Near Waterloo Bridge, the **South Bank Arts Centre**, including the **National Theatre**, contains some of the more controversial 20thC buildings along its banks. Farther downstream, the Gothic **Southwark Cathedral**, by London Bridge, is one of the most important medieval buildings in London. London's bridges are impressive and the recently opened **Tower Bridge Museum** (☎ *(01) 407–0922*) illustrates their history as well as displaying the workings of Tower Bridge itself.

The river offers one of the best ways to appreciate London's character. Boat trips leave frequently from piers at Westminister and the Tower of London.

1 Apsley House, Wellington Museum	**10** Royal Academy
2 British Museum	**11** St Paul's Cathedral
3 Buckingham Palace	**12** Tate Gallery
4 Courtauld Institute	**13** Tower of London
5 Imperial War Museum	**14** Victoria and Albert Museum
6 London Dungeons	**15** Wallace Collection
7 Madame Tussaud's	**16** Westminster Abbey
8 National Gallery, Trafalgar Sq.	**17** Westminster, Palace of
9 Natural History and Science Museums	**18** The Zoo

Tower of London 🏛 ★
Tower Hill, EC3 🕾 *(01) 709–0765* 🍽 *✗ Open Mar–Oct Mon–Sat
9.30am–5pm, Sun 2–5pm; Nov–Feb 9.30am–4pm (closed Sun).
Advisable to visit near opening time. Tube Tower Hill.*

Originally a wooden structure founded by William the Conqueror, the
castle was later transformed by Edward I into a full-fledged medieval
castle. It consists of the great stone **White Tower** completed in 1097, a
moat which is now grassed over, and a curtain wall with 12 towers begun
in the late 12thC. The tower was a royal residence and has also been a
prison for kings, queens, bishops and traitors. It contains a superb
collection of arms and armor.

The **Crown Jewels** are perhaps the greatest single attraction. Major
items include the **Royal Sceptre**, the **Imperial State Crown**, **'King
Edward's' crown**, which was in fact made for Charles II, and the **Queen
Mother's crown** containing the fabulous Kohinoor diamond. The
elaborate coronation robes are also displayed.

On **Tower Green**, near the Tower, a brass plate marks the spot where
Anne Boleyn, Catherine Howard and Lady Jane Grey and others met
their death on the scaffold.

Trafalgar Square
Nelson's Column, towering 170ft (52m) above Trafalgar Square,
dominates the square as Nash intended it to when he redeveloped the
land in the 1820s. Later additions including the **National Gallery** and
Admiralty Arch detract somewhat from the triumphal statement, but
the **Landseer lions** and the superb church of **St Martin-in-the-Fields**
add to the splendor.

Victoria and Albert Museum ★
Cromwell Rd., SW1 🕾 *(01) 589–6371* 🔯 🅿 *Open Mon–Thurs,
Sat 10am–6pm, Sun 2.30–6pm. Closed Fri. Tube South Kensington.*

The 'V & A' is probably the world's greatest museum for the decorative
arts. Founded on the initiative of Prince Albert with the profits of the
Great Exhibition of 1851, the collection was dedicated to 'fostering the
application of fine art to objects of utility.' It developed into a collection
of anything esthetic or of historical interest, and now includes paintings,
sculpture, furniture, ceramics, jewelry, stained glass, woodwork,
complete rooms from great houses, musical instruments and a widely
renowned costume collection. The **Boiler-house Project** in the
basement (opened 1982) has temporary exhibitions relating to art and
design in modern industry, thereby reviving the museum's original
purpose.

Westminster Abbey 🏛 † ★
Broad Sanctuary, SW1 🕾 *(01) 222–5152* 🍽 *Royal chapels* 🎫 *✗
Mon–Sat 10am–4pm. Closed Sun except for services. Tube
Westminster.*

Westminster Abbey, scene of coronation, marriage and burial of many
British monarchs, is also a place of tribute to Britain's heroes.

The exact date of the abbey's foundation is unknown, but there was a
religious foundation here by the 9thC and in 1050 Edward the Confessor
built a new abbey church which became a Benedictine monastery
attached to the Palace of Westminster. Building continued well into the
12thC, and in 1245 Henry III began a vast new building program in the
French Gothic style; by 1259 the chancel, transepts, part of the nave and
the chapter house were complete. When work was resumed in 1375 the
rest of the nave was built in this style. Sir Christopher Wren began the
designs for the w towers and facade in 1698. Nicholas Hawksmoor then
carried out his plans, which are pseudo-Gothic in style but sit uneasily on
the original structure.

On entering the abbey from the w there is a magnificent view along the
nave, with its piers of dark Purbeck marble sweeping up to the triforium,
clerestory and gracefully vaulted ceiling. Immediately ahead set in the
floor is the first of many superb monuments, a memorial to Winston
Churchill, with the **Tomb of the Unknown Warrior** behind.

The rest of the abbey is reached through a gate in the N aisle where
memorials and plaques commemorate 19thC statesmen, scientists
including Newton and Darwin, and musicians including Elgar and
Benjamin Britten.

The jewel in the abbey's crown, **Henry VII's chapel** (in fact completed
in 1512 by Henry VIII), is richly elaborate in the Gothic style.

Edward the Confessor's shrine, behind the altar of the main abbey, contains the **coronation throne** with the legendary coronation stone of Scottish kings, the **Stone of Scone**. This throne has been used for the coronation of almost every monarch since William I.

The exquisite **chapter house** is approached from the E side of the cloister; beyond the chapter house is the **Norman Undercroft** containing the **Abbey Museum**.

Westminster, Palace of 🏛 ★
Parliament Sq., SW1 ☎ *(01) 219–4272 (House of Lords)* ☎ *(01) 219–3107 (House of Commons)* 🔲 🎫 🎟 *Visiting arrangements subject to repeated change, so check first. During parliamentary sittings admittance to public galleries from St Stephen's entrance. Tube Westminster.*

This immense riverside complex of buildings has come to symbolize the very system of government. The oldest part of the former Royal Palace is **Westminster Hall**, built by William Rufus in 1097–99. It was here that medieval kings would call their councils of noblemen, forerunners of the House of Lords. In 1265 Simon de Montfort began the practice of calling additional councils of knights and burghers to represent the shires and towns, and subsequently the House of Commons was formed.

Much of the medieval palace was destroyed by fire in 1834 and was rebuilt in Gothic style by Sir Charles Barry with A.W.N. Pugin. The regular facade with its asymmetrical towers – **Victoria Tower** to the S, and **Clock Tower** containing Britain's most authoritative clock, generally known as **Big Ben**, to the N – is best seen from **Westminster Bridge** or across the river.

The high point of the interior is the medieval **Westminster Hall**, one of the world's greatest timber constructions, with a hammerbeam roof that represents the apogee of English Gothic architecture.

Tours of the palace, which are sometimes allowed, start at the **Norman Porch**, next to Victoria Tower. Visitors see the **House of Lords**, a stunning facade surrounded by sumptuous red leather benches, and the **House of Commons** itself. In this part of the complex, rebuilt after air raids in 1941, the governing party sits on one side and the opposition on the other.

Whitehall
The center of British government and administration, this area contains some outstanding buildings and several places of interest. Among these are **Downing St.**, home of the Prime Minister and the Chancellor of the Exchequer, at nos.10 and 11 respectively; **Horse Guards Parade**, scene of the Trooping the Colour ceremony in June; Inigo Jones' **Banqueting House** containing ceiling decorations by Rubens; and the **Cenotaph** of 1919 commemorating Britain's war dead.

The Zoo 🏛 ☆
Regent's Park, NW1 ☎ *(01) 722–3333* 🔲 🎟 🖵 🍴 *Open 9am–6pm. Tube Regent's Park, Mornington Crescent.*
The Zoological Society of London, as the zoo is more formally known, was founded in 1826; since then it has expanded enormously to include 5,000 species (some of which are in Whipsnade Park Zoo – see *St Albans*). In most cases, the iron cages have been replaced with large compounds reflecting the animals' natural habitats. Notable features include the **Michael Sobell Pavilion**, the **giant pandas**, the **Moonlight World** in which nocturnal animals behave as if it were the dead of night, and the **Snowdon Aviary**. There is also a **children's zoo**.

Hotels
London's hotels were described in one well-bruited year as the most expensive in the world, then 12 months later found themselves in a less-publicized 22nd position in the same *Financial Times* table. However, it is also the case that London has some of the world's grandest hotels.

The one which has inspired the fiercest loyalties is the **Savoy Hotel** (*Strand, WC2* ☎ *(01) 836–4343* 🏷), owned originally by Richard D'Oyly Carte, who introduced the operettas of Gilbert and Sullivan in the *en suite* theater. The Savoy remains wonderfully stylish.

Most of the other grand hotels are in Mayfair, presided over by **Claridge's** (*Brook St., W1* ☎ *(01) 629–8860* 🏷) and the

Connaught (*16 Carlos Pl., W1* ☎ *(01) 499–7070* ▦).
Claridge's is too dignified even to have a bar, although drinks
are served in the sitting room. The Connaught has a clubbier,
rather male, restrained elegance, and one of London's finest
restaurants. In the same style, but rather less grand, is
Brown's (*22–24 Dover St., W1* ☎ *(01) 493–6020* ▦), flagship
of the Trust House Forte Group. The hotel which bears the
name of this opulent swath of London, the **May Fair** (*Stratton
St., W1* ☎ *(01) 629–7777* ▦), belongs to the Inter-Continental
group.

A Continental flourish was brought to the heart of London
when César Ritz opened his British branch in the early 1900s.
The Ritz (*Piccadilly, W1* ☎ *(01) 493–8181* ▦) looks as though
it belongs in the Rue de Rivoli, and has a stunning interior to
match. Nearby is the smaller, superbly run **Athenaeum** (*116
Piccadilly, W1* ☎ *(01) 499–3463* ▦), owned by Rank.
Britain's grandest privately owned hotel, the **Park Lane** (*Brick
St., Piccadilly, W1* ☎ *(01) 499–6321* ▦) is also, confusingly,
on this stretch of road.

Park Lane itself is lined with luxury hotels. The greatest
landmark among these is the **Dorchester** (*Park Lane, W1*
☎ *(01) 629–8888* ▦), looking like a beached ocean liner. It is
the most opulent of London hotels, with a fine *nouvelle cuisine*
restaurant. Its neighbor, the **Inter-Continental** (*1 Hamilton Pl.,
Hyde Park Corner, W1* ☎ *(01) 409–3131* ▦), follows a similar
culinary philosophy with great success.

The latest international name to arrive on the London hotel
scene is Hyatt, through its acquisition of the **Carlton Tower**
(*2 Cadogan Pl., SW1* ☎ *(01) 235–5411* ▦), whose Chelsea
Room restaurant is superb.

The most fashionable hotel in London is the somewhat
theatrical **Blakes** (*33–35 Roland Gdns., SW7* ☎ *(01) 370–6701*
▦). The most luxurious smaller hotels are perhaps the **Capital**
(*22 Basil St., SW3* ☎ *(01) 589–5171* ▦), the **Basil Street
Hotel** (*8 Basil St., SW3* ☎ *(01) 581–3311* ▯), and **Dukes**
(*34–36 St James's Pl., SW1* ☎ *(01) 491–4840* ▦). The most
discreet are the **Alexander** (*9 Sumner Pl., SW7* ☎ *(01)
581–1591* ▯) and **Eleven Cadogan Gardens** (*11 Cadogan
Gdns., SW3* ☎ *(01) 730–3426* ▦).

There are, of course, many less expensive hotels, and the
London Tourist Board (*26 Grosvenor Gdns., SW1W 0DU* ☎ *(01)
730–0791*) will provisionally reserve one if you write at least
six weeks in advance, indicating preferred price bracket and
location. There are also instant-reservations booths in the tourist
information centers at Victoria Station and Heathrow Airport.

Restaurants

London has at least 2,000 restaurants, representing about 50
culinary styles, ethnicities and nationalities, from American to
Vietnamese. Inevitably, in such a large city, choice must be
dictated not only by palate and pocket but also by geographical
convenience. Theaterland is served by the wine-bars and
restaurants of Covent Garden, and by Soho, with its moderately
priced Italian restaurants in the area of Old Compton St. and
inexpensive Chinese restaurants around Gerrard St. Shoppers
in Oxford St. might consider an inexpensive Greek-Cypriot
meal at one of the many small restaurants around Charlotte St.,
but those patronizing Bond St. may have to pay the
considerable price of eating in Mayfair. Farther w,
Knightsbridge, Chelsea and Kensington have a cosmopolitan

array of good eating places. Bayswater, especially Westbourne Grove, seems to have become a center for Indian restaurants.

Haute cuisine in London began belatedly to win international recognition in the 1980s through the efforts of restaurateurs like the Roux brothers, whose Mayfair mascot **Le Gavroche** (*43 Upper Brook St., W1* 🕿 *(01) 408–0881* ▥▥▥) offers contemporary French cuisine of the highest standard. Gastronomically, the greatest challenger to the Roux brothers is one of their former chefs, Pierre Koffman, whose **La Tante Claire** (*68 Royal Hospital Rd., SW3* 🕿 *(01) 352–6045* ▥▥▥ *to* ▥▥▥) is a temple dedicated to creative French cooking. Gastronomes will also want to investigate the robust **Ma Cuisine** (*113 Walton St., SW3* 🕿 *(01) 584–7585* ▥▥▥); the uncompromising **Chez Nico** (*129 Queenstown Rd., SW8* 🕿 *(01) 720–6960* ▥▥▥), just across the river from Chelsea; or a rising star, **L'Arlequin** (*123 Queenstown Rd., SW8* 🕿 *(01) 622–0555* ▥▥▥).

Brasserie dining is a style which established itself in London during the early 1980s. The original and best is **Langan's Brasserie** (*Stratton St., W1* 🕿 *(01) 493–6437* ▥▥▥), off Piccadilly. In Knightsbridge, food critic Quentin Crewe was one of the founders of **Brasserie St Quentin** (*243 Brompton Rd., SW3* 🕿 *(01) 589–8005* ▥▥▥). In Soho, a similar style is enjoyed by film and publishing people upstairs at **L'Escargot** (*48 Greek St., W1* 🕿 *(01) 437–2679* ▥▥▥ *to* ▥▥▥); a more authentic brasserie is downstairs.

English food of the highest standard emerges from the imaginative kitchen at the somewhat sepulchral **Leith's** (*92 Kensington Park Rd., W11* 🕿 *(01) 229–4481* ▥▥▥), in Notting Hill. A more traditional, even Georgian, style of cooking is maintained at the **English House** (*3 Milner St., SW3* 🕿 *(01) 584–3002* ▥▥▥) in Chelsea, while smart shoppers in Sloane St. head for the more informal **English Garden** (*10 Lincoln St., SW3* 🕿 *(01) 584–7272* ▥▥▥). For genuine English grandeur, and superb oysters, there is **Wilton's** (*27 Bury St., SW1* 🕿 *(01) 930–8391* ▥▥▥).

Fish restaurants have always been a London tradition. Oyster bars such as **Bill Bentley's** (*202 Bishopsgate, EC2* 🕿 *(01) 734–4756* ▥▥▥), in the City, maintain the tradition. So do English fish restaurants such as **Sheekey's** (*28 St Martin's Court, WC2* 🕿 *(01) 240–2565* ▥▥▢) and the grander **Scott's** (*20 Mount St., W1* 🕿 *(01) 629–5248* ▥▥▥) in Mayfair. An Italian flavor is provided by the moderately priced **Manzi's** (*1 Leicester St., WC2* 🕿 *(01) 734–0224* ▥▥▢) in Soho.

Nightlife

London offers a choice of nightlife to suit all tastes. The many theaters and cinemas in the West End present a wide variety of productions; for details see national or London-oriented newspapers or magazines. Theater tickets can be obtained in advance from the box office, from theater ticket agencies (see Yellow Pages in telephone book) or, on the day and for half price, from a booth on the w side of Leicester Sq.

Specific theaters worth mentioning are the three at **The National Theatre** (*Upper Ground, South Bank, SE1* 🕿 *(01) 928–2252*) which present classical and modern, British and international plays, and the **Barbican Theatre** (*Barbican Centre, EC2* 🕿 *(01) 628–8795*), home of the Royal Shakespeare Company. The Royal Ballet and Royal Opera Companies perform at the **Royal Opera House** (*Bow St., WC2* 🕿 *(01) 240–1066*), and the Sadler's Wells Royal Ballet Company can be seen at **Sadler's Wells Theatre** (*Rosebery Ave., EC1* 🕿 *(01) 278–8916*). The two most important places for concerts are the **Royal Albert Hall** (*Kensington Gore, SW7* 🕿 *(01) 589–8212*) and the **Royal Festival Hall** (*South Bank, SE1* 🕿 *(01) 928–3191*).

The most exclusive and well-known nightclubs such as **Annabel's** (*44 Berkeley Sq., W1* ☎ *(01) 629–3558*), **Raffles** (*287 King's Rd., SW3* ☎ *(01) 352–1091*) and **Tokyo Joe's** (*Clarges St., W1* ☎ *(01) 409–1832*) require an introduction from a member. Nightspots open to anyone include **Dingwalls** (*Camden Lock, NW1* ☎ *(01) 267–4967*) for live music, **Legends** (*29 Old Burlington St., W1* ☎ *(01) 437–9933*) with disco and French cuisine, and **Stringfellows** (*16 St Martin's Lane, WC2* ☎ *(01) 240–5534*) for good, loud music. Jazz venues include **Ronnie Scott's Club** (*47 Frith St., W1* ☎ *(01) 439–0747*), **Pizza Express** (*10 Dean St., W1* ☎ *(01) 439–8722*), **Pizza on the Park** (*11 Knightsbridge, SW1* ☎ *(01) 235–5550*) and **Kettners** restaurant (*29 Romilly St., W1* ☎ *(01) 734–6112*). Major rock concerts are staged at the **Odeon**, Hammersmith (*Queen Caroline St., W6* ☎ *(01) 748–4081*) and the **Earls Court Exhibition Centre** (*SW7* ☎ *(01) 385–1200*), while pubs such as the **Half Moon** (*93 Lower Richmond Rd., SW15* ☎ *(01) 788–2387*) feature live rock groups. **The Venue** (*160–62 Victoria St., SW1* ☎ *(01) 828–9441*) and the **Marquee** (*90 Wardour St., W1* ☎ *(01) 437–6603*) also promote lesser-known groups.

Shopping

Knightsbridge is dominated by **Harrods**, the world-famous department store; other highly regarded shops here are **Harvey Nichols**, **The Scotch House**, and **Laura Ashley**, queen of country-style fashions. Nearby in Sloane Sq., the reliable **Peter Jones** department store and the **General Trading Co.** contrast with the trend-setting and often bizarre **King's Rd.** clothes shops.

In the **West End** the smartest area is **Bond St.**, home of **Bill Gibb**, **Gucci** and **Hermes**; nearby South Molton St. has more financially accessible clothes shops including **Browns** and **Monsoon**. N of this area runs the more democratic **Oxford St.**, with many department stores including **Selfridges**, **John Lewis** and **Marks & Spencer**. **Regent St.**, running s from Oxford Circus, has **Liberty's** department store, renowned for its fabrics; **Hamleys**, the biggest toy shop in the world; and **Aquascutum**, known for its coats. Several shops for china and glass are interspersed among these major shops.

Piccadilly contains **Hatchards** well-stocked bookshop, **Fortnum & Mason's** aristocratic department store with its exotic food department, and **Simpson**, noted for its menswear. Close by, in **Jermyn St.** or **Savile Row**, a gentleman will find everything from badger-hair shaving brushes to made-to-measure suits, shirts and shoes.

Covent Garden has out-of-the-ordinary gifts and clothes shops in and around the piazza, and there are market stalls, mostly selling handmade goods, in the central area.

Street markets are still a colorful feature of London life. The best-known are **Portobello Rd.**, a Saturday antiques market; **Petticoat Lane**, in Middlesex St. in the East End, selling bargain goods on Sunday; **Camden Passage** on Wednesday morning and Saturday, for antiques; and **Camden Lock**, by the Regent's Canal, selling an entertaining mix of secondhand goods on Sunday.

Longleat House and Safari Park ☆

Map 4L7. Wilts. Off A362, 30 miles (48km) NW of Salisbury ☎ *(09853) 551 (house) or 328 (safari park). House* ▨ 🎟 ■ ＊ ⇔ *open Easter–Sept 10am–6pm, Oct–Easter 10am–4pm. Safari Park* ▨ ＊ *open Mar–Oct 10am–6pm or sunset if earlier.*

Once a priory stood here, but after the Dissolution the estate came to the Thynne family (marquesses of Bath since 1789) and Longleat has remained their seat ever since. Sir John Thynne, the first owner, apparently designed this magnificent Elizabethan mansion himself. Inside there are tapestries, Spanish leather hangings, paintings by such masters as Titian and Reynolds, 19thC hand-molded ceilings and a wealth of art treasures.

The **Safari Park** is one of Europe's finest, having several special features such as a picnic area, a large herd of giraffe, a

safari boat and a gorilla island. Longleat's other attractions
include the formal gardens and the park landscaped by
Capability Brown, the maze, dollhouses, boat rides, animal
rides, a lakeside train, and a variety of events in the summer.

Ludlow
*Map 9I6. Shropshire. 24 miles (38km) N of Hereford.
Population: 161,500 i Castle St.* ☎ *(0584) 3857.*

Sprawled over a steep hill above two small rivers, Ludlow is a
town with very ancient roots (it is known that both prehistoric
and Roman ways crossed this hill). It is a place not only of royal
associations but also one in which the building craftsmen of
successive periods have left their mark – the Norman **castle**,
medieval parish church, Tudor half-timbered houses, Georgian
facades and Victorian market all contribute to make it a town of
real character. Much of what is best is within a central muddle
of sometimes narrow streets most enjoyably explored on foot.

The **museum** (*Buttercross* ☎ *(0584) 3857* 🖾 *open
Easter – Sept Mon – Sat 10.30am – 12.30pm, 2 – 5pm, Sun
10am – 1pm, 2 – 5pm*) concentrates on local history from
prehistoric to Victorian times. Its well-known collection of
more than 30,000 fossils (*in Old St.*) may be seen by
appointment.

Ludlow Castle
NW corner of the upper town ☎ *(0584) 3947* 🖾 *Open May – Sept
10am – 6pm; Oct – Apr 10.30am – 4pm.*

Started in the early 12thC – the keep and the unusual round chapel are
the principal survivors from this Norman period – Ludlow's castle has
been home to two sad royal couples. For several years the two young sons
of Edward IV lived in the **Pendower Tower**, but on their father's death
in 1483 their uncle, Richard of Gloucester, moved them to the Tower of
London where they disappeared. And it was here, in 1501 – 2, that two
other children enjoyed brief happiness: Prince Arthur, aged 14 and elder
son of Henry VII, and Catherine of Aragon, his 16yr-old bride. Less than
six months after the wedding Arthur died and Catherine was later
handed on to Arthur's brother, Henry VIII.

Sights nearby
Croft Castle
9 miles (14.5km) SW of Ludlow ☎ *(056885) 246. NT* 🖾 👄 *Open
Apr, Oct Sat, Sun 2 – 5pm; May – Sept Wed – Sun and bank holidays
2 – 6pm.*

Fine avenues of trees, an ancient castle with Georgian interior
decoration, and a large Iron Age hillfort are the lures here. The hillfort,
Croft Ambrey, is about 1 mile (1.5km) from the castle and is known to
have been in use in the 4thC BC.

Stokesay Castle ☆
Stokesay, on the A49, 6 miles (9.5km) NW of Ludlow 🖾 👄 *Open
Mar, Oct 10am – 5pm (closed Mon, Tues); Apr – July, Sept
10am – 6pm (closed Mon except bank holidays, Tues); Aug
10am – 6pm (closed Tues). Closed Nov – Feb.*

Started in the 13thC and completed in 1305, Stokesay is England's oldest
and perhaps most satisfying example of a fortified manor house. Note
especially the half-timbered Elizabethan **gatehouse**, the projecting wood
structure of the **north tower**, and the beamed ceiling of the **hall**.

Ⓗ **The Feathers**
The Bull Ring, Ludlow, Shropshire SY8 1AA ☎ *(0584) 2919*
🈺 *28905* 🅸 🎏 *35* 🛏 *35* 🍴 🖚 ➡ AE CB 🅳 🅾 VISA

Location: Corve St., just N of Bull Ring crossroads. With elaborate
half-timbering and an interior known for its plasterwork, woodcarving
and antiques, this hotel, built in 1603, has rooms bearing such names as
the Richard III Restaurant and the James I Lounge which foster a sense
of royal association.
❑ 🍴 🖚 👥

Lyme Regis
Map 4M6. Dorset. On the coast, 24 miles (38km) w of Dorchester. Population: 3,400 **i** *The Guildhall, Bridge St.* ☎ *(02974) 2138.*

This charming seaside resort was given its royal title by Edward I. The harbor is protected by a long, curved breakwater known as the **Cobb**, which was immortalized by Jane Austen in *Persuasion* and has more recently attracted attention because of the film *The French Lieutenant's Woman*.

Sight nearby
Forde Abbey
Near Chard, 12 miles (19km), N of Lyme Regis ☎ *(0460) 20231* ▨ ▤ ☛ *House and gardens open Easter, May–Sept Wed, Sun, bank holidays 2–6pm; gardens only open Mar–Apr, Oct Sun 2–4pm. Visitors can pick fruit and vegetables according to the season.*

Visited principally for its noted **Mortlake tapestries**, this gracious, long, low mansion successfully blends building styles ranging from the original Cistercian abbey of 1138 (much of which survives) up to reconstructions of the 16th–17thC.

For garden lovers there are 25 acres including several lakes, all set along the pastoral valley of the little river Axe, while a touch of history is provided by the fact that the Duke of Monmouth stayed here in 1680 when seeking support for his ill-fated cause.

Ⓗ **Alexandra** (*Pound St., Lyme Regis, Dorset DT7 3HZ* ☎ *(02974) 2010* ☐ *to* ☐); **Devon** (*Uplyme, Lyme Regis, Dorset DT7 3TQ* ☎ *(02974) 3231* ☐ *to* ☐).

Malvern Hills
Map 4J7. H and W. Between Hereford and Worcester **i** *Winter Gardens, Grange Rd., Great Malvern* ☎ *(06845) 4700.*

The highest point, the **Worcestershire Beacon**, is a modest 1,395ft (425m) but nevertheless these brown hills rise sharply enough out of the Severn plain to impress as a miniature mountain range. Although encircled and crossed by roads, the hills should really be regarded as ideal, if by some standards tame, walking country offering exceptional views; 15 counties, three cathedrals and several abbeys can be seen from the top of the Beacon on a good day. **Great Malvern** at the N end is the principal town, while toward the S end the earthworks of the Iron Age **British Camp** (Herefordshire Beacon) invite exploration. Medicinal springs and innumerable schools complete the scene.

Event Mid-May to early June, Malvern Festival. The main themes are Bernard Shaw's plays and Elgar's music.

Restaurant
Malvern Wells (*on A4532, 10 miles/16km sw of Worcester*).

Ⓡ **Croque-en-Bouche**
221 Wells Rd. ☎ *(06845) 65612* ▥▥▥ ▩ ▤ Ⓐ Ⓒ ⊕ ⓒ ⓥⒾⓈⒶ *Last orders 9.15pm. Closed lunch except Sun; Mon, Tues; Wed following bank holiday; Sun dinner.*

A very French restaurant, run by an English couple. The French mood starts with an unusually complete list of aperitifs, including Suze, Picon, Lillet, Chambèryzette, ratafia and pineau. It proceeds through a five-course set menu which is limited but well-balanced, and which might feature *lotte à l'américaine*, pheasant *truffe*, or chocolate almond cake, before reaching a well-fed conclusion with a choice of about 50 Cognacs, Armagnacs, Calvados and eaux-de-vie. There is also a wine list which leaves no region unturned, with more interesting Californians than most, and even Lebanese Cabernets.

Manchester
*Map **10F7**. Greater Manchester. 30 miles (48km) E of
Liverpool. Population: 544,000. Airport* ☎ *(061) 437–5233;
railway station* ☎ *(061) 832–8353; coach station* ☎ *(061)
228–3881; bus inquiries* ☎ *(061) 226–8181* **i** *Magnum
House, Portland St., Piccadilly* ☎ *(061) 247–3694 or Town
Hall Extension, Lloyd St.* ☎ *(061) 236–1606.*

Commerce is what counts here, natural enough in a city which,
notwithstanding its Roman origins, is essentially a product of
the Industrial Revolution and especially of the cotton industry.
The Ship Canal, which when opened in 1894 made the city into
a major inland port, and the extensive postwar redevelopments
including the shopping precincts off Market St., claiming to be
among Europe's largest, round off the picture of modern
Manchester.

But if commerce represents the work of the Mancunians,
books and music epitomize their culture, for the city enjoys
wide renown in both these fields. There are three major public
libraries, all open to visitors. These are the **Central Library**, in
a rotunda of 1934 and one of Europe's largest municipal
libraries; **Chetham's Hospital** (a foundation of *c.*1420, a school
and library since 1653, with buildings spanning the whole
period), one of the oldest free libraries in Britain; and the **John
Rylands Library** (*Deansgate* ☎ *(061) 273–3333* ☑ *open
Mon–Fri 9.30am–5.30pm, Sat 9.30am–1pm, closed Sun*),
containing priceless manuscripts and early printed books. For
music lovers, Manchester is the home of the famed Hallé
Orchestra (see *Nightlife*, below).

Event In early Aug, Manchester Show at Platt Fields.

Sights and places of interest
City Art Gallery
Mosley St. ☎ *(061) 236–9422* ☑ *Open 10am–6pm. Closed Sun.*
This clean, classical building (dating from 1829 and held by many to be
Manchester's finest) is a fitting setting for the city's collections of
paintings, sculpture and applied art. The rooms are opulent and well-lit
but tend to be cluttered, sometimes with pictures hanging too high to be
properly enjoyed. The paintings span from the Old Masters to modern
art; if selections have to be made, they should include the **Pre-
Raphaelites** (Holman Hunt's *The Light of the World* is one of the
gallery's best-known paintings) and George Stubbs' *Cheetah and Stag
with Two Indians*. The gallery has frequent temporary exhibitions.

Gallery of English Costume
Platt Hall, Platt Fields, Rusholme. 2½ miles (4km) s of city center
☎ *(061) 224–5217* ☑ *Open Apr–Sept 10am–6pm. Closed Mon,
Sat, Sun.*
Here, in an elegant house dating from 1764, the ever changing course of
English fashion from the 16thC to the present day can be traced. Exhibits
include clothes designed by Mary Quant and Zandra Rhodes.
Temporary exhibitions on various aspects of fashion such as shoes and
underwear are a regular feature.

Gallery of Modern Art
*Princess St., next to City Art Gallery. Entry details as for City Art
Gallery.*
The gallery is devoted to 20thC paintings and drawings, sculpture,
ceramics and decorative arts, by artists ranging from Sickert to Hockney.
The permanent collections periodically cede place to temporary
exhibitions.

Manchester Cathedral †
Near the river Irwell at Victoria Bridge ☎ *(061) 834–7503.*
This cathedral – a 15th and 16thC collegiate parish church raised to its
present status in 1847 – claims the curious distinction of being the
broadest in England, its width amounting to almost half its length.
However, visitors are more likely to come here to see the early 16thC

choir stalls ☆ which, with their intriguing misericords (depicting animal scenes including bear-baiting, unicorns and monsters), rank high among Europe's best.

There is also a **Brass Rubbing Centre** (☎ (061) 834–9031 🔲 open *Easter–Oct 10am–4pm, Nov–Easter 11am–3pm, closed Sun, Mon*).

Town Hall
Albert Square ☎ *(061) 236–3377* 🔲 🔣 *Guided tours Mon–Fri 10am and 2.30pm lasting about 1hr.*

Designed by Alfred Waterhouse and completed in 1877, Manchester's town hall is a Neo-Gothic proclamation of the confidence and established order of that date. Inside, the principal features of interest are an exhibition of the city's charters and plate, and the murals by Ford Madox Brown illustrating Manchester's history and achievements.

Whitworth Art Gallery
Oxford Rd., nearly 2 miles (3km) s of city center ☎ *(061) 273–4865* 🔲 🚶 *Open Mon–Wed, Fri, Sat 10am–5pm, Thurs 10am–9pm. Closed Sun.*

The four principal collections here – any one of which is reward enough for the journey out from the center of the city – are **British Watercolors** (Blake, Pre-Raphaelites, Turner, and World War II artists); **Contemporary British Art** (Hockney, Lowry, Nash, Spencer); **Sculpture** (Epstein, Hepworth, Moore); and **Textiles** ☆ of wide provenance and beautifully displayed.

Sights nearby

Dunham Massey
12 miles (19km) sw of central Manchester ☎ *(061) 941–1025. NT* 🔲 🏛 🚶 ➡ *Open Apr–Oct: house 2–6pm, garden and domestic quarters 11am–6pm. Closed Fri.*

In this beautifully proportioned, moated, red-brick mansion, an early 18thC rebuilding of an Elizabethan predecessor and until 1976 seat of the earls of Stamford, somewhat somber rooms contain 18thC furniture and many good portraits (Van Dyck, Lely, Kneller, Romney). On Wed, the **Elizabethan mill** on the grounds is shown in action.

Salford City Art Gallery and Museum
The Crescent, Peel Park, Salford. On A6, 2 miles (3km) nw of city center ☎ *(061) 736–2649* 🔲 🚶 *Open Mon–Fri 10am–5pm, Sun 2–5pm. Closed Sat.*

Admirers of L.S. Lowry will head for this gallery which shows the largest public collection of his works. **Lark Hill Place**, on the ground floor, is a full-scale late 19thC period street scene of shops and houses.

Styal
Wilmslow, 10 miles (16km) s of Manchester ☎ *(0625) 527468. NT* 🔲 🏛 🚶 *Open Apr–June, Sept 11am–5pm (closed Mon except bank holidays); July–Aug 11am–5pm; Oct, Nov, Mar noon–4.30pm (closed Mon); Dec–Feb Sat, Sun noon–4.30pm. Country Park always open during daylight.*

The specific site is **Quarry Bank Cotton Mill**, the heart and *raison d'être* of a complete and little-altered Industrial Revolution mill colony, which recalls not only the practical realities of ensuring a work force but also the advanced and humane attitude of Samuel Greg who built his mill here in 1784. At first he relied largely on pauper children (for whom he built the **Apprentice House**), but later, as business prospered and demanded more labor, Greg and his successors bought or built the houses, cottages, shop, school and chapel which make up much of the village of Styal.

Quarry Bank Mill today serves as an unusual museum in which live demonstrations back up displays illustrating all aspects of Styal – technical, commercial and human – as well as the mill's place in the growth of the cotton industry. Samuel Greg's large estate is now a country park of riverside woodland.

Tatton Park
12 miles (19km) sw of Manchester ☎ *(0565) 3155. NT* 🔲 🏛 🚶 ➡ *House, garden, park, Old Hall and farm all open different times – telephone for exact times.*

With a medieval manor, a stately home (the estate belonged to the Egerton family from 1598–1958), famous gardens and a huge deer park, Tatton is just the place for a family outing on a fine day. In **Old Hall**, the restored medieval manor, exhibits tell the story of the early days of the estate. **Tatton Hall**, the manor's eventual successor dating from

1774–1825, epitomizes the social pattern in stately homes of the 19th and early 20thC, with on the one hand exquisite decoration and priceless possessions and on the other the extensive domestic quarters. Within the 60 acres of **gardens** ☆ are woodland, a maze, a rose garden, an exotic fernery and a Japanese garden complete with its Shinto temple, while the park includes **Tatton Mere**, a large lake where visitors can swim, fish, sail or just enjoy the many wildfowl.

Hotels

Ⓗ **Piccadilly**
Piccadilly Plaza, Manchester M60 1QR ☎ *(061) 236–8414*
⑩*668765* ▥▥▥ ➎ *250* ▭ *250* ━ ⇌ Ⓐ Ⓔ Ⓒ Ⓑ Ⓓ Ⓓ ⓋⒾ *Closed*
Christmas.
Location: In the heart of the city, near tourist office. As a modern, city-center hotel, the Piccadilly has more facilities than any other in the North. It is very much an executive's hotel, with its large lounge, three bars and coffee shop. The hotel's **Ambassador** restaurant takes a particular pride in its roast beef, carved at the table, but also has daily specials ranging from Lancashire hotpot to whiting *en croûte*. There is also a specialty table of appetizers and an à la carte menu.
♨ ☐ ⊿ 《 👥 ⍩ *Sat.*

Ⓗ Other hotels: **Grand** (*Aytoun St., Manchester M1 3DR* ☎ *(061) 236–9559* ⑩*667580* ▥▥▥); **Midland** (*Peter St., Manchester M60 2DS* ☎ *(061) 236–3333* ⑩*667797* ▥▥▥); **Portland** (*Portland St., Piccadilly Gardens, Manchester M1 6DP* ☎ *(061) 228–3400* ⑩*669157* ▥▥▥).

Hotel/restaurant nearby
Birtle (*9 miles/14.5km* N *of Manchester*).

Ⓗ Ⓡ **Normandie**
Elbut Lane, Birtle, near Bury, Greater Manchester BL9 6UT
☎ *(061) 764–3869* ▥▥▥ ➎ *20* ▭ *3* ⇌ Ⓐ Ⓔ ⓋⒾ
Ⓡ ▭ ⇌ ☐ *Last orders 9pm. Closed Sat lunch, Sun, Jan 1, Dec 26.*
Location: 2 miles (3km) E *of Bury on B6222, then 1 mile (1.5km)* N *up Elbut Lane.* A gastronomic delight in the most unlikely of places: tucked underneath an utterly basic motel in a hard-to-find hamlet between the old cotton towns of Bury and Rochdale. Excellent French cooking from a Moroccan chef who knows how to buy and handle meat and does not stint on quantity. A good, interesting cheese board and an astonishing wine list, with 120 Bordeaux and 60 Burgundies, not to mention more than 40 Cognacs. The motel backs directly onto the Pennines, from which there are deep, valley views of the towns Lowry painted.
⌂ ♨ ☐ ⊿

Nightlife
The **Free Trade Hall** (*Peter St.* ☎ *(061) 834–1712*) is the home of the Hallé orchestra and venue for the Hallé Proms (late June to early July) and for rock and folk concerts; the **Library Theatre** (*St Peter's Sq.* ☎ *(061) 236–7110*) has a resident theatrical company, while the **Palace Theatre** (*Oxford St.* ☎ *(061) 236–9922*) has visiting companies including the Royal Ballet, Glyndebourne Opera Company and the National Theatre. The **Royal Exchange Theatre** (*St Ann's Sq.* ☎ *(061) 833–9333*) has a stage built in-the-round inside the old cotton exchange; it presents touring plays. The **Royal Northern College of Music** (*124 Oxford St.* ☎ *(061) 273–4504*) puts on concerts, operas and ballet performed by the students or by visiting companies.
Soigné nightclubs in town include the **Playboy** (*10 Canal St.* ☎ *(021) 228–3141*), with a restaurant, casino and nightclub; the **Millionaire** (*West Mosely St.* ☎ *(021) 236–2466*), restaurant and disco; and **Fagins** (*Oxford St.* ☎ *(021) 236–9971*), restaurant and nightclub.

Shopping
The **Arndale Centre** in the city center, off Market St., is an enormous shopping complex including major department stores. A much smaller and more exclusive shopping area is **St Ann's Sq.**, the Bond St. of Manchester. The Royal Exchange contains many interesting shops.

The Marches
Map **9**. _Cheshire, Shropshire, H and W. Lining the Welsh border._

The Marches is a name of great historical meaning, for these were the turbulent lands which William the Conqueror handed over to three of his barons, offering virtual independence provided only that they kept their domains quiet. And this in varying degree is just what the earls of Chester, Shrewsbury and Hereford did for the next 500yrs.

Today the Marches are toured for their beautiful countryside, for their many picturesque and often historic towns and villages, for stately homes and castles, and for their wealth of black-and-white, half-timbered houses, many of the best of which will be found at such places as **Weobley**, **Eardisley** and **Pembridge**, all to the NW of Hereford.

A main road links _Hereford, Ludlow,_ **Stokesay**, _Shrewsbury,_ and **Whitchurch** and _Chester,_ but this spine, typical although much of it is, should be treated as no more than a convenient axis from which to make excursions, for it is along the side roads that the best will be found. The choice of side-trips is continual, but two at least demand mention. One is westward from Hereford to the **Golden Valley** below the **Black Mountains** of Wales; the other is across the **Long Mynd** above Church Stretton (between Ludlow and Shrewsbury), a bare moorland ridge offering wide views, some breezy walking and several prehistoric sites.

Marlborough
Map **5K8**. _Wilts. 35 miles (66km) w of Reading. Population: 6,100_ _**i**_ _St Peter's Church, High St._ ☎ _(0672) 53989._

Named after Maerl's Barrow, a prehistoric mound supposed to be Merlin's burial place, Marlborough is now a thriving and attractive market town. An impressive wide street lined with charming old buildings and with a church at each end provides the center of the town and the venue for the market (_Wed, Sat_).

Sight nearby
Littlecote
9 miles (14.5km) NE of Marlborough ☎ _(0488) 82170 or 82528 on weekends_ 🖭 _separate tickets for each sight_ 🍴 🌸 🚗 _House, Villa, Frontier City all open different times (closed Oct–Mar). Telephone for exact times._

The contrasts could hardly be greater: a Roman villa, a mellow Tudor mansion, and the Wild West. The villa complex (500yds/450m from the house) is still being excavated; it includes a temple of unusual form containing a large **Orpheus mosaic**. The principal feature of the early 16thC house is its **Tudor hall** which shows arms and armor of the Civil War period, including well-preserved buffalo-skin jerkins. The house also has an austere **Cromwellian chapel** and a gruesome ghost story. For children, there is a replica **Wild West** township, the scene of gunfights and other contemporary excitements.

Hotel and restaurants nearby
Kintbury (_13 miles/21km E of Marlborough_).

Ⓗ Ⓡ **Dundas Arms**
Kintbury, Berks RG15 0UT ☎ _(0488) 58263_ 🛏☐ 🍴 6 🛏 6 🚗 ⇥
🆎 ⓞ ⓒⓓ 🆅🆂🅰 _Closed Sun, Mon, one week at Christmas._
Ⓡ 🍽 ⌂ ⬛ ⚊ _Last orders 9.15pm._
Location: On edge of village. A riverside pub which has been turned into a stylish country restaurant. The menu features fish dishes and game, although by no means exclusively.
🍴 ⴵ 🥢 ◁⊏

Pewsey (*on A345, 6 miles/9.5km S of Marlborough*).

⊞ **The Close**
River St. ☎ *(06726) 3226* ⅢⅢ ▢ ▆▆ ⇌ AE ⊙ ⊚ VISA *Last orders*
9.30pm. Closed Mon, Sun dinner, two weeks in Feb.
Hearty but adventurous, and thoroughly dependable, with very
competitive prices. The Close is in the village which gives its name to the
Vale of Pewsey, dotted with thatched cottages and orchards. Its staple
dishes, with apple a favorite ingredient, are simple enough – main
courses might be loin of pork, lamb with tarragon butter, or guinea fowl
with juniper berries; casseroles and duck dishes also feature strongly –
but the enthusiastic proprietors also enjoy serving confections from Asia
and Africa with their fixed-price Sunday 'tiffin' (lunch).

The Mendip Hills
Map 4L6. Somerset. Between Weston-super-Mare and
Wells ***i*** *The Library, Union St., Cheddar* ☎ *(0934) 742769.*
This limestone ridge some 15–20 miles (24–32km) in length is
known for its walks, its caves, Cheddar cheese, and above all for
the **Cheddar Gorge** (along B3135 to the NE of the small town of
Cheddar), a narrow ravine below precipitous cliffs rising to
around 430ft (130m) above the road.
  For hotels, see *Wells*, to the SE of the hills.

Sights and places of interest
Cheddar Caves
S end of Cheddar Gorge ☎ *(0934) 742343* ▧ *separate charge for*
each attraction or inclusive discount tickets available ◪ *for Gough's*
Cave ▣ ✳ ⇌ *Gough's Cave and Cox's Cave open Easter–Sept*
10am–5pm, Oct–Easter 11am–5pm. Other attractions open Easter
to mid-Oct 10am–5pm.
There is plenty of evidence that these caves were used by prehistoric man
and by animals now long extinct in Britain. **Gough's Cave** is the larger of
the two and involves a conducted tour. In **Cox's Cave**, with its good
limestone formations, visitors are on their own with a taped
commentary. Other attractions include the **Fantasy Grotto**, a man-
made cave with tableaux; **Jacob's Ladder**, steps to the top of the gorge;
and a **museum** and **exhibition** with artifacts, dioramas and the skeleton
of Cheddar Man, found in Gough's Cave and said to be around 10,000yrs
old.
Chewton Cheese Dairy
Chewton Mendip, on A39, 5 miles (8km) N of Wells ☎ *(076121)*
560 ▧ ⇌ *Shop open Mon–Fri 8.30am–5pm, Sat 9am–5pm, Sun*
9am–1pm. Closes 4pm Jan–Mar.
Here is an opportunity to see the famed Cheddar cheese being made
(*telephone for exact time*). The shop sells cheese, butter and cream, and
cheese can be sent to almost any address in the world.
King John's Hunting Lodge (*Axbridge Museum*)
Market Square, Axbridge ☎ *(0934) 732012. NT* ▣ *Open*
Apr–Sept 2–5pm.
A crazily picturesque late 15thC building that has nothing to do with
King John, who merely owned land in these parts. It houses a museum of
local archeology and history.
Wookey Hole
Just NW of Wells ☎ *(0749) 72243* ▨▨ ◪ *for caves and papermill*
(about 1hr) ▣ ✳ ⇌ *Open Apr–Sept 10am–6pm, Oct–Mar*
10am–4.30pm.
The vast and spectacular caves formed by the river Axe are the main draw
here. In one of the caverns visitors see the **Witch of Wookey**, today a
stalagmite but once a witch until she was petrified by a courageous
Glastonbury monk. Included in the entrance fee is a mill at which paper
is made by hand as it has been since the 17thC; a collection of old
fairground figures, beautifully carved and painted; the bizarre storeroom
belonging to Madame Tussaud's (see *Sights* in *London*) which also runs
this complex; and a caves museum.

Newcastle-upon-Tyne
*Map 15C8. T and W. On the NE coast. Population: 222,000.
Airport* ☎ *(0632) 860966; railway station* ☎ *(0632) 326262;
coach station* ☎ *(0632) 616077; bus information* ☎ *(0632)
325325* **i** *Central Library, Princes Sq.* ☎ *(0632) 610691, and
Blackfriars, Monk St.* ☎ *(0632) 615367.*

A place of often startling contrasts, Newcastle offers two totally
different first impressions. When approached from the N,
seemingly endless suburbs give way to the green **Town Moor**,
beyond which the visitor is confronted by the **Civic Centre**, a
clean and effective modern achievement (1968) with several
striking features. The approach from the S, on the other hand,
will satisfy those with set ideas about what a northern
industrial center should look like, for here something of the
grime survives where three adjacent bridges span the Tyne – the
Tyne Bridge now carrying the superhighway bypass; the Swing
Bridge (1876); and Robert Stephenson's split-level (road and
rail) High Level Bridge of 1849. Between these extremes of old
and new (the bridges and the Civic Centre) lies central
Newcastle, with its network of fine Victorian streets (**Grey St.**
is incomparably the best) which, despite fringe encroachment
by modern town planners, have kept their dignity.

There are contrasts of detail, too. The medieval **castle** has
been split in two by a railway. The beautifully balanced
medieval stone lantern tower on the **cathedral** (*St Nicholas St.*)
is 400yrs older than the Civic Centre's copper lantern. An
ancient Dominican friary, **Blackfriars** (*Monk St.*), is home now
to modern craftsmen who both work and sell their wares here.
And a mellow 17thC almshouse, home of the charming **John G.
Joicey Museum** ☆ (*City Rd.* ☎ *(0632) 324562* ▣ *open
10am–5.30pm, closed Sun*) which tells the social story of the city
and has exceptionally well-designed period rooms as well as
arms and armor, is reached through dreary subways of mindless
graffiti. (For details of Newcastle's wide range of other
museums, see below.)

Sights and places of interest
Newcastle's museums
The Greek Museum (*The Quadrangle, Newcastle University* ☎ *(0632)
328511* ▣ *open Mon–Fri 10am–4.30pm*) is devoted to Greek and
Etruscan art. The exhibits span from Minoan to Hellenistic.

The Hancock Museum (*Barras Bridge, Newcastle University*
☎ *(0632) 322359* ▣ ➹ *open Mon–Sat 10am–5pm; and Sun
Easter–Sept 2–5pm*) has displays of natural history and ethnography of a
caliber way above most museums of this kind. The **Northumberland** and
Geology halls and the **John Hancock Collection** of birds all deserve
special mention.

The Hatton Gallery (*The Quadrangle, Newcastle University* ☎ *(0632)
328511* ▣ *open Mon–Fri 10am–5.30pm, Sat during term 10am–5pm,
closed Sun*) has a permanent collection of paintings (mainly Italian) and
sculpture spanning from the 14thC to the present day, including the last
relief of the Dadaist, Kurt Schwitters, built from odd fragments of junk
and tattered symbols of western culture. The gallery also has a
continuous program of temporary exhibitions.

The Laing Art Gallery (*Higham Place* ☎ *(0632) 327734* ▣ *open
Mon–Sat 10am–5.30pm, Sun 2.30–5.30pm, bank holidays
10am–5.30pm*) has applied art on the lower floor and British paintings,
17th–20thC, on the upper floor. Among the pictures is an outstanding
selection ☆ of the melodramatic works of John 'Mad' Martin
(1789–1854), including *Belshazzar's Feast* and *The Bard*. Other British
artists represented are Richard Wilson, the Pre-Raphaelites, portraitists
(Reynolds, Lawrence, Raeburn) and modern painters such as Stanley
Spencer.

The Museum of Antiquities (*The Quadrangle, Newcastle University* ☎ *(0632) 328511* ◙ *open 10am–5pm, closed Sun*) is of particular interest to anyone planning to visit *Hadrian's Wall*. A vivid picture of how it all looked in Roman times is gained from excellent models including one which shows the entire length of the wall. There are also prehistoric and Anglo-Saxon exhibits.

Sights nearby

Beamish North of England Open Air Museum ☆

Beamish Hall, Stanley. 5 miles (8km)s of central Newcastle ☎ *(0207) 31811* ▨ ▬ ✳ ▭ *Open Apr–Sept 10am–6pm; Oct–Mar 10am–5pm (closed Mon). Some attractions summer only.*

The theme here, in a setting of some 200 acres, is life in the N of England in the early 20thC, illustrated tangibly and wherever possible in action. Older visitors may see things they never thought to see again, younger ones may be forgiven some disbelief. Ambitious plans for the future include the reconstruction of a whole section of a market town, but here are just a few of the experiences that await today's visitor: a complete railway station, with the possibility of a steam train ride; a colliery where visitors can see how coal was mined about 1900, while meticulously furnished cottages show how the miners lived; a ride on a 1920s tram; a transportation exhibition; or a stroll around a farm. There may even be a band playing in the Victorian bandstand.

Washington Old Hall

The Avenue, Washington. 7 miles (11km) SE of Newcastle-upon-Tyne ☎ *(0632) 466879. NT* ▨ *Open Mar–Oct noon–5pm or sunset if earlier (closed Wed); Nov–Feb Sat, Sun 2–4pm.*

In 1183 William de Hertburn acquired this property, building a house (some parts of the original can still be seen although there was much rebuilding in the 17thC) and changing his name to the local Washington, or Wessyngton as it then was. Thus this is an ancestral home of George Washington. Although his personal link is remote since the family sold the house in 1613, some 40yrs before his great-grandfather emigrated, there are Washington relics, and it is fascinating to see that the family's arms incorporate three stars and two stripes.

Hotels

☒ **Newcastle Crest** (*Newbridge St., Newcastle-upon-Tyne, Tyne and Wear NE1 8BS* ☎ *(0632) 326191* ☏ *53467* ◫); **Royal Turks Head** (*Grey St., Newcastle-upon-Tyne, Tyne and Wear NE1 6EL* ☎ *(0632) 326111* ◫); **Swallow** (*Newgate Arcade, Newcastle-upon-Tyne, Tyne and Wear NE1 5SX* ☎ *(0632) 325025* ☏ *53168* ◫).

Hotel/restaurant nearby

Longhorsley (*20 miles/32km N of Newcastle-upon-Tyne*).

☒ ☒ **Linden Hall** ☙ ▥

Longhorsley, Morpeth, Northumb NE65 8XF ☎ *(0670) 56611* ☏ *538224* ▩ *to* ◫ ▭ *45* ▭ *45* ▭ ▭ ▭ ᴀᴇ ᴄʙ ◉ ◉ ᴠɪsᴀ ▩ ▭ □ ▭ *Last orders 9.30pm.*

Location: Just N of Longhorsley, on A697. The game-shooting weekends at Linden Hall provide some indication of the style of country life in Northumberland, a majestic but under-appreciated county which is in parts as Scottish as it is English. The 3,000-acre estate has a Northumbrian character, too, not least in the work of the county's great architect John Dobson, who helped build the house in 1812. Bedrooms are individually furnished, and Linden Hall even has its own inn, with cask-conditioned ale. The restaurant's specialties include seasonal game, lamb in Madeira sauce and veal *cassis*.

▱ ✇ ⚲ □ ▱ ⚓ ⚔ ⚜ ☡ ⚘ ▭ ⚱

Nightlife

City Hall (*Northumberland Rd.* ☎ *(0632) 612606*) is the main venue for concerts, both orchestral and rock. The productions at the **Newcastle Playhouse** (*Gulbenkian Studio, Barras Bridge* ☎ *(0632) 323421*) are mostly presented by the TyneWear Theatre Company and are of a high standard. The main theater is the **Theatre Royal** (*100 Grey St.* ☎ *(0632) 322061*) where the major productions include ballet, plays and opera by leading touring companies.

Shopping

The **Eldon Square Shopping Precinct**, one of Europe's largest city-center shopping precincts, incorporates the traditional **Green Market**; adjacent to it is the Victorian **Grainger Market**. These complexes provide Newcastle with an efficient shopping area in which national department stores and local shops can be found.

The New Forest

Map 5M8. Hants. Between Southampton and Bournemouth **i** *Main parking lot, Lyndhurst* ☎ *(042128) 2269.*

Although not a forest in the full sense of the word (in fact this term, dating from the time of William the Conqueror, means no more than that this was a royal hunting preserve), there is nevertheless plenty of mixed woodland here as well as open heath, and the great charm of the area, covering nearly 300sq. miles (780sq.km), is that it can be enjoyed both by the motorist and the walker for whom there await inviting tracts of road-free countryside. Other features are deer, semi-wild ponies, and the many beautifully sited and tended Forestry Commission picnic and camping sites (see *Sports and activities*, below).

Sights and places of interest

Beaulieu Palace House, Abbey and Motor Museum ☆

Beaulieu, on B3056 ☎ *(0590) 612345, or for medieval banquets 612165* 🔳 *for major sights. Voucher Books for all extra features, or individual tickets available* 💷 ✳ 🚗 ⇥ *Open Easter–Sept 10am–6pm; Oct–Easter 10am–5pm.*

Since 1538 the home of the Montagu family, Beaulieu is one of the best developed and most popular of England's stately home complexes. The three principal attractions are the ruined **abbey**, the **motor museum** and the **Palace House**, but there are all sorts of other lures, such as a monorail, a veteran bus ride, and an annual program of special events.

The **abbey** was a Cistercian house founded in 1204 and destroyed at the Dissolution. The cloisters and archways of the chapter house are still identifiable, but the real survivor is the refectory which now serves as the parish church, known for its evocative reader's pulpit.

The **National Motor Museum** ★ ranks among the world's finest and illustrates the progress of motoring from 1895 until the present day. In addition to more than 200 vehicles there are special displays.

The **Palace House** was originally the abbey gatehouse. In spite of extensive Victorian Baronial additions, it is nevertheless a gracious enough place. Family relics and portraits can be seen, while tableaux in some of the rooms reflect facets of the lives of past generations.

One of the more exciting ways of getting to Beaulieu is on the Orient Express. (*For further details* ☎ *(01) 928–5837.*)

Buckler's Hard ☆

Beside the river, 2 miles (3km)s of Beaulieu ☎ *(059063) 203* 🔳 💷 🚗 *Open Easter–May 10am–6pm; June–Sept 10am–9pm; Oct–Easter 10am–4.30pm.*

A 'hard' is a slipway and what can be seen here beside the Beaulieu river is an 18thC shipbuilding village, one moreover that built ships for Nelson. Among the features (some with wax figures and not unrealistic sound effects) are the New Inn, a laborer's cottage, a shipwright's cottage, and a **maritime museum**. In summer there are boat trips. See also *Hotels*, below.

New Forest Butterfly Farm

Longdown, Ashurst ☎ *(042129) 2166* 🔳 💷 ✳ 🚗 *Open early Apr–Oct 10am–5pm.*

This, to quote the official leaflet, is 'an indoor tropical garden filled with exotic free-flying butterflies and moths from around the world.' Less attractive, and happily less free, are scorpions, tarantulas and such. A large picnic area, a shop and an adventure playground round off this out-of-the-ordinary place.

Rufus Stone

Just N of A31, a short way NE of Stoney Cross. Always accessible.

The stone records the death here in 1100 of William II (Rufus), slain by an arrow while out hunting. Whether he was killed by accident or design or by whom nobody knows. Various names have been suggested (William was unpopular both as a man and as king), the favorite being Walter Tirel who, guilty or innocent, wisely fled the country.

Hotels and restaurants
Beaulieu *(5 miles/8km NE of Lymington)*.

H Montagu Arms

Palace Lane, Beaulieu, Hants S04 7ZL ☎ *(0590) 612324* ▯▮ ⌂ 26
🛏 26 ⟵ 🅿 ⌂ *winter* ⇌ AE CB ⊕ ⊙ VISA

Location: Village center. An inviting, ivy-clad, brick building with a paneled and chintz interior. Bedrooms are individually styled, some with four-poster beds and some with pleasant views of the abbey and river.

⌂ ▢ 🖼 ⚓ ⚐ 🎿

Buckler's Hard *(7 miles/11km NE of Lymington)*.

H Master Builder's House

Buckler's Hard, Beaulieu, Hants SO4 7XB ☎ *(059063) 253* ▮▯
⌂ 23 🛏 17 ⟵ ⇌ AE CB ⊕ ⊙ VISA

Location: Beside the 18thC village site. This hotel was the home of the prosperous Henry Adams, the best known of the local 18thC shipbuilders. Skillful renovations, including an unobtrusive modern extension, have ensured that little of the place's gracious riverside charm has been lost. The restaurant, overlooking the river, specializes in English dishes such as venison and game in season.

♿ ▢ ⚓ ⚐ 🎿 🎿

New Milton *(5 miles/8km W of Lymington)*.

H R Chewton Glen 🏨 ⛳

Christchurch Rd., New Milton, Hants BH25 6QS ☎ *(04252) 5341*
✆41456 ▮▮▮ ⌂ 52 🛏 52 ⟵ ⇌ AE CB ⊕ ⊙ VISA
R ▮▮▮ ⌷ 🖼 ⇌ 🚗 *Last orders 9.30pm.*

Location: On A337 between New Milton and Highcliffe. One of the best-known country house hotels, and the one which most strives to offer also the full services of a metropolitan hotel. The glen itself is a small, wooded ravine, through which it is an easy walk to the sea at Christchurch Bay. Historically, this was smuggling country, and the naval writer Captain Frederick Marryat, who is today better remembered for his *The Children of the New Forest*, lived in the house in the 1840s. The building was remodeled in Queen Anne style in the early 20thC, and has been extended in more recent years. Shuttered windows and formal gardens add an Italianate mood, although touches such as the coachlamps in the corridors gild the lily. Rooms are extremely well-equipped and comfortable, with white-painted bamboo furniture and restful color schemes with lots of pastel blues.

Outstanding cuisine in the Marryat Room includes local sea bass with salmon mousse; *foie gras* and chicken; calf's sweetbreads with assorted seasonal mushrooms and home-made noodles; and Scottish fillet steak in pastry *Périgourdine*. There is an extensive wine list.

⌂ ▢ 🖼 🍴 ⚐ 🎿 ≈ 🏊 〰 ✓ 🚶 🏌 🎿

Sports and activities
Camping Camping is only allowed on camp sites which are either privately owned or run by the Forestry Commission. (*Details can be obtained from tourist information centers or the Forestry Commission, Queens House, Lyndhurst.*)
Fishing The Avon is a good fishing river offering trout, roach, grayling, chub and pike and salmon (strictly preserved). Compulsory permits are available from most inns, the Angling Club in Ringwood or from Hunter's Hardware (*High St., Fordingbridge*). Alternatively, there is sea fishing both from the beach and from boats.
Riding The New Forest is ideal country for riding, and the tourist office has a list of recommended riding establishments.

Norfolk Broads

Map 13H12. Norfolk. NW and S of Great Yarmouth **i** *East Anglia Tourist Board, 14 Museum St., Ipswich, Suffolk* ☎ *(0473) 214211.*

In all there are some 130 miles (200km) of boating waterways mainly in Norfolk but also in Suffolk. These shallow, reedy meres or sluggish streams offer windmills, waterbirds, nature reserves, some attractive villages and not infrequent pubs. But although nature is placid here, man may not be so, and in summer there can be a lot of people around. A number of firms including **Blakes Holidays Ltd** (*Wroxham, Norwich* ☎ *(06053) 3226*) and **Hoseasons Holidays Ltd** (*Sunway House, Lowestoft, Suffolk* ☎ *(0502) 62101*) rent out a variety of boats.

Northampton

Map 6I9. Northants. 67 miles (107km) NW of London. Population: 150,000 **i** *21 St Giles St.* ☎ *(0604) 22677.*

A manufacturing town of no obvious character, Northampton is today best known for shoemaking, and any visitor with such an esoteric interest should make for the **Central Museum** (*Guildhall Rd.* ☎ *(0604) 34881* 🖭 *open 10am–6pm, closed Sun*) where the principal display tells the story of boots, shoes and leather, not just locally but worldwide. There are examples of footwear from, for example, Africa, China and America, while 19thC Northampton is brought to life through a reconstruction of a cobbler's shop, *c.1860*. A subsidiary museum is the **Museum of Leathercraft** (*60 Bridge St.* ☎ *(0604) 24881* 🖭 *open 10am–1pm, 2–5.30pm*).

Sight nearby
Althorp

Althorp, 6 miles (9.5km) NW of Northampton ☎ *(060125) 209* 🔲 🔳 🚗 *House and grounds open Sept–July Tues–Thurs, Sat (June, July grounds only), Sun 2.30–5.30pm; Aug 2.30–6pm; bank holidays 11.30am–6pm. Closed Mon.*

A mansion of some contemporary interest, since 1508 it has been the seat of the Spencer family and thus, more recently, the home of the Princess of Wales before her marriage. For specialized tastes there is fine French furniture and porcelain, but the majority of visitors come to enjoy the splendid collection of pictures, especially portraits, by a dazzling company of artists including Lely, Reynolds and Gainsborough.

Ⓗ Angel

Bridge St., Northampton NN1 1NA ☎ *(0604) 21661* 🌐 *25971* 🔲 🍴 51 🛏 9 ⟷ ➡ 🆎 ⓐ ⓓ 🆅

Location: Central. This one-time coaching inn is the oldest hostelry in the town. With its warm woodwork and welcoming pub-like bars it carries on a tradition of hospitality reaching back to the 16thC.
🔲 💺

Ⓡ Vineyard ⬤ ♣

7 Derngate ☎ *(0604) 33978* 🔲 🔲 🔳 ➡ ⓐ ⓓ 🆅 *Last orders 10.30pm. Closed Mon dinner, Sat lunch, Sun, bank holidays, one week at Christmas.*

Wine is one passion of the owner Jim Ainsworth, who came here from the groves of academe. Although his list is extensive, he emphasizes wines that are interesting and of good quality but not necessarily famous and expensive. Cheese is another passion, with England notably well represented. In the kitchen, he is an unrepentant campaigner for the use of offal. Those who do not have such bourgeois tastes can still enjoy an excellent meal inexpensively. Prices and atmosphere are especially good at lunchtimes.

Restaurant nearby
Horton (*on B526, 6 miles/9.5km SE of Northampton*).

R **French Partridge**
Newport Pagnell Rd. ☎ *(0604) 870033* ▥ ■ ➥ ⇦ *Last orders*
9.30pm. Closed Sun, Mon, Easter week, mid-July to early Aug, two
weeks at Christmas.
A French restaurant, run by a couple whose surname is Partridge. Fish
and game dishes are outstanding, and there is an extensive, well-chosen
wine list with some excellent values.

Shopping
An open market is held in **Market Sq.**, one of the largest squares in the
country, on Wed, Fri and Sat. Major shopping streets include **The**
Drapery, **Gold St.**, **St Giles St.** and **Abington St.**, while the **Grosvenor**
Centre adjacent to Market Sq. is a covered shopping precinct.

Northumberland National Park
Map 15B7. Northumb. NW of Newcastle-upon-Tyne,
between Hadrian's Wall and the Scottish border
i Eastburn, South Park, Hexham, Northumb NE46 1BS
☎ *(0434) 605555.*
Virtually the most northern slice of England, it is also the
loneliest, a 398sq. mile (1,030sq.km) area of rolling moor and
mountain bounded by *Hadrian's Wall* to the s and the **Cheviot**
Hills to the N. These broad-shouldered upland tracts beckon
the walker or the pony trekker rather than the motorist, for,
although the more adventurous will penetrate on minor roads,
only one main one crosses the park – the A68, climbing and
dipping from **Otterburn** to high-perched **Carter Bar**, a place at
which to draw breath and scan the great northern arc that is
historic lowland Scotland.
  Border Forest Park, which extends the SW sector of
Northumberland's park, contains Western Europe's largest
reservoir, **Kielder Water**.
  A useful leaflet, *Walks, Trails and Events* is available from
the tourist office. For a list of pony trekking centers contact
Tynedale District Council (*Tourist Information Centre, The*
Manor Office, Hallgate, Hexham ☎ *(0434) 605225*).

North Yorkshire Moors National Park ★
Map 16E9. North Yorks. Inland from Whitby and
Scarborough i The Old Vicarage, Bondgate, Helmsley,
North Yorks YO6 5BP ☎ *(0439) 70657; otherwise Danby*
Lodge National Park Centre (see below).
The essence of this park of over 500sq. miles (1,295sq.km) is a
heart of high, wide, open moorland crumbling around the edges
into pastoral, wooded dales along which await pleasant small
towns and villages together with the ruins of castles and abbeys;
the most remarkable examples, **Rievaulx** and **Whitby**, are
described below, but others such as **Helmsley Castle**, with its
lofty, turreted, ruined keep, and **Byland Abbey** at the s edge of
the park, best known for its well-preserved 12thC glazed tiles,
are worth a detour. **Mount Grace Priory** at Osmotherley, to the
W of the park, is also of interest; its quite substantial ruins are
the best remains in Britain of a Carthusian house.
  Both the E and the W flanks of the park are spectacular; the
former has some of the boldest cliff scenery along England's
eastern coast, while to the W lies **Sutton Bank**, an escarpment
affording a panoramic vista across the Vale of York to the
promise of the Pennines beyond. The park's principal towns are
Helmsley and **Pickering** to the s, **Scarborough** to the SE, and,
farther up the coast, **Whitby**, picturesquely clustering along the
steep sides of the tidal Esk. Eight miles (13km) SW of Whitby,

155

near **Goathland**, over a mile (1.5km) of genuine Roman road has been uncovered.

Danby Lodge National Park Centre (*at Danby, in N central part of park* ☎ *(02876) 654* ▨ ▣ ☛ *open Easter – Oct 10am – 5pm, Mar and Nov Sat, Sun 10am – 5pm*) is the best place at which to start a visit to the park. An exhibition, lectures and films tell all about it, and all manner of leaflets including suggestions for local walks are available.

Sights and places of interest

North Yorkshire Moors Railway

*Map **16E9**. Pickering (to Grosmont)* ☎ *(0751) 72508 or 73535 for recorded timetable* ▨ ▣ ☀ ☛ *Railway operates Apr – Oct (about 1hr in each direction). Telephone for exact times.*

Closed by British Rail in 1965 but reopened by private enterprise eight years later, this line through the heart of the National Park is one of the world's earliest. Built by George Stephenson in the 1830s, its coaches and freight cars were drawn by horses for the first ten years. The locomotives date from 1890 to the present day. Journeys can be broken at **Levisham**, **Newtondale** and **Goathland**, while at **Grosmont** maintenance can be watched from a viewing gallery. Most trains have a bar and there is a splendid Pullman diner service on Wed evenings, mid-June to mid-Sept (*reservations advised*).

Rievaulx Abbey ☆

*Map **16E9**. Off B1257, 2½ miles (4km) NW of Helmsley* ☎ *(04396) 228. DOE* ▨ ☛ *Open mid-Mar to mid-Oct Mon – Sat 9.30am – 6.30pm, Sun 2 – 6.30pm except Apr – Sept 9.30am – 6.30pm; mid-Oct to mid-Mar Mon – Sat 9.30am – 4pm, Sun 2 – 4pm.*

This beautifully sited Cistercian house was founded in 1132, today's considerable remains standing witness to its one-time importance.

To the s, **Rievaulx Terrace** (☎ *(04396) 340. NT* ▨ ☛ ◁ɛ *open Apr – Oct 10.30am – 6pm*), laid out in the 18thC, affords superb and carefully planned views down to the abbey below.

Whitby Abbey

*Map **16D9**. Whitby* ☎ *(0947) 3568. DOE* ▨ ☛ *Open mid-Mar to Apr – Sept 9.30am – 6.30pm; mid-Oct to mid-Mar Mon – Sat 9.30am – 6.30pm, Sun 2 – 4pm.*

High on their windswept clifftop, these mainly 12th–13thC ruins are a gaunt reminder that this is a place whose story reaches deep into the roots of early English Christianity. Founded in the 7thC, Whitby was one of the first mixed houses – moreover one whose monks and nuns were ruled by a woman, St Hilda – and it was the venue of the synod of 664 which in effect established the supremacy of Catholicism in Northumbria for around 900yrs. But in 867 the Danes destroyed Whitby and two centuries passed before Benedictine monks returned to re-establish their ancient abbey.

Restaurant

Fadmoor (*7 miles/11km NE of Helmsley*).

ℝ **Plough**
Fadmoor ☎ *(0751) 31515* ▮▯ ▩ ▤ ☛ *Last orders 8.30pm. Closed lunch, Sun, Mon, Jan 1; also one week in mid-Feb, mid-May and mid-Oct, Christmas.*
A pub on the moors, recommended for the variety, quality, inventiveness and value of its substantial, three-course set menu.

See also *Castle Howard*.

Norwich

*Map **13I12**. Norfolk. 115 miles (184km) NE of London. Population: 122,000* **i** *Augustine Steward House, 14 Tombland* ☎ *(0603) 20679.*

With no actual center or main street, Norwich can be a confusing place to visit, but those who abandon their cars can

wander through the ancient streets (**Elm Hill** is one of the best
examples, with cobblestones and well-preserved old houses)
that wind their way here and there between the city's three
important focal points: the **cathedral**, the **castle** and the
market place. This last, crammed with stalls every weekday, is
surrounded by several distinguished buildings, such as the
15thC flint **Guildhall** and the modern **City Hall** (1938).
Event In late June, Royal Norfolk Show at Agricultural
Showground.

Sights and places of interest
Bridewell Museum
Bridewell Alley, Bedford St. ☎ *(0603) 611277* 📷 *Open
10am–5pm. Closed Sun.*

Starting as a merchant's home in the 14thC, becoming a 'bridewell' or
vagrants' prison in 1583 (the wretches' scratched initials and dates can be
seen in the courtyard), then a factory from 1828–1923, this ancient
building finally became a museum of local crafts and industries in 1925.
Exhibits cover innumerable activities such as shipping, food,
shoemaking and printing and include some astonishing early machinery.
Before leaving, glance at the building's N wall which is an outstanding
example of early flintwork.

Norwich Castle and Castle Museum
Castle Meadow, Market Avenue ☎ *(0603) 611277* 📷 📼 *Open
Mon–Sat 10am–5pm, Sun 2–5pm.*

This huge motte, thrown up soon after 1066, supported a wooden
fortress until *c.*1130 when Henry I built the massive stone keep which
today survives as such a prominent central feature of the city. Its external
facade, although dating from the 19thC and in different stone, is a
reproduction of the original Norman blind arcading. The interior is
every bit as impressive, not least for the deep well, now cleverly lit.

The **museum** covers many fields including archeology, social history
and natural history; the most outstanding exhibits are some admirable
dioramas of Bronze and Iron Age scenes. The museum's art gallery
shows paintings by the Norwich school with particular emphasis on John
Crome and John Sell Cotman.

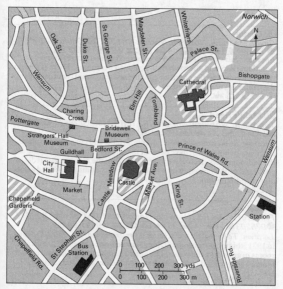

Norwich Cathedral 🏛 ✝
450yds (140m) NE of the castle ☎ *(0603) 20715.*

Essentially this is an achievement of Norman simplicity, a legacy
bequeathed by two men: Bishop Losinga who started to build in 1096
and was responsible for the choir, transepts and E bays of the nave, and
his successor Bishop Eborard who completed the bulk of the nave.
Floodlit all these centuries later, their combined masterpiece assumes a
quality they may perhaps have glimpsed by moonlight. The cathedral's
soaring spire was added in the 15thC.

Vault bosses are a feature of the interior, notably in the nave and in the
cloisters, although the former, illustrating events in the Bible, are not
easy to see. The cloister bosses present no problem, however, and with
their sometimes quite detailed representations of the contemporary daily
round are the more entertaining. The **Bishop's Throne** also demands
attention, a unique survival from the 8thC and so positioned that its
occupant could dominate the length of the nave.

Sainsbury Centre for Visual Arts
University of East Anglia, 1½ miles (2.5km) w of city center
☎ *(0603) 56060* 🎫 ▣ 🍴 *Open noon–5pm. Closed Mon.*

In 1973 Sir Robert and Lady Sainsbury presented their private
collections to the university and these are now shown in an award-
winning building (a steel structure with aluminum and glass panels)
which is also used for frequent temporary exhibitions. The Sainsbury
taste spanned a remarkably wide field embracing medieval and modern
European art, and the art of the American Indians, Eskimos and tribal
Africans. The Anderson Collection of Art Nouveau works and the
University of East Anglia's collection of 20thC Constructivist Art can
also be seen here.

Strangers' Hall
Charing Cross ☎ *(0603) 611277* 🎫 *Open 10am–5pm. Closed Sun.*

Originally a rich merchant's home, this rambling old house (much added
to since it was begun in about 1320) is an appropriate setting for the
sequence of 17 period rooms which encompass Tudor to Victorian times
and which, together with other exhibits, make up a vivid museum of
English domestic life. In the coach house, visitors can see a splendid
Panhard–Levassor car dating from 1898.

'Strangers' was the name given to the immigrant weavers of the 14thC,
for whom this hall later served as a center.

Hotels

Ⓗ Castle
Castle Meadow, Norwich, Norfolk NR1 3PZ ☎ *(0603) 611511*
Ⓣ*975582* ▯ 🛏 *79* 🚪 *26* 🚗 🔲 ≈ AE CB ⓓ ⓓ VISA
Location: Just SW of the castle. A good, average hotel with rather
functional bars and cheerful, well-equipped bedrooms. There is a useful
snack shop and, in the main, air conditioned restaurant, beef carved on
the trolley is a popular feature.
✦ ㋔ ☐ 🖃 🏊

Ⓗ Maid's Head
Tombland, Norwich, Norfolk NR3 1LB ☎ *(0603) 28821* Ⓣ*975080*
▯ ▮ 🛏 *82* 🚪 *78* 🚗 🔲 AE ⓓ ⓓ VISA
Location: By the cathedral. A solid, comfortable and conservative place,
successor to inns which have been on this site for some 700yrs. Some of
the bedrooms lack decorative imagination, but the restaurant is red-
plush and sophisticated, with a set menu of outstanding value and a good
dry white house wine.
✦ ☐ 🏊

Ⓗ Nelson
Prince of Wales Rd., Norwich, Norfolk NR1 1DX ☎ *(0603) 28612*
Ⓣ*975203* ▯ 🛏 *94* 🚪 *94* 🚗 🔲 ≈ AE ⓓ ⓓ VISA
Location: To the E of the town, beside the river and near the station. Opened
in 1971, this is a purpose-built, long, low red-brick hotel with several
rooms overlooking the water. The hotel's name and various nautical
touches are justified by the fact that Lord Nelson attended school in
Norwich.
✦ ㋔ ☐ 🖃 🖊 ◁≪ 🏊

Restaurant nearby
Guist (*on A1067, 18 miles/29km NW of Norwich*).

ⓡ The Tollbridge
Dereham Rd. ☎ *(036284) 359* ⅢⅡ ▭ ■■ ▬ ⌂ ⌐ *Last orders*
9.30pm. Closed Sun, Mon, last three weeks in Jan, first week in Oct.
At this 18thC tollhouse on the river Wensum, freshwater fish feature on
the menu whenever possible. Excellent and imaginative cooking in a
charming restaurant which also makes something of a specialty of its
desserts. Cask-conditioned Adnams' beer is available here.

Nightlife
The **Theatre Royal** (*Theatre St.* ☎ *(0603) 28205*) is renowned for its
enterprising repertoire which includes pre-West End plays and hit
shows. There is also the excellent **Norwich Puppet Theatre** (*St James,
Whitefriars* ☎ *(0603) 29921*).

Shopping
Major shopping streets in the center are **St Benedict St.**, **Pottergate**,
Elm Hill and **London St.** with many shops housed in medieval
buildings. The **Bridewell Alley** medieval thoroughfare has become a
center for crafts and antiques with **The Mustard Shop** (and museum)
selling Colman's mustard, and **Hovells** specializing in baskets, pine and
cane furniture. The **Anglia Sq.** shopping center in the N is less exclusive.
There is a colorful market on weekdays in **Market Pl.**

Nottingham
Map 11H9. Notts. 25 miles (40km) N of Leicester.
Population: 300,000. East Midlands Airport ☎ *(0332)*
810621; railway station ☎ *(0602) 46151; coach and bus*
station ☎ *(0602) 48007* **i** *18 Milton St.* ☎ *(0602) 40661.*
Nottingham's most famous associations are lace and Robin
Hood. Lace can be seen at the **Lace Centre** (*Castle Rd.*
☎ *(0602) 413539* ▣ *open 10am – 5pm*), a 15thC building
moved to this site in 1969, and at the adjacent **Museum of
Costume and Textiles** (*41 – 53 Castlegate* ☎ *(0602) 411881* ▣
open 10am – 5pm), which also has costumes of the 17th – 19thC,
including accessories and underwear, charmingly shown in
period rooms. The Lace Centre also sells Nottingham lace.
　Robin Hood, the outlaw who lived in nearby **Sherwood
Forest** and spent his time robbing the rich to feed the poor, is
more elusive, although his statue stands beside Castle Rd. In the
forest, a peaceful area for walks and picnics, the **Major Oak**
with its vast girth is more than 1,000yrs old.
　The town center is **Old Market Sq.** For the visitor, however,
Nottingham's main interest focuses on the **castle**, some 600yds
(550m) to the SW. While in this quarter, visitors can have a
drink at an inn that dates back to the 12thC, The Trip to
Jerusalem (see *Nightlife*, below).
Event First Thurs in Oct for 3 days, **Goose Fair**. Spectacular
funfair with games and merry-go-rounds for all ages; originally
a 13thC market for the buying and selling of geese.

Sights and places of interest
Brewhouse Yard Museum
At s foot of castle ☎ *(0602) 411881* ▣ *Open 10am – noon, 1 – 5pm.*
As its name suggests, this was once the site of the castle's maltings and
brewhouse. However, a row of houses was built here *c.*1670, and these
now provide a pleasing setting for a variety of imaginative displays,
including period rooms and shops, illustrating many aspects of
Nottingham's story over the past three or more centuries. The garden
has some unusual local plants.

Nottingham Castle Museum
In the sw quarter of the town ☎ *(0602) 411881* 🄾 *but* 🄿 *on Sun and bank holidays* 🄿 *Open Apr–Sept 10am–5.45pm; Oct–Mar 10am–4.45pm.*

The Norman castle crowning this steep sandstone rock was razed by Cromwell. What is seen today is the rather pompous, one-time residence of the dukes of Newcastle, built first in the 17thC by a Reform mob in 1831, rebuilt by Nottingham Corporation, and in 1878 opened as England's first provincial **museum** of fine and applied art. The collections are wide-ranging – ceramics, silver, glass, ethnology, local archeology – while the **art gallery** shows works by local artists.

Sights nearby
Newstead Abbey
On A60, 9 miles (14.5km) N of Nottingham ☎ *(06234) 2822* 🄿 🄿 🥩 *Grounds open 10am–6pm or sunset if earlier. Abbey open Easter–Sept 2–6pm.*

Once a 12thC Augustinian priory, this lovely place came to the Byron family in 1540, passing to the poet in 1798 when he was only ten and frequently visited by him until he sold it in 1817. Byron enthusiasts will arrange to come here when the house is open, to see the poet's bedroom (little changed), some of his furniture, books, manuscripts and other relics, while the more imaginative will be able to people the corridors and rooms with the young set who held wild parties here, sometimes dressed as the monks of old. But Newstead is well worth a visit at any time; a gracious, rambling stone building in a tranquil setting of lawns and lakes and romantically incorporating the 13thC w facade of the original abbey church. Near the house, a memorial to Lord Byron's dog, Boatswain, is inscribed with lines written by the poet.

Wollaton Hall
A609, 3 miles (5km) w of town center. Natural History Museum ☎ *(0602) 281333. Industrial Museum* ☎ *(0602) 284602* 🄾 🄿 🥩 *Natural History Museum open Apr–Sept Mon–Sat 10am–7pm, Sun 2–5pm; Oct–Mar Mon–Sat 10am–sunset, Sun 1.30–4.30pm. Industrial Museum open Apr–Sept Mon–Sat 10am–6pm, Sun 2–6pm; Oct–Mar Thurs, Sat 10am–4.30pm, Sun 1.30–4.30pm.*

This rather pretentious Elizabethan mansion houses a natural history museum while the stables contain an industrial museum. The park has a golf course, fishing lake, nature trail and 19thC camellia house.

Hotel

Ⓗ **Victoria** ✿
Milton St., Nottingham NG1 3PZ ☎ *(0602) 49561* 🕿 *37401* 🔳 ☎ *167* 🛏 *167* 🚗 ⚌ 🄰🄴 ⓞ 🄲🄾 *VISA*
Location: Immediately w of Victoria Centre and adjacent to Tourist Information. A solid, conservative and spacious hotel with a sumptuous Edwardian touch.
✦ ⬜ 🖼 🎿

Hotel nearby
Castle Donington (*10 miles /16km SW of Nottingham*).

Ⓗ **Donington Manor**
High St., Castle Donington, Derby DE7 2PP ☎ *(0332) 810253* 🕿 *377208* 🔳 ☎ *39* 🛏 *35* 🚗 ⚌ 🄰🄴 ⓞ 🄲🄾 *VISA* *Closed late Dec.*
Location: On A453, in the town center. This Regency building was built as a coaching inn in 1794 and retains much of its original style, such as bow windows with curved glass, plasterwork, and an elegant dining room. The restaurant specializes in game dishes in season.
⬜ 🎿 ⚓ 🎿

Restaurant

Ⓡ **Le Têtard** 🍽
10 Pilcher Lane ☎ *(0602) 598253* 🔳 ⬜ 🍴 ⚌ 🚗 ⓞ 🄲🄾 *VISA*
Last orders 10.30pm. Closed Sun, bank holidays lunch, one week at Christmas.

'The tadpole' does, indeed, serve frogs' legs, and the menu at this French-run restaurant in Nottingham's Lace Market is determinedly

Gallic. Too ambitious to be regarded as a bistro (although in France it probably would be), its specialties include poached *langouste*, turbot Hollandaise and *escalope de veau forestière*. An interesting wine list.

Nightlife
At the **Nottingham Playhouse** (*Wellington Circus* ☎ *(0602) 45671*), one of England's top repertory companies performs enterprising and often controversial plays. The new entertainment complex, the **Royal Centre**, comprises the **Theatre Royal** (*Theatre Sq.* ☎ *(0602) 42328*) which has been restored to its Victorian opulence and puts on comedy, opera, ballet, plays, one-man shows and pantomime, and the **Royal Concert Hall** (*Theatre Sq.* ☎ *(0602) 42328*), venue for concerts, ballet, dance companies and rock. Other features of the complex include discos, cinemas, cabaret spots and pubs.

A good wine-bar, and popular meeting place, is **Brown's** (*17–19 Goosegate*). Set into the castle rock is **The Trip to Jerusalem**, dating from 1189 and reputed to be the oldest inn in the country. It was said to have been patronized by the Crusaders, hence the name.

Shopping
The traditional shopping area of Nottingham centers on **Old Market Sq.** and the surrounding streets. More modern shopping areas include the huge **Broad Marsh Centre** to the s and the **Victoria Centre** with its indoor market to the N. **Sneinton Market**, slightly farther out, sells country produce on Tues, Thurs and Fri, other goods on Mon and Sat.

Places nearby
Newark-on-Trent (*20 miles (32km) NE of Nottingham*). The main feature of Newark, apart from its Georgian houses and cobbled marketplace, is its large 12th–15thC **castle** (*no admission*), best seen across the river when approaching the town from the N. Often visited by King John, who died here in 1216, the castle successfully withstood three sieges during the Civil War, but was dismantled in 1646. Fortunately an impressive **Norman gatehouse** (1170) has survived.

Southwell (*12 miles/19km NE of Nottingham*).
Southwell Minster †
☎ *(0636) 812649.*
Roman paving between the s transept pews; a **rood screen** bearing an array of carved human heads, over 200 of them and expressing almost as many moods; and a **chapter house** in which the intricately sculpted foliage ranks among the earliest of its kind in England – these are just some of the curiosities to be seen in this robust minster, built in the 12th–14thC but possibly dating back to the mid-7thC.

Ⓗ **Saracen's Head**
Market Place, Southwell, Notts NG25 0HE ☎ *(0636) 812701*
☎858875 ⫴⏢ ⫴ 23 ⬜ 23 ➞ ⇌ ⊨ AE CB Ⓘ ⓘ VISA
Location: Close to the minster. Here the traveler will find modern facilities within the setting of a 16thC (or older) coaching inn. Outside, in the picturesque half-timbered yard, it is easy to imagine coaches, horses and hostlers where cars now park, while, inside, guests can picture Charles I dining here during the dark days of 1646.
◨ ⮕ ☙

Oxford ★
Map **5K8**. *Oxon.* *56 miles (90km) NW of London.*
Population: 108,800. Railway station ☎ *(0865) 722333; coach and bus station* ☎ *(0865) 240504* ⓘ *St Aldates* ☎ *(0865) 726871.*

It does not take long to discover that there are two Oxfords: that of the colleges, aloof behind those sometimes discouraging gates (this Oxford is first mentioned in the 12thC), and, outside, a harsher Oxford of traffic wardens and shopping centers, successor to a settlement named in the Anglo-Saxon Chronicle of 912. Unlike Cambridge, Oxford's colleges are not conveniently sited in one main area. They are in fact scattered around the city, but the network of linking streets hides many an unexpected delight.

For the best view across the city, it is worth ascending the tower of **St Mary the Virgin** in the High St.

Event On May 1, May Day celebrations. Choirboys sing madrigals from Magdalen Tower at dawn; there is also morris dancing.

Sights and places of interest
Colleges

Of Oxford's 35 colleges only a selected few can be described here, but this should not deter the enthusiast from exploring further, for there are hardly any which do not have something to attract the discerning eye. It should be remembered, however, that the colleges are private centers of learning, under no obligation to admit outsiders. Nevertheless most do so, usually free of charge. As a general guide many colleges are closed in the morning, while most (though not necessarily their chapels, libraries and halls) are open in the afternoon. Many colleges' opening hours vary from term to vacation; the terms run approximately from mid-Jan to mid-Mar, mid-Apr to late June and Oct to early Dec. Visitors with a particular interest or those intent on studying Oxford in depth should try to avoid mid-May to late June, when some colleges close for the degree examinations.

Christ Church College and Cathedral †
St Aldates ☎ *(0865) 242201. Open 9.30am–12.30pm, 2–5pm. Entrance by Meadow Gate to the s, but by the main gateway on Sun.*

First, Cardinal Wolsey founded Cardinal College in 1525, razing most of the priory which stood here at that time. Four years later everything stopped when Wolsey fell from power, but in 1532 Henry VIII stepped in to found his own college. Soon, however, this was suppressed to give way in 1545 to the new college of Christ Church, now the largest Oxford college.

Assuming entry by Meadow Gate, visitors first reach the **cathedral**. The smallest in England and enjoying the curious status of being both the city's cathedral and the college's chapel, the building (generally 12thC Norman) is virtually all that survives of the priory razed by Wolsey, although he did manage to pull down the w bays of the nave. Among a number of points of note are the alternating round and octagonal **nave piers**, the late 15thC **choir ceiling**, and the **cloister**, scene of Cranmer's humiliation when his head was shorn and his vestments were stripped from him.

While in this part of the college, have a look into the **hall** (1529), the largest in Oxford and gallery for a notable collection of portraits, including those of *King Henry VIII*, *Queen Elizabeth I* and *Cardinal Thomas Wolsey*.

From the rather gloomy confinement of the cathedral and hall the visitor moves into the huge, open **Great Quadrangle** or Tom Quad, much of it dating from Wolsey's time. On its w side, the college's principal entrance is provided by Wolsey's gateway topped by **Tom Tower** (Wren, 1681), famous for its great bell which each evening tolls 101 times in honor of each member of the original foundation.

See also *Christ Church Picture Gallery*, below.

Magdalen College
E end of High St. ☎ *(0865) 241781. Open 2–6.15pm.*

A foundation of the 15thC (on the site of a Hospital of St John) and with most of its buildings dating from about the same era, this college (pronounced Mordlen) is best known for its lofty tower beside the river Cherwell from which choirboys sing on May Day morning. The college has long enjoyed something of an upper-crust flavor which stems from its close association with royalty and the aristocracy, and not least from the unstinting support it gave to Charles I to whom it rashly presented much of its silver. Traces of the original Hospital of St John can be found in the **Chaplain's Quadrangle** and perhaps in the kitchen, but one of the most picturesque parts of the college is the **Cloister Quadrangle** (15th–16thC) in which the often amusing grotesques on the buttresses certainly merit individual study.

All are welcome at the chapel's beautiful choral services.

Merton College

Merton St. ☎ *(0865) 249651. Open Mon–Fri 2–4pm, Sat, Sun 10am–4pm.*

Although University and Balliol Colleges can claim slightly earlier endowment, Merton is not only the university's oldest foundation (the deed of 1264 in the college archives proves it) but also the place which set the pattern for all future Oxford and Cambridge colleges. This mellow and picturesque place should be visited for its early 14thC **Mob Quad** ☆ – a retreat which more than anywhere else in Oxford evokes an aura of medieval scholarship. The **chapel** is the university's oldest, and the **library** (1378) claims the curious distinction of being the first to remove its books from chests and store them upright on shelves.

New College

Holywell St. ☎ *(0865) 248451. Open during term Mon–Fri 2–5pm, Sat, Sun noon–6pm; during vacation 11am–6pm.*

In spite of its name this is one of the older colleges, founded in 1379 by William of Wykeham, Bishop of Winchester, as the next educational step for the scholars of the college he was building at Winchester; indeed, until the 19thC no one else was admitted and New College achieved a prestigious reputation it still tends to cherish. A man of great wealth and influence, William was well able to achieve his aim, and the range of buildings that await the visitor beyond the modest entrance stand as distinguished examples of late 14thC Perpendicular architecture. The buildings apart, there are three things worth seeking out: in the chapel, with its Victorian interior, a painting, *St James*, by El Greco and *Lazarus*, a statue by Epstein, and in the garden a section of the **13thC city wall**.

All are normally welcome at the choral services.

St John's College

St Giles ☎ *(0865) 247671. Open 1–7pm.*

Keen gardeners and botanists head for this college's spacious grounds – generally accepted as the finest in Oxford – in which a huge, immaculate lawn sweeps away from the college's mature 17thC eastern facade. The college, founded in 1555, is principally associated with Archbishop Laud who was president from 1611–21; unacceptably High Church, he was executed by the Puritans in 1645 and is buried in the chapel.

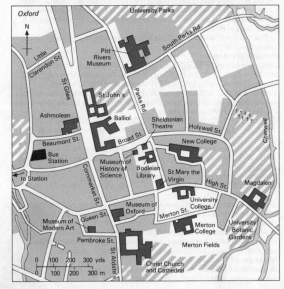

Other sights
Ashmolean Museum ★
Beaumont St. ☎ *(0865) 512651* 📷 *Open Tues–Sat 10am–4pm,
Sun 2–4pm. Closed Mon and during St Giles Fair (Mon and Tues
following first Sun after Sept 2).*

This is the home of the university's priceless collections of art and
antiquities. With departments spread around three floors and a
confusing arrangement of some 50 rooms, it is no place for aimless
wandering; the wise visitor will devise a route with the help of the clear
floor plan available at a nominal price.

On the ground floor the principal antiquities departments are
Classical Sculpture, Egyptian, Far Eastern and **Medieval**. Any choice
from this wealth can only be as inadequate as it is subjective, but
nevertheless there are two exhibits which appear to have become the
stars. These are the **Shrine of Taharqa** of the 7thC BC in the Egyptian
Sculpture Gallery and the exquisite **Alfred Jewel** (9thC) in the Medieval
Room. On the first floor there are prehistoric European, Roman,
Anglo-Saxon and Near Eastern antiquities, the last of these including the
famous Arthur Evans material from Knossos in Crete.

The artists whose paintings hang in the ten galleries devoted to fine art
are representative of periods spanning from early Italian to 20thC
English. Here are the principal classifications and just a few names.
Italian Renaissance: Paolo Uccello's *Hunt in the Forest* ★ a work of fairy-
tale quality. **Venetian:** Tintoretto, Mantegna. **Netherlands:** Rubens,
Van Dyck. **Europe (17th–18thC):** Canaletto, Poussin. **England
(18thC):** Hogarth, Reynolds. **Pre-Raphaelites:** Millais, Holman-Hunt,
Burne-Jones. **France (19thC):** Corot, Daubigny, Pissaro (*Portrait of
Jeanne with a Fan* ★), Fantin-Latour.
Bodleian Library
Broad St. ☎ *(0865) 244675* 📷 *Open Mon–Fri 9am–5pm, Sat
9am–12.30pm. Closed Sun.*

One of the world's oldest and most distinguished libraries, the Bodleian
owes its origin to Humphrey, Duke of Gloucester (1391–1447), who
presented the first books. Tragically this collection was largely dispersed
at the Reformation and the library was not refounded until 1602 when
the diplomat and scholar Sir Thomas Bodley handed over his collections
to the university. So far as today's visitor is concerned the principal
feature is the 15thC **Divinity School**, famed for its elaborate vaulted
ceiling and notorious as the scene of the examination in 1555 of Bishops
Cranmer, Ridley and Latimer, all burned at the stake opposite nearby
Balliol College. The school is now used for permanent and temporary
exhibitions of Bodleian treasures.

Just s of the Bodleian, the **Radcliffe Camera** library is a magnificent
rotunda of 1749.
Botanic Gardens
Magdalen Bridge ☎ *(0865) 242737* 📷 *Open Apr–Sept Mon–Sat
8.30am–5pm, Sun 10am–noon, 2–6pm; Oct–Mar Mon–Sat
9am–4.30pm, Sun 2–4.30pm. Greenhouses open 2–4pm.*

Founded in 1621 as the medical faculty's Physick Garden, these gardens
are among the oldest in Britain. The gateway (1630) is by Nicholas Stone.
Christ Church Picture Gallery
Christ Church College ☎ *(0865) 242102* 📷 *but* 📷 *Thurs. Open
10.30am–1pm, 2–4.30pm. Usual entrance by Canterbury Gate from
Oriel St.*

The finest college collection of paintings, with an emphasis on
14th–17thC Italian artists, including Leonardo da Vinci, Michelangelo
and Raphael.
Museum of the History of Science
Broad St. ☎ *(0865) 243997* 📷 *Open 10.30am–1pm, 2.30–4pm.
Closed Sat, Sun.*

There is a double interest here, the museum as such and its attractive
building put up in the 17thC to house the collections of Elias Ashmole,
thus becoming the doyen of British public museums. In the 19thC these
collections moved to the Ashmolean's present site, while since 1937 this
Broad St. building has housed material on a wide range of scientific
subjects, such as sundials, microscopes, clocks and cameras.
Museum of Modern Art
30 Pembroke St. ☎ *(0865) 722733* 📷 📢 *Open Tues–Sat
10am–5pm, Sun 2–5pm. Closed Mon.*

Changing exhibitions, films and lectures take place in a converted brewery building.

Museum of Oxford
St Aldates ☎ *(0865) 815559* 📷 *Open Tues–Sat 10am–5pm. Closed Sun, Mon.*
The theme here is the story of the city of Oxford, imaginatively told through models, old prints and maps as well as special exhibitions.

Pitt Rivers Museum
South Parks Rd. ☎ *(0865) 512541* 📷 *Open 2–4pm. Closed Sun.*
More than one million objects, including items brought back by 18th–19thC explorers, make up this anthropological and ethnographic collection, which began with bequests from General Augustus Pitt Rivers in the late 19thC.

Sheldonian Theatre
Broad St. ☎ *(0865) 241023. Open 10am–12.45pm, 2–4.45pm.*
Until the mid-17thC **St Mary's** church served as the venue for most university occasions, but in 1663–69, thanks to the generosity of Gilbert Sheldon (then Warden of All Souls) and the architectural genius of Christopher Wren (then Professor of Astronomy), Oxford received this splendid theater. Inspired by Rome's Theater of Marcellus, it is semi-circular at one end and has a superb painted ceiling. It is used for university ceremonies, including the conferring of degrees.

Hotels

🇭 **Eastgate**
The High, Merton St., Oxford OX1 4BE ☎ *(0865) 248244*
🖀 *858875* 🍽 ⚬ *46* 🛏 *20* 🚗 🚆 AE CB ◉ ◉ VISA
Location: Just s of High St. and E of the Examination Schools. With its entrance in quiet Merton St., overlooking the 19thC Examination Schools, the Eastgate combines a touch of academic ambience with the convenience of being beside High St. If the brochure's equation of the interior with that of a don's study is a trifle fanciful, the style here is nevertheless one of unforced traditional comfort.
‡ 🕭 ⊡ ☞ 🏛

🇭 **Randolph**
Beaumont St., Oxford OX1 2LN ☎ *(0865) 247481* 🖀 *83446* 🍽
⚬ *109* 🛏 *109* 🚗 🚆 AE CB ◉ ◉ VISA
Location: Opposite the Ashmolean Museum. Built in 1864, the Randolph meets all modern needs within a setting of confident Victorian grandeur.
‡ 🕭 ☞ 🏊 🏛

Restaurant

🇷 **Elizabeth** 🍴
84 St Aldates ☎ *(0865) 242230* 🍽 🍷 🍽 🍽 AE ◉ VISA ◁ *Last orders 11pm. Closed Mon, lunch Tues–Sat, last two weeks in Aug, two weeks at Christmas.*
Made famous by Kenneth Bell before he went to Thornbury Castle, near Bristol, the Elizabeth (now owned by Antonio Lopez) has sustained its reputation and become an institution. The cooking is as fine as ever, in a broadly classical French style. Friendly staff; a large, superb wine list.

Hotel and restaurants nearby
Clanfield (*on A4095, 20 miles/32km w of Oxford*).

🇷 **The Plough**
☎ *(036781) 222* 🍽 🍷 🍽 🛏 🚗 AE ◉ *Last orders 9.30pm.*
Although this Elizabethan manor house is reminiscent of a village inn, and is robustly English enough to serve Wadworth's cask-conditioned ale, its well-respected restaurant is Anglo-German and French, with an excellent wine list which is naturally dominated by France. The German touches in the kitchen reflect the ethnic background of Hedy Barnes, who owns the Plough with her husband Tony. Diners travel from far and wide to sample her cooking.

Given the antiquity of the place, the six bedrooms are inevitably small (🍽), but they are perfectly comfortable.

Great Milton (*10 miles/16km* E *of Oxford*).

Ⓗ Ⓡ **Manoir aux Quat'Saisons** 🏨 ⌂ 🏛
Great Milton, Oxford OX9 7PD ☎ *(08446) 230* ▥ ❧ 10 ▭ 10 ➡
➤ Ⓐ Ⓒ Ⓥ *Closed Christmas to early Jan.*
Ⓡ ▥ ▭ ━ ➤ ⌂ *Closed Sun dinner, Mon.*
Location: At w *end of village.* Having established what was arguably the
best restaurant in Britain outside London – Les Quat'Saisons in Oxford –
Raymond Blanc in 1983 turned his attention to a country house hotel, in
a 16thC manor. With a far bigger kitchen and a lovely old fireplace, he
argues, he can now do spit-roasts. No doubt the rest of his cuisine, and
the portions, will remain as delicate as ever and as responsive to the
seasons.
🏞 ▢ ⬚ 🏊 ⚓ ⟨≡ ⇌ ⁑ 🏌 👥

Nightlife
The **Apollo Theatre** (*George St.* ☎ *(0865) 244544*) stages rock and
classical concerts, plays, musicals and ballets. The **Playhouse** (*Beaumont
St.* ☎ *(0865) 247133*) is the university theater and stages productions by
visiting professional and amateur companies and by the students
themselves. **Holywell Music Room** (*Holywell St.* ☎ *(0865) 247069*) has
been the place for classical concerts on a small scale since 1748. (*For
information and reservations: Tickets in Oxford* ☎ *(0865) 727855.*)

   Oxford's well-known pubs act as lively meeting places for students and
inhabitants alike: they include the thatched **Perch**, on the river at Binsey
Lane, 1 mile (2km) outside town; The **Trout** at Godstowe; The **Turf**
(which serves mead) in New College St.; and the **Mitre** (which has folk
music) in the High St. Wine-bars include the **Emperor** in Broad St., and
Bacchus in George St. **Browns** is a very popular café/restaurant in action
all day and evening.

Shopping
Queen St. and **Cornmarket** are the major shopping streets. The
Covered Market (*entrance off Market St.*) contains interesting shops
including many gourmet food shops. **Little Clarendon St.**, beyond St
Giles, is full of unusual craft and gift shops, boutiques and wine-bars.
Blackwell's bookshops (divided into Art, Paperback and Children's
bookshops) in **Broad St.** and the **Music Shop** in Holywell St. must rank
almost as sights in Oxford, and the secondhand bookshops, also in Broad
St., are treasure troves of collectors' items.

Sports and activities
Boating   Punts can be rented during the summer from Folly Bridge,
Magdalen Bridge and Bardwell Rd. (*For all boat inquiries* ☎ *(0865)
511161.*)

Peak District National Park ★
Maps 10G7, 11G8. Mainly Derby. E *and* SE *of Manchester
and* w *and* sw *of Sheffield* 𝒊 *For postal inquiries: National
Park Office, Baslow Rd., Bakewell DE4 1AE; for personal
inquiries: Old Market Hall, Bridge St.* ☎ *(062981) 3227.
Additionally, Castle St., Castleton* ☎ *(0433) 20679.*
Visitors often ask 'Which is the Peak?' and the answer is that
there is none. Mountain, certainly – the desolate peat plateau of
Kinder Scout reaches 2,088ft (637m) – but no peak as such,
and indeed the name Peak District is thought to derive from
that of an ancient tribe that once inhabited these parts.

   In fact there are two districts, one to the N and one to the S of
A625 which links the small towns of Hathersage and Chapel-en-
le-Frith. To the N of this road rises the High or Dark Peak, in
large part a waste of upland moor (much above 2,000ft/605m,
and including Kinder Scout) but softened by **Derwent Dale**
running from N–S with its string of reservoirs and for the
motorist conveniently crossed by A57 between Hathersage and
Glossop. To the S of A625, however, there is an altogether
gentler landscape of downland, much of it patterned into small

fields by drystone walling. It is this Low or White Peak region which attracts the most visitors – far too many during vacation periods when cars clog the narrow roads and every skyline silhouettes its trail of walkers – for here are not only the easiest and safest rambles but also such lures as small towns, stately homes, caverns (the best are around Castleton) and museums.

Much of the best of the Peak District is under the protection of the National Trust, whose three most notable properties are **Hope Woodlands** (where there is little wood but plenty of peat) straddling A57 and embracing parts of Kinder Scout; **Edale**, straddling A625 and including aptly named **Mam Tor** – aptly because the name means Shivering Mountain and this is just what its slithering shale corries appear to be doing; and, most popular of all, **Dovedale** (parallel to and just w of A515) where man all too often swamps nature. The **Pennine Way**, a 250-mile-long (400km) walkers' route to the Scottish border, starts from Edale.

Among the district's important centers are **Bakewell**, famed for a tart first made in 1860 at the Rutland Arms; **Buxton**, faded as a spa but still determinedly Edwardian; **Castleton**, cavern center of the Peak and source of Blue John, one of Britain's rarest and most attractive semi-precious stones; and **Hathersage**, model for Morton in Charlotte Brontë's *Jane Eyre*. Lastly, **Matlock** and adjacent **Matlock Bath** with their museums and other attractions are a magnet for buses and crowds.

Events   From Ascension Day to September, well dressing. Wells in certain villages are decorated with panels made up of flowers, leaves and other natural materials. Exact dates and locations available from tourist offices.

Sights and places of interest

Blue John Cavern
Map 11G8. On A625, at top of Mam Tor Pass w of Castleton
☎ *(0433) 20638* 🔲 🛈 🅿 ➤ *Open 9.30am–sunset.*
Although the best known of the Peak District's caverns and also a principal source of Blue John, this cavern can be disappointing. Virtually no Blue John is seen and there is also little in the way of geological formations, so visitors have to content themselves with the boast that they have been down one of the deepest caverns in England (240 steps).

Buxton Museum and Art Gallery
Map 10G7. Terrace Rd., Buxton ☎ *(0298) 4658* 🔲 *Open Tues–Fri 9.30am–5.30pm, Sat 9.30am–5pm. Closed Sun, Mon.*
The art gallery here has some good pictures (including works by de Wint and Brangwyn) while the museum instructively fills in the local story with finds from caverns and examples of Blue John ware.

Dinting Railway Centre
Map 10G7. Dinting Lane, Dinting, near Glossop, off A57
☎ *(04574) 5596* 🔲 🅿 ✳ ➤ *Open 10.30am–5pm. Locomotives in steam Mar–Oct Sun.*
A railway museum with engines, track, brake-van rides and an exhibition hall. Train rides on Sun, lasting approximately 5mins, are available all day.

Great Rutland Cavern and Nestus Mine
Map 11G8. Heights of Abraham, Matlock Bath ☎ *(0629) 2365* 🔲 🅿 ✳ ➤ *Open Easter–late Oct 10am–6pm.*
Lead mining has been a Derbyshire industry for around 2,000yrs and this mine shows how it was done. The mine (almost level, so easily accessible) is believed to have been worked since Roman times. It is in the woodland above the village, where there is also a tower offering a fine view and, for children, a Tree Tops play area.

   The Peak District Mining Museum (*Pavilion Building, Matlock Bath* ☎ *(0629) 3834* 🔲 ➤ *open 11am–4pm or later in summer*) tells more of the mining story and also displays a huge water pressure pumping engine (1819), believed to be the only survivor of its kind.

Haddon Hall
Map 11G8. On A6, just s of Bakewell ☎ *(062981) 2855* 🚗 💷
*Open Apr−Sept Tues−Sat, bank holiday Mon 11am−6pm, bank
holiday Sun 2−6pm. Closed Sun, Mon.*
A notably complete and picturesque example of a stone medieval manor,
Haddon was built during the 13thC although it was added to and altered
until the 17thC. The **Banqueting Hall** of about 1370 is the oldest
virtually unchanged room.

National Tramway Museum
Map 11G8. Crich, near Matlock ☎ *(077385) 2565* 🚗 💷 ⚹ 🚶
*Open Easter−Sept Mon−Thurs 10am−4.30pm, Sat, Sun and bank
holiday Mon 10.30am−5.30pm (closed Fri); Oct Sat, Sun
10.30am−5.30pm.*
The 30 or more vintage trams, both British and foreign, and the
opportunity to take a clanking scenic ride are the main reasons for
coming here. Additional attractions are an Edwardian street scene and a
Peak District Mining Exhibition. A **Grand Transport Extravaganza**
involving a fair, a market and other festivities, is held on August bank
holiday weekend.

Peak Cavern
Map 11G8. Castleton, on A625 ☎ *(0433) 20285* 🚗 🎫 ⚹ 🚶 *Open
Easter to mid-Sept 10am−5pm.*
With its contorted limestone formations this is the most spectacular and
also one of the largest of the Peak District caverns.

Poole's Cavern
Map 10G7. Green Lane, Buxton, off A515 ☎ *(0298) 6978* 🚗 🎫
💷 ⚹ 🚶 *Open Easter−early Nov 10am−5pm. Closed Wed except
mid-July to early Sept.*
This is the place to see stalagmites and stalactites with little effort, for
here the formations are in a virtually level cavern with no more than 16
steps.

Riber Castle Wildlife Park
Map 11G8. Just se of Matlock ☎ *(0629) 2073* 🚗 💷 ⚹ 🚶 *Open
Easter−Oct 10am−5pm; Nov−Easter 10am−4pm.*
Not just another wildlife park, but rather a scientific center emphasizing
the survival of rare European breeds, both wild and domestic. The stars
are the lynxes, but the eagles and snowy owls run a close second, while
many less dramatic creatures − rare breeds of sheep, cattle, pigs, goats
and even poultry − also demand attention.
 Riber's many other attractions include full-scale models of prehistoric
monsters, a vintage car collection, a live butterfly display, a children's
playground and the shell of the 19thC castle.

Speedwell Cavern
Map 11G8. Winnats Pass, near Castleton ☎ *(0433) 20512* 🚗 🎫
💷 ⚹ 🚶 *Open 9.30am−6pm.*
The exciting thing about this cavern is that the visit involves a boat trip
(along a deep underground lead mining gallery) as far as a pothole
described with good reason as a bottomless pit; in spite of attempts using
rockets, its depth has never been determined.

Treak Cliff Cavern
Map 11G8. Castleton, on A625 ☎ *(0433) 20571* 🚗 🎫 🚶 *Open
Easter−Sept 9.30am−4pm; Oct−Easter 9.30am−4pm.*
With rich veins of Blue John, this cavern, known to miners since the
18thC, also has good limestone formations.

 See also *Chatsworth House.*

Hotels and restaurants
Baslow (*4 miles/6.5km NE of Bakewell*).

🅷 🆁 Cavendish 🛏 ⌂
Baslow, Derby DE4 1SP ☎ *(024688) 2311* ⫽⫽⫽ 🔌 *13* 🛏 *13* 🚗 ⌂
🍽 🅰🅴 🆅🅸🆂🅰
🅱 ⫽⫽⫽ 🖥 📺 🚗 *Last orders 10pm.*
Location: On A619. Cavendish is the family name of the dukes of
Devonshire, owners of the Chatsworth estate, parts of which can be seen
from every room. There is trout fishing on the estate, too, for guests who
come during the season (mid-Apr to mid-Oct), and home-smoked trout,
and Chatsworth game such as hare and venison feature on the menu.

Despite its age, the hotel (originally a village inn) is bright and airy, with every modern convenience. There is even a cocktail bar, with a good selection of malt whiskies and brandies, and cask-conditioned local ale.
🏠 ⬜ 🖼 🥄 ⚓ 🔫 ⚔ ✒ 🍴 ♟ ▼

Hathersage (*8 miles/13km N of Bakewell*).

Ⓗ **George** ♣
Main Rd., Hathersage, Sheffield, Derby F60 1BB ☎ *(0433) 50436*
Ⅱ◫ 🍽 18 🛏 18 🚗 ⬛ AE ⬤ VISA
Location: On A625 at village center. Dating in part from the 16thC, this is an exceptionally charming small hotel; the George Bar with its natural stone walls, beams and open fire is especially inviting. In 1845 the landlord, James Morton, was a popular local character whose name Charlotte Brontë adopted for the village in *Jane Eyre*. Home-made pies are among the specialties of the restaurant.
⬜ ▼

Rowsley (*4 miles/6.5km NW of Matlock*).

Ⓗ **Peacock**
Bakewell Rd., Rowsley, Matlock, Derby DE4 2EB ☎ *(062983) 3518*
Ⅱ◫ 🍽 20 🛏 15 🚗 ⬛ AE CB ⬤ ⬤ VISA
Location: At edge of village. Modern facilities in the gracious 17thC setting of what was once a dower house of Haddon Hall. The hotel has its own fishing, and local Wye trout are a feature of the menu. .
⬜ 🖼 ⚓ 🍴

Peterborough
Map 12I10. Cambs. 35 miles (56km) NW of Cambridge.
Population: 102,500 ℹ *Town Hall, Bridge St.* ☎ *(0733)*
63141.
There is one compelling reason for visiting this city, and that is to see the **cathedral** with its magnificent, Early English W front – a screen wall featuring three huge arches. The **nave ceiling** ☆ dating from *c.*1220, is a very rare example of a medieval painted ceiling (repainted in the 19thC) and one that is unique in England.

Ⓗ **The Bull**
Westgate, Peterborough, Cambs PE1 1RB ☎ *(0733) 61364* Ⅱ◫
🍽 114 🛏 107 🚗 ⬛ AE ⬤ ⬤ VISA
Location: City center, just NW of the cathedral. Behind the clean Georgian facade of this former coaching inn are plush, Neo-Edwardian public rooms and modern-style bedrooms. The restaurant, of good local repute, is a notably successful refurbishment.
⬜ 🖼

Plymouth
Map 3N4. Devon. On the S coast. Population: 240,000.
Railway station ☎ *(0752) 21300; coach and bus station*
☎ *(0752) 64011* ℹ *Civic Centre, Royal Parade* ☎ *(0752)*
264849.
Sir Francis Drake showing his contempt for the Spanish Armada in 1588 by completing his game of bowls on The Hoe, the Pilgrim Fathers sailing from here in the *Mayflower* in 1620 – these must be the instant pictures evoked in most people's minds by the name Plymouth. These, and a naval association centuries old and in 1982 movingly reaffirmed by the cheers greeting the ships returning from the Falklands.

Little of Plymouth's Elizabethan and Jacobean past survives, for what time had not removed was destroyed in 1941 when bombs devastated much of the city center. Today, although rebuilt with admirable clarity of vision, this part of Plymouth with its huge shopping center is likely to attract the tourist less than either the historic and beautiful **Hoe** or old Plymouth, known as the **Barbican**. The former, some 350yds (320m) s of Derry's Cross (the town center) by Armada Way, is a splendid hillside expanse of open green above **Plymouth Sound**, the great natural anchorage to which Plymouth owes its existence.

The Barbican quarter, about 300yds (275m) SE of Derry's Cross, runs down to the waterfront between the impressive 17thC **Citadel** (*fortress usually open for tours May–Sept 2–5pm*) and Sutton Harbour. Here **Island House** is said to be where the Pilgrim Fathers lodged (a board lists their names), while the adjacent **Mayflower Stone and Steps** commemorate their departure. Close by, the **Elizabethan House** (*32 New St.* 🖾 *open Easter–Sept Mon–Sat 10am–1pm, 2.15–6pm, Sun 3–5pm; Oct–Easter Mon–Sat 10am–1pm, 2.15–4.30pm, closed Sun*) has been skillfully restored and retains many of its original features.

A panoramic view of Plymouth and its surroundings can be seen from the 14th-floor Roof Deck of the **Civic Centre** (*Royal Parade, open Apr–Sept, Mon–Fri 10am–4pm*). On the first floor, temporary exhibitions of various kinds are mounted in the Exhibition Gallery.

Sights and places of interest
City Museum and Art Gallery
Drake Circus 🕿 *(0752) 668000* 👁 *Open 10am–6pm. Closed Sun.*
The portrait painter Joshua Reynolds was born in what is now the suburb of Plympton in 1723 and spent much of his time in Devonshire, so it is not surprising that Reynolds relics are an interesting aspect of this museum. Other material includes Old Master drawings, local porcelain and exhibits of regional historical interest.

Guildhall
Opposite Civic Centre 🕿 *(0752) 264849* 👁 *Open when not in use 10am–4pm.*
It is worth glancing in here if only to see a hall nearly 50yds (45m) in length and lit by modern stained-glass windows illustrating the history of Plymouth. Built in 1874 and badly damaged by wartime bombing, the Guildhall was rebuilt by 1959.

Merchant's House
33 St Andrew's St. 🕿 *(0752) 668000* 🖾 *Open Mon–Sat 10am–6pm, Sun 3–5pm.*
A notable survivor of its kind, this 16thC house was owned and modernized in the 17thC by William Parker, a seafaring adventurer who later became mayor of Plymouth. Much of the interior detail is untouched or well restored, and the surprisingly spacious rooms house material illustrating the city's early history.

Prysten House
By St Andrew's Church, Royal Parade 🕿 *(0752) 661414* 🖾 *Open 10am–4pm. Closed Oct–Easter Sun.*
What is certain is that this house, the oldest in Plymouth, was built in about 1498 by a merchant called Thomas Yogge, who secured himself a footnote in history through being the man who gave Catherine of Aragon a hogshead of Bordeaux when she reached Plymouth in 1501. What is open to dispute is the popular belief that the house served as a hospice for chantry priests ('prysten') of adjacent St Andrew's Church.

Smeaton's Tower
The Promenade, The Hoe 🕿 *(0752) 264840* 🖾 *Open May–Sept 9.30am–sunset.*
Since 1696 there have been four Eddystone lighthouses 14 miles (22km) s on the Eddystone reef, and this tower, or at least its upper part, was the third. Built by John Smeaton in 1759, it was moved to this spot in 1882 because the sea was eroding the rock on which it had been planted. On a clear day the keen-eyed should be able to identify the base of the tower beside the present Eddystone lighthouse.

Sights nearby
Buckland Abbey
Yelverton, 11 miles (17km) N of Plymouth ☎ *(0822) 853607. NT*
📷 💷 🚙 *Open Easter–Sept Mon–Sat 11am–6pm, Sun 2–6pm;*
Oct–Easter Wed, Sat, Sun 2–5pm.

Cistercian monks and Tudor seafarers have left their mark here. The monks built in this green and wooded valley in the 13thC; an immense **tithe barn**, still with its original roof timbers, dates from this era. Three hundred years later, Buckland was converted from monastery to country house, and in 1581 the property was bought by Sir Francis Drake. His ownership is now remembered by a **Drake Collection**, the most popular item being the legendary Drake's Drum.

Mount Edgcumbe House and Country Park
Across the Tamar, ¾ mile (1.2km) from Plymouth by Cremyll pedestrian ferry, or 24 miles (32km) by car via A374 and B3247 from the Torpoint ferry ☎ *(0752) 822236* 📷 *house* 🏛 *country park* 💷 🚙 *House open May–Sept Mon, Tues 2–6pm. Country park always open.*

On a fine day the park is the real attraction here, with formal gardens, more than 800 acres of woodland and other countryside, and scenic walks along some 10 miles (16km) of coastline. The house, Tudor in origin, was gutted by bombing in 1941 but restored by 1960.

Saltram House
3¼ miles (6km) E of Plymouth ☎ *(0752) 336546. NT* 📷 💷 🚙 〰
Open Apr–Oct: house 12.30–6pm, kitchen and art gallery 11am–6pm (closed Mon except bank holidays), garden 11am–6pm. Nov–Mar garden open 11am–sunset.

Robert Adam and Joshua Reynolds are the two illustrious names associated with this Georgian mansion built around a Tudor core; Adam because his rich interior decoration ranks among his most meticulous and brilliant work, Reynolds because he frequently visited here and Saltram houses no less than 14 of his portraits.

Hotels

Ⓗ Duke of Cornwall
Millbay Rd., Plymouth, Devon PL1 3LG ☎ *(0752) 266256* 📠 *45424*
Ⓘ 🌂 67 🛏 67 🚙 🍴 〰 AE ① ⑩ VISA *Closed Christmas.*
Location: Opposite the Exhibition Centre. Occupying what Sir John Betjeman has described as 'The finest Victorian Gothic building in Plymouth,' this spacious hotel is well sited both for the Exhibition Centre and for the continental ferries.
‡ ♿ ▢ 📷 ♣

Ⓗ Other hotels: **Astor** (*Elliot St., The Hoe, Plymouth, Devon PL1 2PS* ☎ *(0752) 25511* Ⓘ); **Holiday Inn** (*Armada Way, Plymouth, Devon PL1 2HJ* ☎ *(0752) 662866* 📠 *45637* Ⓘ); **Strathmore** (*Elliot St., The Hoe, Plymouth, Devon PL1 2PP* ☎ *(0752) 662101* Ⓘ).

Restaurant nearby
Gulworthy (*on A390, 18 miles/29km N of Plymouth*).

Ⓡ Horn of Plenty
☎ *(0822) 832528* 〰 ▢ 📷 🍽 🚙 🚙 ◁ *Last orders 9.15pm. Closed Thurs, Fri lunch, Christmas.*
The name strikes a less corny note when it is recalled that the proprietors were originally professional musicians. Today, they are gastronomic stars. Patrick Stevenson is a resounding character in the dining room, and his wife Sonia has been described as 'an intuitive cook.' Influences may range from Old Cornish cookbooks to Escoffier to Elizabeth David, but today Sonia Stevenson's gastronomic reputation is her own. Specialties include Cornish sea bass, *quenelles* of salmon, lamb *en croûte* and venison with pine nuts. The restaurant has beautiful views over the Tamar valley.

Nightlife
The New Palace (*Union St.* ☎ *(0752) 25622*) presents professional touring productions, and pantomimes at Christmas. The **Theatre Royal**

(*Derry's Cross* ☎ *(0752) 669595*) was opened in 1982; the modern complex – theater, restaurant, shop, exhibition hall – is one of the largest of its kind in the country and a showpiece along Royal Parade.

Shopping
The four parallel streets of **Mayfair St., Cornwall St., New George St.** and **Royal Parade** form the central shopping area. The covered market (*closed Sun*) at **Frankfurt Gate** (*at the w end of New George St.*) sells locally grown produce and general goods. Older streets in the Barbican area, such as **Southside St.** contain small specialty shops. **Drake Circus,** to the E of the central area, contains several large stores.

Portsmouth (and Southsea)
Map 5M9. Hants. On the s coast. Population: 198,000. Railway station ☎ *(0705) 825771; coach and bus station* ☎ *(0705) 696911 i Civic Offices, Guildhall Sq.* ☎ *(0705) 834092 and Castle Buildings, Clarence Esplanade, Southsea* ☎ *(0705) 826722.*

The spirit of Portsmouth (a naval town even before Henry VII founded his dockyard here) is epitomized by the city's star attraction, Nelson's *Victory.* Yet *Victory* is a star now facing competition from the much older if historically less distinguished *Mary Rose.* In July 1545 this 700-ton war vessel set sail to meet the French, but minutes later she caught the wind, heeling over and sinking as the sea flooded through her gun ports. Successfully raised in 1982, she will go on show (in the dockyard) as soon as possible, and visitors will be able to watch conservation work in progress.

This amalgam of several towns divides into four districts: **Portsmouth** proper, inland and with a modern Civic Centre, tourist office and the railway station; **Portsea** to the NW, home of the dockyard and of HMS *Victory;* **Old Portsmouth** to the SW, by far the most picturesque quarter, where in spite of wartime devastation some old houses and the 15thC **Round Tower,** Portsmouth's first real coastal defense, still stand; and lastly **Southsea,** an elegant resort lining the shore behind its wide common and gardens.

Fort Widley (*on Portsdown Hill Road, N of the town* 🔲 🔲 ⬚ *open for tours Apr–Sept 1.30–5pm*) was built by Lord Palmerston in the 1860s. It provides a superb view of the city below.

Sights and places of interest
Charles Dickens' Birthplace Museum
393 Old Commercial Rd. ☎ *(0705) 827261* 🔲 *Open 10.30am–5.30pm.*
Dickens was born here on Feb 7 1812, but the family moved away when he was about 2yrs old, leaving no trace of their occupation. There is, however, a small exhibition of Dickensiana, together with some pictorial material, but primarily this house is decorated and furnished to show how a lower-middle-class family would have lived in the early 19thC.
City Museum and Art Gallery
Museum Rd., Old Portsmouth ☎ *(0705) 827261* 🔲 ▣ ⬚ *Open 10.30am–5.30pm.*
Opened in 1972 this museum and art gallery is still growing. The Decorative Art collections show representative furniture, glass and ceramics of the 17th–20thC, while the Fine Art galleries have 20thC British prints, drawings, paintings and sculpture. Local history from Roman times and social history of the 18th–19thC round off the museum.
Cumberland House Museum and Aquarium
Eastern Parade ☎ *(0705) 827261* 🔲 *Open 10.30am–5.30pm.*
A museum of local natural history which outstrips many of its kind in imaginative display. The freshwater aquarium, for instance, is designed to appear as a natural stream, while a diorama illustrates the life of the

river bank above; the woodland displays are centered on a beech tree; and the Geological Gallery includes a mock tunnel through a chalk hillside dotted with fossils, leading to a panoramic view at the top.

HMS Victory ★
Dockyard, The Hard ☎ *(0705) 822351* 📷 💺 ✳ *Open Mar–Oct Mon–Sat 10.30am–5.30pm, Sun 1.30–5pm; Nov–Feb Mon–Sat 10.30am–4.30pm, Sun 1–4.30pm.*

Nelson's flagship at the Battle of Trafalgar (1805) is a sight to quicken the most sluggish imagination. Visitors can stand where Britain's great naval hero fell, and can see the cockpit in which he died. Still commissioned and manned, this historic ship has been superbly restored.

Royal Naval Museum
Dockyard, The Hard 📷 💺 *See 'HMS Victory' for* ☎ *and entry details.*

If possible visit this museum before boarding HMS *Victory*; the huge panoramic display of the Battle of Trafalgar will help give a picture of that day's events. Additionally the museum houses relics of Nelson, Trafalgar and the Napoleonic wars, while other permanent and temporary exhibitions portray many aspects of naval life.

Southsea Castle and Museum
Clarence Esplanade, Southsea ☎ *(0705) 827261* 📷 🚗 *Open 10.30am–5.30pm.*

The castle, built by Henry VIII but much modified later, is chiefly of interest for the *Mary Rose* exhibition, held in the Western Galleries.

Sights nearby

HM Submarine Alliance and Submarine Museum
Haslar Pontoon, Gosport, 13 miles (21km) by road from Portsmouth ☎ *(07017) 29217. Ferry from pontoon by the Hard* 📷 *for submarine* 📷 *for museum* 💺 🚗 *Open 9.30am–4.30pm.*

Here is an opportunity to board a submarine built at the end of World War II, and to see what living conditions were like on one of these craft. The nearby museum illustrates the history of submarines.

Portchester Castle ★
Off A27 on N shore of Portsmouth Harbour bay, 8 miles (13km) NW of Portsmouth ☎ *(0705) 378291. DOE* 📷 🚗 *Open mid-Mar to mid-Oct Mon–Sat 9.30am–6.30pm, Sun 2–6.30pm except Apr–Sept 9.30am–6.30pm; mid-Oct to mid-Mar Mon–Sat 9.30am–4pm, Sun 2–4pm.*

Not just another castle, but a fascinating site whose earthworks and stones recall some 1,100yrs of history. Fearful of Saxon invasion, the Romans of the 4thC threw up a series of great forts along this vulnerable shore; this one, Portus Adurni, is of particular interest for still being beside the water. Perhaps a century and a half later, after the Romans had gone, the Saxons settled on this site, and yet more centuries on Henry II built a castle here, later to be chosen by Henry V as the base for his invasion of France prior to Agincourt. Today, impressive evidence of the Roman and Plantagenet presence can still be seen – the Roman remains, although with medieval strengthening, are second only to *Hadrian's Wall* – while, dependent on current excavation, something of Saxon settlement is also visible.

Ⓗ **Pendragon**
Clarence Parade, Southsea, Hants PO5 2HY ☎ *(0705) 823201* Ⓣ *86376* 🛏 *56* 🛏 *36* 🍽 ⇌ AE CB ⓐ ⓓ VISA

Location: *Seafront, almost opposite Southsea Castle.* With good views of the Solent from the upper rooms, the Pendragon is externally typically Victorian and wholly in sympathy with its setting. The interior is spacious and cheerful and likely to appeal to families.
🏃 □ 🖂 🦯 ☕ 🎿

Nightlife
Major rock and classical concerts are staged at the **Guildhall Concert Hall** (*Guildhall Sq.* ☎ *(0705) 824355*). The main theater is the **Kings Theatre** (*Albert Rd.* ☎ *(0705) 828282*).

Shopping
The most central of Portsmouth's many shopping areas is the area around **Commercial Rd.** and **Charlotte St.** incorporating the **Tricorn Centre**. Most nationally-known chain and department stores will be

found here as well as the open-air general market (_Charlotte St.,
Thurs–Sat_). More major stores are found in Southsea's **Palmerston Rd.**,
while **Marmion Rd.** and **Osborne Rd.** which run off it contain some
unusual and interesting shops.

Richmond

_Map 15D8. North Yorks. 30 miles (48km) s of Durham.
Population: 7,000 i Friary Gardens, Queen's Rd. ☎ (0748)
3525._

Although known best for its **castle**, Richmond is in its own
right a small hilltop town of real character, well worth a visit if
only for its cobbled market square. All other Richmonds,
whether London suburb or in Virginia, are children of this one,
for the earldom was created in 1071, its seat remaining here
until Henry VII, also Earl of Richmond, transferred it to his
new palace in Surrey.

Sights and places of interest
Georgian Theatre
Victoria Rd. ☎ _(0748) 3021_ 🔳 _Open Easter and May–Sept
Mon–Fri, Sun 2.30–5pm, Sat, bank holiday Mon 10am–1pm,
2.30–5pm._

Built in 1788, this is the oldest theater in England in its original form.
There is also a **museum** which displays original playbills and the oldest
(1836) complete set of painted scenery in Britain.
Richmond Castle
Town center ☎ _(0748) 2493. DOE_ 🔳 _Open mid-Mar to mid-Oct
Mon–Sat 9.30am–6.30pm, Sun 2–6.30pm except Apr–Sept
9.30am–6.30pm; mid-Oct to mid-Mar Mon–Sat 9.30am–4pm, Sun
2–4pm._

Spectacularly planted above the river Swale and best seen, at least in
part, from the bridge below, this castle merits a visit if only to peer over
the precipitous edge of its courtyard. Dating from _c._1070, and thus one
of the oldest in the country, the castle got its huge keep (over the earlier
gatehouse) just a century later.

🅷 **The Frenchgate**
59–61 Frenchgate, Richmond, North Yorks DL10 7AE ☎ _(0748)
2087_ 🔳 ♙ _12_ 🔲 _6_ 🚗 🅿 🚬 _Restaurant closed Sun to
non-residents._
Location: N quarter of the town. This is a charming house in an equally
charming cobbled street, both wholly appropriate to an ancient town like
Richmond. The resident owners rightly emphasize their personal service
and the excellence of their cuisine, enhanced by the elegant Georgian
dining room.
🖼 ⚓

Hotel/restaurant nearby
Coatham Mundeville (_16 miles/26km NE of Richmond_).

🅷 🆁 **Hall Garth**
Coatham Mundeville, Darlington, Co. Durham DL1 3LV ☎ _(0325)
313333_ 🔳 ♙ _19_ 🔲 _19_ 🚗 🚬 _Closed Christmas to early Jan._
🆁 🔳 🔲 🚬 _Last orders 9.15pm. Closed Sun, first Mon in May._
Location: Just off A167 in the village. There is an earthy, matter-of-fact
quality about Hall Garth which presents a northern, altogether less
precious face than many another country house hotel. The pantiled
roofing on the stables and the scattered old farm buildings give the place
a rather French appearance. Inside, the bedrooms are unpretentious and
the house rambling. With an adjoining pub (offering cask-conditioned
McEwans) to run as well, _patron_ Ernest Williamson bustles around with
a pencil tucked into his beard, relaxing only over a glass of wine in the late
evening. Sitting on wooden settles in the cramped bar, his customers join
him in a nightcap from the good selection of cognacs and malt whiskies.
Janice Crocker's cooking is hearty and enjoyable.
🖼 🔲 🖼 ⚓

Ripon
Map 15E8. North Yorks. 25 miles (40km) NW *of York.*
Population: 11,000 i *Wakeman's House, Market Pl.*
☎ *(0765) 4625.*

There is one particular reason for staying the night and that is to
be present at the 1,000yr-old ceremony of the sounding of the
Wakeman's horn. Right up until the early 17thC the official
responsible for law and order was the Wakeman, whose evening
watch with a group of constables was proclaimed by blowing a
horn at each corner of the Market Cross. Today the horn is still
sounded each evening at 9pm, although the cross has been
replaced by an 18thC obelisk. In 1976 replica horns were
presented to Ripon, Wisconsin, and Ripon, California.

Apart from this ceremony, the main reason for visiting Ripon
is the city's small but superb **cathedral** in Kirkgate. Its ancient
and famous **Saxon crypt** ☆ was built by St Wilfrid in 672 and
here the visitor can still stand within Wilfrid's walls, the only
real change being that diocesan treasures have now replaced the
saintly relics of the past. The cathedral's structure is of many
architectural periods ranging from Norman to Perpendicular,
and the most outstanding feature is perhaps the Decorated east
end of the choir.

Ⓗ **Unicorn**
Market Pl., Ripon, North Yorks HG4 1BZ ☎ *(0765) 2202* ⅠⅠ ☜ 27
▭ 14 ◨ ☲ AE ◉ ⦿ VISA
Location: Market Pl. In this old-style inn with all the necessary modern
touches, the oak-panelled restaurant and the beamed, pub-like Tom
Crudd Bar are particularly welcoming.
▢ ⬈ ⚟ ☲

See also *Fountains Abbey*.

Rochester
Map 7K11. Kent. On the Medway, 31 miles (50km) E *of*
London. Population: 56,000 i *Eastgate Cottage, Eastgate,*
High St. ☎ *(0634) 43666.*

After the **castle** and **cathedral**, both outstanding of their kind,
Charles Dickens tends to take over; and rightly so, since the
novelist spent many years near here and based several of his
books on Rochester and its surroundings. But there is more to
Rochester than this, and although forming part of a large
conurbation the city has retained much of its 17th–19thC
character, not to mention sections of Roman and medieval wall.
An admirable official leaflet, *A Walk around the City*, leads to
some intriguing corners and will particularly reward Dickens
enthusiasts.
Event Four days in early June, Dickens Festival. Dickens-
related festivities with much of the population of Rochester
taking part and wearing Dickensian costume.

Sights and places of interest
Charles Dickens Centre
Eastgate House, High St. ☎ *(0634) 44176* ▨ *Open*
10am–12.30pm, 2–5.30pm.
The house (1591) features in *The Mystery of Edwin Drood* as the Nun's
House and in *The Pickwick Papers* as Westgate House, while in the
garden stands the chalet which the novelist used as his study when he
lived at Gad's Hill Place near Rochester. But the main attraction – and
surely this would have appealed to Dickens – is a theatrical display of
many Dickensian characters and scenes, brought pretty close to life by a
clever marriage of sound and light.

Rochester Castle

At nw end of the city, beside the river Medway ☎ *(0634) 42852.
DOE* 🏛 �::: *Open mid-Mar to mid-Oct Mon–Sat 9.30am–6.30pm,
Sun 2–6.30pm except Apr–Sept 9.30am–6.30pm; mid-Oct to mid-
Mar Mon–Sat 9.30am–4pm, Sun 2–4pm.*

Set within bailey walls of 1087 (to some extent following the course of
Roman walls), this lofty many-storied keep (1127) ranks among the
largest in the country; it is also unusual for being in two parts and for still
showing its Norman piers and arches, the latter retaining their typical
dog-tooth decoration. There are nearly 150 steps to the top, but the
Medway view rewards the effort.

Rochester Cathedral †

Beside the castle at nw of the city ☎ *(0634) 43366* ✗

After *Canterbury*, Rochester ranks as the oldest bishopric in England.
Consecrated by St Augustine in about 604, the first bishop built a modest
cathedral, part of which is marked out on the floor just inside the w door.
There followed another Saxon cathedral and then a Norman one (started
in 1082 by Bishop Gundulf), before work started in about 1200 on the
Gothic aspects seen today. Of the Norman cathedral (much refurbished
and added to in the 12thC) the principal remains are **Gundulf's Tower**
beside the N transept, the w bays of the nave, the fine crypt and – the star
feature of the cathedral – the w front (1160) with its recessed and
elaborate **doorway** ☆

Sight nearby

Lullingstone Roman Villa

Eynsford, 15 miles (24km) w of Rochester ☎ *(0322) 863467. DOE*
🏛 �::: *Open mid-Mar to mid-Oct Mon–Sat 9.30am–6.30pm, Sun
2–6.30pm except Apr–Sept 9.30am–6.30pm; mid-Oct to mid-Mar
Mon–Sat 9.30am–4pm, Sun 2–4pm.*

Roman villas are not normally associated with Christianity, but murals
here prove that this villa's 4thC occupants were Christians. There is some
good mosaic flooring, and identifiable features include the baths and a
granary.

Upnor Castle

Upnor, on Medway w bank, 3 miles (5km) N of Rochester.
☎ *(0634) 78742. DOE* 🏛 �::: *Open mid-Mar to mid-Oct Mon–Sat
9.30am–6.30pm, Sun 2–6.30pm.*

Upnor is not so much a castle as a glorified gun platform, first built in
1559 to defend the approach to the increasingly important dockyard of
Chatham. It is situated beside the river at the foot of **Upnor** village's
quaint little High St. (*no cars*) and contains an interesting exhibition
describing the Medway defenses from Elizabethan times onward.

Hotel nearby

Gravesend (*4 miles/6.5km w of Rochester*).

Ⓗ **The Inn on the Lake** ✿

Shorne, Gravesend, Kent DA12 3HB ☎ *(047482) 3333* ▥▯ ☎ *78*
▤ *78* ═ ☰ *AE* Ⓞ Ⓞ *VISA*

Location: On A2. Even though it costs more, insist on a lakeside room at
this long, low, modern hotel in which picture windows overlook twin
lakes backed by woods and waterscaped with a fountain and torrents.
The restaurant is outstanding for both food and service.

♿ 🖼 🏊 ⚓ ⛷ ⛵

Shopping

The attractive cobbled **High St.** with its Victorian lampposts contains
shops selling antiques, paintings, crafts, china and glass (notably **Reeves
& Sons** at No.142). A general market is held in **Corporation St.**
(*parallel to the High St.*) on Fri and an antiques market on Sat.

Romsey

*Map 5L8. Hants. 5 miles (8km) nw of Southampton.
Population: 10,000* ⓘ *King John's House, Church St.*
☎ *(0794) 512200.*

Romsey is a pleasant small town on the edge of *The New Forest*,
known primarily for the Norman abbey around which it grew

and for **Broadlands**, the beautiful Georgian home of Lord
Palmerston and Lord Louis Mountbatten.

Romsey Abbey ☆ in the center of the town began as a
nunnery in *c*.910, although the present building dates from
around 1130. Lord Louis Mountbatten's grave is in the s
transept, and a Saxon cross at the E end of the s choir aisle is
probably contemporary with the original church.

Broadlands

A31, on s edge of the town ☎ *(0794) 516878* 🖼 💻 🚗 *Open
Apr–July 10am–6pm (closed Mon except bank holidays); Aug–Sept
10am–6pm.*

Lord Louis Mountbatten, owner of Broadlands from 1939 until his death
in August 1979, is the name most associated with this place, and he is
remembered by an exhibition in the William and Mary stable building.

Originally a manor belonging to Romsey Abbey, Broadlands was
transformed into the distinguished Palladian mansion that stands here
today by Capability Brown and Henry Holland the Younger, at the
instigation of the 2nd Viscount Palmerston. The rooms are a light and
elegant decorative delight, frames for many treasures which include
ancient Greek and Roman marbles, four paintings by Van Dyck, a
portrait of Lady Hamilton by Lawrence and relics of the 3rd Lord
Palmerston, Prime Minister from 1855–58 and 1859–65.

Sight nearby

Mottisfont Abbey

Mottisfont, w of A3057, 5 miles (8km) NW of Romsey ☎ *(0794)
40757. NT* 🖼 🚗 *Open Apr–Sept: grounds 2.30–6pm (closed Sun,
Mon); house (Rex Whistler Room and Cellarium only) open Wed, Sat
2.30–6pm.*

An Augustinian priory from the 12thC until the Dissolution, Mottisfont
was then successfully transformed into a private mansion. Further
alterations took place in the 18thC, and in 1939 the drawing-room was
decorated with remarkable *trompe l'oeil* work by Rex Whistler. The
walled garden is known for its old-fashioned roses.

Ⓗ **White Horse**
Market Pl., Romsey, Hants SO5 8ZJ ☎ *(0794) 512431* ⅢⓂ 🔑 33
🛏 33 🚗 ⬛ 🆎 ⒸⒷ 💲 ⓞ 🆅🆂🅰

Location: Central Romsey. Although it has a Georgian facade this is a
much older place. Two of Cromwell's soldiers are said to have been
hanged from the iron sign bracket, but morbid thoughts are brushed
aside by the hotel's pleasant atmosphere.
&️ ⬜ 📷 🐾 ⛷

Ⓡ **Old Manor House**
21 Palmerston St. ☎ *(0794) 517353* ⅢⓂ 🍽 🔑 🛋 🚗 🆎 💲 ⓞ
🆅🆂🅰 *Last orders 10.30pm. Closed Sun dinner, Mon, Easter Sun,
Christmas.*

A friendly place, well run by wry owner-chef Mauro Bregoli, whose
kitchen is Italian and French. Great attention is paid to raw materials,
and cooking is skillful, with *nouvelle* touches. The menu changes
frequently. Bregoli is especially proud of his *turbot au matignon de
légumes*: 'The chef reserves the rights to the specifications of this
dish.'

Royal Tunbridge Wells   See *Tunbridge Wells*.

Rye

*Map 7L11. East Sussex. 10 miles (16km) NE of Hastings.
Population: 4,500 i Council Offices, Ferry Rd.* ☎ *(0797)
222293.*

If ever a town beckoned the visitor simply to wander around
and explore all its corners, it must surely be Rye. This is a place
of steep little cobbled streets and alleys and of picturesque old
houses of many types and periods. Do not miss either **Mermaid
St.** ★ or **Watchbell St.**, both as captivating as their names.

177

Sights and places of interest
Lamb House
West St. ☎ *(0892) 890651. NT* 🖾 *Open Apr–Oct Wed, Sat 2–6pm.*

This Georgian house – built by a distinguished citizen, George Lamb, in 1723 – was the home of the American writer Henry James from 1898–1916 and after that of the novelist E.F. Benson. The garden-room in which James worked and which was immortalized in Benson's Mapp and Lucia books, was destroyed by a bomb in 1940, but memorabilia are shown in the house.

Rye Museum
Ypres Tower, SE quarter of the town ☎ *(0797) 223254* 🖾 *Open Easter to mid-Oct Mon–Sat 10.30am–1pm, 2.15–5.30pm, Sun 11.30am–1pm, 2.15–5.30pm.*

Dating from the 13thC this tower houses a museum of local history, but its main attraction is as a point affording a fine view across Romney Marsh and the river Rother.

Sight nearby
Smallhythe Place
On B2082, near Tenterden, 6 miles (9.5km) N of Rye ☎ *(05806) 2334. NT* 🖾 *Open Mar–Oct 2–6pm or sunset if earlier. Closed Tues, Fri.*

The actress Ellen Terry lived in this 16thC, half-timbered house from 1899 until her death in 1928. Today, it is a theatrical museum devoted to her memory; there are also relics of other famous thespians such as Irving, Garrick and Mrs Siddons.

Ⓗ **George**
High St., Rye, East Sussex TN31 7JP ☎ *(0797) 222114* 🔳 🍴 *20* 🛏 *20* 🚗 ➡ 🆎 ⒸⒷ ⏀ ⒾⒹ 𝖵𝖨𝖲𝖠

Location: At the junction of High St. and Lion St., opposite the Old Grammar School. Over 400yrs old and full of oak beams – some said to come from Elizabethan ships – the George is a place of much character. The restaurant is good, especially for fish dishes.
🔲 📷 🦷 🏛

Ⓗ **Mermaid**
Mermaid St., Rye, East Sussex TN31 7EU ☎ *(0797) 223065* ☎ *957141* 🔳 🍴 *29* 🛏 *22* 🚗 🏠 ➡ 🆎 ⒸⒷ ⏀ 𝖵𝖨𝖲𝖠

Location: Central, just NW of Lamb House. This enchanting place is one of the oldest inns in England. A hostelry of shadowy date – although it is reported that a Mermaid Inn stood here in 1300 – it is known to have been rebuilt in 1420. The interior, with its beams, panelling and mullioned windows, fully lives up to the promise of the half-timbered exterior.
🦷 🏛

Ⓗ Ⓡ **The Monastery**
6 High St., Rye, East Sussex BN31 7JE ☎ *(0797) 223272* 🔳 🍴 *8* 🛏 *7* 🚗 ➡ *Closed Apr–Nov Tues; Dec–Mar Sun–Tues.*
Ⓡ 🔳 🍽 🍷 🎵 *on weekends. Closed Apr–Nov Tues; Dec–Mar Mon–Tues and Sun dinner.*

Location: In town center. An Augustinian friary built in the 1300s stood on this site, and the Gothic tracery of the chapel survives vestigially to provide an interesting garden view from the restaurant and most of the rooms. The historical interest thus provided is apposite in a little town dense with antiquity.

A good sense of location is provided, too, in the English menu: the best lamb in England comes from this part of the country, and features here as 'Romney roast,' a dish for two, comprising boned loin stuffed with orange and rosemary. Other specialties include fried oysters in Guinness, rump of beef in puff pastry with onion sauce, and raspberry and almond flan.
🍽 ◀€ ✓

Shopping
The main shopping streets are **Cinque Ports St.**, **High St.**, **Tower St.** and **The Landgate**. An antiques and bric-à-brac market is held in Cinque Ports St. (*Thurs, Sat*) and a general market is held in the **Cattle Market** (*to the N of the town, Thurs*).

St Albans

Map 6K10. Herts. 20 miles (32km) N of London.
Population: 52,000 **i** *37 Chequer St.* ☎ *(0727) 64511.*
Once an important Roman provincial capital called
Verulamium, St Albans (named after the first Christian martyr
in Britain) is visited for its impressive, basically Norman, abbey
church which became a **cathedral** in 1877, and its **Roman
remains**. Around the cathedral lie several well-preserved old
streets, such as **French Row**, **Fishpool St.** and **George St.**
Wander down **Abbey Lane**, which turns off George St., and
you come to **The Fighting Cocks**, an octagonal, timber-framed
inn, one of the oldest inhabited licensed houses in England.

Sights and places of interest
St Albans Cathedral Ⅲ †
Just w of city center crossroads ☎ *(0727) 52120.*
In 793 Offa of Mercia discovered the remains of St Alban (beheaded for
concealing the priest who had converted him) and built a Benedictine
monastery to shelter them. By medieval times the monastery had become
one of the most powerful in Britain, but today all that remains are its
gatehouse and church. The latter, rebuilt by the Normans, has the
longest nave in Europe, and its Norman tower, central nave and
transepts are, to a large extent, built of Roman material removed from
Verulamium. Among points of particular interest inside are the **13thC
murals** on the Norman piers; the E wall of the S transept which may be a
relic of the Benedictine abbey; and **the shrine of St Alban** with, beside it,
the oak loft of c.1400 from which the monks kept continuous watch over
the saint's relics. In the N aisle, just behind the watching-tower, there are
some fragments of a shrine said to be that of St Amphibalus, the priest
who converted Alban.
Verulamium
*w of the cathedral. The Roman Theatre and Verulamium Museum
are w of the park, reached by car via Verulam Rd. to a traffic circle,
and then left along Bluehouse Hill to St Michael's Church* ← *Site:
Always open. Roman Theatre* ☎ *(0727) 54051* ◫ *Open Mar–Sept
10am–5pm; Oct–Feb 10am–sunset. Verulamium Museum*
☎ *(0727) 54659* ◫ *Open Apr–Oct Mon–Sat 10am–5.30pm, Sun
2–5.30pm; Nov–Mar Mon–Sat 10am–4pm, Sun 2–4pm.*
Verulamium, built soon after the arrival of the Romans, was sacked by
Boadicea but soon rebuilt, and flourished until the early 5thC. Today,
this once bustling Roman city is just a public park sheltering little more
than lengths of wall, a hypocaust (heating system), and (on the other side
of Bluehouse Hill – see above for directions) the remains of the
Roman theater, unique in Britain for having a stage rather than the usual
amphitheater. The **museum**, in which everything is exceptionally well
explained, has some excellent models, coffins complete with skeletons,
and many fine mosaics that can be studied at close range.

Sights nearby
Hatfield House Ⅲ ☆
5 miles (8km) E of St Albans ☎ *(07072) 62823* ◫ **K** *Mon–Sat* ◫
◫ *House open late Mar–early Oct Tues–Sat noon–5pm, Sun
2–5.30pm, bank holiday Mon 11am–5pm (closed Mon). Park open all
year; East Gardens Mon 2–5pm; West Gardens, open when house is
open and Mon 2–5pm.*
Robert Cecil, 1st Earl of Salisbury, built this palatial mansion with its
fine **Great Hall** and remarkable carved staircase in 1607–11 as a fitting
establishment for one who was chief minister to James I, and Hatfield has
been the home of the same family ever since. Nevertheless it is
Elizabethan associations that seem strongest here, for this was the site of
the royal palace of 1497, where Queen Elizabeth I spent much of her
childhood, and it was here that she learned of the death of Mary Tudor
and thus of her own accession. Robert Cecil's father, William, became
the queen's chief minister. A wing of the old palace still stands and
Elizabethan banquets are held here (☎ *(07072) 62055*). The main house
– rich in paintings, tapestry and furniture – shows some notable portraits
of the queen as well as other contemporary material, including some of
Elizabeth's personal possessions.

Knebworth House
15 miles (24km) NE of St Albans ☎ *(0438) 812661* 🚇 📽 ♿ 🚍
Park open 11am–6pm, house 11.30am–5pm: Apr–Sept (closed Mon except bank holidays); Oct park open Sun only.

Knebworth's Tudor origins were heavily disguised by the Victorian novelist and statesman, Sir Edward Bulwer-Lytton, who had the strange idea of loading the exterior with decoration. Luckily he did not touch the splendid Jacobean panelling of the **Banqueting Hall**, the principal feature of the interior.

In the park, Knebworth offers many amusements, mostly for children. Telephone for dates of jousting displays.

Luton Hoo
8 miles (13km) N of St Albans ☎ *(0582) 22955* 🚇 📽 🚍 *Open Easter–early Oct Mon, Wed, Thurs, Sat and Good Fri 11am–5.45pm, Sun 2–5.45pm.*

Considering that it was begun in 1767 by Robert Adam, completed in 1816 by Robert Smirke, seriously damaged by fire in 1843, and remodeled early this century, Luton Hoo has managed to retain a surprisingly well-proportioned balance. The house, however, is of less importance than its contents, the **Wernher Collection** of fine and decorative art. Rembrandt and Titian are among the artists whose works hang here, while tapestries, medieval ivories, porcelain and the exquisite jeweled creations of **Carl Fabergé** ☆ are among other treasures.

Shaw's Corner
Ayot St Lawrence, 5 miles (8km) N of St Albans ☎ *(0438) 820307. NT* 🚇 🚍 *Open 11am–1pm, 2–6pm or sunset if earlier: Mar and Nov Sat, Sun; Apr–Oct closed Mon except bank holidays, Tues.*

George Bernard Shaw spent the last 44yrs of his long life in this modest Victorian house. Little has changed here since he died in 1950. The revolving hut in which he wrote still stands, and the house is filled with memorabilia.

Whipsnade Park Zoo
Whipsnade, 13 miles (25km) NW of St Albans ☎ *(0582) 872171* 🚍 📽 ♿ 🚍 *Open Mon–Sat 10am–6pm or sunset if earlier, Sun and bank holidays 10am–7pm or sunset if earlier.*

A finely located and famous zoo in which animals and birds live in large open-air enclosures. Well-known for its conservation work, the zoo has several rare species, while special features include a children's zoo, white rhinos, wild horses and dolphins. A narrow-gauge railway takes visitors through the African section (*Apr–Oct*).

Ⓗ **St Michael's Manor**
Fishpool St., St Albans, Herts AL3 4RY ☎ *(0727) 64444* ⫽⫽ 🍴 *22*
🛏 *14* 🚍 🛋 ⇌ AE ⓒ VISA

Location: Between the cathedral and the Verulamium Museum. Within comfortable walking distance of the cathedral and the Roman remains, this is a hotel of high standards and elegant setting. The building is a successful grafting of later periods onto an early 16thC original and the interior reflects the past with fine plasterwork, panelling and chandeliers.
🍽 ▭ 🖼 ⚓ 🔧 🎭

Shopping
The main streets, **St Peter's St., Chequer St., Hatfield Rd.** and **Catherine St.**, form the central shopping area while the streets around the cathedral – **Holywell Hill, George St.** and **Fishpool St.** – contain many antique shops. **Maltings, Heritage Close** and **Gentle's Yard** are recently developed shopping precincts. An extensive general market is held in **Market St.** and **St Peter's St.** (*main day Sat*).

St Ives
Map 2N2. Cornwall. On the N coast, 15 miles (24km) NE of Land's End ℹ *The Guildhall, Street-an-Pol* ☎ *(0736) 796297.*

With its reputation for clear light, this attractively situated and picturesque small coastal resort has been a favorite with artists since the 19thC; the works of painters, sculptors, potters and other craftsmen are on show and for sale all over the place.

Sights and places of interest
Barbara Hepworth Museum
Barnoon Hill ☎ *(0736) 796226* 🔲 *Open Apr–June, Sept 10am–5.30pm (closed Sun); July–Aug Mon–Sat 10am–6.30pm, Sun 2–6pm; Oct–Mar 10am–4.30pm (closed Sun).*

A place for those who appreciate modern sculpture. Dame Barbara Hepworth lived here from 1949 until her death in 1975, and visitors can see her studio and examples of her work, as well as memorabilia. There is also a Hepworth *Madonna* in the parish church.

Barnes Museum of Cinematography
44 Fore St. 🔲 *Open Apr–Sept 11am–1pm, 2.30–5pm.*

As its name implies, the museum has all sorts of exhibits telling the story of photography and especially of moving pictures.

Ⓗ Tregenna Castle
St Ives, Cornwall TR26 2DE ☎ *(0736) 795254* ⓣ *45128* ▥ 🏴 *83* 🔲 *70* 🍴 ▣ ▣ ▣ ▣ *VISA*

Location: On a hill overlooking St Ives. Looking almost like a toy castle with its turrets and battlements, this Georgian house stands on 100 acres of grounds high on a hill overlooking the sea. Tregenna Castle has no great gastronomic pretensions and lists no specialties, although the cuisine is competent. Cornish cream teas are served. Rooms are spacious and comfortable, and Tregenna is a convenient hotel on the less busy of Cornwall's two coasts.

🏠 ⚓ ♿ ▢ ⛵ ⛷ ⇌ 🎣 ⤢ ✓ 🐴 🚣 ⛹ 🎿

Restaurant nearby
Botallack *(on B3306, 9 miles/14.5km sw of St Ives).*

Ⓡ The Count House
☎ *(0736) 788588* ▥ 🔲 ▭ ▬ ◁ ▣ *AE* *CB* ▣ ▣ *VISA* *Last orders 10pm. Closed lunch Mon–Sat, dinner Sun–Tues and at Christmas.*

The name refers to the administrative offices of a once-famous tin mine on a rugged clifftop. In winter a log fire warms diners as they tuck into the Count House's home-made bread, large helpings of pâté, and main courses which show great care in preparation. The fresh vegetables are outstanding and the desserts and coffee are excellent, too. A sound wine list includes one of the few English reds.

Sports and activities
St Ives and the surrounding area are renowned for their good beaches, many of which are patrolled by lifeguards during the summer. Surfing and other water-sports are also extremely popular.

St Michael's Mount
Map 2N2. Cornwall. On the s coast, 3 miles (5km) E of Penzance ☎ *(0736) 710507. Access on foot at low tide. Also in summer by ferry at high tide. NT. Castle* 🔲 🎭 *Nov–Mar* 🎥 ◁ *Open Apr–May Mon, Wed, Fri 10.30am–5.45pm; June–Oct Mon, Tues, Wed, Fri 10.30am–5.45pm; Nov–Mar, tours leave Mon, Wed, Fri at 11am, noon, 2pm, 3pm, 4pm, weather and tide permitting.*

This dramatic cone erupting some 200ft (61m) out of the tidal sands is best seen from the shore. Nevertheless, such a place beckons almost irresistibly and anyone who succumbs will be well rewarded by the views of **Land's End** and *The Lizard* and will also be able to visit the **castle**. Originally a Benedictine chapel founded in 1047 by Edward the Confessor and placed under the care of the Benedictine monks of Mont St Michel in Normandy, it was later developed into a castle, and since 1657 has been a private house. Further back in time this rock seems to have been the Roman Ictis, and also, if tradition is to be believed, the refuge in the 5thC of St Keyne and thus one of the earliest English Christian sites.

Salisbury
Map **5L8**. Wilts. 20 miles (32km) NW of Southampton.
Population: 35,000 *i* City Hall, Fisherton St. ☎ (0722)
27676.

Salisbury, a particularly pleasant market town known for its old
buildings many of which are hotels, pubs and restaurants, has a
precise year of birth: 1220 when the bishopric was transferred
from **Old Sarum** (see below) and work started on the **cathedral**.
This – an edifice of perfect proportion, an immaculate example
of Early English design, and with a famous spire – is the
compelling reason for coming to Salisbury. What is more, it
stands within a close of rare charm – the largest in England, yet
a tranquil place of lawns and trees and period houses
(13th–20thC) in part protected by a 14thC wall built with stone
from Old Sarum.

    Salisbury Plain is the bare chalk downland that extends N to
Devizes and E–W between Andover and Warminster. Here the
principal tourist objective is *Stonehenge*.

Sights and places of interest
Mompesson House
The Close ☎ (0722) 5659. NT ▨ Open Apr–Oct, 12.30–6pm or
sunset if earlier. Closed Thurs, Fri.
Of the many gracious old houses around the cathedral close, Mompesson
stands out as a Queen Anne gem. While many may be content simply to
enjoy it from the outside, those who go in will be rewarded by some really
splendid 18thC plasterwork and a unique collection of English drinking
glasses of the same period.

Salisbury Cathedral † ★
Just s of the city center ☎ (0722) 28726.
The only medieval cathedral in England to have been built as a totally
new conception rather than as a replacement for a previous building,
Salisbury is a triumph of unity. The soaring spire (404ft/123m) which is
the cathedral's daring signature was added a century later in *c*.1334.

    Inside, Salisbury has something sadly lacking in so many other
cathedrals, namely an unimpeded vista from end to end, one moreover
which today reaches a spectacular finality in the glorious blue of the
Prisoners of Conscience window (1980).

    Morbid though it may sound, tombs are important here and several are
painted in what were probably their original colors. But the two main
features, both within the body of the cathedral, are **Magna Carta ★** –
one of the four surviving originals of 1215, shown in a special case in the
NE transept – and the celebrated **ancient clock** mechanism. The latter
(nave N aisle) dates from at least 1386 and is the oldest working clock
mechanism in England, if not in the world.

    Lastly, both the **cloister** and **chapter house** deserve a visit, the former
astonishingly large for a church that was not monastic, the latter known
for its 13thC sculptured scenes, every one of which repays detailed study.

Salisbury and South Wiltshire Museum
The King's House, 65 The Close ☎ (0722) 332151 ▨ Open May,
*June, Sept 10.30am–5pm (closed Sun); July, Aug Mon–Sat
10.30am–5pm, Sun 2–5pm; Oct–Apr 10.30am–4pm.*
This museum is of particular interest for its archeological material,
especially that from *Stonehenge* and *Old Sarum*, and can be
recommended to anyone also visiting these sites.

Sights nearby
Old Sarum
A345, 2 miles (3km) N of Salisbury ☎ (0722) 5398. DOE ▨ ▬
*Open mid-Mar to mid-Oct Mon–Sat 9.30am–6.30pm, Sun
2–6.30pm except Apr–Sept 9.30am–6.30pm; mid-Oct to mid-Mar
Mon–Sat 9.30am–4pm, Sun 2–4pm.*
Although there is little to be seen here now – earthworks, a mound on
which stood a Norman castle and, to its NW, the foundations of a once
great cathedral – this often windswept downland site was once the walled
city of Sarum. Iron Age people, Romans, Saxons and Normans all lived
here, but after the castle passed to the Crown in the 12thC there was such

strife with the Church that eventually a decision was made to build a new cathedral 2 miles (3km) away. This was the beginning of the end for Sarum as more and more people moved out, finding the valley site of new Sarum altogether more fertile and congenial. Yet deserted Old Sarum continued to send two members to parliament until 1833.

Wilton House ☆
3 miles (5km) w of Salisbury ☎ *(0722) 743115* 🔲 🔳 🖩 💻 🚗 ⇌
Open Easter–Sept Tues–Sat and bank holiday Mon 11am–6pm, Sun 1–6pm.

Designed by Inigo Jones (with 19thC alterations and additions), Wilton has sumptuous rooms with rich and riotous yet brilliantly conceived decoration, priceless furnishings, and paintings by a seemingly endless catalogue of great masters. And if all this fails to please, then there are 7,000 tin soldiers populating 16 dioramas and five tableaux.

🅷 **King's Arms**
St John's St., Salisbury, Wilts SP1 2SB ☎ *(0722) 27629* 🟠 *25971*
🔳 🍴 *16* 🛏 *5* 🚗 🖂 ⇌ 🔳 ⏣ 🔲 🆔 𝚅𝙸𝚂𝙰
Location: 300yds (275m) NE of the cathedral. Outside, half-timbering. Inside, black beams, low ceilings, crooked passages and leaning walls. The pub-like bars fit in well, and it is not hard to picture supporters of Charles II meeting here, as they did, to further his escape after his defeat at Worcester. But the building is older than this and in part possibly even contemporary with the cathedral.
👥

🅷 **White Hart**
1 St John's St., Salisbury, Wilts SP1 2SD ☎ *(0722) 27476* 🔳
🍴 *72* 🛏 *56* 🚗 🔳 🔲 ⏣ 🔲 𝚅𝙸𝚂𝙰
Location: 350yds (320m) NE of the cathedral. An imposing Georgian facade with a pillared portico surmounted by a white hart marks the entrance to this hotel in which a welcoming lounge with open fires sets the tone.
□ ◪ 🕊 👥

Shopping

Most of Salisbury's shops, including several antique shops and bookshops (many selling antiquarian books) and nationally known stores, are in the small area bordered by **Blue Boar Row**, **Queen St.** running into **Catherine St.**, **New St.** and **High St.** Within this area are two pedestrian precincts: the modern **Old George Mall** and the restored Tudor **Cross Keys Mall.** Salisbury's large general market (*Tues, Sat*) is held in Market Sq. where it has been sited since 1227. Notable shops are **Beach's**, a bookshop by the cathedral, and **Watsons** (*Queen St.*), in the ancient House of John O'Port, for china.

Scarborough

*Map **16**E10. North Yorks. On the coast between the Tees and the Humber. Population: 44,500* ℹ *St Nicholas Cliff* ☎ *(0723) 72261.*

Sprawled over the cliffs and overlooking the headland (known to have been used by Iron Age people, Romans, Saxons and the Normans who built the **castle**), Scarborough became a spa in the 17thC and has remained an elegant and conservative resort ever since. It overlooks two safe and sandy bays, the southern one being the smarter. Brontë fans can visit Anne's grave in the churchyard of **St Mary's** on the headland.

Scarborough Castle
On the point between N and s bays ☎ *(0723) 72451. DOE* 🔲 🚗
Open mid-Mar to mid-Oct Mon–Sat 9.30am–6.30pm, Sun 2–6.30pm except Apr–Sept 9.30am–6.30pm; mid-Oct to mid-Mar Mon–Sat 9.30am–4pm, Sun 2–4pm.

Balanced some 300ft (90m) above the sea this castle nevertheless succumbed to at least three sieges, one in 1312 and two during the Civil War. The jumbled confusion of forbidding ruins comprises mainly a 13thC barbican and a 12thC keep.

H Royal

St Nicholas St., Scarborough, North Yorks YO11 2HE ☎ *(0723) 64333* ⊙ *52472* ▯▯ ⋈ *137*⬜ *137* 🚗 ⇌ AE ⊕ ⊙ VISA

Location: Above South Bay. Nothing could be more in keeping with the spirit of Scarborough: an elegant Regency building sheltering an unashamedly Palm Court ambience, below a galleried foyer complete with wrought-iron stairs and a lofty glass dome. There are sea views, a sun terrace, Victorian pictures, summer entertainment, and facilities for children which even extend to a special dining room.

↨ ⊡ 🕹 ≼ 🖅 🏊 ⋔ ⅋

Nightlife

Shows and musicals, involving top stars, and both rock and pop concerts take place throughout the summer at the following places: **Floral Hall Theatre** (*Queens Parade* ☎ *(0723) 72185*), **Royal Opera House** (*St Thomas St.* ☎ *(0723) 69999*), and **Futurist Theatre** (*Foreshore Rd.* ☎ *(0723) 60644*). The **Stephen Joseph Theatre-in-the-Round** (*Valley Bridge Rd.* ☎ *(0723) 70541*) is an intimate theater renowned for its plays by local playwright, Alan Ayckbourne.

Shaftesbury

Map 4L7. Dorset. 20 miles (32km) w of Salisbury.
Population: 4,000 ℹ *County Library, Bell St.* ☎ *(0747) 2256.*

Occupying a 700ft (212m) spur thrown out from Salisbury Plain (see *Salisbury*), Shaftesbury makes good use of this scenic eminence, one of the town's most popular strolls being along **Park Walk**, a pedestrian terrace riding the escarpment's southern rim. The **abbey ruins** are here, while, opposite, **Gold Hill** drops steeply away, cobbled, picturesque and much loved by film directors. The name most likely derives from 'guild,' a reminder that this was where craftsmen once worked. And there is another reminder in the small **museum** on Gold Hill, where a collection of buttons recalls a cottage industry which from the 17th–19thC earned Shaftesbury and other Dorset towns a worldwide reputation – until a button-making machine was shown at Prince Albert's great exhibition of 1851.

Abbey Ruins

Park Walk ☎ *(0747) 2910* 🖼 *Open Easter–Oct 10am–6.30pm.*
This quiet, rather lost corner has known three kings – Alfred the Great who founded a Benedictine nunnery here in 888; Edward the Martyr, murdered in 978 at the age of 16 and buried here (in 1931 a casket was found which contained the bones of a youth); and Canute who died here in 1035. The abbey was dissolved in 1539, and its stones soon disappeared into local housing. A small **museum** helps to conjure up the past.

Sight nearby

Stourhead ☆

9 miles (14.5km) nw of Shaftesbury ☎ *(0747) 840348. NT* 🖼 🖼
Garden open 8am–7pm or sunset if earlier. House open 2–6pm: Apr, Oct (closed Tues, Thurs, Fri); May–Sept (closed Fri).
Although the 18thC Palladian house is not without interest, Stourhead is most famous for its landscaped garden. Not that this is a garden in the accepted sense, but rather a romantic bowl of woods, shrubs, temples and gentle walks above the lake (with its grotto, bridges and islands) which gives birth to the river Stour.

H Grosvenor

The Commons, Shaftesbury, Dorset SP7 8JA ☎ *(0747) 2282* ▯▯
⋈ *48*⬜ *42* ⇌ AE CB ⊕ ⊙ VISA

Location: Town center. There was a time when coaches clattered into the courtyard of what was then the Red Lion, thankful to have completed the long, steep drag from the plain. Today this same courtyard, now part of a modernized hotel that has preserved its period atmosphere, is a pleasant place to indulge in a Dorset cream tea on a summer afternoon.

▢ ⊡ 🕹 ↯

Sheffield
Map 11G8. South Yorks. 30 miles (48km) s of Leeds.
Population: 520,000. East Midlands Airport ☎ (0332)
810621; railway station ☎ (0742) 26411; coach station
☎ (0742) 754905; bus station ☎ (0742) 28631 i Central
Library, Surrey St. ☎ (0742) 734760.

A surprising city, Sheffield has little of the grime the stranger
could be forgiven for expecting of a great industrial complex
famed for its cutlery since at least the 14thC and for its steel
since the 18thC. Justly proud of its clean air, it is in fact a place
of daring architectural effects and fast-moving traffic through
an imaginatively redeveloped city center. By way of contrast,
there are still those confident Victorian edifices such as the
Cutlers' Hall (1832) and the **Town Hall** (1897), while the
Georgian oasis of **Paradise Square** survives to the N of the much
modified but basically 14th–15thC **cathedral**, which contains
(in the **Shrewsbury Chapel**) a monument to the 6th Earl of
Shrewsbury, custodian of Mary, Queen of Scots.

Sights and places of interest
Abbeydale Industrial Hamlet
Abbeydale Road South, in sw suburbs ☎ (0742) 367731 ▨ ▣
▰ Open Mon–Sat 10am–5pm, Sun 11am–5pm.

Here, in the period setting of an 18th–19thC scythe works, something of
Sheffield's industrial past lives on. One of the more notable exhibits is a
crucible steel furnace of the early 19thC (developed from a design of
1742). But this is not just a museum of dead machinery – waterwheels
turn, there are special working days, there is a crafts fair in summer, and
the human aspect is here in a manager's house of 1890 and a workman's
cottage of 1840.

City Museum
Weston Park, in w quarter ☎ (0742) 27226 ▣ Open June–Aug
Mon–Sat 10am–8pm, Sun 11am–5pm; Sept–May Mon–Sat
10am–5pm, Sun 11am–5pm.

The two most prestigious collections here are, appropriately, those of
Sheffield plate and Sheffield cutlery. Archeology, geology and natural
history are among the themes of other galleries.

Graves Art Gallery
Central Library, Surrey St. ☎ (0742) 734781 ▣ Open Mon–Sat
10am–8pm, Sun 2–5pm.

Although Chinese, Indian, Islamic and African works are all represented
here, the emphasis of the gallery is on European art, notably English
watercolors. Just a few names – Corot, Cézanne, Matisse, Murillo,
Turner, Constable, Wilson – must suffice to point the standard.

Industrial Museum
Kelham Island, on the river off Alma St. ☎ (0742) 22106 ▨ ▣ ▰
Open bank holiday Mon, Wed–Sat 10am–5pm, Sun 11am–5pm.
Closed Mon, Tues.

Kelham was the town armorer in the 17thC, the island was man-made,
and for centuries this quarter has supported all manner of trades ranging
from iron-founding to silk and cotton, so this is an appropriate spot for a
museum of things made in Sheffield over the past 300yrs.

Mappin Art Gallery
Weston Park in w quarter ☎ (0742) 26281 ▣ Open June–Aug
Mon–Sat 10am–8pm, Sun 2–5pm; Sept–May Mon–Sat
10am–5pm, Sun 2–5pm.

A gallery devoted to British art of the 18th–20thC. Artists such as
Millais, Turner and Constable represent the painters, Chantrey and
Henry Moore the sculptors.

Sight nearby
Hardwick Hall ☆
19 miles (30km) s of Sheffield, just E of M1 ☎ (0246) 850430. NT
▨ ▣ ▰ ▰ Open Apr–Oct Wed–Thurs, Sat–Sun, bank holidays
1–5.30pm or sunset if earlier; garden open daily noon–5.30pm; park
open all year.

It is said that Bess of Hardwick was convinced she could not die so long as she was building, so at the age of 70, when she had just been widowed by her fourth husband, the Earl of Shrewsbury, she started work on this splendidly pretentious hilltop home proclaiming its ownership from the rooftops in stone initials. The interior comprises huge tapestry-hung rooms, at least two of which, the **Great Hall** and **Long Gallery**, were specially designed to house tapestries already owned by Bess.

The grounds include fine walled gardens, orchards and a notable herb garden, and 300 acres of parkland containing a lake (fishing and boating available) and rare breeds of cattle and sheep.

H **Grosvenor House**
Charter Square, Sheffield, South Yorks S1 3EH ☎ *(0742) 20041*
🛏54312 ⅢⅡ ⊖ 🍴 121 ⛨ 102 ⇌ ☰ ⥂ AE CB ⊕ ⊙ VISA
Location: City center. A high-rise convenient hotel with adjoining indoor parking. Some of the bedrooms have fine city views.
🛗 ⚕ 🖥 🖾 ⚄ ≪ 👥

Nightlife
The City Hall (*Barkers Pool* ☎ *(0742) 735295*) stages concerts by well-known orchestras (*Sept–May on alternate Fri and Sat*) as well as lighter entertainment including rock and brass band concerts. The modern **Crucible Theatre** (*Norfolk St.* ☎ *(0742) 79922*) is the home of the repertory company and provides a variety of good quality entertainment.

Shopping
The central shopping area stretches for over a mile (1½kms) from **The Moor**, up **Pinstone St.** and **Fargate**, and along the **High St.** World-famous Sheffield plate cutlery and silverware is easily available in its town of origin, and one of the best-known shops is **Mappin & Webb** (*14 Fargate*). Interesting markets include **Castle Market** (*Exchange St., closed Thurs, Sun*) for meat, fish and general goods; **Sheaf Market** (*Dixon Lane, closed Thurs, Sun*) for vegetables and general goods; and **The Setts** open-air market (*Exchange Pl.*) for antiques and secondhand goods (*Mon*) and general items (*Tues, Fri, Sat*).

Sherborne
Map 4L6. Dorset. 5 miles (8km) E of Yeovil. Population: 7,000 **i** *Hound St.* ☎ *(093581) 5341.*
Sherborne is an unspoiled, charming town which has the air of a small cathedral city. The focal point is the **abbey church**; in addition there are some medieval buildings, two castles, and a well-known school which in part occupies the former abbot's hall and monastic buildings.

Sights and places of interest
Abbey Church †
Church Lane.
The exceptionally rich fan vaulting is the main reason for visiting this church which, although of the 13th–16thC, is last in a succession which started in 705 when Sherborne became a bishopric (the see was transferred to Old Sarum in the 11thC but restored in 1925); in 998 a Benedictine monastery was established here. Some remains of earlier churches can still be found: a Saxon doorway at the w end of the N aisle, and the s porch which belonged to the Norman church of the 12thC.

The abbey has some unusually interesting monuments, and the late medieval **roof bosses** depict flowers, foliage, animals, humans and even a mermaid.
Old Castle
A short way N of the new castle ☎ *(093581) 2730. DOE* 🖾 ⇔
Open mid-Mar to mid-Oct Mon–Sat 9.30am–6.30pm, Sun 2–6.30pm except Apr–Sept 9.30am–6.30pm; mid-Oct to mid-Mar Mon–Sat 9.30am–4pm, Sun 2–4pm.
These ruins represent the fortified palace built by the Norman Bishop of Salisbury in about 1110. In 1591 Elizabeth I gave the estate to Sir Walter Raleigh, but when his efforts to make this place habitable failed he built the central block of what is now the new castle (see below).

Sherborne Castle
E across the railway ☎ *(093581) 3182* 🎫 🅿 🚃 *Open Easter–May
Thurs, Sat, Sun, bank holiday Mon 2–6pm; June–Sept 2–6pm.*

An Elizabethan hall, a Jacobean oak room, a Georgian library and a
Victorian solarium all tell the story of the growth that took place around
the central block built by Sir Walter Raleigh in 1594. It was here in the
gardens of his new home that he is said to have been doused by a servant
who found him smoking.

Sights nearby
Cadbury Castle
South Cadbury, 5 miles (8km) N of Sherborne. Always open.
If there ever was such a place as King Arthur's Camelot, then this ancient
hillfort is the most popular claimant. Today no more than tumbled
earthworks, it has at least been established that this place was inhabited
in Arthurian days (around AD500).

Compton House *(Worldwide Butterflies)* ☆
On A30 near Nether Compton, 4 miles (6.5km) W of Sherborne
☎ *(0935) 74608* 🎫 🏃 🚃 *Open Apr–Oct 10am–5pm.*
Here is something far from ordinary: in a 16th–19thC mansion exotic
and delicate butterflies and moths live in special environmental
conditions. What was once the dining room is now the breeding hall, the
home of chrysalids and caterpillars; the drawing room and conservatory
have been converted into a **jungle and palm house** in which flamboyant
tropical vegetation supports its equally flamboyant lepidoptera.

Upstairs, the **Lullingstone Silk Farm** (founded in the 1930s at
Lullingstone Castle in Kent) shows how silk is made. Lullingstone has
often provided silk for royal occasions and in 1981 the silk for the
Princess of Wales' wedding dress came from here.

Montacute
Somerset. N of A3088, 10 miles (16km) W of Sherborne ☎ *(0935)
823289. NT* 🎫 🅿 🚃 *Open Apr–Oct 12.30–6pm. Closed Tues.*
Dating from the 1590s, this house is an exquisite example of the good
taste of a leading Elizabethan lawyer and politician, Sir Edward Phelips.
Montacute now contains a remarkable collection of 16th–17thC Tudor
and Stuart **portraits** ☆ belonging to the National Portrait Gallery (see
Sights in *London*) and superbly displayed in the impressive 180ft (54m)
Long Gallery.

Ⓗ **Eastbury**
Long St., Sherborne, Dorset DT9 3BY ☎ *(093581) 3387* ☐ 🌂 15
🖃 🚃 🎫 🚃

Location: E of the abbey church. Backed by a large walled garden, this
informal hotel – largely Georgian in character – is run by its resident
owners and provides a comfortable, relaxed base from which to explore
Sherborne and its surroundings.
💐 👪

Hotel/restaurant nearby
Near **Sturminster Newton** (*10 miles/16km E of Sherborne*).

Ⓗ Ⓡ **Plumber Manor**
Hazelbury Bryan Rd., Sturminster Newton, Dorset DT10 2AF
☎ *(0258) 72507* 🏠 🌂 12 🛏 12 🚃 🚃 *Closed Jan, Feb.*
Ⓡ 🔳 🍴 🚃 *Last orders 9.30pm (Sun 9pm). Closed lunch; Jan,
Feb; Sun, Mon Nov–Mar.*

*Location: 1¼ miles (2.5km) S of Sturminster Newton, towards Fifehead
Neville.* The respect inspired by old families can do them an injustice. An
old tire hanging from a tree as a swing shows that Plumber Manor is a
family home in the full sense of both words, even if the Prideaux-Brunes
have been there since the early 17thC. Such touches of family life soften
the mood of the well-kept, sturdy little manor house, standing alone
among dairy pastures. It is more of a country house hotel now that
Richard Prideaux-Brune has added a half-dozen more rooms in a
converted stable but the family, with brother Brian in the kitchen, prefer
to think of it as a restaurant, and have the gastronomic reputation to
match, manifest in their specialties such as veal, chicken and mushroom
mousseline, lemon sole with leek purée, and English lamb Shrewsbury.
They also choose their wines well.
🍽 ☐ 💐 ⁑ 🚃

187

Shrewsbury
Map **10H6**. *Shropshire. Between Chester and Hereford.*
Population: 56,200 **i** *The Square* ☎ *(0743) 52019.*

In those dark days that followed the Roman departure from
Britain, security was what mattered, and a site such as this, high
above an almost complete river loop, was an obvious choice for
settlement, particularly in a region bordering the lands of the
ever-restless Welsh. However, by Tudor and Elizabethan times
this had become a prosperous community living in the fine
half-timbered houses which today draw so many visitors. Three
of the best groupings are **Ireland's Mansion** and **Owen's
Mansion** in High St.; **St Mary's Cottage** and **Draper's Hall**
near St Mary's Church, with the **Prince Rupert Hotel, Abbot's
House** and 14thC **Bear Steps** just to the sw; and, below the
junction of Dogpole and Wyle Cop, the house at which Henry
Tudor lodged.

Apart from the old houses, Shrewsbury has a **castle**, dating
mainly from the early 14thC, and a part-Norman **abbey church**
(*just E of English Bridge*), known for its 14thC reader's pulpit;
standing all alone on the s side of the main road, this pulpit
should be pictured as being in the refectory of the monastery
founded here in 1083.

Sights and places of interest
Clive House Museum
College Hill ☎ *(0743) 54811* 📷 *Open May–Oct Mon noon–6pm,
Tues–Sat 10am–6pm, 2–6pm; Nov–Apr Mon noon–4.30pm,
Tues–Sat 10am–4.30pm. Closed Sun.*
This Georgian house –named after Lord Clive (of India) who lived here
when mayor of Shrewsbury in 1762 – is now an elegant setting for a
museum of general interest in which the most notable collections are
those of Caughley and Coalport china and of church silver.
Rowley's House Museum ☆
Barker St. ☎ *(0743) 61196* 📷 *Open 10am–5pm. Closed Sun.*
The building – offering the opportunity to see inside one of the
picturesque old houses in which Shrewsbury abounds – was built in the
16thC as a warehouse and will enthrall anyone with a love of woodwork
and huge beams.

The museum theme is largely Roman, and specifically *Viroconium*
(see below) from where there is a wealth of material.
St Mary's Church †
St Mary's St.
Some of the finest **stained glass** ☆ in Europe is the great attraction here,
and the windows are all well-indicated and explained. Collectors of daft
events will appreciate the daring if disastrous experiment described on a
plaque on the church's w exterior wall.
Sight nearby
Viroconium Romano-British Town ☆
Wroxeter, 4 miles (6.5km) SE of Shrewsbury. ☎ *(0743) 75330.*
DOE 📷 🚶 *Open mid-Mar to mid-Oct Mon–Sat 9.30am–6.30pm,
Sun 2–6.30pm except Apr–Sept 9.30am–6.30pm; mid-Oct to mid-
Mar Mon–Sat 9.30am–4pm, Sun 2–4pm.*
Viroconium was in fact more British than Roman, at least as regards its
inhabitants, for when the Romans abandoned their fort here in *c.*AD90
the site provided the nucleus for a large town developed by the local
tribe. Interestingly, after so short a period of Roman presence, the town
was developed along Roman lines with all the standard features; the
public baths area provides the most important visible remains, including
a Roman wall more than 20ft (6m) high.

🇭 Lion
Wyle Cop, Shrewsbury, Shropshire SY1 1UY ☎ *(0743) 53107*
☎35648 ▮▯ 🛏 60 ⬛ 60 ⬌ AE CB ◑ ⬤ 🍴
Location: Top of the hill descending to English Bridge. The Lion will appeal
to those who desire comfortable surroundings yet would like to identify

with the past, or at least with the 18th and 19thC. Park the car in what was once stabling for 100 horses and then walk into a hostelry which was known to de Quincey, Charles Dickens and his illustrator 'Phiz,' Disraeli, Madame Tussaud (she came to Shrewsbury to put on a wax show here in 1830) and Paganini.

‡ □ ☞ ☙

Ⓗ **Prince Rupert**

Butcher Row, Shrewsbury, Shropshire SY1 1UQ ☎ *(0743) 52461*
Ⓥ*35438* Ⅱ □ ☎ *64* ⊡ ☎ ⊒ AE ⊙ ⊙ VISA
Location: Just sw of St Mary's Church. Half-timbering, oak beams, sagging floors; these are all part of the character of this fine 15thC hotel in which the dashing Prince Rupert (nephew of Charles I) slept in 1644.

‡ ঙ □ ☞

Shopping

Pride Hill and **Castle St.** form the main shopping area, while the **High St.**, running up to Pride Hill, contains smaller shops, and the tiny passages between the major streets contain many exclusive boutiques and antique shops. The **Victorian Shopping Arcade** (*between Hills Lane and Mardol*) and the precinct in the old Royal Shropshire Infirmary (*St Mary's Pl.*) are notable for their small exclusive shops. At the **St Julian's Craft Centre** (*off the High St.*) local craftsmen make and sell their wares. A general market with a few antiques stalls is held at **Market Hall** (*Fri and Sat*).

Southampton

Map 5M8. Hants. On the s coast, opposite the Isle of Wight. Population: 215,000. Airport ☎ *(0703) 612341; railway station* ☎ *(0703) 29393; coach station* ☎ *(0703) 23222; bus station* ☎ *(0703) 26235; city buses* ☎ *(0703) 553011 ɪ Above Bar Quay* ☎ *(0703) 23855.*
Home of the great liner *Queen Elizabeth II* (the main attraction of harbor boat trips when she is in port), Southampton has several rather special features. The **medieval walls** are superior to most in interest and setting; of several museums, no less than four are housed in medieval buildings which rank among the most important in England; and of the 47 pubs which are said to have marked the route between **West Gate** and **Bargate**, at least two survive and deserve mention – the **Duke of Wellington** (*Bugle St.*), rebuilt in *c*.1490 on 12thC foundations, and the **Red Lion** (*High St.*) with a 12thC cellar.
Event In mid-Sept, Southampton International Boat Show.

Sights and places of interest

Bargate Guildhall Museum
High St. ☎ *(0703) 22544* ⊡ *Open Tues – Sat 11am – noon, 1 – 5pm, Sun 2 – 5pm. Closed Mon.*
An earthwork and wood structure until it was rebuilt in stone in the 12thC, Bargate was medieval Southampton's North Gate, a narrow passageway which, astonishingly, remained in use until the 1930s. Nevertheless, the gate was frequently added to and altered, most notably in the 13thC when it was given its two drum towers and provided with an upper hall. The latter, for long a guildhall, is used today for exhibitions.
God's House Tower Museum
Town Quay ☎ *(0703) 20007* ⊡ *Open first Sat in each month 11am – 1pm, 2 – 5pm.*
The name is taken from a neighboring hospice founded in the 12thC, but this tower, built in 1417, had two entirely secular functions: improved defense and, by means of a tunnel below, the regulation of tidal flow so that it could drive the town mill. After use as a piggery, prison and warehouse, the tower (with the gallery joining it to the town wall) was opened in 1960 as a museum of local archeology, covering not only prehistory but also modern Southampton's Roman, Saxon and medieval predecessors.

HMS Cavalier
Berth 45, Ocean Dock, Eastern Docks (Access Gate 4). This berth is temporary pending opening of a permanent site off Mayflower Park ☎ *(0703) 37522* 🖼 ✱ *Open Mar–Sept 10am–6pm; Oct–Apr 10am to ½hr before sunset.*

Launched in 1944, this destroyer saw active service first in northern waters and then in the Far East. Finally retired, she has been saved from the scrapheap by the HMS Cavalier Trust. Visitors can explore the ship; highlights include the operations room, the open bridge with its equipment, and the guns, missiles and anti-submarine weapons.

Southampton Art Gallery
Civic Centre, Commercial Rd. ☎ *(0703) 23855* 🔲 ⬤ *Open Tues–Sat 11am–5.45pm, Sun 2–5pm. Closed Mon.*

The gallery's excellent collections range from early Italian (an altarpiece of *c.*1320) to very modern. Within this span are British schools of the 18th–20thC, a Burne-Jones series of mythical subjects, French Impressionists, Dutch and Flemish Old Masters, and 19th–20thC sculpture.

Tudor House Museum
St Michael's Sq. ☎ *(0703) 24216* 🔲 ⬤ *Open Tues–Sat 11am–5pm, Sun 2–5pm. Closed Mon.*

As a museum this is of mainly local interest – bygones, musical instruments, paintings and decorative art – but the picturesque old house, built in the late 15th or early 16thC, and the small garden recently laid out as a **Tudor knot garden**, both certainly merit a visit. At the garden's edge, forming part of the city wall, visitors can look down into the shell of an even earlier house, that of a merchant of the mid-12thC.

The walls
Around the inner town s of Bargate. Always accessible.

Although there are good stretches to the NE and E, the walls to the w of the city centre are the most rewarding. There are many access points; alternatively the whole western length can be explored in a walk of some 900yds (820m) between **Bargate** and the water, passing historic **West Gate**, once serving a quay which probably saw the departure of Henry V's army in 1415 and certainly that of the Pilgrim Fathers in 1620.

Wool House Maritime Museum
Bugle St. ☎ *(0703) 23941* 🔲 ⬤ *Open Tues–Sat 11am–1pm, 2–5pm, Sun 2–5pm. Closed Mon.*

Southampton's only surviving medieval warehouse, dating from the 14thC, is a beautiful place with stone walls and ancient timbering. As its name suggests, it was a store for the wool that was Southampton's chief export, but during the Napoleonic wars it held French prisoners. The exquisite bone models they carved are among the many models of ships to be seen in the museum of maritime history which is housed here now.

Hotel

Ⓗ Dolphin
High St., Southampton, Hants SO9 2DS ☎ *(0703) 26178* Ⅲ▯
🛏 72 ▭ 72 ⬤ ═ AE CB ① ⓭ VISA

Location: s of Bargate. Although it dates from the 13thC, the Dolphin was largely rebuilt in 1751 and is thus sheer Georgian from its distinctive bow-windowed facade to the plasterwork and panelling of the interior. A place in which to expect, and get, high standards – as did, doubtless, Jane Austen and Queen Victoria when they visited here.

⇕ ⅋ ▢ ◨ 🕭 🖐

Hotel nearby
Hedge End (*5 miles /8km E of Southampton*).

Ⓗ Botleigh Grange
Hedge End, Southampton, Hants SO3 2GA ☎ *(04892) 5611* Ⅲ▯
🛏 47 ▭ 30 ⬤ ═ ① VISA

Location: Grange Rd., Hedge End (off A334). Run by the same resident owners for some 30yrs, this is a gracious, ivy-clad country house set in extensive grounds. Everything is spacious here, including some large and pleasantly old-fashioned bedrooms overlooking the gardens.

▢ ◨ ⚓ ∿ 🖐 🖐

Nightlife

The **Nuffield Theatre** (*University Campus* ☎ *(0703) 555028*) has a resident repertory company and has put on some excellent new productions. The **Gaumont Theatre** (*Commercial Rd.* ☎ *(0703) 29772*) is the center for rock concerts and musicals. The **Turner Simms Concert Hall** (*University Campus* ☎ *(0703) 555028*) stages classical concerts.

Two nightspots worth mentioning are **Casino Silhouette Club** (*4 St Michael's Sq.* ☎ *(0703) 23990*), situated in an attractive part of town, with cabaret and guest artists as well as gambling, and **Club Tiberius** (*11a Cranbury Terrace* ☎ *(0703) 37469*), which has gambling, a restaurant and dancing.

Shopping

The main shopping area in the heart of the city includes the **Above Bar Shopping Precinct**. The area around **Northam Rd.** to the E of the precinct specializes in antiques. The **Kingsland Sq.** market (*Fri, Sat*) sells mainly fruit and vegetables.

Stamford

Map 12H9. Lincs. 10 miles (16km) NW of Peterborough.
Population: 14,500 ℹ *Council Offices, St Mary's Hill*
☎ *(0780) 64444.*

This confidently dignified town has managed to preserve much of its early street plan and is remarkable also for its many mellow stone buildings, both private and municipal, ranging from medieval to the 18thC. Saxon, Danish and Norman in turn, old walled Stamford occupied a comparatively small area to the N of the river; it is here that the best of the old buildings can be seen.

Stamford Museum (*Broad St.* ☎ *(0780) 55611* ▥ *open 10am–12.30pm, 1.30–5pm, closed Mon except bank holiday, Sun*) has examples of local stone used for building, and displays explaining its use. Additionally, there are examples of Stamford pottery (made between 850–1250), exhibits relating to 19thC industries, and other material relevant to the story of Stamford.

Nearby, on the other side of All Saints Place, a complete Victorian steam brewery has been re-opened as a **Brewery Museum** (*All Saints St.* ☎ *(0780) 52186* ▥ ▣ *open Apr–Sept 10am–4pm, closed Mon except bank holidays, Tues*) and, even though it is no longer brewed here, beer drawn from the wood can still be enjoyed in the refreshment room. Visitors can also watch a cooper, saddler and wheelwright plying their trades.

Sights nearby

Burghley House ▥ ☆
1 mile (1.5km) SE of Stamford ☎ *(0780) 52451* ▥ ▣ ⚊ *Open Apr–Sept Mon–Sat 11am–5pm, Sun 2–5pm.*
The most imposing survivor of England's great Elizabethan country houses, Burghley was built by courtier and statesman William Cecil and now contains what is probably the world's largest private collection of Old Masters, particularly Italian.

Capability Brown designed the Orangery, and Grinling Gibbons' carved woodwork can be seen throughout the house.

Burghley Horse Trials take place in the grounds in early Sept.

Rockingham Castle
Off A6003, 15 miles (24km) SW of Stamford ☎ *(0536) 770240* ▥ ▣ *Castle and gardens open 2–6pm: Easter–Sept Thurs, Sun, bank holiday Mon and following Tues.*
Entered through massive twin drum towers, Rockingham, although of many periods, is essentially Tudor within Norman walls built by William the Conqueror on the site of an earlier fortification. The attractions here, all unusually well explained, include a picturesque cobbled street which once led up to the keep; chests belonging to King John and Henry V; the Long Gallery with portraits by Reynolds and Zoffany among others; and the 400yr-old yew hedge clipped into the shape of elephants.

H **George of Stamford**
St Martins, Stamford, Lincs PE9 2LB ☎ *(0780) 62101* 📞 *32578* ▮▮▯
📞 *45* 🛏 *39* ⊟ ⊨ AE ⊕ ⊚ VISA
Location: s of the river. Once the Hospice of the Holy Sepulchre stood
here, a sort of youth hostel for young pilgrims, but by the late 16thC it
had been replaced by the present building which soon became known as
one of the leading coaching inns on the Great North Road. Today an
attractive stone-walled bar-lounge with a log fire gives the modern guest
as warm a welcome as any enjoyed by his coach-weary forebears.
□ ☙ ☗

H **Lady Anne's**
37–38 High St., St Martins, Stamford, Lincs PE9 2BB ☎ *(0780)*
53175 📞 *32376* ▮▯ 📞 *18* 🛏 *15* ⊨ AE ⊕ ⊚ VISA
Location: s edge of the town on the approach to A1. Named after Lady Anne
Cecil of Burghley House who lived here for some years in the late 18thC,
this gracious country house has airy public rooms and old-fashioned
bedrooms of a size and elegance all too rarely found. Children are
especially welcome and will enjoy the large garden, while the restaurant
offers a wide choice ranging from snacks to gourmet dishes.
□ ⤴ ☙ ☗

Hotel/restaurant nearby
Hambleton (*12 miles/19km w of Stamford*).

H R **Hambleton Hall** 🏨 ⌂
Hambleton, Oakham, Leics LE15 8TH ☎ *(0572) 56991* ▮▮▮▮ to ▮▮▮▮
📞 *13* 🛏 *13* ⇨ ⌷ ⊨ AE ⊕ ⊚ VISA
R ▮▮▮▮ ▬ *Last orders 9.30pm.*
Location: On peninsula in Rutland Water, 3 miles (5km) off A606. Down a
thickly wooded, winding drive, Hambleton Hall finally appears in its
slightly cranky Queen Anne splendor. House-martins nest in the roof,
English chintz curtains frame windows overlooking Rutland Water, and
young owner, Tim Hart, bobs about with almost diffident solicitude.
Bedrooms are spacious and comfortable, and public rooms show
evidence of Hart's interest in antiques as well as food and wine, especially
Bordeaux. Before moving to Hambleton in 1980, not long after it
opened, chef Nick Gill trained at Maxim's. His specialties include hot
mousseline of Rutland Water pike and fresh crabmeat, warm salad of
pigeon breast, *paillard* of pork *poire Williams* and hot praline soufflé.
⌂ ⬆ □ ⤴ ⚱ ☙ ⪡ ♪ ⋎ ⛟ ☀ ☗

Stoke-on-Trent
Map **10H7**. Staffs. E *of M6, between Manchester and*
Birmingham. Population: *265,000* i *Central Library,*
Bethesda St., Hanley ☎ *(0782) 21242.*
Confusingly, Stoke-on-Trent is not only the umbrella name for
six towns but is also one of the six. These towns – often known
as The Potteries – are, from N to S, **Tunstall**, **Burslem**, **Hanley**,
Stoke, **Fenton** and **Longton**.
Pottery has been the business of this district since at least the
16thC, but it was in the 18thC that the industry really got going,
establishing such names as Wedgwood, Minton and Spode.
The tourist office in Hanley provides two useful leaflets listing
possible factory visits and pottery shops.

Sights and places of interest
Chatterley Whitfield Mining Museum
Chatterley Whitfield Colliery, Tunstall ☎ *(0782) 813337* 🚆 ▤
🚃 *Museum open 9.30am–4.30pm (closed Mon except bank*
holidays). Underground trips to the mine ▰ 🎫 *Last trip 3.30pm.*
Here (for those over the age of ten) is an opportunity to don helmet and
cap lamp and go down a coal mine with a former miner as a guide. The
tour lasts 1hr, but those with neither the time nor the inclination to
descend can visit an interesting surface exhibition.

City Museum and Art Gallery
Broad St., Hanley ☎ *(0782) 29611* ⬛ 🖭 *Open Mon, Tues,*
Thurs–Sat 10.30am–5pm, Wed 10.30am–8pm. Closed Sun.

A large and important **ceramics collection** ☆ (of worldwide provenance
but with the emphasis on Staffordshire) is at the heart of this bright,
modern museum. Archeology, costumes, glassware, local social history,
and local natural history are among other themes.

Gladstone Pottery Museum ☆
Uttoxeter Rd., Longton ☎ *(0782) 319232* ⬛ 🖭 🖛 *Open*
Apr–Sept Mon–Sat 10.30am–5.30pm, Sun, bank holidays 2–6pm;
Oct–Mar Tues–Sat 10.30am–5.30pm, Sun, bank holidays 2–6pm
(closed Mon).

There is a strong sense of period about this Victorian pottery with its
large bottle-ovens and mid-19thC workshops. Never achieving
household-name status, Gladstone survived for around 200yrs as a
typical, unmodernized, modest pottery until it was closed in the 1960s.
Rescued by a trust, it now serves as a museum that allows its setting to
live; former workers explain arcane processes and craftsmen can be
watched at their finicky tasks of making china flowers and decorating
china and earthenware. Exhibition galleries include the Historical
Gallery, Ceramic Tiles, Ceramic Sanitaryware, Colour and Decoration,
and Clay as a Building Material, and there is also a popular shop.

Sights nearby
Little Moreton Hall ☆
Congleton, E of A34, 7 miles (11km) N of Stoke-on-Trent
☎ *(02602) 2018. NT* ⬛ 🖭 *Open 2–6pm or sunset if earlier:*
Mar, Oct Sat–Sun only; Apr–Sept (closed Tues).

Started in 1480 and completed a century later, this moated manor must
be one of the country's craziest examples of half-timbering. Nor does the
intricacy end here, for it is carried through to the patterned windows and
the elaborate woodwork of the interior where the hall and wainscoted
gallery are the principal features.

Wedgwood Visitor Centre ☆
Barlaston, E of A34, 5 miles (8km) s of Stoke-on-Trent ☎ *(078139)*
3218 ⬛ 🖭 🖛 *Open 9am–5pm. Closed Sat, Sun.*

This is not the Wedgwood factory, but a special center (set in lovely
parkland) in which the essence of this prestigious firm can be appreciated
both comfortably and conveniently. The four main sections are the
cinema, showing a film (*20mins*) which provides an admirable
introduction; the **museum**, telling the story of Wedgwood and showing a
wide range of the firm's creations; the **Demonstration Hall** in which
skills such as throwing, ornamenting and various intricate forms of
decorating can be studied at close range; and the large **shop** (goods can be
sent worldwide).

Ⓗ **Grand** ♣
Trinity St., Hanley, Stoke-on-Trent, Staffs ST1 5NB ☎ *(0782)*
22361 ⬛❚ 🕭 *90* 🍽 *90* 🖛 ═⬛ 🅰🅴 ⓘ ⓘ 🆅🅸🆂🅰

Location: w side of Hanley. This solid, self-assured, pleasantly old-
fashioned hotel has a good restaurant with an imaginative salad bar, and,
at breakfast, a generous self-service buffet. In the lobby, guests can help
themselves to coffee at all times.
♨ ⬛ 🖾 🎓

Nightlife
Victoria Theatre (*Hartshill Rd.* ☎ *(0782) 615962*) is the main theater
for the Potteries and Newcastle-under-Lyme region.

Stonehenge ★

Map 4L7. Wilts. Junction of A303 and A344, 10 miles
(16km) N of Salisbury ☎ *(09802) 3108. DOE* ⬛ 🖭 🖛
Open mid-Mar to mid-Oct 9.30am–6.30pm; mid-Oct to
mid-Mar 9.30am–4pm.

Europe's most famous prehistoric site is exciting, mysterious,
aloof and entirely satisfying.

Essentially, Stonehenge is a rampart and ditch circle,
approached from the NE by an earthwork avenue and having at

its center a complex of great monoliths, generally arranged in circular form. Created in three main stages over a period of more than 1,000yrs from *c.*2800BC, it remained in use for at least another 500yrs.

What it was used for is more of a puzzle. The generally accepted verdict is that it was a temple, and certainly it would seem that only people driven by some fearful religious compulsion could have erected a monument such as this; the great blue-stones were brought all the way from the *Preseli Hills* in SW Wales (see *Wales A–Z*).

However, to what god or gods the temple was dedicated will probably never be known, although the sun will always be a favorite choice, obvious in itself and also because on midsummer day it rises directly over the stone in the avenue (the so-called Heel Stone).

Stratford-upon-Avon ★

Map 5J8. Warwicks. Between Oxford and Birmingham. Population: 19,500 i 1 High St. ☎ (0789) 293127.

A cynic might suggest that Stratford represents one of the most successful municipal public relations exercises of all time; one that has conjured the world's premier literary shrine out of little more than the house in which William Shakespeare was born and spent his youth, the foundations of the one he built in his later years, his tomb and the homes of his relatives.

Essentially what Stratford provides – and provides superbly – is a glimpse (if inevitably only in terms of architecture and period interiors) of the Tudor world of the prosperous provincial market town in which Shakespeare lived and worked. At every turn the visitor is confronted by half-timbered houses which, although wildly picturesque to modern eyes, must have been commonplace to Shakespeare.

Sights and places of interest

Hall's Croft

Old Town. Shakespeare Birthplace Trust ☎ (0789) 204016 ▣
Open Apr–Sept Mon–Sat 9am–6pm, Sun 2–6pm; Oct Mon–Sat 9am–5pm, Sun 2–5pm; Nov–Mar 9am–12.45pm, 2–4pm (closed Sun).

This was the pleasant home of Dr John Hall and his wife Susanna, Shakespeare's elder daughter. They lived here until they moved to **New Place** on Shakespeare's death in 1616, and Susanna can be pictured busy in the kitchen or maybe enjoying the walled garden, while her husband attended to his patients in his dispensary, doubtless using equipment very similar to that seen here today.

Harvard House

High St. ☎ (0789) 204507 ▣ Open Apr–Sept Mon–Sat 9am–1pm, 2–6pm, Sun 2–6pm; Oct–Mar 10am–1pm, 2–4pm (closed Sun).

Now owned by Harvard University, this house dating from 1596 is noteworthy both as the most elaborate timber-framed building in Stratford and also for having been the home of Katharine Rogers, wife of Robert Harvard and mother of John (1607–38), founder of the American university. There is also an association with the novelist Marie Corelli, who was responsible for preservation carried out in 1909.

Holy Trinity Church †

Trinity St., at s end of Old Town ☎ (0789) 66316 ▣ for Shakespeare's tomb.

The main reason for coming to this 13th–15thC church is to see **Shakespeare's tomb**, together with a bust-monument which, erected by his family in 1623 (only 7yrs after his death) may well be a good likeness. And why dispute the popular belief that the bard himself composed the doggerel rhyme that marks his grave? Several of his family lie here too – his wife Anne, his daughter Susanna and her husband John Hall, and Thomas Nash who was the first husband of Susanna's daughter.

Also of interest in the church are the font in which Shakespeare was probably baptized; photographs of pages from the parish register recording his baptism and burial; and a chained Bible of 1611.

Motor Museum
1 Shakespeare St. ☎ *(0789) 69413* 🔲 *Open Apr−Oct 9.30am−6pm; Nov−Mar 10am−4pm.*

Scenes and sounds from the Roaring Twenties provide the setting for a collection of flamboyant, classy and grand vintage cars from the Golden Age of Motoring.

New Place
Chapel St. Shakespeare Birthplace Trust ☎ *(0789) 204016* 🔲 *Open Apr−Sept Mon−Sat 9am−6pm, Sun 2−6pm; Oct Mon−Sat 9am−5pm, Sun 2−5pm; Nov−Mar 9am−12.45pm, 2−4pm (closed Sun).*

Although only the foundations and the well survive of the house which Shakespeare bought in 1597 (it was demolished in 1759), it is not too hard to picture what must have been a substantial Tudor residence of a kind still to be seen around the town. The purchase made, Shakespeare began to establish himself as a respected local citizen, a role he fulfilled until his death here in 1616. In a way the gardens too are a survival, for what is now called the **Great Garden** occupies the poet's orchard and kitchen garden, while an **Elizabethan knot garden** recalls a style of his time.

The foundations and gardens are reached by passing through **Nash's House**, once owned by Thomas Nash (who married Shakespeare's granddaughter) and now a museum of local history.

Royal Shakespeare Theatre Gallery
Waterside ☎ *(0789) 296655* 🔲 *✗* 🔲 *Open Mon−Sat 9am−6pm, Sun 11am−4pm.*

Paintings of scenes from past productions, portraits of Shakespeare and of some of the distinguished actors and actresses who have interpreted his works, and memorabilia of theater personalities make up the gallery's permanent collection, and there are temporary exhibitions of costumes and props on loan from other theaters.

Tours of the gallery and theater backstage area are available at 1.30pm, 5.30pm (except for matinée days) and after evening performances.

Shakespeare's Birthplace
Henley St. Shakespeare Birthplace Trust ☎ *(0789) 204016* 🔲 *Open Apr−Sept Mon−Sat 9am−6pm, Sun 10am−6pm; Oct Mon−Sat 9am−5pm, Sun 10am−5pm; Nov−Mar Mon−Sat 9am−4.30pm, Sun 1.30−4.30pm.*

John Shakespeare – glover and general merchant – was probably living in and trading from these premises as early as 1552, and since his son was born 12yrs later it seems safe enough to accept that the event took place here. That this occurred in what is unashamedly called the **Birthroom** is more a matter of long-standing tradition. In those days the property was divided into the family home and business wing – a division which generally applies today, with the former furnished in period style while the latter (later used as an inn with the curious name of *Swan and Maiden Head*) houses a **museum** and **visitor center**. In the garden there are trees, plants, herbs and flowers mentioned in Shakespeare's plays.

The World of Shakespeare
Waterside ☎ *(0789) 69190* 🔲 *Open Apr−Sept 9.30am−8.30pm; Oct−Mar 9.30am−5pm (closed Mon). Show every ½hr.*

In a darkened auditorium, 25 tableaux supported by dramatic light and sound effects illustrate life in the 16thC. Among the subjects are the London plague, Elizabethan sports, Queen Elizabeth I's journey from London to Kenilworth, and bear-baiting.

Sights nearby
Anne Hathaway's Cottage ☆
Shottery, 1 mile (1.5km) w of Stratford-upon-Avon. Shakespeare Birthplace Trust ☎ *(0789) 204016* 🔲 *🛶 Open Apr−Sept Mon−Sat 9am−6pm, Sun 10am−6pm; Oct Mon−Sat 9am−5pm, Sun 10am−5pm; Nov−Mar Mon−Sat 9am−4.30pm, Sun 1.30−4.30pm. Buses from Bridge St., or walk along footpath from Evesham Pl.*

With its half-timbering, thatch and old-time garden – not to mention an interior that is as 'period' as anyone could wish – this cottage is almost too picturesque to be true. Add that it was here that Anne Hathaway was born in 1556 and here too that she was courted by Shakespeare whom she married in 1582, and the place becomes irresistible.

Mary Arden's House
Wilmcote, 3 miles (5km) NW of Stratford-upon-Avon. Shakespeare Birthplace Trust ☎ (0789) 204016 ▨ ⌖ Open Apr–Sept Mon–Sat 9am–6pm, Sun 10am–6pm; Oct Mon–Sat 9am–5pm, Sun 10am–5pm; Nov–Mar Mon–Sat 9am–4.30pm, Sun 1.30–4.30pm. Train to Wilmcote, or Stratford–Birmingham bus which passes within 1 mile (1.5km).

Shakespeare's mother, one of the eight daughters of Robert Arden, lived in this prosperous farmstead until her marriage to John Shakespeare in 1557. Little-changed architecturally, the house with its period furnishings and utensils is an effective reminder of Mary Arden's days. Visitors can wander around the hall, kitchen, servants' room and massively beamed upper rooms. Outside there are a dovecote, cider mill, pump and, in the outbuildings, a **farming museum** in which some of the items date back to Tudor times.

Hotels

⒣ Alveston Manor
Clopton Bridge, Stratford-upon-Avon, Warwicks CV37 7HP ☎ (0789) 204581 ◎31324 �|||| ⌖ 112 ▭ 112 ⌖ ⥤ AE CB ⓓ ⓒ VISA

Location: E of river bridge. The name reaches back to Saxon times, the attractive building represents periods spanning from Elizabethan to Queen Anne, and, if local tradition can be accepted, the grounds saw the first performance of *A Midsummer Night's Dream*. Attractions today include a restaurant which provides an early theater dinner.
ᇰ ☐ ⧗ ⌄ ⛱

⒣ Arden
44 Waterside, Stratford-upon-Avon, Warwicks CV37 6BA ☎ (0789) 294949 ◎291855 |||| ⌖ 63 ▭ 43 ⌖ ⥤ AE CB ⓓ ⓒ VISA

Location: Close to Royal Shakespeare Theatre. A restful, pleasant hotel occupying a modernized Regency building. Ideal for theatergoers.
☐ ⧗ ⌄ ⛱

⒣ Shakespeare
Chapel St., Stratford-upon-Avon, Warwicks CV37 6ER ☎ (0789) 294771 ◎311181 |||| ⌖ 66 ▭ 66 ⌖ ⥤ AE CB ⓓ ⓒ VISA

Location: 300yds (275m) w of the Royal Shakespeare Theatre. Dating from the 16thC, this hotel with its rambling, low-ceilinged rooms, leaded windows and some crazy floors, has been sensitively modernized.
⧘ ☐ ⧗ ⛱

Restaurant nearby
Henley-in-Arden (*on B4480, 8 miles/13km NW of Stratford-upon-Avon*).

⒭ Le Filbert Cottage
65 High St. ☎ (05642) 2700 |||| ☐ ▦ ⓒ VISA Last orders 10.30pm. Closed Sun, Jan 1, Dec 26.

A timbered cottage seems an appropriate place in which to eat in what remains of the Forest of Arden. No filberts (cultivated hazelnuts) evident on the menu, although there are *noisettes* (of venison) which might have pleased Shakespeare. Le Filbert is, of course, French, and intensely so. To be more precise, its background is Breton, hence many fine fish dishes, and *Armoricaine* sauce for the sea bass. The menu has seasonal variations, but numbers among its specialties *velouté de crustaces et poissons, gratin de fruits de mer*, and *medaillon de veau à la crème*.

Nightlife

Royal Shakespeare Theatre
Waterside ☎ (0789) 292271.
Opened in 1932, this not unattractive riverside building is successor to the Memorial Theatre, completed in 1879 but burned down in 1926. It is

home of the world-famous Royal Shakespeare Company, and at least five
Shakespeare plays are produced here annually between about mid-Apr
and the following Dec or Jan.

The **Box Tree** restaurant overlooking the river is both popular and
good, and the **River Terrace** is open all day for lighter fare

The Other Place
Southern Lane ☎ *(0789) 292271.*
The Royal Shakespeare Company's 'other place' is a smaller theater
presenting Shakespeare, classics and modern works.

Shopping
The main shopping streets are **Bridge St.**, **High St.**, **Wood St.**, **Henley
St.**, **Sheep St.** and **Rother St.** A small arcade off **Meer St.** also contains a
few antique shops. The **Rother Market** (*in Rother St., Fri*) sells local
produce and general goods.

Tewkesbury
*Map 4J7. Glos. A38, 10 miles (16km) N of Gloucester.
Population: 8,700 i Tewkesbury Museum, 64 Barton St.*
☎ *(0684) 295027.*
There is still a field here known as the **Bloody Meadow**, a grim
reminder of that May day in 1471 when York's defeat of
Lancaster and the death of the Prince of Wales ended one phase
of the Wars of the Roses. And a bloody day it was, even at the
abbey church in which the Lancastrian survivors sought
sanctuary, only to be dragged out and killed. Today the town is
tranquil and picturesque, with its half-timbered houses and its
narrow alleys running down to the placid river.

Tewkesbury Abbey †
On main through-road (A38) ☎ *(0684) 292896.*
Tewkesbury's Benedictine abbey was founded in the early 8thC, but the
church seen today was started some 350yrs later in 1092. In spite of
restoration and some additions (notably the 14thC choir chapels) it has
retained much of its splendid Norman character, enhanced by memorials
to resounding Norman names such as Despenser, Beauchamp and de
Clare. There is much else of interest inside: the Norman piers with their
many masons' marks; the ornamentation in the tower vaulting glorifying
York's annihilation of Lancaster and below, perhaps symbolically, the
traditional resting place of the young Lancastrian Prince of Wales; the
tomb of the Duke of Clarence, executed in 1478 (that he asked to be
drowned in Malmsey wine is the colorful if unsubstantiated tradition);
and, in the Lady Chapel, a painting, *Madonna del Passeggio*, by Raphael.

Beside the abbey, an attractive row of medieval cottages can be seen in
Church St.

Ⓗ Royal Hop Pole
Church St., Tewkesbury, Glos GL20 5RT ☎ *(0684) 293236* ▯▯▯
🛏 *29* ▭ *29* ▬ ▬ ▭ ⒶⒺ ⒸⒷ ⓥⒾⓈⒶ
*Location: On the main through-road (A38), between the town center and the
abbey church.* Half-timbered and quietly old-fashioned, this hotel is
thoroughly in keeping with the town. It was here that Mr Pickwick and
Mr Ben Allen partook of 'more bottled ale,' which the modern guest can
still do in the Pickwick Bar.
▱ ⬀ ⬇ ⛵

Ⓡ Wheatsheaf
132 High St. ☎ *(0684) 292034* ▯ ▭ ▬ ▬ ⒶⒺ ⒸⒷ ⓥ ⓦ ⓥⒾⓈⒶ
Last orders 10.30pm. Closed Mon.
This 15thC shop has been a French restaurant for a couple of years, and
now specializes not only in *nouvelle cuisine* but also in *minceur*. In spite of
proprietor John Hawkes' proselytizing zeal, he still manages more
English dishes such as Stilton mousse, kidneys in port, pork in cider and
sirloin in Guinness.

The Thames Valley

Map 6K9. London, Berks, Bucks, Oxon. Between London and Oxford **i** *Thames and Chilterns Tourist Board, 8 Market Pl., Abingdon, Oxon OX14 3UD* ☎ *(0235) 22711.*

If only because it flows through London to debouch as the gaping estuary which gives SE England its distinctive outline, the Thames is indisputably Britain's best-known river. Rising in the Cotswolds, the river's length is some 210 miles (338km), but it is only the central course between Oxford and Hampton Court which is known as the Thames Valley. Here the normally placid stream meanders through typically quiet English countryside with low wooded hills and lush meadows, broken by comfortable small towns, among which stately and not so stately homes spill their lawns and gardens down to the water's edge.

The larger places of interest – *Oxford*, *Windsor* and Eton, and Hampton Court (see **Sights** in *London*) – appear as individual entries, but there is scarcely a spot along the river's length that is without its claim to individuality of some kind. **Abingdon**, **Dorchester** with its abbey church, and **Wallingford** behind its ancient earthworks are all historic places; names such as **Henley**, **Hurley**, **Marlow** and **Maidenhead** conjure up pictures of riverside elegance, regattas, stylish inns and idle waterborne hours; and proud **Cliveden**, once the glittering home of the Astors, is now leased to California's Stanford University. Approaching London, **Runnymede** is immortal as the meadow where in 1215 the barons forced King John to sign Magna Carta, and there is also a memorial to President John F. Kennedy.

By far the best way to enjoy the river is by boat. *The Thames, Royal River* booklet available from tourist offices gives details of boat services along this stretch of the Thames.

Tintagel

Map 2M3. Cornwall. On the N coast, between Newquay and Bude ☎ *(0840) 770328. Castle: DOE* ▦ *Open mid-Mar to mid-Oct Mon–Sat 9.30am–6.30pm, Sun 2–6.30pm except Apr–Sept 9.30am–6.30pm; mid-Oct to mid-Mar Mon–Sat 9.30am–4pm, Sun 2–4pm. ½-mile walk (1km) from the village.*

There is magic in this name. Beyond the village with its old **post office** and teashops, **Tintagel Castle** on its wild headland was, according to popular legend, the birthplace of King Arthur. Romantics will have no difficulty in accepting this, but in fact the castle was built by the Earl of Cornwall in *c*.1150, at least 500yrs after Arthur's death. Over the centuries the castle has been cleft in two by the sea, leaving one half on the mainland, the other on a small island.

Torquay

Map 3M5. Devon. On the S coast, 18 miles (29km) S of Exeter. Population: 109,000 **i** *Vaughan Parade* ☎ *(0803) 27428.*

This smart, beautifully located and lively resort is renowned for its equable climate. The constant comparison to the Mediterranean may be overdone but, protected from all winds other than those from the balmy south, it can boast palm trees and subtropical gardens. As well as safe beaches, a colorful harbor and a hinterland as lovely as the coast, Torquay has hotels and shops of international distinction.

Sights and places of interest
Aqualand
Beacon Quay, Harbour ☎ *(0803) 24439* 🖼 ⚹ *Open Apr–Oct 10am–10pm, but may close earlier in Apr, May, Sept, Oct.*
The largest and most attractive aquarium in the West Country, Aqualand shows both local and exotic marine life, including one of the country's largest collections of tropical fish. The **otter pool** is another popular and unusual attraction.

Kent's Cavern
Ilsham Rd. ☎ *(0803) 24059* 🖼 📷 💺 ⚹ 🚌 *Open Easter to mid-June 10am–6pm; mid-June to mid-Sept Mon–Fri, Sun 10am–9pm, Sat 10am–6pm; mid-Sept to Easter 10am–5pm. Tours lasting 40mins start every few minutes.*
It is a sobering thought that today's visitor, here to admire the cleverly illuminated stalagmites and stalactites, is treading ground well known to his primitive ancestors of a staggering 100,000 years ago. Here prehistoric man lived and worked, leaving behind his tools, the bones of the now extinct animals on which he fed, and even his own bones.

The best finds are now in the **Torquay Natural History Museum** (*529 Babbacombe Rd.* ☎ *(0803) 23975* 🖼 *open 10am–4.45pm: Mar–Oct Mon–Sat, closed Sun; Nov–Feb Mon–Fri, closed Sat, Sun*), but some representative specimens are shown here at the cave.

Torre Abbey
Torre Abbey Meadows ☎ *(0803) 23593* 🖼 *Open Easter–Oct 10am–1pm, 2–5.30pm.*
Here are the remains of an abbey founded in 1196, a 12thC tithe barn and, in an 18thC house grafted onto the abbey remains, the municipal collections of pictures, furniture and decorative art.

Sights nearby
Compton Castle
Compton, 4 miles (6.5km) w of Torquay ☎ *(08047) 2112. NT* 🖼 🚌 *Open Apr–Oct Mon, Wed, Thurs 10am–noon, 2–5pm.*
Built in three consecutive centuries – 1320, 1440 and 1520 – Compton ranks as one of the country's finest and least altered fortified manors. The owners installed all the comforts available in their day while at the same time portcullises, towers, battlements and a great enceinte showed their determination to defend them. The owner during the 16thC was Sir Humphrey Gilbert, colonizer of Newfoundland; his half-brother Sir Walter Raleigh was a frequent visitor to this pleasing place.

Model Village
Hampton Ave., Babbacombe, 1¼ miles (2.5km) NE of Torquay ☎ *(0803) 38669* 🖼 ⚹ 🚌 *Open Easter to mid-Oct 9am–10pm; mid-Oct to Easter 9am–5pm.*
Described as a 'masterpiece of miniature landscaping,' these gardens include literally thousands of dwarf conifers, shrubs and flowers, among which a model railway, village, town, farms and churches can be seen.

Torbay Museum
Higher Blagdon, near Paignton, off A385 ☎ *(0803) 553540* 🖼 ⚹ 🚌 🍽 *Open Apr–June, Sept–Oct 10am–6pm; July–Aug 10am–7pm.*
Military aviation and daring feats of the past are the main theme. Some 18 complete aircraft represent the 1920s–50s, while special features include The Red Baron, Fighter Aces of World War I, and Escape and Evasion. There is also a model railway and a costume collection.

🏨 **Cavendish** (*Belgrave Rd., Torquay, Devon TQ2 5HN* ☎ *(0803) 23682* ◫); **Grand** (*Seafront, Torquay, Devon TQ2 6NT* ☎ *(0803) 25234* ❂42891 ◫ *to* ◫); **Imperial** (*Park Hill Rd., Torquay, Devon TQ1 2OG* ☎ *(0803) 24301* ❂42849 ◫).

Restaurant nearby
Dartmouth (*on A379, 1 mile/1.5km s of Torquay*).

🍴 **Carved Angel** ⌂
2 South Embankment ☎ *(08043) 2465* ◫ ▢ ▤ ◁ *Last orders 10pm. Closed Sun dinner, Mon and bank holidays; Jan.*
A sister restaurant to the Riverside at Helford (see *Truro*), with a comparable gastronomic reputation. Run by perfectionists for diners

who share that attitude, so that the engrossing view of the Dart estuary is almost an unwelcome distraction, although it is a reminder that local seafood contributes greatly to the menu. There are some interesting Rhône and Loire wines on an extraordinarily comprehensive list.

Nightlife
The **Princess Theatre** (*Torbay Rd.* ☎ *(0803) 27428*) and **Babbacombe Theatre** (*Babbacombe Downs Rd.* ☎ *(0803) 38385*) are the venues for summer season celebrity shows. Torquay's casino is **Newton's** in Union St. Best of the discos and clubs and the most expensive is **La Pigalle** in the *Imperial* hotel (see above).

Shopping
Strand, Fleet St. and **Union St.**, running inland from the harbor, and the new **Haldon Shopping Centre** contain department stores and nationally known shops. The upper part of Union St., in the **Torre** area, has several antique shops. Other more exclusive shops can be found along the seafront, particularly on **Victoria Parade** and in the **Wellswood** area, toward Babbacombe. A covered market selling local produce and general goods is held in **Market St.** (*off Union St., closed Sun*).

Truro
Map 2N3. Cornwall. 52 miles (83km) w of Plymouth. Population: 14,800 **i** *Municipal Building, Boscawen St.* ☎ *(0872) 74555.*

Home of Cornwall's only cathedral, Truro is also the county's administrative center. Its Georgian houses have been particularly well preserved, especially in **Lemon St.** and **Boscawen St.**

The **cathedral**, with its three spires, was built at the turn of the 19th–20thC on the site of the 16thC parish church, nearly all of which was demolished.

The **County Museum and Art Gallery** (*River St.* ☎ *(0872) 2205, open 9am–1pm, 2–5pm, closed Sun and bank holidays*) is best known for its collection of Cornish minerals. It also has material illustrating Cornish life through the ages, and paintings by, among others, Kneller (*The Cornish Giant*), Hogarth, Gainsborough and John Opie, the 'Cornish Wonder.'
Event On May 8, or nearest Sat, in Helston (17 miles/27km sw), townsfolk, and even the mayor, take to the streets to perform traditional dances.

Sight nearby
Cornish Engines Museum
Pool, 15 miles (25km) w of Truro ☎ *(0209) 3150. NT* 🔲 ⬤ *Open Apr–Oct 11am–6pm or sunset if earlier.*
One does not have to be an engineer to be impressed by the sheer size and the functional simplicity of these great 19thC engines which were so much a part of the Cornish tin-mining industry. They pumped water, they wound men up and down, and they brought the ore to the surface.

Hotels and restaurants nearby
Helford (*off B3293, 22 miles/35km sw of Truro*).

Ⓗ Ⓡ **Riverside** △
Helford, Helston, Cornwall TR12 6JU ☎ *(032623) 443* ▯ ☜ 6
🛏 6 ⬤ ᗱ *Closed Nov–Feb.*
Ⓡ △ 🎞 ▢ ▬ ▬ ⬤ *Last orders 9.30pm. Closed for lunch.*
Location: On the estuary. Gastronomic trailblazer George Perry-Smith moved here from his famous Hole-in-the-Wall restaurant, in Bath. There can be the occasional quibble, but as might be expected, the Riverside provides a truly outstanding meal. 'French provincial' it might be, with welcome Gallic touches like the offer of cheese before dessert, but the biscuits are Bath Olivers and there is home-made walnut bread,

walnut treacle tart, too, and home-made fudge with the endless good coffee.

The hotel has half a dozen sizeable, well-equipped bedrooms.

Newtown-in-St-Martin *(off B3293, 19miles/30km SW of Truro)*.

R Anthea's
Glenesk House ☎ *(032623)* 352 □ ■■ ▰ *Last orders 10pm. Open Easter–Oct Wed–Sat dinner only.*
Sustaining home-made breads, soups, casseroles and *cassoulets* have become something of a specialty at Anthea France's bistro, where Gallic food is served in Celtic surroundings (an old Cornish cottage with an open fire). The dishes feature local produce, with a sensible emphasis on fish, although a favorite *cassoulet* features duck, pork, lamb and garlic sausage. No license, so take your own wine.

St Martin-in-Meneage *(20 miles/32km SW of Truro)*.

H Boskenna ✿
St Martin-in-Meneage, Helston, Cornwall TR12 6BS ☎ *(032623)* 230 □ ❧ 3 ▭ 1 ▰ ⇌ *residents only.*
Location: In the middle of the village, off B3293. A small Georgian house in a pretty village, run as an extension of their own home by the endlessly obliging John and Patricia Munro. The Munros are excellent and ambitious cooks (they started the *Riverside* at Helford – see above). Sad to say, their dining room is open only to residents. The restaurant is not licensed but guests may bring their own wine.

St Mawes *(19 miles/30km S of Truro)*.

H R Tresanton ▨
St Mawes, Cornwall TR2 5DR ☎ *(0326)* 270544 ▥▥ ❧ 21 ▭ 21 ▰ ⇌ 🅰 [VISA] *Closed Nov–late Mar.*
R ▥▥ ▭ ■■ ⇌ *Last orders 8.45pm.*
Location: On the hill overlooking the harbor. In a pretty house directly overlooking the sea, this is a peaceful, old-fashioned hotel, pleasantly secluded, with lots of flowers, trees and terrace views.

The reliable restaurant features local seafoods, such as Tresanton smokies, Cornish crab dishes, and sea scallops in vol-au-vent.

Tunbridge Wells
Map 7L11. Kent. 36 miles (58km) S of London. Population: 44,600 **i** *Town Hall* ☎ *(0892) 26121.*
Known officially as Royal Tunbridge Wells, this elegant spa is famous for its **Pantiles,** a promenade of colonnaded houses and shops begun in the 17thC and added to in the 18th–19thC. Close by, the church of **King Charles the Martyr** should be seen for its plaster ceiling and wooden cupola.

Sights nearby
Chartwell
Near Westerham, 13 miles (21km) NW of Tunbridge Wells
☎ *(0732) 866368. NT* ▨ ▦ ⇌ ▰ *House open Mar–Nov on following days, garden and studio open Apr to mid-Oct on following days: Mar–June, Sept–Nov Tues–Thurs 2–6pm or sunset if earlier, Sat, Sun, bank holidays 11am–6pm or sunset if earlier; July–Aug Tues 2–6pm, Wed–Thurs, Sat, Sun, bank holidays 11am–6pm. Closed Mon, Tues after bank holidays, Fri, Dec–Feb.*
Winston Churchill bought this beautifully situated house in 1922, making it his home from 1924 onward. The rooms evoke much about the man and his family and also, indirectly, a whole era of British political and social history. Two rooms serve as a museum, and paintings by Sir Winston are displayed in the **Garden Studio**. Churchill personally built the wall that surrounds what was once the kitchen garden.

Knole ☆

14 miles (22km) N of Tunbridge Wells ☎ *(0732) 453006.* NT 🔲 🎦
🔳 *Oct–Nov except Sat, Sun* 🔂 *Open Apr–Sept Wed–Sat and bank holidays 11am–5pm, Sun 2–5pm; Oct–Nov Wed–Sat 11am–4pm (tour only). Sun 2–4pm. Closed Mon except bank holidays, Tues.*
Chimneys, battlements and countless gables surmount this enormous private house. Started in 1456, Knole was much enlarged when grabbed by Henry VIII and again after 1603 when granted by Elizabeth I to Thomas Sackville, whose descendants have lived here ever since. Virginia Woolf, friend of Vita Sackville-West who was born and brought up here, used Knole as the model for the house in *Orlando*.

Today the State Rooms serve largely as a museum of priceless furniture, portraits and a unique collection of 17th and 18thC textiles ☆

Penshurst Place ☆

Penshurst, 5 miles (8km) NW of Tunbridge Wells ☎ *(0892) 870307*
🔳 🔳 🏃 🔂 *Open Apr–first Sun in Oct, grounds 12.30–6pm, house 1–5.30pm. Closed Mon except bank holidays.*
Penshurst, birthplace of Sir Philip Sidney (1554), is one of England's most splendid country houses, yet it delights through its mellow stone and brick restraint rather than overawing through pretentious grandeur. The s front (the visitors' entrance) represents the original house of c.1340, and it must be counted something of a miracle that the various owners who during the 15th and 16thC added new wings and who later carried out extensive restoration did so with such sensitive good taste. The glory of Penshurst is its **Great Hall ★** of 1340, incomparably the finest of its kind and period in the country, with a lofty chestnut roof and primitive central fireplace.

There are other attractions here too: a costume exhibition, a toy museum, rare breeds of sheep, a nature trail, a countryside exhibition, and a Venture Playground.

Sissinghurst Castle ☆

Off A262, Cranbrook, 17 miles (27km) E of Tunbridge Wells.
☎ *(0580) 712850.* NT 🔲 🔳 🔂 *Open Apr to mid-Oct Tues–Fri 1–6.30pm, Sat, Sun, Good Fri 10am–6.30pm. Closed Mon.*
The gardens here were the creation in the 1930s of Vita Sackville-West and her husband Harold Nicolson. This is no scenic concept, but rather several small gardens – including an almost magical **white garden** and a **cottage garden** – each with its own theme.

The castle, once a Tudor manor with a moat, is now no more than a gatehouse and tower, but the mellow brick buildings add to the special atmosphere here. In the tower, the study where V. Sackville-West wrote some 20 books between 1930–62 can also be seen.

🏨 **Calverley** (*Crescent Rd., Tunbridge Wells, Kent TN1 2LY* ☎ *(0892) 26455* 🔳).

Hotel/restaurant nearby

Near **East Grinstead** (*14 miles/22km W of Tunbridge Wells*).

🏨 🍽 **Gravetye Manor** 🏰 🔼
East Grinstead, West Sussex RH19 4LJ ☎ *(0342) 810567*
🕐 *957239* 🔳 🔳 🍴 *14* 🛏 *14* 🔳 ➡
🍽 🔳 🔳 ⊟ *Last orders 9.30pm.*
Location: 1 mile (1.5km) s of B2110. Gravetye sits grandly among dense acres of the forest which once covered this part of Sussex. It has its own spring, to provide a water more local than Perrier at the dining table, and to supply a tank where trout and crayfish are held. Fish dishes at Gravetye are superb, but so is everything, and perhaps especially the desserts. This kitchen lost its last chef to the Ritz in London but his deputy and successor Allan Garth has quickly won comparable respect. The wine list is one of the finest in Britain, the house beautifully maintained and the bedrooms individually furnished.
🔲 🔳 🔳 🌿 ⚓ 🎿 🔳 ✓ 🏇 ⛵ 🎿

Shopping

The main shopping thoroughfare runs down from **Calverley Rd.** in the N to the **Pantiles** with its specialized and more exclusive shops and restaurants. The sprawling streets surrounding this thoroughfare are

worth exploring for their small and interesting shops. A general market is
held in **Victoria Rd.** (*N of Calverley Rd., Wed*) and an antiques and
bric-à-brac market in the adjacent **Drill Hall** (*Wed*).

Warwick
*Map 11I8. Warwicks. 8 miles (13km) NE of Stratford-upon-
Avon. Population: 18,500* **i** *Court House, Jury St.* ☎ *(0926)
492212.*

Although the huge **castle** dominates the town both historically
and as a tourist attraction, Warwick itself is a charming,
unspoiled place, known for its timbered houses, most of which
were built in the late 17th–early 18thC after a fire in 1694 had
destroyed many of the medieval buildings. **Castle Bridge** offers
the best view of the castle, while nearby **Bridge End** is an
enchanting row of old houses. **Mill St.**, running from Castle
Hill up to the castle, has the town's best preserved black and
white timbered buildings.

Sights and places of interest
Lord Leycester's Hospital
West Gate ☎ *(0926) 492797* 🖼 💶 ⊸ *Open Apr–Sept Mon–Sat
10am–5.30pm (closed Sun); Oct–Mar 10am–4pm.*
In 1571 Robert Dudley, Earl of Leycester (or Leicester) converted a
group of late 14thC buildings, incorporating the town's **West Gate**, into
a home for retired military people, and today this homey half-timbered
row still serves the same purpose. Visitors are allowed into the restored
Great Hall, the **Guildhall** (once used by the medieval town council) and
the **Chaplain's Dining Hall**.

Market Hall County Museum
Market Pl. ☎ *(0926) 493431* 🔲 *Open May–Sept Mon–Sat
10am–5.30pm, Sun 2.30–5pm; Oct–Apr Mon–Sat 10am–5.30pm
(closed Sun).*
Displays illustrating town and county history, geology, archeology and
natural history are housed in the former market hall, built in 1670.
  St John's House (*Coten End* ☎ *(0926) 493431* 🔲 *open May–Sept
Tues–Sat 10am–12.30pm, 1.30–5.30pm, Sun 2.30–5pm, closed Mon;
Oct–Mar Tues–Sat 10am–12.30pm, 1.30–5.30pm, closed Sun, Mon*) is
part of the County Museum. A fine Jacobean mansion, it contains
musical instruments and a folk and costume collection.

Oken's House Dolls Museum
Castle St. ☎ *(0926) 495546* 🖼 ✻ *Open Mon–Fri 10am–5pm, Sat,
Sun 11am–5pm. Closed Jan, Feb.*
This quaint little building, once the home of Thomas Oken, a successful
merchant and local benefactor who died here in 1573, houses a collection
of dolls made of china, wood, wax and metal. The stars of the collection
are the mechanical and musical dolls.

St Mary's Church †
Northgate.
Although this imposing church was largely rebuilt after the disastrous
town fire of 1694, the **Norman crypt** and the 15thC **Beauchamp Chapel**
survived. The chapel, an outstanding example of contemporary
Perpendicular work, contains the tomb of the chapel's patron Richard
Beauchamp, Earl of Warwick, who died in 1439, and some superb
stained glass.

Warwick Castle ☆
Castle Hill ☎ *(0926) 495421* 🖼 ⊸ *Open Mar–Oct 10am–5.30pm;
Nov–Feb 10am–4.30pm.*
The superb, largely 14thC exterior with its battlemented towers
contrasts strikingly with the sumptuous interior which dates from the
late 17thC and the late 19thC. Built on the site of defenses put up by
Alfred the Great's daughter in *c*.915, the castle has a colorful history; it
was sacked and besieged at various times and has belonged both to
royalty and to those who plotted against them.
  Among the many features offered the visitor are the **Great Hall** with a
fine collection of arms and armor; the **State Rooms** with their splendid
paintings and other art treasures; the **barbican, rampart walk, dungeons**
and **torture chamber**; and the extensive riverside grounds.

Sight nearby
Kenilworth Castle
On E edge of Kenilworth, 5 miles (8km) N of Warwick ☎ *(0926)*
55581. DOE 🔲 ➿ *Open mid-Mar to mid-Oct Mon–Sat*
9.30am–6.30pm, Sun 2–6.30pm except Apr–Sept
9.30am–6.30pm; mid-Oct to mid-Mar Mon–Sat 9.30am–4pm, Sun
2–4pm.

Thanks largely to Cromwell's officers, Kenilworth is no more than a
ruin, but it is an exceptionally imposing one as befits a place that has
known kings and queens. Started in *c*.1120, it was later visited by Henry
II (who built the present keep), John and Henry III; Edward II signed
his abdication here; *c*.1400 John of Gaunt converted Kenilworth from
fortress to palace; and in the 16thC, Robert Dudley, Earl of Leicester,
lavishly entertained Elizabeth I here on no less than four occasions
between 1565–75.

Ⓗ **Lord Leycester**
Jury St., Warwick CU34 4EJ ☎ *(0926) 491481* 🔳 ➾ *43* 🔲 *13* ➿
🔲 ➿ *AE* *CB* *ⓞ* *VISA*
Location: Town center. A pleasantly informal hostelry within easy
walking distance of the castle entrance.
🔳 🛁

Hotel/restaurant nearby
Near **Bishop's Tachbrook** (*3 miles/5km SE of Warwick*).

Ⓗ Ⓡ **Mallory Court**
Harbury Lane, Bishop's Tachbrook, Leamington Spa, Warwicks
CV33 9OB ☎ *(0926) 30214* 🏵 ➾ *7* 🔲 *5* ➿ ➾ *AE* *CB* *ⓞ* *VISA*
Closed one week at Christmas.
Ⓡ 🔳 ⏹ ➿ ➖ *Last orders 9.45pm. Closed Sat lunch, Sun dinner.*
*Location: 2 miles (3km) S of Leamington Spa, turn off A452 toward
Harbury.* The admirer who said this was the best hotel in England is
clearly a lover of faultless refinement. It is a fastidious place, with cut
flowers and potpourri everywhere, cottage-style bedrooms, and rather
hushed service in a dining room which serves superb classical French and
nouvelle cuisine. Behind stern gateposts, the house has a prim,
Elizabethan look, although it was built in 1915 and was once the luxury
home of an automobile magnate. Since Jeremy Mort and Allan Holland
opened it as a hotel in 1976, it has developed an outstanding reputation.
The rolling countryside in which it is set gradually blends into the Forest
of Arden and the northern edge of the Cotswolds.
🔲 ⬜ 🔳 🔌 ⚓ ⟨⟨ ⇒

Shopping
There are several antique shops on **High St.**, including the **Warwick
Antique Market** on the corner of Swan St. Other small shops including
boutiques, craft shops and galleries are on **Swan St.**, **Smith St.** and **New
St.** A small precinct off **Market Pl.** (*general market held on Sat*) has some
small chain stores.

Wells
Map **4**L**6**. Somerset. 20 miles (32km) S of Bristol.
Population: 9,000 *i Town Hall* ☎ *(0749) 72552.*
For the locals Wells is a lively market, shopping and general
center. For the tourist the name is synonymous with the
world-famous **cathedral**.
Event In June, Royal Bath and West Agricultural Show held
near Shepton Mallet, 6 miles (9.5km) E of Wells.

Sights and places of interest
Bishop's Palace
On S side of the cathedral ☎ *(0749) 78691* 🔲 *Open 2–6pm:
Easter–July, Sept–Oct bank holiday Mon, Thurs, Sun; Aug.*
The core of this impressive palace was built in the 13thC by Bishop
Jocelin, a measure of the esteem in which he must have held himself, yet
appropriate enough for the man able to conceive the cathedral's W front.

More than a century later another bishop had such a tense relationship with the town that he deemed it wise to dig a moat with a drawbridge.

The principal aspects on show are **Bishop Jocelin's Hall**, the ruined **Bishop Burnell's Hall** (late 13thC) and **Bishop Burnell's Chapel**. And watch the swans in the moat; when hungry they may ring a bell on the gatehouse wall.

Wells Cathedral † ★
City center, beside Market Pl. ☎ *(0749) 74483.*
Held by many to be the loveliest cathedral in England, the present edifice was begun by Bishop Reginald in *c.*1176, although a see had been established here as early as 909. Reginald's successor Jocelin gave the cathedral its spectacular **west front** ★ Twice as wide as it is high (an effect achieved by placing the towers outside the lines of the aisles), this astonishing wall of masonry still carries some 300 of its original 400 sculptures. And if it is breathtaking now, think what it must have been like in its original full color.

Inside the cathedral there is another architectural surprise, the strange arrangement of so-called scissor-arches (best seen from the transepts) which, today as in 1338, still successfully shift the tower's weight from the W, where the foundations were sinking, to the more solid ground on the E side. There is much else of interest in this cathedral, but only a few highlights can be mentioned here: the ancient **14thC clock** in the N transept; **Bishop Bytton's tomb** in the choir s aisle, long held to cure toothache; the magnificent **Jesse east window**; and the satisfyingly simple flight of steps which climb to what is widely accepted as the finest Decorated **chapter house** in the country.

Just N of the cathedral lies the charming and surely unique little 14thC street known as the **Vicars' Close** ✿

Sight nearby
Wootton Vineyard
North Wootton, 3 miles (5km) SE of Wells ☎ *(074989) 359* 🔲 🚗
Open Mon–Sat 10am–1pm, 2–5pm.
First planted in 1971, Wootton Vineyard enjoys the cachet of having won the English Vineyards Association's trophy for the year's most distinguished wine in 1982. Visitors are welcome to walk around the vines climbing the slopes of this tranquil, lost valley and to visit the winery where stylish white wines and Somerset Punch can be bought.

Ⓗ **Crown**
Market Pl., Wells, Somerset BA5 2RP ☎ *(0749) 73457* 🔳 🍴 14
🛏 8 🚗 🚆 🚄 AE ⦿ ⦿ VISA
Location: Close to the cathedral. This 15thC building with Elizabethan additions has a proud American connection since it was from a window here in 1695 that William Penn preached to a large crowd. A snug old-world atmosphere characterizes the interior.
🔲 🗲 ⚓

Ⓗ **Star**
High St., Wells, Somerset BA5 2SQ ☎ *(0749) 73055* 🔳 🍴 22 🛏
7 🚄 AE ⦿ ⦿ VISA
Location: Near to the cathedral. This one-time coaching inn dates back to the 16thC and is a picturesque place clustered around a cobbled courtyard.
🔲 ⚓

Shopping
The **High St.** runs into **Market Pl.**, where a general and food market is held on Wed and Sat. Market Pl. and **Sadler St.** (which runs from the NE corner) contain antique shops, boutiques and delicatessens.

The West Country
Map 2,3&4. Avon, Cornwall, Devon, Dorset, Somerset, Wilts. sw England i West Country Tourist Board, Trinity Court, 37 Southernhay East, Exeter, Devon EX1 1QS ☎ *(0392) 76351.*
All six West Country counties abound in places of beauty or interest, many of which appear as individual *A–Z* entries. Here

it must suffice to mention some principal features, starting with two generalizations about Cornwall and Devon, the two counties that – particularly in July and August – attract the largest number of tourists: first, the s coasts tend to be wooded, sheltered, even intimate, while the N are barer, bolder and lined by superb beaches; second, both counties make rich clotted cream, which the gourmet eats piled high on a scone with jam.

Of **Avon** no more need be said than that it is largely made up of *Bath* and *Bristol*.

Cornwall – the last Celtic outpost in England – tapers toward Land's End, the dramatic, windswept rocks that are the country's most westerly point. Inland, Cornwall has many reminders of its religious and secular past: Celtic crosses mark ancient tin holy sites or graves, while the distinctive outlines of disused tin mines (some of which are now being re-opened) dot the landscape. Around Cornwall's famous coast there are cheerful resorts, quaint coves and fishing villages and, above all, rugged cliff scenery, best on *The Lizard* to the s and between Newquay and *Tintagel* to the N.

Glorious **Devon** is a county as lushly lovely along its coasts as it can be inland; within a small compass it offers bold red-sandstone cliffs, sunken lanes linking lost villages, rich red acres, and, high above, the startling contrast that is Dartmoor (see *Dartmoor National Park*).

If Devon is red, then **Dorset** is brown, green and white, a land of plow, dairy farms and breezy chalk downs, of long views and sudden wooded valleys.

Somerset, famed for cider and Cheddar cheese, offers its contrasts too; acres of apple orchards, the high uplands of Exmoor (see *Exmoor National Park and environs*) and the *Mendip Hills*, and the wetland flats of peaty Sedgemoor.

Wiltshire – scenically dominated by Salisbury Plain (see *Salisbury*), forbidding, bleak and military – may fairly be described as a transit county, yet one which briefly halts thousands to stand in awe at *Stonehenge* or *Avebury Circle* before hastening on to the more comfortable attractions beyond the chalk downs.

Westonbirt Arboretum

Map 4K7. Glos. A433, 7 miles (11km) N of motorway M4 (Exit 17) ☎ *(066688) 220* 🏨 ▆ ⬥ *Open 10am–8pm or sunset if earlier. Visitor Centre and cafeteria close 5.30pm.*

Although some knowledge of rare species trees obviously adds to the enjoyment of a visit here, the trees are so magnificent (the first were planted in 1829) and the whole site so beautiful that even the most botanically ignorant will be amply rewarded.

Ⓗ **Hare and Hounds**
Westonbirt, Tetbury, Glos GL8 8QL ☎ *(066688) 233* 🏷️💵 🏩 *23* 🖭 *19* ⬥ 🖾 🖾 🖾 🅒🅓 *VISA*

Location: At the crossroads a short way E of the Arboretum. This is a stylish, conservative and very English country hotel, with three bars, log fires and an inviting restaurant which offers a particularly good English wine.
▢ 🖾 ⚓ ⤵ ✦ 🐎

Winchester

Map 5L8. Hants. 10 miles (16km) N of Southampton. Population: 31,000 ℹ *The Guildhall, The Broadway* ☎ *(0962) 68166.*

Egbert, Alfred the Great, Canute, William the Conqueror – these are just some of the royal names associated with one of

England's most ancient and historic cities. A busy market town in Roman times, Winchester later became the capital of Wessex and then, under William the Conqueror, the joint (with London) capital of England. Little survives from pre-Norman days, yet there is much in Winchester that is both old and picturesque. The **cathedral** was started as long ago as 1079; the hilltop fortress of the Normans is recalled both by fragments of wall and by the early 13thC **Great Hall**; the **Pilgrims' Hall** in The Close, worth visiting for its hammer-beam roof, and the **Hospital of St Cross** are medieval; and, if the leap is made to more modern times, the city has several charming Queen Anne and Georgian streets.

Sights and places of interest

City Museum
The Square ☎ *(0962) 68166* 🔜 *Open Apr–Sept Mon–Sat 10am–5pm, Sun 2–5pm; Oct–Mar Tues–Sat 10am–5pm, Sun 2–4pm (closed Mon).*

The place for those wishing to see physical evidence of Winchester's past, including a 3rdC mosaic floor and reconstructions of old shops.

Great Hall ☆
w end of High St. ☎ *(0962) 4411* 🔲 *Open Apr–Sept Mon–Fri 10am–5pm, Sat and bank holidays 10am–6pm, Sun 2–6pm; Oct–Mar Mon–Fri bank holidays 10am–5pm, Sat, Sun 2–5pm.*

William the Conqueror built the first fortress here but, around 150yrs later, Henry III enlarged and dramatically changed it. Virtually all that survives today is this Great Hall, after London's Westminster Hall undoubtedly the finest medieval hall in Britain. High on one wall hangs a famous **round table**, officially dating from *c.*1335 and thus, although it tantalizes with a picture of Arthur and the names of his knights, sadly not the table around which the chivalry of Camelot may have gathered some eight centuries earlier.

Westgate Museum
High St. ☎ *(0962) 69864* 🔜 *Open Apr–Sept Mon–Sat 10am–5pm, Sun 2–5pm; Oct–Mar Tues–Sat 10am–5pm, Sun 2–4pm (closed Mon).*

The building, the medieval **West Gate** (13th–14thC) which was later used as a prison, is of as much interest as the collection of arms and armor which it now houses.

Winchester Cathedral † ☆
A short way sw of The Guildhall ☎ *(0962) 3137 Crypt* 🔜 🎫 *10.30am, 2.30pm, available Easter–Oct. Library* 🔜

Before going in, pause at a distance and contemplate the squat length of this sober edifice, built between 1079 and the late 15thC and ranking as Europe's longest medieval church. Reflect too that the area to the immediate N was in turn the Roman forum and then the site of the 7thC Saxon minster, one of the bishops of which was St Swithin, of whom the doggerel runs 'St Swithin's day if thou dost rain, For forty days it will remain' – and all because 40 days of rain in 971 delayed the removal of his remains from the outside to the inside of the minster (perhaps a meteorological protest from a man whose wish had been to lie outside).

Inside, the main architectural attractions are the impressive Perpendicular **nave** which was grafted into the earlier Norman work, the largely **Norman transepts** and what is probably the oldest **Norman crypt** in England. There are also mortuary chests holding the remains of Egbert, Canute and other Dark Ages rulers, and the supposed tomb of the uncouth William II (Rufus), victim in 1100 of a carelessly, or perhaps deliberately, aimed arrow; a library containing the famous 12thC illuminated **Winchester Bible**; a 12thC carved font made of black Tournai marble; **Jane Austen's** burial place; and windows by Burne-Jones in the **Epiphany Chapel**.

Winchester College
College St., s of the cathedral ☎ *(0962) 64242* 🔲 ✗ *for small fee Apr–Sept. Open Apr–Sept Mon–Sat 10am–6pm, Sun 2–6pm; Oct–Mar Mon–Sat 10am–4pm, Sun 2–4pm.*

One of Britain's earliest public schools, the college was founded in 1382 by Bishop William of Wykeham (former pupils are called Wykehamists) who was largely responsible for the Perpendicular nave in the cathedral. Much of the college's 14th and 15thC structure has been preserved.

Just NW of the college are the house in which Jane Austen died (it is marked by a plaque) and also **Kingsgate** (13thC), which contains the church of St Swithin.

Sights nearby
Hospital of St Cross ☆
St Cross Rd., 1¼ miles (2.5km) s of the city center ☎ (0962) 51375
▓ *Open Apr–Sept Mon–Sat 9am–12.30pm, 2–5pm; Oct–Mar Mon–Sat 10.30am–12.30pm, 2–3.30pm.*

One of the oldest almshouses in Britain and today still in use as such. In fact there are two foundations here, that of St Cross founded in 1136 by Henry de Blois, grandson of William the Conqueror, and that of Noble Poverty, the gift in 1445 of Cardinal Beaufort for 'those who once had everything handsome about them, but had suffered losses.' Most of the buildings clustering around the peaceful close are from Beaufort's time, although part of the chapel survives from the 12th and 13thC. Stand in the close, visit the hall, kitchen and chapel, and chat with the quaintly garbed brothers, and only the most stolid of visitors will fail to sense the ghosts of medieval charity. Wayfarer's dole (bread and ale) is still given to travelers who ask for it.

Jane Austen's House
Chawton, 18 miles (29km) NE of Winchester ☎ (0420) 83262 ▓
🛦 *Open Apr–Oct 11am–4.30pm; Nov–Mar 11am–4.30pm (closed Mon–Tues).*

The Rev Austen having died in 1805, the Austen ladies – Jane, her mother and her sister Cassandra – settled in this red-brick house in 1809. It was in this placid genteel setting that Jane wrote *Emma* and *Persuasion* and revised *Mansfield Park, Sense and Sensibility* and *Pride and Prejudice.* The house has been left much as it was in the author's day.

Ⓗ Wessex
Paternoster Row, Winchester, Hants SO23 9LQ ☎ (0962) 61611
⬛47419 ▥▥ 🖾 94 ▭ 94 ⟵ ⟹ 🄰🄴 🄲🄱 🄳 🄾 🆅🅸🆂🄰
Location: Just NE of the cathedral. A modern (1960s) hotel, very central and unobtrusively overlooking the cathedral green.
‡ & ▢ ▨ ▨ ⚓ ⫷ ⟨⟨

Hotel/restaurant nearby
Sparsholt (*3 miles/5km NW of Winchester*).

Ⓗ Ⓡ Lainston House ▦ ✿ ▥
Sparsholt, Winchester, Hants SO21 2LT ☎ (0962) 63588
⬛477375 ▥▥ to ▥▥ 🖾 28 ▭ 28 ⟵ ⟹ 🄰🄴 🄾 🄾 🆅🅸🆂🄰
Ⓡ ▥▥ ▭ *Last orders 10.30pm.*

Location: Between A272 and Sparsholt. This hotel was born with a fine pedigree. It was founded by Marie-Jose Seiler, a member of the Swiss hotel-owning dynasty and her husband, the former Managing Director of the Dorchester, London. They acquired Lainston, a good-looking William and Mary house set in 63 acres of grounds, in 1980, and furnished it in a beautifully understated country house style.

The same easy, relaxed atmosphere pervades the restaurant, where prices are very reasonable; specialties include *émincé de veau Zurichoise* and *rösti,* and the short wine list is well-chosen and helpful.
⌂ & ▢ ▨ ▨ ⚓ ⫷ ✷ ⸾ ⬳ ⟨⟨

Shopping
The **High St.** is the main shopping area. More exclusive shops can be found in **The Square** (*between the High St. and cathedral*) and in **Parchment St.** (*off the High St.*), while the **Kings Walk** shopping precinct (*off Middle Brook St.*) has an antiques and crafts market.

Windsor
Map 6K9. Berks. 20 miles (32km) w of London. Population: 30,000 **i** *Central Station* ☎ (07535) 52010.

Windsor Castle dominates this busy and pleasant town both physically and emotionally. The sense of history and royal

occasion can be overwhelming, but given time and good
weather a trip on the river can provide a tranquil antidote.

Events In mid-May, Royal Windsor Horse Show held in
Home Park.

Late Sept to Oct, Windsor Festival. Classical music
performed at sites throughout Windsor.

Mon–Sat at 11am, Changing of the Guard at Windsor Castle.

Sights and places of interest
Guildhall
High St. ☎ *(07535) 66167* 🕮 *Open Apr–Sept 1.30–4.30pm.*
The collection of royal portraits is the main attraction of this guildhall,
started in 1686 and completed by Wren a few years later.
Household Cavalry Museum
Combermere Barracks, St Leonard's Rd. ☎ *(07535) 68222* 🔲
*Open mid-Apr to early Sept Mon–Fri 10am–1pm, 2–5pm, Sun
10am–1pm, 2–4pm (closed Sat and bank holiday Mon); early Sept to
mid-Apr Mon–Fri 10am–1pm, 2–5pm (closed Sat, Sun and bank
holiday Mon).*

Many visitors to Windsor will have already enjoyed the pageantry
provided by the Household Cavalry in London. Here is the opportunity
to learn something of the story of this colorful and gallant corps.
Royalty and Railways Exhibition
Windsor Station ☎ *(07535) 60655* 🕮 🅿 🚗 *Open
9.30am–5.30pm.*

Windsor Station, built for Queen Victoria's Diamond Jubilee, is a fitting
setting for this Jubilee exhibition (organized by Madame Tussaud's)
which includes a full-size replica of the royal train as well as figures of
leading Victorian personalities.
Windsor Castle ★
Town center ☎ *(07535) 68286. All or parts of the castle may be
closed on short notice; telephone for details.*

Started by William the Conqueror in *c.*1070 and added to or altered by
eight later monarchs, Windsor is the world's largest inhabited castle.
The Royal Family spends Christmas at Windsor and often entertains
visitors at the castle during the year. Tourists come to Windsor Castle by
the thousand, not surprising since, quite apart from its royal
associations, this is a truly stupendous edifice, best viewed from the
Long Walk in **Windsor Great Park**.

The **Curfew Tower** (🕮 *open 11am–1pm, 2–4pm, closed Sun, Mon*)
remains virtually the same as it was when built (1227–30) by Henry III to
defend this NW corner of the castle, although a rather absurd roof was
added in the 19thC.

St George's Chapel (🕮 *open early Apr to Sept Mon–Sat
10.45am–4pm, Sun 2–4pm; Oct to early Apr Mon–Sat 10.45am–3.45pm,
Sun 2.15–3.45pm*), built 1475–1528, is visited as a notable example of
Perpendicular architecture and rich vaulting, for its association with the
Order of the Garter and for its several royal tombs. Well-meaning Henry
VI (1422–61) heads the list of kings who lie here; his probable murderer
Edward IV (1461–83) who started the building of this chapel lies on the
other side of the choir. But if in life Edward was the winner, the role was
reversed in death and it was to the miracle-working tomb of Henry that
the pilgrims flocked, placing their gifts in the intricate alms box that still
stands here. In one vault the uncouth Henry VIII (1509–47) and the
fastidious Charles I (1625–49) make improbable companions, while not
far away lie poor mad George III (1760–1820) and his sons George IV
(1820–30) and William IV (1830–37). Finally, from the 20thC, there are
Edward VII, George V and George VI.

The **Albert Memorial Chapel** (🔲 *open 10am–1pm, 2–3.45pm, closed
Sun*) was 13thC in origin. Queen Victoria remodeled it as a memorial to
Prince Albert who died in 1861, but today this eerie place is dominated
by the tomb of his grandson, the Duke of Clarence, who died in 1892.

Queen Mary's Dolls' House (🕮 *open Apr 10.30am–5pm, closed Sun;
May to late Oct Mon–Sat 10.30am–5pm, Sun 1.30–5pm; late Oct to Mar
10.30am–3pm, closed Sun*), given to Queen Mary in 1923, was designed
to a scale of 12:1 by the eminent architect Sir Edwin Lutyens. Its
treasures include miniature original works by such writers and painters
as Chesterton, Kipling, Orpen and Munnings.

The **Exhibition of Drawings** (⬛ _open Apr 10.30am–5pm, closed Sun; May to late Oct Mon–Sat 10.30am–5pm, Sun 1.30–5pm; late Oct to Mar 10.30am–3pm, closed Sun_) includes works by Leonardo da Vinci, Holbein and other masters.

The **State Apartments** (_entry details as for Queen Mary's Dolls' House but also closed when the Royal Family is in residence, usually Apr and for periods during Mar, May, June and Dec_), although dating in part from the 12thC, essentially represent Charles II's palace as remodeled by George IV. A room with nine Van Dycks; another filled with Canalettos; one splendid hall aglow with portraits (mostly by Lawrence) of the high and mighty of Europe who had played a part in the overthrow of Napoleon; another resplendent with Stuart and Hanoverian Sovereigns of the Order of the Garter – this list may indicate the riches awaiting the visitor in this sequence of sumptuous rooms bearing such resounding titles as the **Garter Throne Room**, **St George's Hall**, the **Queen's Presence Chamber** and the **King's State Bedchamber**.

Finally, in the **Royal Mews** (_open late Mar–Apr, Sept–Oct 10.30am–5pm, closed Sun; May–Aug Mon–Sat 10.30am–5pm, Sun 10.30am–4pm; Nov to late Mar 10.30am–3pm, closed Sun_) there are royal coaches and carriages, paintings of the Royal Family with their horses, and an exhibition of gifts received by the Queen on the occasion of her Silver Jubilee in 1977 and throughout her reign.

Sights nearby
Eton College
Eton, ¼ mile (1km) N of Windsor Castle, on N side of the river
☎ (07535) 63593 ⬛ _Open in term 2–5pm; Easter holidays (late Mar to late Apr) 10.30am–5pm; summer holidays (early July to early Sept) 9am–5pm ✗ Apr to mid-Oct 2.15pm, 3.30pm._

Founded by Henry VI in 1440 and now surely the world's most famous school, Eton can claim to be one of the few really successful achievements of that well-meaning but ineffectual monarch. Even here things went wrong, however, for when Henry was deposed by Edward IV his plans were so drastically modified that the Gothic Chapel finished up only half the length planned. The 16th–17thC schoolyard, the chapel, and the cloisters, one of the oldest parts of the college, are the principal areas accessible to visitors.

Windsor Safari Park
On B3022, 3 miles (5km) SW of Windsor ☎ (07535) 69841 ▦ ▣ ✦
🐘 _Open 10am–5pm or sunset if earlier._

A drive-through safari park. Other attractions are the **Seaworld** with a killer whale and regular dolphin shows, a children's farmyard and a children's amusement complex.

Ⓗ Castle
High St., Windsor, Berks SL4 1LJ ☎ (07535) 51011 ☏ 849220 ▥▯
⇔ 85 ▭ 85 ◁ ⊏ AE CB ⓓ ⓒ VISA
Location: Opposite the castle. Once a Georgian coaching inn, the Castle retains much of the elegant character of those days, but it also offers thoroughly modern facilities.
‡ ▢ 👪

Restaurants nearby
Bray-on-Thames (_near A308, 6 miles/9.5km NW of Windsor_).

Ⓡ Waterside Inn ⌂
Ferry Rd. ☎ (0628) 20691 ▦ ▭ ▆ ⏚ ◁⏚ AE ⓓ ⓒ VISA _Last orders 10pm. Closed Mon, Tues lunch, Sun dinner (Nov–Easter), one week at Christmas._

Britain's most honored chefs, the Roux brothers, have their regal-but-relaxed country outpost right on the water's edge at Bray. Hardly surprisingly, the restaurant is extremely well patronized, and it is advisable to reserve a few days in advance. A splendid pike mousse _cervelas_ has been known to feature on the menu, and fish _mousselines_ are something of a Roux specialty, but diners might also remember that the brothers come from the cattle-rearing Charolles and are the sons of a _charcutier_. Albert's devotion is to pastry and Michel's to spectacular presentation. Michel is in charge at the Waterside; Albert at Le Gavroche, their _London_ flagship restaurant.

Burghfield (*near M4 and A33, 19 miles/30km sw of Windsor*).

R **Knights Farm**
Berrys Lane ☎ *(0734) 52366* ▥ ▆ ▬ ⬤ **VISA** *Last orders 9pm.
Closed Sat lunch, Sun, Mon, first two weeks in Aug, two weeks at
Christmas.*
The menu always contains a meatless main course and the Trevor-
Ropers, owners of this pleasant restaurant in a Queen Anne farmhouse,
are happy to provide alternatives for customers with stricter dietary
beliefs. There is, however, a fish course and no less than three meat
selections on the menu, which changes monthly to suit seasonal produce.
Dishes are cooked with sunflower oil in preference to hard fats, and
indeed full, fresh flavors come out of the kitchen. Fruit wines are
included on an extensive list.

Nightlife
The **Theatre Royal** (*Thames St.* ☎ *(07535) 53888*), a charming theater
with a beautifully decorated interior, stages a good selection of well-
known plays.

Shopping
Curfew Yard off Thames St., the **High St.**, **Castle Hill** and the streets
running off it contain antique shops, gift shops and fine boutiques. The
real antiques center, however, is **Eton High St.** Windsor's central
shopping street is **Peascod St.**

Woburn Abbey ★
*Map 6J9. Beds. w of M1 (Exits 12 or 13), 13 miles (21km) s
of Bedford* ☎ *(052525) 666* ▣ ✳ ⇌ ▬ *Abbey* ▩ *Open Jan
1, Feb–Easter, Nov 1–4.45pm; Good Fri–Oct Mon–Sat
11am–5.45pm, Sun 11am–6.15pm. Small extra charge for
the private apartments. Park* ▩ *(but no charge to visitors
buying abbey entrance ticket). Open Jan 1, Feb–Easter, Nov
noon–3.45pm; Easter–Oct Mon–Sat 10am–4.45pm, Sun
10am–5.45pm. Animal Kingdom* ☎ *(052525) 246* ▩ *Open
10am–sunset.*
The Canalettos alone richly reward a visit to Woburn. These
(there are more than 20 of them) hang in the elegant **Canaletto
Dining Room**, one of the private apartments. Stunning
although these are, they represent only a part of Woburn's
fine-art collection, which includes works by a dazzling galaxy of
great masters. Other treasures to be found in this basically
mid-18thC, exquisitely decorated mansion (built on the site of a
12thC abbey) are tapestries, chinoiserie, porcelain, a
sumptuous Sèvres dinner service, silver and gold vaults, and
one of the world's finest exhibitions of model soldiers. On a
more prosaic level, there is a garden center, a pottery, an
antiques center with original shopfronts, shops, restaurants and
a pub.
   The **park** supports nine species of deer (the most interesting
are the Père David which Woburn has saved from extinction),
while the **Animal Kingdom** is Britain's largest and most
exciting drive-through safari park.

Sights nearby
Ascott
Wing, 8 miles (13km) sw of Woburn ☎ *(029668) 242. NT* ▩ ▬
*House and garden open Apr–July Wed, Thurs, Sat 2–6pm; Aug–Sept
Wed, Thurs, Sat and Aug bank holiday 2–6pm. Garden also open
Apr–Sept last Sun in each month 2–6pm.*
This 19thC, half-timbered mansion contains the priceless **Anthony de
Rothschild collections** of Oriental porcelain, fine furniture and
paintings (for example Gainsborough and Stubbs and, from Holland,
Cuyp and Hobbema). The extensive grounds include a topiary sundial.

H Bedford Arms
George St., Woburn, Milton Keynes, Beds MK17 9PX ☎ _(052525)_
_441_ ⑩ _825205_ ⫸ ⊷ _40_ ⊟ _40_ ⊶ ⇌ ⊷ AE ⊕ ⓒ VISA
Location: In the village. Dating from 1678 or earlier, much of this
Georgian coaching inn was later redesigned by Henry Holland, his touch
being particularly apparent in the elegant **Holland's** restaurant. This is a
hotel which in all ways blends perfectly into this quiet Georgian village.
□ ⏏ ⚓ ⚊

Worcester
_Map **4J7**. H and W. w of M5 between Birmingham and
Cheltenham._ _Population: 75,500_ _i Guildhall, High St._
☎ _(0905) 23471._

Known for its porcelain, its **cathedral** and as the site of the
defeat of Charles II in 1651, Worcester also has a number of old
houses, notably the 16thC timbered buildings on **Friar St.**
Event In Aug, the Three Choirs Festival takes place in the
cathedral every 3yrs, alternating with Hereford and Gloucester.
In Worcester in 1984.

Sights and places of interest
City Museum and Art Gallery
Foregate St. ☎ _(0905) 25371_ ⊡ _Open Mon–Wed, Fri
9.30am–6pm, Sat 9.30am–5pm. Closed Thurs, Sun._
Man in the Severn valley, and especially at Worcester, is the principal
theme here. There is also a complete and authentic turn-of-the-century
pharmacy.
The Commandery
Sidbury ☎ _(0905) 355071_ ▨ _but_ ⊡ _Oct–Mar_ ⓟ _Open
Easter–Sept Tues–Sat 10.30am–5pm, Sun 3–6pm; Oct–Mar
Tues–Sat 10.30am–5pm (closed Sun). Closed Mon._
Once a hospice for the sick and needy, this _c._1500 building with its
splendid **Great Hall** was the Royalist headquarters at the Battle of
Worcester (1651). Today the Commandery serves as a museum of local
history.
Guildhall
High St. ☎ _(0905) 23471_ ⊡ _Open Mon–Fri 9.30am–5pm._
This elaborate but handsome building dates from 1723. Inside, the
elegant **Assembly Room** amply fulfills the promise of the exterior where
statues of Charles I and Charles II (with Cromwell's head nailed by the
ears, above) recall the city's staunchly Royalist sympathies.
Royal Worcester Porcelain Works
Severn St. ☎ _(0905) 20272_ ⓟ ⊷ _Factory_ ▨ 🔨 _Open Mon–Fri
10–11.45am, 2–3.45pm or 2.45pm on Fri. Reservations advisable.
Dyson Perrins Museum_ ⊡ _Open Apr–Sept Mon–-Sat 10am–1pm,
2–5pm (closed Sun); Oct–Mar Mon–Fri 10am–1pm, 2–5pm (closed
Sat, Sun). Showroom and seconds shop open Mon–Sat 9am–5pm._
Britain's oldest porcelain works (1751) was founded, rather improbably,
by a fellow of Merton College, Oxford; it was John Wall's insistence on
always combining quality with innovation that set the pattern followed to
this day. The factory tour (_1hr_) shows how this is achieved and the
museum displays what has been created over more than 230yrs.
Tudor House Museum
Friar St. ☎ _(0905) 25371_ ⊡ _Open 10.30am–5pm. Closed Thurs,
Sun._
Both building and museum merit a visit; the former for its molded
plaster ceiling and exposed sections of 16thC wattle-and-daub work, the
latter for its displays (with period rooms) illustrating local domestic life
from Elizabethan times onward.
Worcester Cathedral †
College Green, by the river ☎ _(0905) 28854._
There were several false starts here, beginning with a Saxon cathedral in
the 7thC which 300yrs later gave way to a new one. The Danes soon
destroyed this, so in the 1080s Bishop Wulstan put up a Norman edifice,
destined however to go up in flames in 1113, 1147 and finally in 1203.
Luckily Wulstan's tomb began to work miracles in the early 13thC, so he

was quickly canonized and from then on pilgrims justified and financed the fine new cathedral which (with much 19thC restoration) stands here today.

The 11thC **crypt**, 14thC **cloisters** noted for their vault bosses, the **chapter house** (1150–1400; a very early, if not the earliest, example of arches flowering gracefully from a central shaft), and **King John's tomb** are the main features of interest. The hapless Prince Arthur (see *Ludlow*) rests near the High Altar, and there are two other curious tombs in the nave N aisle: that of the Beauchamps where painted effigies rest on black swans, and that of Nicholas Bullingham whose body is uncomfortably split into two pieces.

Sights nearby
Elgar's birthplace
Lower Broadheath, off A44, 3 miles (5km) w of Worcester
☎ *(090566) 224* 🚇 *Open May–Sept 1.30–6.30pm, bank holidays 10.30am–12.30pm, 1.30–6.30pm; Oct–Apr 1.30–4.30pm, bank holidays 10.30am–12.30pm, 1.30–4.30pm. Closed Wed.*
Musical scores, photographs and general memorabilia of the composer Sir Edward Elgar are shown here in the house in which he was born in 1857.

Lower Brockhampton ☆
Near Bromyard, 11 miles (17km) w of Worcester ☎ *(08852) 2258.*
NT 🚇 🚶 *Open Apr–Oct Wed–Sat, bank holidays 10am–1pm, 2–6pm, Sun 10am–1pm. Closed Mon, Tues.*
A photographer's delight, this 14thC half-timbered moated manor and its 15thC detached gatehouse nestle in a lost valley at the end of a long, narrow private road.

Ⓗ Giffard
High St., Worcester, H and W WR1 2QR ☎ *(0905) 27155* Ⓣ*338869*
▥▥ ⊷ *104* 🛏 *104* ⊷ ▦ Ⓒ🅱 ⦿ 🆅🆂🅰
Location: City center, just N of the cathedral. This is a hotel grafted onto a shopping mall, but with a particularly attractive long restaurant overlooking the cathedral.
⥮ ⛓ ☐ ⌨ 😋

Ⓡ Brown's
24 Quay St. ☎ *(0905) 26263* ▥▥ 🍽 ⊱ 🚶 🅰🅴 ⦿ 🆅🆂🅰 *Last orders 9.45pm. Closed bank holiday Mon, Sat lunch, Sun dinner, two weeks at Christmas.*
On the banks of the river Severn, this 18thC corn mill has been converted into an airy, spacious restaurant, famous in the area for its fish dishes, although the owners also like to draw attention to their vegetables. They are too modest to mention their skill in the kitchen, and the generous portions of such specialties as fresh fish that changes daily, scampi *en croûte* in a curried sauce, veal with pine nuts and Strega, Malakoff pudding and home-made ice creams. There is an excellent wine list, with good Italian house wines.

Hotel/restaurant nearby
Abberley (*12 miles/19km NW of Worcester*).

Ⓗ Ⓡ The Elms Hotel 🏨 △
Abberley, Worcester, H and W WR6 6AT ☎ *(029921) 666*
Ⓣ*337105* ▥▥ ⊷ *20* 🛏 *20* ⊷ 🚶 ▦ 🅰🅴 Ⓒ🅱 ⦿ 🆅🆂🅰
Ⓡ ▥▥ ☐ 🍽 ⊱ 🚶 𝄞 *sometimes. Last orders 9pm.*
Location: In village. A good, old-fashioned country house hotel, with an outstanding chef. Perhaps it is the enormous beds that make the bedrooms seem a little small, but they are wonderfully comfortable, with large, airy bathrooms. The writing room and library bar are grand, but warm and welcoming. The dining room is graced on occasions by a harpist, although no siren song is needed to attract guests to the work of Paris-trained Scotsman Murdo MacSween, whose style is classical and modern French, with much use of local produce. A magnificent herb garden grows in the small but leisurely grounds of the Queen Anne house and the hotel is in a richly green stretch of thinly populated countryside between Worcester and the Welsh border.
🌄 ☐ ⌨ 🎿 🐎 ≪ 🎣 ⛳ 🚣 🏹 ● 😋

Shopping

Notable among Worcester's china shops are **G.R. Pratley & Sons** (*The Shambles*), and the **Royal Worcester Porcelain shop**. Other specialty shops, including several selling antiques, can be found on the historic streets to the s such as **College St.**, **Friar St.**, **Corn Market** and **New St.** Department stores and chain shops are in the **High St.**, **Lychgate** precinct, and **Blackfriars Sq.** which also holds a general market (*Wed–Sat*). An outdoor market is held in **Corn Market** (*Fri, Sat*), and another covered market is held in **The Shambles** (*Mon–Sat*).

York ★

Map 11E9. North Yorks. 22 miles (35km) NE of Leeds. Population: 105,000 i de Grey Rooms, Exhibition Sq. ☎ *(0904) 21756.*

If ever a city was a museum, it must be York; although it is also, it should quickly be made clear, a busy administrative, commercial and university center. The museum aspect – the walls, towers, gates, old buildings and churches that crowd the city – is all clearly identified by descriptive plaques.

Known in Roman times as Eboracum, it grew into a city of such importance that three emperors – Hadrian, Septimius Severus and Constantine the Great – came here. Angles came after the Romans, followed in 867 by the Vikings or Danes who developed Jorvik as an important inland port on the river Ouse and gave York its name.

Recently, archeologists uncovered a superbly preserved Viking neighborhood. The ancient buildings have been incorporated into the ultra-modern **Jorvik Viking Centre** (*opening Apr 1984, ask tourist office for details*).

Next came the Normans, raising two castles, strengthening and extending the **city walls** ☆ (still visible near the minster and to the SE of the city) and eventually merging into the later medieval people who bequeathed the majestic **minster** and, on a more intimate scale, the highly picturesque old houses which characterize **The Shambles** ☆

As a background to a tour of the sights, the **Heritage Centre** (*Castlegate* ☎ *(0904) 28632* ▨ *open Mon–Sat 10am–5pm, Sun 1–5pm*) tells the story of York in a strikingly presented audio-visual show.

Sights and places of interest

Castle Museum ☆

Tower St. ☎ *(0904) 53611* ▨ ✸ 🚗 *Open Apr–Sept 9.30am–6.30pm, Sun 10am–6.30pm; Oct–Mar 9.30am–4.30pm, Sun 10am–4.30pm.*

Britain's largest and best folk museum is based on the collections of an irascible country doctor, Dr Kirk (1869–1940), who hated mass production and decided to preserve the physical evidence of a way of life that was fast vanishing.

The **period rooms** span more than three centuries, right up to the coronation year of 1953; **Kirkgate**, the star of the museum, is a cobbled street, complete with shops, fire and police stations and even horse carriages; **Half Moon Court** is a rebuilt Edwardian street. Additionally there is a Yorkshire crafts and agriculture section with a weaver's cottage and a farm kitchen; a costume gallery; a military collection; a children's gallery; and a mill which actually makes and sells flour.

City Art Gallery

Exhibition Sq. ☎ *(0904) 23839* ▨ *Open Mon–Sat 10am–5pm, Sun 2.30–5pm.*

Paintings here are from the 14th–20thC and include works by distinguished representatives of most Western European schools. The pride of the gallery is the **Lycett Green Collection** of Old Masters presented in 1955. British works (16th–20thC) are prominent, including many by the York artist William Etty (1787–1849).

Clifford's Tower

Tower St. ☎ *(0904) 58626. DOE* 🖼 🚻 *Open mid-Mar to mid-Oct Mon–Sat 9.30am–6.30pm, Sun 2–6.30pm except Apr–Sept 9.30am–6.30pm; mid-Oct to mid-Mar Mon–Sat 9.30am–4pm, Sun 2–4pm.*

Here is a perfect example of a keep crowning a motte, the latter dating from 1069. The 13thC stone keep succeeded the wooden fortress erected here by William the Conqueror. The arrangement was typical motte-and-bailey, with a large bailey defended by a wall, towers and moat enclosing the area on which now stand the **Assize Courts** and the *Castle Museum*.

Holy Trinity Church †

Goodramgate.

In total contrast to the majestic minster, here is a simple and quaint place of worship, built in the 14thC but visited today for its 18thC box-pews and its double-decker pulpit.

King's Manor

Exhibition Sq. ☎ *(0904) 59861* 🖼 *Open 10am–5pm.*

Splendidly restored and now part of York University, this building which was once the residence of the Abbot of St Mary's was largely rebuilt at the Dissolution in order to serve as the meeting-place of the resoundingly titled King's Council of the North. Since then it has received many high-ranking visitors, possibly including Henry VIII and Catherine Howard, James VI of Scotland on his way s to be crowned James I of England, and Charles I.

Merchant Adventurers' Hall

Fossgate ☎ *(0904) 54818* 🖼 *Open Easter–Oct 10am–4.30pm; Nov–Easter 10am–3pm (closed Sun). May be closed at any time for official functions.*

The Company of Merchant Adventurers, the city merchants principally concerned with cloth export, was formed in 1357 and, although no longer commercially active, survives today. Visitors see the **Undercroft** (1357), also known as Trinity Hospital, which until well into the 19thC was divided into cubicles in which lived needy men and women supported by the Company; the fine, timbered **Great Hall** (mainly 15thC); the modern **Governor's Parlour**; and **Trinity Chapel**, restored in 1411 but now 17thC in spirit.

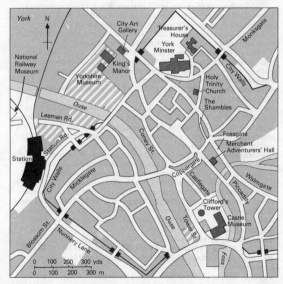

National Railway Museum
Leeman Rd. ☎ *(0904) 21261* 🔲 ▪ ✦ ← *Open Mon–Sat 10am–6pm, Sun 2.30–6pm.*

The theme of this enormously popular museum is the story of Britain's railways from the horse-drawn contraptions of long ago up to today's most advanced ventures. Real locomotives and rolling stock stand alongside all manner of displays – technical, social and economic.

Treasurer's House
Chapter House St. ☎ *(0904) 24247.* NT 🔳 *Open Apr–Oct 10.30am–6pm.*

Dating mainly from the 17th–18thC and visited for its period decoration, furnishing, pictures and objets d'art, this house stands on a site where once a Roman home and, centuries later (1100–1547), the official residence of the Treasurer of the minster once stood.

York Minster † ★
Just E of tourist information office. Chapter House, Undercroft Museum and Treasury, Central Tower all 🔳 *Normally open Mon–Sat from 10am, Sun from 1pm. Closing times vary with the time of year and are displayed on notice boards.*

Outside, inside and even underneath this is the largest and most exciting church edifice in Britain, a huge complex of massed Gothic grandeur which has rested for over seven centuries above the still visible foundations and walls of the Roman *principia*, or headquarters.

It was the decision in 627 of Edwin of Northumbria to embrace Christianity that brought the first wooden chapel here. Three churches followed before the York Minster of today was begun in 1220; it took 250yrs to build and combines all stages of Gothic from Early English to Perpendicular.

The minster's triple-towered exterior should be seen both by day (best from the **city walls**) and also at night, when floodlighting miraculously bestows an ethereal quality on a place essentially massive.

Move into the cathedral and the instant impression is of openness and space and, at the crossing, even of humbling grandeur. Yet even as the visitor stands here dwarfed his eye is carried to detail, to the little sculpted scenes which are such a delightful feature of York. Note, too, the cathedral's window glass, in particular the strange **Five Sisters Window** in the N transept (containing eerie grisaille glass of the 13thC as well as a single stained panel which survives from the Norman church) and the immense **east window** (early 15thC).

The **Undercroft Museum and Treasury ★** is a truly unique place where the visitor actually walks through the remains of the Roman *principia*, while at the same time enjoying a museum and treasury arranged around the massive 20thC steel and concrete structures which have doubled the strength of the minster's foundations.

The 13thC **Chapter House** is notable on three counts: it is octagonal; it has no central pillar, relying instead on external buttresses; and its stalls are adorned with carved human heads, each a work of art.

Yorkshire Museum and Gardens
Museum Gardens ☎ *(0904) 29745. Museum* 🔳 *Open Mon–Sat 10am–5pm, Sun 1–5pm.*

As its name implies, this museum is concerned more with the county than with the city although inevitably some emphasis is laid on the latter, especially the Roman and Viking aspects. Among the fields covered are geology, natural history, prehistoric antiquities and decorative art, notably regional ceramics.

When sated with all this, escape into the **gardens** ✿ bounded on the W and E by medieval and in part Roman walls and forming a beautifully landscaped oasis enhanced by peacocks and ancient buildings and ruins, notably those of **St Mary's Abbey**. The buildings of Roman, Dark Ages and medieval masons cluster together at the E of the gardens, forming a group that spans around 1,000yrs. The pivot is the **Multangular Tower** (*c*.300), still stoutly the W corner tower of Roman York and much of it, with the adjacent wall, still of that distinctive Roman construction.

Sights nearby
Beningbrough Hall
Shipton, 8 miles (13km) NW *of York* ☎ *(0904) 470715.* NT 🔳 ▪ ← *Open Apr–Oct noon–6pm, bank holiday Mon 11am–6pm. Closed Mon, Fri.*

The hall, built in 1716, has been turned into a theme museum, giving

fascinating insight into 18thC domestic life. This is achieved through audio-visual presentations, and above all through about a hundred pictures from the National Portrait Gallery; these alone are a compelling reason for coming here.
Selby Abbey 🏛 † ☆
Selby, 12 miles (19km) s of York ☎ *(0757) 703123.*
This solid great church, part of a Benedictine abbey founded in 1069, is predominantly Norman. Note in particular the N porch with its fine doorway.

The arms of the Washington family form part of a window of the S choir clerestory, and have done so since 1584 and perhaps considerably earlier. The window is best seen from a special vantage point in the N choir aisle where everything is explained.

Ⓗ **Abbots Mews**
6 Marygate Lane, Bootham, York YO3 7DE ☎ *(0904) 34866* ▯
🐎 *27* ▭ *27* 🚗 🖾 ⇌ *AE* ⊕ *CB* *VISA* *Closed late Dec.*
Location: Near the Ouse, a short way w of Museum Gardens. Although the rooms are fairly small and cluttered, the hotel has a certain tucked-away charm as well as a good restaurant. The minster area can be reached by a pleasant walk across Museum Gardens.
🛏 🖾 ⚓ ⚓

Ⓗ **Dean Court**
Duncombe Place, York YO1 2EF ☎ *(0904) 25082* ⑩ *57450* ▥▯
🐎 *35* ▭ *35* 🖾 ⇌ *AE* *CB* ⊕ *CB* *VISA*
Location: Immediately sw of the minster. A converted Victorian place retaining something of the best of its former atmosphere. No parking at the hotel, but a locked parking lot is available in Bootham Row (5mins' walk away); collect the key before parking.
‡ ▢ 🖾 ⚒

Nightlife
The **Theatre Royal** (*St Leonard's Pl.* ☎ *(0904) 23568*) is popular, and puts on good productions, often with well-known names. **Central Hall** and **Lyons Concert Hall** (*University Campus, Heslington* ☎ *(0904) 59861*) are the places for rock and classical concerts. The **Arts Centre** (*Micklegate* ☎ *(0904) 27129*) has music, theater, films, and exhibitions by local artists.

Shopping
Coney St. is York's main shopping street, with department stores and chain shops. The streets to the E, notably **Stonegate**, **High Petergate**, **Low Petergate**, **The Shambles** and **Goodramgate** contain smaller, specialty shops. A large open-air market (*off Parliament St., closed Sun, Mon*) sells general goods and local produce.

Yorkshire Dales National Park ★
Map 15E7&8. Mainly North Yorks. NW of Leeds **i** *For postal inquiries and personal visits (Apr–Sept): Colvend, Hebden Rd., Grassington BD23 5LB* ☎ *(0756) 752748; also Apr–Sept Malham Information Centre, near Skipton* ☎ *(07293) 363.*
Yorkshire Dales National Park embraces over 25 named dales. If each dale has its individuality, there is also a common pattern – a valley in gentle green pastoral and perhaps wooded country, narrowing to a riverside climb, rarely very steep, which breaks out onto broad expanses of bare, brown fell. The three best-known dales are (from N to S) **Swaledale**, **Wensleydale** and **Wharfedale**. Of these Swaledale is the wildest; Wensleydale, known for its cheese, is the broadest, green and pastoral for most of its length and with the most sites of interest; while Wharfedale is not unlike Wensleydale although more wooded and climbing into sterner country. Features of the dales are sheep, drystone walls, remains of medieval castles and religious houses, tumbling streams and waterfalls.

217

Visitors who simply drive the lengths of the valleys may well be disappointed. They will see much that is lovely, less though that is wild or grand. This lies to either side and the real rewards – the long vistas, the exhilarating sense of space – go to the motorist, and even more to the walker, who escapes from the confined valleys. There can, for instance, surely be no disappointment halfway between Wensleydale's **Castle Bolton** and Swaledale's **Reeth**; even less on the breathtaking **Buttertubs Pass** between **Hawes** and **Thwaite**. And while there, stop and have a look at a buttertub, strange limestone columns rising from black depths.

Sights and places of interest
Bolton Castle
Map 15E7. Castle Bolton, Wensleydale ☎ *(0969) 23408* ▓ ▄
▅ *Open Apr–Sept 10am–5.30pm; Oct–Mar 10am–3pm. Closed Mon except bank holidays.*
Today, this grim, part-ruined, 14thC stronghold contains a restaurant (*telephone for opening hours*) offering the opportunity to lunch or dine within the walls which for six months confined Mary, Queen of Scots.
Ingleborough Cave
Map 15E7. Clapham, off A65 between Ingleton and Settle ☎ *(04685) 242* ▓ *Open Mar–Oct 10.30am–5.30pm. One mile (1.5km) walk from the village.*
Beneath **Ingleborough Hill**, a North Yorkshire landmark (those who climb to the 2,373ft/725m summit are rewarded with a superb view and the remains of an **Iron Age** fort), Ingleborough cave has good stalagmites and stalactites.
Jervaulx Abbey
Map 15E8. Wensleydale, on A6108 between Masham and Leyburn ▣ *Always open.*
Founded in *c.*1144 near Askrigg higher up the dale, this Cistercian house quickly moved down to this more hospitable site. Today Jervaulx is no more than confused and picturesque ruins, but visitors should be able to pick out the cloister, the chapter house, some tombs and the church.
Middleham Castle
Map 15E8. Middleham, Wensleydale ☎ *(0904) 22902. DOE* ▓ ▄ *Open mid-Mar to mid-Oct Mon–Sat 9.30am–6.30pm, Sun 2–6.30pm; mid-Oct to mid-Mar Mon–Sat 9.30am–4pm, Sun 2–4pm.*
The castle is closely associated with the enigmatic Richard III who spent much of his time here (he married Lady Anne Neville whose family had long owned the place) and whose only legitimate son was born and died in the huge keep, built in *c.*1170 and one of the largest in England.
Upper Dales Folk Museum
Map 15E7. Hawes, Wensleydale ☎ *(09697) 494* ▓ ▄ *Open Apr–Sept Mon–Sat 11am–5pm, Sun 1–5pm; Oct Tues, Sat 11am–5pm, Sun 2–5pm.*
The theme of this museum is the old way of life throughout the Yorkshire Dales. The domestic scene, cheese and butter-making and farming in general are among the activities recalled.
Yorkshire Museum of Carriages and Horse-Drawn Vehicles
Map 15E7. Aysgarth Falls, Wensleydale ☎ *(0748) 3275* ▓ ✸ *Open Easter–late Oct 11am–5pm.*
In an old mill, a museum devoted to the great days of horse-drawn transportation has around 50 vehicles of various kinds.

See also *Brontë Parsonage*.

Hotels and restaurants
Ilkley (*on A65, 14 miles/20km sw of Harrogate*).

▣ **Box Tree** ⌂
Church St. ☎ *(0943) 608484* ▥▥▥ ▭ ▀ ▄ AE ⦿ ⦿ VISA *Last orders 9.30pm. Closed lunch; Sun, Mon, Jan 1 and Christmas.*
A manicured evergreen seems an appropriate symbol for this perennially honored restaurant, one of the finest in Britain. The Box Tree belongs

to the genteel spa town rather than to its craggy moorlands, and was once a tea shop. Its past is echoed in the clutter of decorative china, although the gilded ceiling fans set a more appropriate tone for the exotic and wonderfully successful interpretations of French classics, which include such specialties as *boudin blanc au Roquefort, melodie de poissons aux julienne de légumes,* and *timbale de fraises.*

Masham (*7 miles/11km NW of Ripon*).

Ⓗ **Jervaulx Hall**
Near Masham, Ripon, North Yorks HG4 4PH ☎ *(0677) 60235* Ⅱ▢
🍲 *9* 🛏 *3* 🚙 ⇌ 🚆 ⓞ 𝘝𝘐𝘚𝘈 *Closed Jan–Feb.*
Location: On A6108, by Jervaulx Abbey. This is a country house hotel of real style and good taste, well sited as a comfortable and quiet base from which to explore both Wensleydale and Swaledale.
⌂ ㅤ 🌡

Pool-in-Wharfedale (*on A659 and A658, 7 miles/11km SW of Harrogate*).

Ⓡ **Pool Court** ⌂
Pool Bank ☎ *(0532) 842288* 𝄃𝄃𝄃 ▢ ▆▆ ⇌ ▤▤ 🚙 *AE* ⓞ 𝘝𝘐𝘚𝘈 *Last orders 9.30pm. Closed Sun, Mon, and for ten days at Christmas.*
Lucky Wharfedale to have not one but two of Britain's most celebrated restaurants, both long established and still in the hands of their relatively young chef-patrons. Pool Court, in an elegantly-furnished Georgian house, offers friendly service but very serious cooking. The style is innovative and cosmopolitan but firmly based on classical French and *nouvelle cuisine.* Specialties include pears poached and served with prawns and crab, bound with cream cheese; saddle of lamb with an apricot and almond dressing; pink roast duck with raspberry vinegar; and fruit pancakes.

Wales A–Z

Aberystwyth
Map 8I4. Dyfed. On the w coast of Cardigan Bay.
Population: 11,000 **i** *Eastgate* ☎ *(0970) 612125.*
Aberystwyth is an undecided kind of place both physically and in spirit, part middle-market resort, part local center, part university town. Behind an open and airy waterfront rounding the castle hillock with its contorted fragments, there hides a fussy, old-fashioned town, while above on Penglais Hill the modern buildings of the **University College** and the **National Library of Wales** hardly seem to belong.

Only picturesque ruins survive of the once powerful **castle** (*New Promenade* 🔲 *always open*), started in 1277 for Edward I and blown up by Cromwell 400yrs later. But on its promontory by the sea this is a pleasant spot for a stroll, picking out the remains of gates, walls and towers.

In the town proper is the **Ceredigion Museum** (*Coliseum, Terrace Rd.* ☎ *(0970) 617911* 🔲 *open 10am–5pm, closed Sun*). Ceredigion means Cardigan (once a county, now a district of Dyfed), and this is the theme of this mainly folk museum.

The **Vale of Rheidol Steam Railway** (*Railway Station, Alexandra Rd.* ☎ *(0970) 612378* 🚃 ✻ 🚙 *open Easter–early Oct, telephone for exact times*) is an entertaining way of traveling nearly 12 miles (19km) up a scenic valley to reach the popular, wooded beauty spot of **Devil's Bridge**. The ride is on British Rail's only remaining steam train, albeit narrow gauge, and takes 1hr in each direction with 1hr's wait between outward and return journeys.

Sight nearby
Strata Florida Abbey
14 miles (21km) SE of Aberystwyth ☎ *(09745) 261. WO* 🖼 🚗
*Open mid-Mar to mid-Oct Mon–Sat 9.30am–6.30pm, Sun
2–6.30pm; mid-Oct to mid-Mar Mon–Sat 9.30am–4pm, Sun
2–4pm.*
The Welsh overran this Norman-occupied land 2yrs after the abbey had
been founded in 1164 by Robert Fitzstephan. Thus the interest of these
ruins – church, cloister and chapter house, spanning the 12th to early
16thC – is that they represent an essentially Welsh Cistercian house; one,
moreover, of such importance that in 1238 Llewellyn the Great chose
Strata Florida as the site for a great gathering of Welsh princes,
summoned to swear allegiance to his son Dafydd.

Hotels nearby
Chancery (*3 miles/5km S of Aberystwyth*).

Ⓗ **Conrah Country Hotel**
Chancery, Aberystwyth, Dyfed SY23 4DF ☎ *(0970) 617941* ▮▯
🍽 *26* 🛏 *19* 🚗 ⬛ AE ⓓ CB VISA
Location: On A487. Large windows in the spacious and thoughtfully
furnished public rooms make the most of the lovely grounds that are such
a feature of this high-lying country house. There is also a motel wing.
🏠 ‡ 🗖 🖾 🎾 ⚓ ⛷ ≈ 🏌

Eglwysfach (*12 miles/19km NE of Aberystwyth*).

Ⓗ **Ynyshir Hall** ✿
Eglwysfach, Machynlleth, Powys SY20 8TA ☎ *(065474) 209* ▮▮▯
🍽 *11* 🛏 *7* 🚗 ⬛ AE CB ⓓ CB *Closed Jan.*
Location: On A487. This gracious white-painted 16thC house set deep in
famous gardens shelters an exceptionally relaxing and relaxing hotel.
The restaurant makes good use of fresh local produce – salmon, seafood,
lamb – while vegetables and some fruit are home-grown. For visitors
interested in birds there is the adjoining Ynyshir reserve.
🏠 🖾 ⚓ ⛷ ✓

Nightlife
The **Arts Centre** (*Great Hall, University Campus* ☎ *(0970) 4277*) puts
on plays, concerts and exhibitions. The **Royal Pier Pavilion** (☎ *(0970)
617000*) has a restaurant and dancing.

Shopping
The main shopping streets are **Great Darkgate St.**, **Terrace Rd.** and
Northgate St.

Anglesey (Môn)
Map 8G4. Gwynedd. Off NW tip of mainland Wales ℹ *Isle
of Anglesey Tourist Association, Coed Cyrnol, Menai Bridge*
☎ *(0248) 712626.*
From the homes and burial places of thousands of years ago to
the nuclear power of today, the choice is the visitor's; in
between there are a great medieval castle, an 18thC stately
home, a grim Victorian jail and numerous almost prim resorts.

But it is for its prehistoric sites that Anglesey is best known.
Burial chambers, earthworks, standing stones and hut circles
abound, these last best seen from the steep, narrow road that
climbs **Holyhead Mountain** above South Stack lighthouse, to
the northwest.

The **Menai Strait** is crossed by Thomas Telford's elegant
suspension bridge of 1826 carrying the A5, and the
Britannia railway bridge of 1850, rebuilt in 1972 following a
fire. From Menai Bridge, the A5 passes the **Anglesey Column**
which commemorates the 1st Marquess of Anglesey. Just

beyond is Llanfairpwllgwyngyllgogerychwyrndrobwll-
llantysiliogogogoch, meaning 'St Mary's Church in a hollow by
the white hazel close to the rapid whirlpool by the red cave of St
Tysilio.'

Sights and places of interest
Beaumaris Castle
Beaumaris, at N end of the town ☎ *(0248) 810361. WO* 🖼 🚗
*Open mid-Mar to mid-Oct 9.30am–6.30pm; mid-Oct to mid-Mar
Mon–Sat 9.30am–4.30pm, Sun 2–4pm.*

The last of Edward I's Welsh castles, now a squat ruin, was built by men
who knew some nasty defensive tricks. The plan is concentric: curved
outer walls ensured good fields of fire, as did inner defenses raised higher
than the outer, while twisted approaches would have given attackers
pause for thought. On a more domestic level, a mental picture of the
scene here and of the size of the ships of the time is conjured by the little
dock, which still has its iron mooring ring.

Beaumaris Jail (*Castle St., in center of the town* ☎ *(0248) 723262* 🖼
open late May–Sept 11am–6pm), with its grim cells, treadwheel and walk
to the scaffold, is certainly not for impressionable children, but will
attract students of 19thC penology.
Bryn Celli Ddu Burial Chamber
Off A4080, 4 miles (6.5km) SW of Menai Bridge. WO 🔲 *Always
open.*

Although much restored, this burial chamber goes some way toward
revealing the importance people attached to burial around 4,000yrs ago,
and the lengths to which they were prepared to go to assemble and
arrange huge stones. It is also worth reflecting that only a fraction of the
original complex survives.
Din Lligwy Iron Age Village
Off A5025, near Moelfre on E coast. WO 🔲 *Always open.*

Some imagination is needed to people these foundations and lower
courses, remnants of what seems to have been a late Iron Age fortified
village. **Lligwy Burial Chamber**, just S, has an unusually large capstone
over a chamber from which the remains of some 30 people were
excavated.
Museum of Childhood
Water St., Menai Bridge ☎ *(0248) 712498* 🖼 ⚽ *Open Easter–Oct
Mon–Sat 10am–6pm, Sun 1–5pm.*

How children have lived since the early 19thC is the captivating theme
here. Dolls mix with ingenious clockwork devices, educational toys with
handwork, magic lanterns with pottery, glass and paintings.
Plas Newydd
On A4080, 3 miles (5km) S of Menai Bridge ☎ *(0248) 714795. NT*
🖼 🚗 ◁€ *Open Apr, Sept–Oct 2–5pm, May–Aug noon–5pm.
Closed Sat.*

Built at the turn of the 18th–19thC by James Wyatt (around a 16thC
manor), Plas Newydd is most associated with that dashing cavalry
commander, the Earl of Uxbridge, later the 1st Marquess of Anglesey,
who inherited the estate in 1812. Perversely, he is known less for his
distinguished military and political exploits than for eloping with
Wellington's sister-in-law and losing a leg at Waterloo. A **cavalry
museum** here is in part devoted to him and even shows his artificial limb.
Another Plas Newydd personality was the artist Rex Whistler
(1905–44). A close friend of the family, he is represented here by several
works, but above all by a huge, romantic *trompe l'oeil* mural ☆ Older
masters hang here too, including Hoppner, Romney and Lawrence.

Outside, from beside the Menai Strait, there are superb views of
Snowdonia, while near the stables stand the remains of a prehistoric
burial chamber.
Wylfa Nuclear Power Station
Cemaes Bay, NW Anglesey ☎ *(0407) 710471* 🚗 *Observation
Tower* 🔲 *Open June to mid-Sept 9am–8pm; mid-Sept to May
10am–4.30pm. Power station* 🖼 🎫 *June to mid-Sept Mon–Fri,
tours at 10am, 2pm. No children under 14.*

The interest here is both technical and scenic, the former catered to by
the power station tour and the exhibition in the Observation Tower, the
latter by the rugged headland where walkers can follow a nature trail.

Hotels
Beaumaris (*4 miles/6.5km NE of Menai Bridge*).

Ⓗ **Bishopsgate House** 🏛
54 Castle St., Beaumaris, Gwynedd LL58 8AB ☎ *(0248) 810302*
▢ 🐾 *11* 🛏 ➡ 🆑 𝗩𝗜𝗦𝗔 *Closed Nov to mid-Mar.*
Location: On the main street, at s end of the town. Both the Georgian
building and the hotel within have a pleasingly unpretentious character.
Antique furniture and some nice china and glass enhance the sense of
modest good taste, and the bedrooms are furnished in a traditional style
too.
👁 ⚘

Ⓗ **Bulkeley Arms**
19 Castle St., Beaumaris, Gwynedd LL58 8AW ☎ *(0248) 810415*
▥ 🐾 *42* 🛏 *18* 🛏 ➡
Location: About halfway along the length of the main street. Behind its
rather daunting exterior and lobby, this is a conservatively comfortable
hotel affording views across the Menai Strait towards Snowdonia.
♨ ⚙ ⚘ ⦉

Bangor
Map **8G4**. *Gwynedd. On the Menai Strait, opposite
Anglesey. Population: 14,500* **i** *Garth Rd.* ☎ *(0248) 52786.*
Strung out along either side of a steep valley, Bangor is
decisively split in two by its lower through-road (Deiniol Rd.),
leaving the university claiming the N while the city crowds the
southern slopes.

The chief attraction of this sober city is its **cathedral** (*off
Glanrafon* ☎ *(0248) 51693*). Although this is a venerable
Christian site reaching back to a 6thC monastery whose founder
(St Deiniol) was created Bishop of Gwynedd, the modest
cathedral seen today was not started until *c.*1180. In later
centuries it was not infrequently wrecked, lying in ruins
throughout the 15thC and being badly damaged during the
Civil War, until it was finally restored, indeed largely rebuilt,
by Sir Gilbert Scott during the 19thC. Inside can be seen some
old inscribed stones, ingenious 'dog-tongs,' Flemish figures of
the 16thC, and some modern furnishings. The adjacent **Biblical
Garden** has flora mentioned in the Bible.

Sight nearby
Penrhyn Castle
At junction of A5 and A55, 3 miles (5km) E of Bangor ☎ *(0248)
53084. NT* 🏰 🖼 🅿 🛏 *Open Apr–May, Oct 2–5pm; June–Sept
11am–5pm.*
There are four different attractions here: a Victorian Neo-Norman pile of
a place, a collection of dolls, an interesting industrial railway museum,
and, the pride of Penrhyn, lots of skillful if somber slate craftsmanship.
The slate-work – here because the owners of this estate developed the
Bethesda quarries – includes a billiard table, a massive bed, dining-room
sideboards and the **Grand Staircase** ☆

Hotel nearby
Talybont (*2 miles/3km SE of Bangor*).

Ⓗ **Ty Uchaf**
Talybont, Gwynedd LL57 3UR ☎ *(0248) 52219* ▢ 🐾 *10* 🛏 *10*
🛏 ➡ 🆑 𝗩𝗜𝗦𝗔 *Closed mid-Dec to mid-Jan.*
Location: On A55, a short way E of junction with A5. A fairly small place
set well above the road, this was first a coaching inn, then later a
farmhouse before becoming a privately owned hotel in 1968. The
spacious grounds make this a peaceful place in which to relax.
👁 ▢ 🖼 ⚙ ⚘ ⦉

Brecon
Map 9J5. Powys. 35 miles (56km) w of Hereford.
Population: 6,000 **i** *Market Car Park* ☎ *(0874) 2485.*

A small cathedral city and center for a large country district,
Brecon can be a crowded, busy place. **Bulwark**, the main street,
has touches of Georgian character (the actress Sarah Siddons
was born at the inn which now bears her name), while in the NW
there are the remains of the 11thC **castle**, in part built with
masonry taken from the Roman fort now known as **Y Gaer** (see
Brecon Beacons National Park).

Sights and places of interest
Brecknock Museum
Captain's Walk ☎ *(0874) 4121* 🖭 🚗 *Open 10am–5pm. Closed
Sun.*

A regional folk and general museum which is outstanding of its kind.
Brecknockshire was the earlier name for Breconshire, a county now
absorbed by Powys.
Brecon Cathedral †
Priory Hill, in the N of the town ☎ *(0874) 3344.*

This imposing church looks rather more venerable and important than it
is, since it was not until the end of the 11thC that a Benedictine
monastery and church were established here. Only a small part of this
survives and today's edifice represents rebuilding of the 13th–14thC,
with some restoration in the 19thC. It became a cathedral only in 1923.
The clear, uncluttered length is the most pleasing feature of the interior,
something for which one may thank the Reformation, since prior to this a
screen barred off the choir and beyond.

🏨 **Nythfa House**
Belle Vue Rd., Brecon, Powys LD3 7NG ☎ *(0874) 4287* ▭ ♟ *14*
🖭 *12* 🚗 ➡ 🍴 ⑩ 𝚅𝙸𝚂𝙰

Location: In the NE quarter. A solid, mainly Georgian stone house tucked
away in its own grounds in a rather lost corner of the town. Squash courts
and a sauna are among the unexpected facilities here.
🍽 ✇ ⚓ ⬗ ♨ ●

Shopping
Bulwark, High St. and **The Struet** contain nationally known shops and
several antique shops. A general market is held in **Market Hall** (*Tues,
Fri*).

Brecon Beacons National Park
*Map 9J5–6. Mainly Powys. Between Brecon and Merthyr
Tydfil, and stretching well to the E and w* **i** *Postal inquiries
and visitor center in summer: 7 Glamorgan St., Brecon,
Powys LD3 7DP* ☎ *(0874) 4437, and Libanus Mountain
Centre, near Brecon* ☎ *(0874) 3366.*

The Brecon Beacons, in fact, can claim only the central core of
this long, narrow park which unwinds all the way from the
Black Mountain in the w to (confusingly) the Black Mountains
in the E where *Offa's Dyke* runs along the English border.
Pastoral around much of its fringe, for the most part this is a
land of high moor and heath, interrupted by valleys and
generously dotted with reservoirs, forests and prehistoric
traces. The park, a favorite with walkers and pony-trekkers,
also serves the motorist well, for few valleys are without a road.
Mynydd Illtyd (*approached by car from Libanus on A470, a short
way s of Brecon*) in a gentle way encapsulates the park, for here
are upland common, ancient earthworks, burial mounds,
standing stones, traces of a Roman road and, to tie it all
together, the informative **Mountain Centre**. Forest lovers can
also head to the **Garwnant Forest Centre** (*off A470, 5
miles/8km N of Merthyr Tydfil*); enthusiasts for the prehistoric

should ask for the official information sheet *Megalithic Monuments*; and those who just want to relax amid water, forest and mountain will go to the **Neuadd reservoirs,** approached by a minor road to the N of Merthyr Tydfil.

Sights and places of interest

Brecon Mountain Railway

Map 9J5. Pant Station, Merthyr Tydfil, on s edge of the park ☎ *(0685) 4854* 🎫 ⬛ ✱ 🍴 *Services daily late May to mid-Sept, Easter holidays, May bank holiday, Christmas and New Year; Sat, Sun only mid-May, mid-Sept to Oct. Telephone for exact times.*

Already running 2 miles (3km) to Pontsticill, and with a further 3½ miles (6km) planned, this narrow-gauge line, which first operated in 1863, provides a novel way of enjoying the lakes and woods at this edge of the park.

Carreg Cennen Castle

Map 8J4. 4 miles (6.5km) se of Llandeilo, on w edge of the park. WO 🅿 ⬛ *Always open.*

Defiantly perched high on a precipitous crag, few ruins can be as visually exciting as these. The castle was built in the 13th–14thC, but this is no place to dispute the tradition that centuries earlier one of Arthur's knights ruled here.

Dan-yr-Ogof and Cathedral caves

Map 9J5. On A4067, 15 miles (24km) sw of Brecon ☎ *(0639) 730284* 🎫 *Combined ticket available* 🎫 *for Dan-yr-Ogof cave* ⬛ ✱ ⬛ 🍴 *Open Easter–Oct 10am–sunset. Telephone for winter times. Tour duration 1½ hrs.*

The Dan-yr-Ogof cave claims to be the longest in Britain accessible to visitors, the Cathedral cave to have the largest single chamber. A craft shop, information center, dinosaur park and museum round off this complex.

Llanthony Priory

Map 9J6. On B4423, on e edge of the park. WO 🅿 ⬛ *Always open.*

The 12thC ruins of this Augustinian priory are modest, but seem in place in this tranquil valley through the heart of the Black Mountains. A short way N, right beside the road, the gatehouse has become part of a barn.

Tretower Court and Castle ☆

Map 9J5. At junction of A40 and A479, 10 miles (16km) se of Brecon ☎ *(0874) 730279. WO* 🎫 ⬛ *Open mid-Mar to mid-Oct Mon–Sat 9.30am–6.30pm, Sun 2–6.30pm; mid-Oct to mid-Mar Mon–Sat 9.30am–4pm, Sun 2–4pm.*

Two adjacent, very different sites for the price of one.

Tretower Court is a mellow medieval fortified manor, especially appealing because of its inviting wall walk, which was originally defensive but later given a roof and windows.

Tretower Castle forms a unique complex of a cylindrical 13thC tower rising within a 12thC enceinte. Doubtless a forbidding place once, Tretower is now tamed, even suffering the indignity of having its outer ward taken over by a farmyard.

Y Gaer Roman Fort

Map 9J5. 3 miles (5km) w of Brecon. WO 🅿 *Always open. Access is across private farmland.*

Although in the 11thC this fort's walls served as a ready source of stone for Brecon's castle, interesting remains can still be seen. Today a tranquil site, in its Roman years (roughly 100–300AD) Cicutium as it may then have been called, thrilled to the sounds of imperial cavalry.

Sports and activities

Boating A variety of boats is available on the Brecon–Pontypool canal, the river Usk and Llangorse Lake. A Waterways Board license is required before putting any craft on the canal.

Fishing A Water Authority license (available from the *Welsh Water Authority, Cambrian Way, Brecon*) and a permit (often available from tackle shops) are needed for fishing on the many salmon rivers, in the trout-stocked reservoirs and for stream fishing.

Information on these and other activities including riding, walking, climbing and caving are available from the National Park offices.

Caernarfon

Map 8G4. Gwynedd. sw end of the Menai Strait.
Population: 9,000 ℹ *The Square* ☎ *(0286) 2232.*

The fascinating thing about Caernarfon is the way in which,
700yrs later, it still so faithfully represents Edward I's concept
of a castle and associated borough together forming one
compact defensive and commercial entity. The citizens –
usually English immigrants – could trade within the protection
of the walls, but in return they were expected to boost the
garrison in an emergency. It can all be seen here; walls and
towers on the N, E and w, the great castle defending the s, and,
within, a town of typically squared-off pattern. This – old
Caernarfon within the walls – is tourist Caernarfon, but go
outside too, down to **Slate Quay**, because only from here can
the true strength of the castle be appreciated.

Sights and places of interest
Caernarfon Castle ☆

Castle Ditch ☎ *(0286) 3094. WO* 🏞 🚶 *Open mid-Mar to mid-Oct*
9.30am – 6.30pm; mid-Oct to mid-Mar Mon - Sat 9.30am – 4pm, Sun
2 – 4pm.

Huge though it is, this historic castle of 1283–1323 is unspectacular from
the town side although very different if viewed from below from the s or
w. From here the towering walls rise sheer, promising an interior of
similar scale. But it is a promise unfulfilled, for the interior is little more
than a shell, although one encased by walls which, with their system of
continuous passages and many towers, irresistibly invite exploration.

To most visitors Caernarfon will spell Prince of Wales, for it was here
that Edward II, the first to bear that title, was born in 1284. More recent
times have seen the investitures here as Prince of Wales of the future
Edward VIII in 1911, and of Prince Charles in 1969.

Of the castle's several towers, the largest and most important is **Eagle
Tower**, containing the room in which Edward II is said to have been
born (in fact it is unlikely that the tower would have reached this level by
that time). Eagle Tower now houses a lively audio-visual presentation.

Segontium Roman Fort

On E side of A487, on SE outskirts ☎ *(0286) 5625. NT* 🅞 *Open*
Mar–Apr, Oct Mon – Sat 9.30am – 5.30pm, Sun 2 – 5pm; May–Sept
Mon – Sat 9.30am – 6pm, Sun 2 – 6pm; Nov–Feb Mon – Sat
9.30am – 4pm, Sun 2 – 4pm.

This far western outpost of Rome's empire was occupied for some 300yrs
(AD80 – 380). Today, however, Segontium is little more than outlined
foundations which the layman visitor may well soon abandon for the
admirable **museum**. Only in part concerned with Segontium as such, the
theme here is the Romans in Britain and particularly in Wales.

Ⓗ **Royal**

North Rd., Caernarfon, Gwynedd LL55 1AY ☎ *(0286) 3184* ⃞⃞
🔑 58 🛏 58 ▦ 🚶 ⇌ AE ⓒ VISA *Closed one week at Christmas.*
Location: At NE end of the town, on road to Bangor. This hotel provides
everything the traveler is likely to want, including a choice of three places
in which to eat: a main restaurant, a grill and fish restaurant which stays
open until late, and a snack bar.
💲 ♿ ⬜ 📷 ✓ 🚶 ⛵

Hotel/restaurant nearby
Llanwnda (*4 miles/6.5km sw of Caernarfon*).

Ⓗ Ⓡ **The Stables**

Plas Ffynnon, Llanwnda, Caernarfon, Gwynedd LL54 5SD
☎ *(0286) 830711* ⃞⃞ 🔑 12 🛏 12 🚶 🚶 ⇌ AE ⓒ VISA
Ⓡ ⃞⃞ ⬜ 🍴 🚶 *Last orders 9.45pm (Sun 8.30pm).*

Horses still graze in the surrounding 13 acres, but the one-time military
stables of Plas Ffynnon, with many of their original features retained,
were in 1973 converted and extended to become a restaurant. The
owners, Richard and Jenny Howarth, provide simple, reliable cooking

specializing in local fish, flambéed dishes and home-made desserts.

In 1979 they added a single-story extension, retaining the stable theme, to provide 12 bedrooms.

 ☺ □ 📷 ⏩ ☒ ≍ ⚰

Shopping
The main shopping streets are **Castle St.**, **Bridge St.**, **Pool St.**, **High St.** and **Bangor St.** There is a lively general and fruit and vegetable market (*Sat*) at **Y Maes**, the square in front of the castle.

Cardiff (*Caerdydd*)
Map 4K6. South Glam. 25 miles (40km) w of the Severn Bridge. Population: 291,000. Rhoose airport ☏ *(0446) 710296; railway station* ☏ *(0222) 499811; coach and bus station* ☏ *(0222) 396521* **i** *3 Castle St.* ☏ *(0222) 27281.*
Many people tend to come to Cardiff, the capital of Wales, thinking in terms of the South Wales industrial belt. In fact in its central area Cardiff is architecturally one of the most distinguished cities in Britain, and a place which within a few paces of the tourist office provides an astonishing variety.

The **castle**, if neither beautiful nor conventionally frowning, is at least a landmark of note, while, just to the NE, **Cathays Park** ☆ speaks volumes for the good taste of the planning authorities and architects of the early years of the 20thC. The word 'park' is misleading; a dignified, much varied grouping of white stone buildings, including the **City Hall**, the **National Museum of Wales** and departments of **University College**, space themselves along avenues and gardens.

To the s of the castle, however, the scene is quite different, for this is downtown Cardiff, a quarter of busy shopping streets, pedestrian precincts and a lively covered market. Go w of the castle and the change is again dramatic, as gardens, parks and playing fields stretch far into the distance on either side of the little river Taff.

Sights and places of interest
Cardiff Castle
Castle St. ☏ *(0222) 31033* 📸 🎥 *castle* ⚑ *Mar–Apr, Oct: castle open 10am–4pm, grounds open 10am–5pm. May–Sept: castle open 10am–5pm, grounds open 10am–5pm. Nov–Feb: castle open 11am–3pm, grounds open 10am–4pm. Sometimes closed for official functions.*
Romans, Normans and others through to the 19thC have all had a hand in the story of this great walled rectangle at Cardiff's center, although most of what is seen today from the outside is of this last period. It is inside, beyond the 13thC gateway (the **Black Tower**), that history reveals itself through a length of Roman wall and, across the green, the 11thC Norman motte, crowned by a keep of about a century later. The buildings at the sw represent the late medieval trend toward more comfortable living than would ever have been found in a drafty, purely defensive keep. Extended in Tudor and Stuart days, they were rebuilt in the 19thC, and should not be missed by anyone with an eye for colorful and highly eccentric interior decoration.
National Museum of Wales ★
Cathays Rd. ☏ *(0222) 397951* 📷 ⚑ *Open Mon–Sat 10am–5pm, Sun 2.30–5pm.*
This is one of Britain's great museums – an art gallery of distinction, too – and although the underlying theme is of course things Welsh, this is as often as not lost in the wealth of wider material. For example, Richard Wilson and Augustus John may be prominent as Welsh artists, but Old Masters and a notable collection of Impressionists are not far away; and if the displays relating to the countryside, archeology and industry are about Wales, complex international science is only around the corner.

Sights nearby
Llandaff Cathedral †
Llandaff, 2 miles (3km) NW of Cardiff ☎ (0222) 562400.
Llandaff's story is a checkered one. A pagan burial site; one or perhaps
two pre-Norman churches; a Norman cathedral (of which the arch
behind the altar is the main survival); addition and alteration throughout
the 13th–14thC; then 300yrs of neglect, Llandaff being of so little
consequence that Cromwell's soldiers used the nave as a pub, and fed
pigs from the font. Restored in the 19thC, reduced again to a shell by
bombing in 1941, the cathedral was finally rebuilt in the 1950s.

Judgment on the interior must rest with the individual, but whatever
else this may be, the central feature – a great concrete arch carrying a
cylindrical organ case with Epstein's aluminum *Christ in Majesty*
uncomfortably stuck onto it – is at least striking. And for those who find
it too much, there is a 10thC Celtic cross to recall the humbler approach
of those who built and worshiped here before even the Normans came.

Welsh Folk Museum
St Fagan's, 3¼ miles (6km) W of Cardiff ☎ (0222) 569441 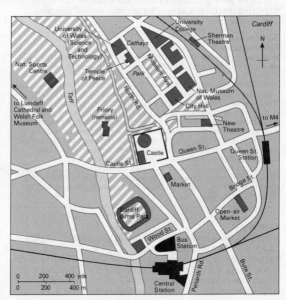
Open Mon–Sat 10am–5pm, Sun 2.30–5pm.
The greater part of this large museum is in the open air, so a fine day can
make all the difference as the visitor wanders around a park in which are
scattered buildings brought from all parts of Wales – for example, mills,
farmhouses, a chapel, a smithy and a tannery.

Indoors there are two quite different areas. One contains galleries on
such themes as agriculture, dress, law and order, the home, and folklore;
the other is **St Fagan's Castle**, an Elizabethan mansion within a Norman
wall which today shows 17th–19thC furnishings.

🄷 Angel
Castle St., Cardiff, South Glam CF1 2QZ ☎ (0222) 32633
☎498132 ▥▥ ⇔ 98 ⬛ 82 ⇔ ⚏ AE ◐ ⓒ VISA Closed Christmas.
Location: Nearly opposite castle entrance. A palatial place, yet the
ambience is homey and relaxing enough, partly the result of careful color
schemes and lighting. The main restaurant is Louis XVI in style; in
contrast, the Tavern Grill in the cellars is informal and intimate.
‡ ઇ ☐ ⌷ ⅔ ≪ ✓ ☝ ⛄ ◑ ⅋ ⸙

H **Beverley**
75 Cathedral Rd., Cardiff, South Glam CF1 9PG ☎ *(0222) 43443*
📖 🍴 *18* 🛏 *18* ⇆ ➔ 🔘 [VISA]
Location: *w of Sophia Gardens, a short way along road to Llandaff.* A staid
Victorian building shelters a crisp, modern, usefully sited hotel.
◻ ⬚ 🎿 ⛱ ⅋

Nightlife
New Theatre (*Park Place* ☎ *(0222) 32446*) is visited four times a year by
the Welsh National Opera; ballet, West End plays and musicals are also
presented here. **Sherman Theatre** (*Senghenydd Rd.* ☎ *(0222) 25855*) is
the university theater; it presents interesting plays, films and
exhibitions. **Chapter Arts Centre** (*Market Rd., Canton* ☎ *(0222)
25776*) has a theater and cinema and puts on exhibitions. **St David's
Concert Hall** (*St David's Centre* ☎ *(0222) 371236*) is a new center for
rock and classical concerts.

Shopping
St Mary St., **Queen St.** and the **St David Shopping Centre** contain the
major shops while the arcades off them contain smaller shops such as
Celtic Crafts (*Castle Arcade*), and **Things Welsh** (*Duke St. Arcade*).
Cardiff Central Indoor Market (*off St Mary St., Mon–Sat*) is a large
general market.

Chepstow
*Map 4K6. Gwent. Just w of the Severn Bridge. Population:
8,500 i Old Arch Building, High St.* ☎ *(02912) 3772.*
An old market town with winding medieval streets, Chepstow is
best known for its **castle** (☎ *(02912) 4065, WO* 🚻 ➔ *open
mid-Mar to mid-Oct 9.30am–6.30pm; mid-Oct to mid-Mar
Mon–Sat 9.30am–4pm, Sun 2–4pm*). Perched precipitously
above the Wye, this long fortress of three wards and a keep is at
its most dramatic if seen from the N side of the nearby river
bridge. Building of the keep started soon after the Norman
conquest, not in the customary wood but in stone, which places
Chepstow among Europe's earliest stone castles. It is worth
exploring the interior, if only for the near vertical glimpses
down to the river.

Sight nearby
Tintern Abbey ☆
Wye Valley, 5 miles (8km) N of Chepstow ☎ *(02918) 634. WO* 🚻
➔ *Open mid-Mar to mid-Oct 9.30am–6.30pm; mid-Oct to mid-Mar
Mon–Sat 9.30am–4pm, Sun 2–4pm.*
Founded in 1131 and rebuilt and extended in the 13th–14thC, Cistercian
Tintern appealed powerfully to Victorian romantics. Serene beside
Wordsworth's 'sylvan Wye,' the majestic church survives as a largely
intact shell still with its splendid w facade and huge E window, while
much of the extensive domestic precincts can be identified around the
main and infirmary cloisters. Beyond, to the NE, the large area of the
abbot's hall and lodging reflects the power of this house and of its rulers,
while near the entrance the large lay brothers' refectory recalls the
Cistercian emphasis on (labor-intensive) agriculture.

H **Castle View** (*16 Bridge St., Chepstow, Gwent NP6 5EZ* ☎ *(02912)
70349* ⓥ *498280* 📖); **George** (*Moor St., Chepstow, Gwent NP6 5DB*
☎ *(02912) 2365* 📖).

Conwy ☆
*Map 9G5. Gwynedd. On the N coast. Population: 12,000
i Castle St.* ☎ *(049263) 2248.*
Visually Conwy is the undisputed star of Wales. Climb up to the
castle's ramparts and all lies spread before you. The three
companion bridges across the river – Telford's graceful
suspension bridge (1826) preserved by the National Trust,

Stephenson's strange railway tube (1848), and the not
unattractive modern road bridge; Edward I's spectacular
circuit of walls and 21 towers climbing across the hill and
enclosing the borough he chartered to support his castle; the
backdrop of wooded hills; the animated quay and the busy
estuary reaching out to the Great Orme (see *Llandudno*).

Exhibitions which throw light on Conwy's past can be seen at
the **Visitor Centre** (*Rosehill St.* ☎ *(049263) 6288* 🖾 *open
July–Aug 10am–9.30pm, Sept–June 10am–5.30pm*) and also at
Aberconwy House (*Castle St.* ☎ *(049263) 2246, NT* 🖾 *open
Apr, May 10am–5.30pm, closed Wed; June–Sept
10am–5.30pm; Oct Sat, Sun 10am–5.30pm*), a late 14thC
house, perhaps originally the home of a prosperous merchant.

Sights and places of interest
Conwy Castle ★
At e end of the town, by the bridges ☎ *(049263) 2358. WO* 🖾 ◔
*Open mid-Mar to mid-Oct 9.30am–6.30pm; mid-Oct to mid-Mar
Mon–Sat 9.30am–4pm, Sun 2–4pm.*

Only 6yrs after building Conwy in 1284, Edward I had the opportunity to
test its strength when he found himself besieged here by the insurgent
Welsh. Although not completed, the castle held. Richard II was not so
lucky in 1399; he ran out of food and soon afterward had to surrender to
Bolingbroke (Henry IV) at Flint. Internally dismantled in 1665, Conwy
is now an imposing shell with walls and towers intact; picturesque, too,
for the way in which four of the towers are carried higher by cylindrical
turrets.

Inside, the best advice is not to spend too much time at ground level,
but to climb to the rampart walk which affords the best picture of the
castle's layout.

Plas Mawr
High St. ☎ *(049263) 3413* 🖾 ▣ *Open Apr–Sept 10am–5.30pm,
Oct–Mar 10am–4pm.*

This immensely satisfying Elizabethan town house, complete with
courtyards, gables and even a watchtower, today provides a gracious
setting for art exhibitions.

The Smallest House
The Quay ☎ *(049263) 3484* 🖾 ✿ *Open Easter–June, Sept–Oct
10am–6pm, July–Aug 10am–9.30pm, otherwise ask for key next
door.*

The smallest house not just in Conwy but in Britain (according to the
Guinness Book of Records), which is still large enough to show a Victorian
Welsh cottage interior.

Sight nearby
Bodnant Garden ☆
On A470, 5 miles (8km) s of Conwy ☎ *(049267) 460. NT* 🖾 ▣ ◔
Open mid-Mar to Oct 10am–5pm.

Lord Aberconway's magnificently situated gardens were started in 1875.
Steeply terraced, with numerous rare plants, the landscaped effects –
both formal and informal – are enhanced by views of Snowdonia.

Ⓗ **Castle** (*High St., Conwy, Gwynedd LL32 8DB* ☎ *(049263) 2324*
🏢); **Llys Gwilym** (*3 Mountain Rd., Conwy, Gwynedd LL32 8PU*
☎ *(049263) 2351* ▢).

Shopping
The main shopping streets are **Castle St.** and **High St.** A general market
is held at **Old Station** (*Sat, also Tues in summer*).

Gower Peninsula
Map 3K4. West Glam. Immediately w of Swansea
i Singleton St., Swansea ☎ *(0792) 50821, or*
Oystermouth Sq., The Mumbles ☎ *(0792) 61302.*

Bays, beaches, grand cliff scenery, nature reserves, caves,
prehistoric remains and resorts such as Oystermouth and
Mumbles are just some of the attractions of this stubby

peninsula. As always in such frequently overcrowded places, those on foot will see the best scenery. The cliff caves (mostly dangerous and not to be attempted without local advice) are archeologically famed for the ancient human and animal bones found here, proof that man was in Gower a staggering 19 millennia ago. Its prehistoric sites include **Parc le Breos** or Giant's Grave (*close to Parkmill, on A4118*) which is a good example of a burial chamber; another, involving an easy upland walk, is **Arthur's Stone** high on central Cefn Bryn; and for those prepared to climb there are **Sweyne's Houses** on Rhossili Down, in the w of the peninsula.

Hotel
Langland Bay (*5 miles/8km sw of Swansea*).

Ⓗ **Osborne**
Rotherslade Rd., Langland Bay, Swansea SA3 4QL ☎ *(0792) 66274* �📶 ⏧ *43* 🛏 *21* 🡒 ⫘ AE CB ⊙ ⊙ VISA *Closed one week at Christmas.*
Location: On the shore. Excitingly perched above the sea, yet with a sheltered sandy bay just below, this is a comfortable, informal hotel with a restaurant known for its seafood.
🏠 🛉 🕭 ▢ 🖾 🥄 🔆 🤸 🏊 ⚓ 🏕 ⛵ 🖤

Holywell
Map 9G6. Clwyd. Near N coast, 15 miles (26km) NW of Chester. Population: 8,500 🛈 *Assembly Hall, High St.* ☎ *(0352) 711997.*
Unless in search of Welsh textiles – and Holywell's popular mill is conveniently close – most people come here for **St Winefride's Well**, visited by pilgrims today as it was for centuries prior to the Reformation, during which it was cared for by the monks of **Basingwerk** (see below). The story of the well begins in the 7thC when a would-be seducer, spurned by Winefride, became so enraged that he slashed off her head. The water which spurted from the spot where her head fell became known for its medicinal properties. Centuries later and long canonized, St Winefride was sufficiently important for her help to be sought by Henry V prior to Agincourt. She also inspired Margaret Beaufort (mother of Henry VII) to finance the building of the **chapel** beside the well. It is not often open, but a fine carved frieze depicting real and mythical animals can be admired on the outside.

Sights nearby
Basingwerk Abbey
1 mile (1.5km) N of Holywell. WO 🄾 *Always open.*
Although now sadly ruined, this Cistercian foundation of 1131 stands in pleasant surroundings and challenges the visitor to identify what is left: the great church, or the domestic quarters around the open space that was once the abbey's busy cloistered heart. Look, for example, for the evidence of a bench around the chapter house, or for the fragment of hatch between the refectory (which has internal arcading on its w wall) and the kitchens.
Grange Cavern Military Museum
Grange Lane, Holway, on A55, just w of Holywell ☎ *(0352) 713455* 🍴 ▣ 🡒 *Open May–Sept 9am–6pm, Oct–Apr 10am–5pm.*
In the 19thC this was a limestone quarry; during World War II bombs were stored here, including the 'bouncers' launched by the Dambusters. Today, with other military material, over 70 vehicles of the past have found a weird home here. Recent acquisitions include an Argentinian anti-aircraft gun brought back from the Falklands War.

Kidwelly Castle

Map 8K4. Dyfed. 10 miles (16km) s of Carmarthen
☎ *(0554) 890104. WO* 🚻 🚗 *Open mid-Mar to mid-Oct*
9.30am–6.30pm; mid-Oct to mid-Mar Mon–Sat
9.30am–4pm, Sun 2–4pm.

Look for three unusual features here in this 12th–14thC castle.
First, the **gatehouse**, sited on the outer rather than the inner
curtain, a sensible economy enabling it to serve also as a part of the
defenses of the adjacent town. Second, the way in which an
inner ward, ringed by an outer one, flanks the river. Third, the
chapel, high in a tower above the water.

Laugharne

Map 8J4. Dyfed. On Carmarthen Bay.

This charming town was the home of the poet Dylan Thomas
(1914–53). For 16yrs he lived and wrote in the **Boat House**
(*Cliff Walk* ☎ *(0267) 7557* 🚻 🅿 *open Easter to mid-Oct*
10am–6pm, 10–15mins' walk from the town), which is perched
on a cliff above the wide tidal estuary. Apart from the house
itself, some original furniture and a few photographs, there is
not much to be seen, and only genuine Dylan Thomas
enthusiasts will find a visit here worthwhile.

Llanberis

Map 8G4. Gwynedd. Snowdonia, 6 miles (9.5km) E of
Caernarfon. Population: 2,000 ℹ *Snowdonia National Park*
and Central Electricity Generating Board Centre, on the road
between the two lakes ☎ *(0286) 870765.*

Slate, electricity and Snowdon are the features here. The slate
quarries may have closed, living on only as a museum or as
features of a country park, but the great gray scars will surely
require centuries to heal. Abandoned, ugly and lowering, yet
insistent and undeniably impressive evidence of human daring
and endeavor, the many-tiered corries will long reach high
toward the valley's rim. But now it is the turn of electricity
generation, with the pumped-storage **Dinorwic Power Station**
claiming to be the largest of its kind in Europe. There are no
external scars from this, however; fed by tunnels and shafts, the
generators are deep in the mountain, in immaculate caverns to
which, from 1984 or 1985, visitors will travel by electric bus.

Snowdonia equals scenic grandeur. Yet, with the exception
of the slate corries, Llanberis at the mountain's foot enjoys little
of this, although it lies waiting just around the corner; a short
walk to the waterfall of **Ceunant Mawr**, a drive up wild
Llanberis Pass, or, best of all, a train ride up to Snowdon's
clustered peaks.

Sights and places of interest
Dolbadarn Castle

SE of the town. WO 💷 🚗 *Always open.*

Although most of the castles seen in Wales were built by Edward I,
Dolbadarn, with its unusual circular tower-keep, is a genuine pre-
Edwardian Welsh fortress, tactically sited to dispute travel through
this pass.

Llyn Padarn

Here, within a well-organized complex, are a lake, a steam railway, a
country park, craft workshops, and a museum which reveals what life
was like in the quarrying communities.

Adults as much as children enjoy a ride along the lakeshore on the
Lake Steam Railway (*N of Llanberis bypass* ☎ *(0286) 870549* 🚻 🅿 ✱
🚂 *trains run fairly regularly Easter–Sept, but closed Sat, Sun early in the*
season; telephone for exact times) in a train pulled by one of the three quaint

engines (1889–1922) which once hauled slate from Llanberis to the
Menai Strait. The view of Snowdon can be splendid, and those who wish
can get off at the halfway station, have a picnic and return by a later train.
Padarn Country Park has way-marked woodland paths, mountain
views, picnic sites, old slate workings and a visitor center (☎ *(0286)
870549* 🖼 ⬤ *open Easter, May–early Oct 9am–5pm*) in the former
quarry hospital.

The slate quarry which gave Llanberis so much of its character closed
in 1969, but clings to life in its workshops of 1870 which now house the
Welsh Slate Museum (☎ *(0286) 870630* 🖼 💻 ⬤ *open Easter–Sept
9.30am–6pm*). There are blacksmiths' hearths, a foundry and a
waterwheel, a gallery illustrating the quarryman's life, and slate-splitting
and trimming demonstrations.

Oriel Eryri
On the bypass ☎ *(0286) 870636* 🖼 ⬤ *Open Mon–Sat
10am–5pm, Sun 2.30–5pm, while exhibitions are in progress.*
Oriel Eryri, which means Exhibition Snowdon, is a regional
environmental interpretation center, opened in 1983 and the most
modern of its kind.

Snowdon Mountain Railway ★
s end of the town ☎ *(028682) 223* 🖼 💻 ✳ ⬤ ⍦ *Open
Easter–early Oct but closed Sat and Sun early and late in the season.
Trains run from 9am and then at roughly ½hr or hourly intervals;
telephone for exact times.*
'Opened 1896 and still puffing' boasts an official leaflet. And, it might be
added, still pulling in the passengers who want to ride on Britain's only
rack-and-pinion track, climbing a spectacular 3,000ft (900m) in 5 miles
(8km). The round trip, including ½hr on the summit of Snowdon, takes
2½hrs.

Ⓗ Dol Peris
High St., Llanberis, Gwynedd LL55 4HA ☎ *(0286) 870350* ❑
🐾 *10* ⬤ ⇥ Ⓔ ⬛Ⓒ
Location: Town center. This is a small, friendly and unpretentious hotel
which makes a point of welcoming children.

Llandudno
Map 9G5. Gwynedd. On the N coast. Population: 16,000
ℹ *1 Chapel St.* ☎ *(0492) 76413.*
Wales' largest and classiest resort seems happy enough to
remember that it was built as such in the second half of the
19thC. The elegant hotel facades that line the gentle arc of the N
beach epitomize the spirit of this place, and if there is anything
vulgar here it is kept well hidden. Yet Llandudno is neither
fusty nor staid. The message is one of tempered vigor, and for
every ancient dreaming on the benches there are ten children
thrilling to donkey rides, Punch and Judy, wading and boating
pools and much else. All this is on the lively N beach; the w
beach, where Lewis Carroll met the child who inspired *Alice in
Wonderland*, is much more peaceful.

The pier, a famous relic of Victoriana, is as cheerful today as
it ever was. Nor should the **Great Orme** be missed, a headland
lifting to nearly 700ft (200m). You can go up by the famous
Great Orme Tramway of 1902, by aerial tramway (the longest in
Britain), by car or on foot. And for those who want to venture
farther afield, there is the marine drive (*toll charged*) around the
headland, while the **Great Orme Nature Trail** takes in geology,
flora, fauna, and even some points of archeological interest.

Three museums merit a visit. For children there is the **Doll
Museum** (*Masonic St.* ☎ *(0492) 76312* 🖼 ✳ *open Easter–Sept
Mon–Sat 10am–1pm, 2–5.30pm, Sun 2–5.30pm*), which has
no less than 1,000 dolls, entrancing in the fashions of their day,
as well as toys, prams, cradles and other nursery items from the
old days. In another room there is a working model railway.

The **Mostyn Art Gallery** (*23 Vaughan St.* ☎ *(0492) 79201* ▣ *open during exhibitions Apr – Sept 11am – 6pm, Oct – Mar 11am – 5pm; closed Sun, Mon*) has temporary exhibitions showing a wide range of contemporary art, including work by artists living in Wales, and exhibitions of both fine and decorative arts of regional interest, while **Rapallo House** (*Fferm Bach Rd., Craig-y-Don* ☎ *(0492) 76517* ▣ *open Apr, Sept – Nov 10am – 12.45pm, 2 – 4pm; May – Aug 10am – 12.45pm, 2 – 5pm, closed Sat, Sun*) has fine and applied art, armor and weapons, Roman relics and a replica of an old Welsh kitchen.

Ⓗ **Cranleigh**
Great Orme's Rd., West Shore, Llandudno, Gwynedd LL30 2AR ☎ *(0492) 77688* ☐ ♻ *13* ▭ *3* ➤ ▣ ⇌ *Closed Nov – Easter.*
Location: At foot of Great Orme, close to w beach. In this bright, modest, family-run hotel it is the personal touch that counts. Convenient for the quiet w beach or for walks on Great Orme, yet less than a mile (1.5km) from the lively area near the pier.
▱ ⚓ ⟨⟨ ⁂ ✓ 🖉 ➤

Ⓗ **Empire**
73 Church Walks, Llandudno, Gwynedd LL30 2HE ☎ *(0492) 79955* ◉*617161* ▮☐ ♻ *56* ▭ *56* ➤ ▣ ⇌ 〔AE〕〔CB〕◉ 〔CO〕〔VISA〕 *Closed for 2 weeks at Christmas.*
Location: 400yds (365m) sw of the pier. An uninspired square block hides a hotel which combines functional efficiency with the informality enjoyed by families. The decor is bold, the rooms well equipped, and the many facilities include a children's pool.
♨ ☐ ▱ ⚓ ≈ ⟨⟨ ✓ 🖉 ♫

Ⓗ Ⓡ **Plas Fron Deg** ▰ ▰
Church Walks, Llandudno, Gwynedd LL30 2HL ☎ *(0492) 77267* ☐ ♻ *8* ▭ *3* ▣ ⇌ 〔AE〕◉ 〔CO〕〔VISA〕
Ⓡ ▮☐ *Last orders 9pm.*
Location: At NW end of town. Welsh specialties have brought acclaim to the kitchen of Margaret Neal, although she is keen to point out that, in addition to its culinary peculiarities, the country simply has fine raw materials, especially lamb and beef. Plas Fron Deg ('Little House on the Hill') is a pretty, Victorian home in the town, not far from the sea. Specialties include Conwy salmon and Welsh lamb Marsala.
▱ ⚓ ⟨⟨ ⁂

Nightlife
The **Pier Pavilion** (*The Promenade* ☎ *(0492) 76258*) and the **Arcadia Theatre** (*The Promenade* ☎ *(0492) 76570*) stage celebrity summer shows.

Shopping
Mostyn St. and the streets running off it contain well-known stores and smaller specialty shops. A general market is held in The Arcade, on Mostyn St. (*Mon – Sat*).

Llangollen
Map 9H6. Clwyd. 10 miles (16km) sw of Wrexham.
Population: 3,000 *i* *Town Hall* ☎ *(0978) 860828.*
For all its setting of vale and mountain, to many people Llangollen means no more than an infuriating traffic bottleneck along A5. But turn off from the main through-road, go down to the river and there are surprises: a 14thC stone bridge; an evocative **Great Western Railway station** (☎ *(0978) 860951* ▦ ▣ *open Sat, Sun 10am – 5pm, also weekdays in high season; telephone for exact times*) complete with steam trains; an unusual exhibition carrying the visitor back to the great days of Britain's canals; and, not far away, the ruins of a Welsh-founded abbey. Above the town, and a perpetual challenge (there is a path),

hangs **Castell Dinas Bran**, in turn Iron Age earthwork, Welsh wooden fortress and 13thC stone keep.

Event In July, International Music Eisteddfod, on N bank of the river. Singing and dancing competitions during the day, concerts at night. Competitors wear national costume.

Sights and places of interest
Canal Exhibition Centre
The Wharf ☎ *(0978) 860702* 🖼️ *Open Easter–Sept 10am–5.30pm.*
Britain's almost forgotten waterways are the theme of this museum. All sorts of aspects are covered, such as how canals were planned and dug, their craft and what they carried, their role in the industrial development of the era and the people who worked on and beside them. There are also horsedrawn boat trips. Three miles (5km) E at **Pontcysyllte**, drop into the valley and marvel at Telford's lofty canal-carrying aqueduct.

Plas Newydd
Butler Hill ☎ *(0978) 860234* 🖼️ 🚶 *Open May–Sept Mon–Sat 10am–7pm, Sun 11am–4pm.*
This highly picturesque half-timbered house was the home, at the turn of the 18th–19thC, of the Ladies of Llangollen, two aristocratic Irish eccentrics who became known for their wit, their outrageous dress, and their collection of bric-à-brac (sadly dispersed after the ladies' deaths) to which visitors were expected to contribute.

Sights nearby
Chirk Castle
5 miles (8km) SE of Llangollen ☎ *(0691) 777701. NT* 🖼️ 🅿️ 🚶
Open Easter–May, Oct Tues–Thurs, Sun 2–5pm; June–Sept Tues–Thurs noon–5.30pm, Sun 2–5.30pm; bank holiday Mon noon–5.30pm. Closed Mon, Fri, Sat.
No towering keep here, no fairy-tale turrets, but a grim, squat, square fortress of massive walls and bastions along an open rise. Inside, however, Chirk softens and provides some startling contrasts. One wing, complete with dungeon, is virtually untouched since the castle was built in 1310 and is just what might be expected within such a forbidding exterior; another is a private house; a third surprises with splendidly decorated and furnished state rooms; and the fourth, to the S, still shows the pattern of gables of a Tudor dwelling.

Over 500yrs earlier a royal builder, Offa of Mercia, was busy here, and a section of his **dyke** runs across the park.

Valle Crucis Abbey
On A542, 1¼ miles (2.5km) NW of Llangollen ☎ *(0978) 860326. WO* 🖼️ 🚶 *Open mid-Mar to mid-Oct 9.30am–6.30pm; mid-Oct to mid-Mar Mon–Sat 9.30am–4pm, Sun 2–4pm.*
Much of both the church and the domestic buildings can be found in these ruins of a Cistercian abbey, founded in this lovely valley in 1201 by a prince of Powys. A very Welsh corner, this, for the tombs in the choir are said to include those of a famous beauty who inspired the bards, while 9thC **Eliseg's Pillar** (*just N beside the road*) honors an early prince who seized Powys from the English.

Ⓗ **Royal**
Bridge St., Llangollen, Clwyd LL20 8PG ☎ *(0978) 860202* |||
🍴 *39* 🛏️ *33* 🚶 🍳 🚭 AE CB ⬦ ⓘ VISA
Location: *By the river bridge.* Once a stop for the Irish mail coaches, the Royal received its name after Princess (later Queen) Victoria and her mother the Duchess of Kent visited here in 1832. Today this modern hotel combines the convenience of being within the town with a superb situation beside the Dee, close to the 14thC bridge.
🏨 ♿ 🖊️ 📷 🏊 🎿 🚣 🎣 🏇

Hotel nearby
3 miles (5km) E of Llangollen, off A539.

Ⓗ **Bryn Howel**
Llangollen, Clwyd LL20 7UW ☎ *(0978) 860331* |️| 🍴 *36* 🛏️ *30*
🚶 🚭 ⓘ VISA *Closed Christmas Day.*
In 1971, a modern wing was added to this gloriously located 19thC

mansion which houses a most comfortably appointed hotel. There are
superb views, notably of Castell Dinas Bran.

⌂ & ▢ ▨ ⚓ ≪ ✦ ⊷ ☲

Shopping
Tweed and other fashion fabrics are woven and sold at the **Llangollen
Weavers** (*Dee Lane, near Llangollen Bridge*).

The Lleyn Peninsula
Map 8H4. Gwynedd. N of Cardigan Bay **i** *The Square,
Caernarfon* ☎ *(0286) 2232, or High St., Porthmadog*
☎ *(0766) 2981.*

Ignore the resorts along the S coast – **Abersoch**, **Pwllheli**,
Criccieth – and the Lleyn is a land apart, Welsh Wales in
language and custom, a place that minds its own business. For
the most part, the scale here is small – small farms, fields, coves,
even small resorts. Yet there can be dramatic exceptions.
Toward the NW, triple-peaked **Yr Eifl**, known as The Rivals,
rises nearly 2,000ft (600m) above the sea; at the peninsula's tip,
beyond quaint **Aberdaron**, the National Trust's breezy, green
cliffland affords views of **Bardsey**, for 1,000yrs the island of
pilgrims (it made both economic and spiritual sense, since three
visits here equaled one to distant Rome); and, just E of
Aberdaron, the road hovers above the perfect sand and cliff
crescent of **Porth Neigwl** before plunging toward the shore.

Sights and places of interest
Criccieth Castle
Map 8H4. Criccieth ☎ *(076671) 2227. WO* ▢ *Open mid-Mar to
mid-Oct 9.30am–6.30pm; mid-Oct to mid-Mar Mon–Sat
9.30am–4pm, Sun 2–4pm.*
An early 13thC Welsh stronghold, Criccieth was reinforced by Edward I
in around 1283. The oldest part, dating from about 1230, is the small but
stoutly built inner ward.
Lloyd George Museum
Map 8H4. Llanystumdwy, 2 miles (3km) w of Criccieth ☎ *(076671)
2654* ▢ ➡ *Open Easter–Sept Mon–Fri 10am–5pm, Sat, Sun
2–4pm.*
The statesman David Lloyd George (1863–1945) spent his early and last
years in the village of Llanystumdwy; he went to school here, he died
here and his grave is beside the river. This museum tells his story.
Penarth Fawr
3 miles (5km) NE of Pwllheli, off A497. WO ▢ *Always open.*
Inside this most unusual and attractive single-room house of the 15thC,
there is a detailed explanation of how a family would have lived here.

See also *Portmeirion*.

Monmouth
*Map 9J6. Gwent. Wye Valley, between Severn Bridge
and Hereford. Population: 6,500* **i** *Nelson Museum, Market
Hall, Priory St.* ☎ *(0600) 3899.*
At the confluence of the Wye and the little Monnow,
Monmouth is best known for the people associated with it, the
earliest of whom was that highly suspect 'historian' Geoffrey of
Monmouth, born here in *c.*1100. Henry V (Harry of
Monmouth) was born in the castle in 1387 and, if Shakespeare is
to be believed, soldiers wearing 'Monmouth caps' fought at
Agincourt. In any event, **Agincourt Square** marks the town
center, and a statue of Henry stands on the **Shire Hall**. Here too
is a statue of C.S. Rolls, born at nearby Hendre and co-founder
of the firm of Rolls-Royce. His mother, Lady Llangattock, was
a great admirer of Lord Nelson; memorabilia collected by her is

on show at the **Nelson Museum** (*Market Hall, Priory St.*
☎ *(0600) 3519* ☒ *open Mon – Sat 10.30am – 1pm, 2 – 5pm, Sun
2 – 5pm, later closing times in July and Aug*).

The town can claim one rare building, namely the fortified
13thC **Monnow Bridge**, a reminder of Monmouth's strategic
importance between two rivers.

Sights nearby
Raglan Castle
Off A40, 7 miles (11km) sw of Monmouth ☎ *(0291) 690228. WO*
☒ ☛ *Open mid-Mar to mid-Oct 9.30am – 6.30pm; mid-Oct to
mid-Mar Mon – Sat 9.30am – 4pm, Sun 2 – 4pm.*
Although Raglan looks strongly fortified, and indeed stands on the site of
a Norman keep, this was no Edwardian 13thC stronghold but rather a
residential palace of the 14th – 16thC, although it was provided, just in
case, with defensive features. This aspect is principally represented by
the so-called **Great Tower**, a detached keep unusual for being
hexagonal, while courts, kitchen, chapel, Great Hall and grand staircase
reflect the castle's preferred function. In fact the defenses were not
required until the Civil War, when in 1646 royalist Raglan held out for
eleven weeks before eventually falling.
Skenfrith Castle
On B4521, 5 miles (8km) nw of Monmouth. NT ☒ *Always open.*
This small 13thC ruin comprises a round tower within a rectangular
curtain. The mound on which the tower stands is not, as might be
supposed, a Norman motte but a defensive device to give a secure field of
fire over and beyond the curtain.

Ⓗ **King's Head**
Agincourt Sq., Monmouth, Gwent NP5 3DY ☎ *(0600) 2177*
☎*497294* Ⅲ ▭ ☎ *29* ▭ *26* ☛ ⇌ ⒶⒺ ◉ ⒸⒹ 𝚅𝙸𝚂𝙰
Location: Town center. This inviting, half-timbered 17thC building has a
warm, stylish and cheerful interior. Note, in one of the bars, a fine
plaster likeness of Charles I.
▢ ▣ 👥

Restaurant nearby
Llandewi Skirrid (*17 miles/27km NW of Monmouth*).

Ⓡ **Walnut Tree Inn**
☎ *(0873) 2797* Ⅲ ▭ ⇌ ☎ ▦ ☛ *Last orders 10.15pm. Closed
Christmas.*
The most famous restaurant in Wales, and there is none better. The
conjunction of an old inn, with a flagstoned, pub-like bar, and a patron
called Franco Taruschio is not as strange as it seems; South Wales has
long attracted distinguished Italian immigrants. In nearly 20yrs at the
Walnut Tree, Taruschio has displayed gastronomic brilliance with
dishes from all over Italy and France, and has more recently been equally
at ease with *nouvelle cuisine*. Interesting wines, including some from
Taruschio's own vineyard.

Newport
*Map 4K6. Gwent. 13 miles (20km) NE of Cardiff.
Population: 112,300.*
This busy industrial and commercial center has a most unusual
attraction, namely the **Transporter Bridge** (*s of Commercial
Rd.*) which carries cars and pedestrians across the Usk estuary
on a moving platform. A good view of the docks can be seen
from the catwalk (☒) reached by a staircase.

The **Museum and Art Gallery** (*John Frost Sq.* ☎ *(0633)
840064* ☒ *open Mon – Fri 10am – 5.30pm, Sat 9.30am – 4pm,
closed Sun*) has displays relating to the docks, Roman material
from **Caerwent** and **Caerleon** (see below), and much else
including sculpture by Epstein and Rodin.

Sights nearby
Caerleon Roman Site
*On the s coast, 2 miles (3km) N of Newport. Amphitheater and
Fortress* ☎ *(0633) 421656. WO* ▨ ☞ *Open mid-Mar to mid-Oct
9.30am–6.30pm; mid-Oct to mid-Mar Mon–Sat 9.30am–4pm, Sun
2–4pm. Legionary Museum* ☎ *(0633) 421462* ☒ *Open Mar–Apr,
Oct Mon–Sat 9.30am–5.30pm, Sun 2–5pm; May–Sept Mon–Sat
9.30am–6pm, Sun 2–6pm; Nov–Feb Mon–Sat 9.30am–4pm, Sun
2–4pm.*

From this fort of Isca, as the Romans called it, the 2nd Legion controlled
southern Wales from roughly the 1st to the late 4thC. For 20thC visitors
the legion has bequeathed the earthwork outline of its barracks, its
sizeable **amphitheater** complete with eight entrances, and the many
objects now shown in the **museum**.
Caerwent Romano-British Town
On A48, 8 miles (13km) E of Newport. WO ☒ *Always open.*
In c.AD75 the Romans confined the local tribe (the Silures) within walls,
so that they could keep an eye on them. Today, 2,000yrs later, there is
still a village here, largely conforming to the original pattern but
retaining the tribal name rather than the Roman Venta Silurum. Visitors
who simply drive through from E to W will see something of the walls;
those with more time should walk along the s wall from the w gate to the E
gate, stopping also at the village church where there are some Roman
inscribed stones.

Hotel nearby
Caerleon (*2 miles/3km N of Newport*).

Ⓗ **Priory**
High St., Caerleon, Newport, Gwent NP6 1XD ☎ *(0633) 421241*
ⅡⒶ ⇌ 25 ▭ 25 ☞ ⊡ 🗗 ☒ 🆎 ⚎ [VISA]
Location: Adjacent to the Roman site. As its name implies, this low,
rambling, stone hotel stands on the site of a Cistercian priory, of
which the main door on High St. and the cellars still survive. Some of the
bedrooms are large and traditional with a garden view.
🏠 □ 🖾 🍴 ⚓ 🛋

Offa's Dyke
*Map 9. Clwyd, Powys, Gwent. At intervals along the English
border from Prestatyn to Chepstow.*
Dug in 784 by Offa of Mercia (and it must have been quite an
undertaking), this earthwork, 167 miles (267km) in length, was
never intended as a defense but rather as a territorial gesture.
For the energetic a path accompanies its length. For others
there are several spots at which the dike can be well seen: in the
park of **Chirk Castle** (see *Llangollen*); at **Knighton** on the
English border, where it crosses the edge of the town; or in the
Black Mountains, where it runs beside the road from **Hay-on-
Wye** to **Llanthony**.

Pembroke (*Penfro*)
*Map 8K3. Dyfed. On Milford Haven, on sw coast.
Population: 14,000* ℹ *Pembrokeshire Coast National Park
Centre, Drill Hall, Main St.* ☎ *(0646) 682148.*
Pembroke is a long, narrow place which, secure within its
13thC walls, once extended the defensive complex of the **castle**
eastward along the ridge. The walls are still here, and to see
them best, aim for the parking lots below to the s; for the town,
walk up one of the access alleys.

Pembroke Castle ☆
w end of the town ☎ *(0646) 684585* ▨ *Open Easter–Sept
10am–6pm; Oct–Easter 10.30am–4pm (closed Sun).*
Roman, Viking and finally Norman fortifications frowned down in turn
from this strategically tempting ridge-promontory above the river. The

Normans were long content with a wood and turf enclosure, and it was probably not until the late 12th or early 13thC that the earls of Pembroke began to spread their great stone fortress eastward along the ridge. Visitors enter at the E end to arrive in the outer ward, defended by five sturdy towers, in one of which Henry VII is said to have been born in 1457. But it is the complex inner ward that is most interesting, for this is the oldest part, cluttered with domestic buildings of all periods and dominated by the formidable, cylindrical **Great Keep** ☆ which with its unusual domed stone roof stood here in 1210, if not earlier.

H **Old King's Arms**
Main St., Pembroke, Dyfed SA71 4JS ☎ *(0646) 683611* 📠 *48598*
🛏 ♨ *21* 🛏 *21* ☎ ⬅ 💳 *VISA Closed two weeks at Christmas.*
Location: On s side of Main St. There is still plenty of old-world style about this ancient coaching inn, in spite of additions made in 1830 and again in recent years. A rustic, almost pub-like ground floor (log fires in winter) contrasts with some modern bedrooms, and the snug, beamed restaurant enjoys local if not wider repute.
🔲 🖼 ⚓

Pembrokeshire Coast National Park and environs
Map 8J3–4. Dyfed. Around the Pembroke peninsula from Cardigan to Amroth **i** *For postal inquiries: National Park Information Office, County Offices, Haverfordwest, Dyfed SA61 1QZ* ☎ *(0437) 3131; visitor center, 40 High St., Haverfordwest* ☎ *(0437) 66141.*

This is a park of infinite variety – bare moorland hills and bold windswept headlands, coves and beaches, beckoning nature reserve islands, cliffs and caves and creeping tidal inlets. A land, too, on which man has left his mark over millennia, from neolithic burial chambers and ritual stones through venerable chapels and medieval castles to the great oil refineries of Milford Haven.

The motorist prepared to venture along the many inviting by-roads can see much of interest; the pony trekker or the walker will see more, the latter especially well catered to by the 168 miles (264km) of the increasingly popular coastal path, or, less ambitiously, by the park information service's program of guided theme walks.

Sights and places of interest
Carew Castle and Cross
Map 8J3. Carew, off A477, 5 miles (8km) w of Tenby 🏛 *Open Easter, June–Sept Mon–Sat 10am–5pm, Sun 2–5pm.*
Viewed casually, this is just another square stronghold with formidable towers at its corners. In fact it presents at least three distinct faces. The earliest is the w side, uncompromisingly a 13thC fortress, defiant with two massive, high-buttressed (a most unusual feature) drum towers. Inside, to the w, there is the 15thC Great Hall, in which the castle's owner, Sir Rhys ap Thomas, received Henry Tudor (Henry VII) before riding on with him to victory at Bosworth Field, while to the N large windows and oriels mark Sir John Perrot's manor of 1558.

Carew Cross (*beside the road at castle entrance*) is a good example of an early Christian wheel-cross. It honors a prince slain in battle in 1035.
Cilgerran Castle
Map 8J4. 3 miles (5km) s of Cardigan ☎ *(0222) 824249. NT/WO* 🏛 *Open mid-Mar to mid-Oct Mon–Sat 9.30am–6.30pm, Sun 2–6.30pm; mid-Oct to mid-Mar Mon–Sat 9.30am–4pm, Sun 2–4pm.*
Richard Wilson and Turner are among the many artists who have been unable to resist these romantic ruins balanced high on a crag above the Teifi river gorge, and it is of course from this side that the castle should be viewed. Cilgerran has in fact been a ruin for much of the past 900yrs. The first castle (11thC) failed to survive repeated assaults; it was rebuilt in 1233, but fell into ruins less than a century later.

Lamphey Bishop's Palace
Map 8K3. Lamphey, on A4139, 2½ miles (4km) E of Pembroke
☎ *(0646) 672224. WO* 🏛 🚶 *Open mid-Mar to mid-Oct Mon–Sat*
9.30am–6.30pm, Sun 2–6.30pm; mid-Oct to mid-Mar Mon–Sat
9.30am–4pm, Sun 2–4pm.
The bishops of St David's did themselves well, having a choice of several
country manors to which they could escape from the rigors of their bleak
cathedral site. In gentle surroundings of orchards and fishponds,
Lamphey was one such, known to have been in use in 1096 although the
ruins that stand here now are of the 13th–16thC and include work
carried out by the Devereux family, earls of Essex, to whom Lamphey
was given after the Dissolution. From W to E the principal sections are the
Camera in which the bishop had his suite on the first floor, leaving the
ground level for staff and servants; the ruined early 13thC **Old Hall**; and
the two-story **Great Hall**.

Manorbier Castle
Map 8K3. On the S coast, 5 miles (8km) SW of Tenby ☎ *(083482)*
421 🏛 *Open for a week at Easter, then late May–Sept 11am–6pm.*
This squat and sturdy 12th–14thC castle – part fortress, part nobleman's
home – is best known as the birthplace in *c*.1147 of Giraldus, a half-
Norman, half-Welsh nobleman, scholar and priest who traveled widely
and made his name through descriptive writings about Wales.

Pentre Ifan Burial Chamber ☆
Map 8J3. On minor road 3 miles (5km) S of Nevern, on N coast.
WO 🔲 *Always open.*
The imagination must work hard to conjure the scene here in 2,000BC or
earlier, when this lonely spot was used for communal burial. The
massive capstone and supports are standard, but Pentre Ifan offers more,
in the form of a detached arrangement of stones on the S side and a single
megalith to the NE.

Picton Castle (and Graham Sutherland Gallery)
Map 8J3. The Rhos, 4 miles (6.5km) SE of Haverfordwest, S from
A40 ☎ *(043786) 201* 🏛 🍴 🚶 *Grounds open Easter–Sept*
10.30am–sunset (closed Mon except bank holidays). Graham
Sutherland Gallery open Easter–Sept 10.30am–5pm (closed Mon
except bank holidays).
The castle, with a history which starts with a Norman motte and ends
with 20thC conversion, is not open to visitors. However, the beautiful
grounds provide picnic areas and woodland walks, while the **Graham
Sutherland Gallery** (a branch of the National Museum of Wales) shows a
range of works by this artist.

St Dogmael's Abbey
Map 8J3. 1 mile (1.5km) W of Cardigan. WO 🔲 *Always open.*
Only fragments remain of the 14th–15thC church and refectory of an
abbey founded in 1115, but the precinct includes the Victorian parish
church housing the **Sagranus Stone**. Bearing both Latin and Ogham
(5thC Gaelic) texts, this stone enabled scholars to work out the Ogham
alphabet in 1848.

St Govan's Chapel ☆ †
Map 8K3. St Govan's Head, Castlemartin peninsula 🔲 🚶
Accessible by steps down a rocky cleft near the parking lot.
Venerable sanctity and legend mix inextricably in this simple, primitive
place wedged halfway down a narrow cliffside cleft. Whether one accepts
that the cliff split open to save the saintly Govan from pirates, that in
gratitude he built his cell here and that in 586 he was laid to rest under the
altar, or whether the 11thC seems a more reasonable if far less interesting
date for this chapel, this remains a place for humility and thought with its
stone altar, small cell and the fissure that will grant your wishes should
you be able to turn around in it.

Hotel and restaurants
Near **Cardigan** (*18 miles/29km* NE *of Fishguard*).

Ⓗ Ⓡ **Rhyd-Garn-Wen**
Cardigan, Dyfed SA43 3NW ☎ *(0239) 612742* 🛏 🔑 *3* 🛏 *3* 🚶
🏛 🏛 🍴 🍴
Ⓡ 📖 🏛 🍴 🍴 🚶 *Last orders 9.30pm.*
Location: On A487, 3 miles (5km) W of Cardigan. 'This is our home, and
our dogs recognize no great difference between family and guests,' says

the enthusiastic Susan Jones, who was a bookseller until she and her husband established their hotel. The bedrooms are large and comfortable, and the book-laden drawing room has an open fire.

The restaurant menu changes every day, and emphasizes local produce and herbs, and vegetables and fruit from the garden. Mr Jones has a serious interest in wines, and has bought very well.

🖼🦞🦅🍷💼🍽

Newport (*7 miles/11km SW of Cardigan*).

Ⓡ **The Pantry**
Market St. ☎ *(0239) 820420* ▥ ▭ ▬ *Last orders 9.30pm. Closed lunch, Sun, Mon and occasional weekends during the winter.*
By common consent one of the best restaurants in Wales. First-class raw materials and extremely conscientious preparation bring an extra dimension to simple dishes like minestrone or shellfish pie. The Pantry likes light touches of curry, too, as in its spiced chicken. Surroundings are rustic and Welsh.

Portmeirion (*Porthmeirion*) 🏛 ☆
Map 8H4. Gwynedd. On the coast, at NE corner of Cardigan Bay ☎ *(0766) 770228* ▨ *except for hotel guests* ▬ ▬ ≡ *Open Apr–Oct 9.30am–6pm.*
Portmeirion, on the eastern fringe of the *Lleyn Peninsula*, is an architectural and planning fantasy, a largely Italianate and entirely artificial private vacation village set higgledy-piggledy around a wooded chine beside a wide tidal estuary. The dream and achievement of the architect Clough Williams-Ellis (1883–1978), the village – built both before and after World War II – is an eclectic yet harmonious patchwork of styles.

Ⓗ **Portmeirion Village Hotel**
Porthmeirion, Penrhyndeudraeth, Gwynedd LL48 6ER ☎ *(0766) 770228* ▣ ☜ *20* ▣ *20 and 16 housekeeping cottages* ▬ 📠 ≡
Ⓐ Ⓔ 💳 🆚 *Closed mid-Oct to Easter.*
Location: At Portmeirion. The hotel proper burned down in 1981. Now it is integral with the village and guests are accommodated in comfortable cottages or villas, each one highly individual. Shops, residents' lounge and bar, and restaurant are all available but in different buildings.
🖼♿🦅≈🍷📺💼🍽👥

Powis Castle
Map 9H6. Powys. On A483, 1 mile (1.5km) s of Welshpool ☎ *(0938) 4336. NT* ▨ ▬ ▬ *Castle and garden open Easter and following week, May–June, Sept 1–6pm (closed Mon, Tues); July–Aug 1–6pm (closed Mon); bank holiday Mon 11.30am–6pm.*
Powis looks the mixture that it is, a 13thC castle later converted to residential use. Late 16thC plasterwork and wood panelling are the main features of the interior, together with paintings and antiques, and there are souvenirs of Clive of India whose son acquired the estate by marriage. The early **18thC gardens** ☆ with their terraces, topiary and statuary are highly rated by connoisseurs. The gardens also contain one of Britain's tallest trees, a 185ft (56m) Douglas Fir.

Preseli Hills
Map 8J3. Dyfed. E of Fishguard.
Enthusiasts of prehistory will head for this bare expanse of high moorland and bog, empty today but – to judge from the tumuli, burial chambers, hill settlement remains, stone circles and lone megaliths – once a rather different place. A **Bronze Age Trail**,

which links A478 at Crymmych with B4329 a short way N of
Greenway, passes places which provided some of the stones of
Stonehenge (see *England A–Z*).

Pumpsaint (and Ogofau Gold Mines)
*Map 8J4. Dyfed. On A482, 20 miles (32km) SE of
Aberaeron. NT* ⌖ ⇌ *Always open.*

Gold has been dug out of these mines on and off since Roman
times, and maybe even earlier, but when they were last worked
(in the 1930s) the returns failed to justify the effort involved.
Visitors may find this a confusing site unless the explanatory
material displayed at the National Trust hut is first studied.
When walking around, stick to the marked walks; shafts and
other features can be dangerous.

The depressions on the **Pumpsaint Stone** here were left by
five (*pump*) saints who used it as a pillow.

Rhyl
*Map 9G5. Clwyd. On N coast of Wales. Population: 34,000
i Town Hall, Wellington Rd.* ☎ *(0745) 31515.*

All along the N coast of Wales the safe, sandy beaches attract
hordes of vacationers. After *Llandudno*, Rhyl with its large
funfairs is one of the most popular.

Colwyn Bay, 12 miles (19km) to the W of Rhyl, has three
miles (5km) of sandy beach and is the home of the **Welsh
Mountain Zoo** (*inland from Colwyn Bay* ☒ *open
10am–sunset*). Here visitors can watch free-flying displays by
eagles, falcons and other birds of prey, or have a meal in the
Safari Restaurant overlooking the lion compound.

Sights nearby
Denbigh Castle
12 miles (19km) s of Rhyl ☎ *(074571) 3979. WO* ☒ ⇌ *Open
mid-Mar to mid-Oct 9.30am–6.30pm; mid-Oct to mid-Mar Mon–Sat
9.30am–4pm, Sun 2–4pm.*

In patriotic Welsh eyes it is the previous castle that stood here that counts
– a ramshackle place no doubt, but one much honored for its stout
resistance to Edward I. Its successor (1282–1322), although irregular in
shape, generally conformed to the contemporary pattern of being
integral with the town walls, a section of which still extends from the
castle. Today the castle is little more than a shell, but its large **gatehouse**
and several towers still stand.

Rhuddlan Castle
At Rhuddlan, just s of Rhyl ☎ *(0745) 590777. WO* ☒ ⇌ *Open
mid-Mar to mid-Oct 9.30am–6.30pm; mid-Oct to mid-Mar Mon–Sat
9.30am–4pm, Sun 2–4pm.*

Edward I made good use of the river here, diverting and canalizing it to
enable ships to dock at his new castle's walls, to protect one side, and to
provide the water for the moat that guarded the other three. The dock
gate and moat inlet together with the remains of their defensive tower can
still be seen. Started in 1277, this was Rhuddlan's third castle; the motte
of its Norman predecessor still stands a short way to the SE.

St Asaph's Cathedral †
6 miles (9.5km) s of Rhyl ☎ *(0745) 583429.*

This is both the smallest cathedral in Wales and also one of the oldest
foundations (560). Whatever edifice stood here in the 13thC was
destroyed by the invading English, and today's cathedral represents
rebuilding ordered by Edward I, although with a good deal of restoration
right up to the 19thC. Connoisseurs of exquisite church art will enjoy a
16thC Spanish ivory *Madonna* in the s transept, while bibliophiles
should ask to be shown the **Chapter Museum** with its early Bibles.

Ⓗ **Westminster** (*10–12 East Parade, Rhyl, Clwyd LL18 3AH*
☎ *(0745) 53171* ▯).

Hotels nearby
Colwyn Bay (*12 miles/19km w of Rhyl*).

Ⓗ **Hopeside** (*63–67 Prince's Drive, Colwyn Bay, Clwyd LL29 8PW*
☎ *(0492) 33244* ☐ *to* Ⅱ☐); **Norfolk House** (*39 Prince's Drive, Colwyn
Bay, Clwyd LL29 8PF* ☎ *(0492) 31757* Ⓥ*61254* Ⅱ☐ *to* Ⅲ☐).

Near **St Asaph** (*6 miles/9.5km s of Rhyl*).

Ⓗ **Oriel House**
Upper Denbigh Rd., St Asaph, Clwyd LL17 0LW ☎ *(0745) 582716*
Ⅲ☐ ⊷ 20 ☐ 20 ⊷ ⇌ Ⓐ Ⓔ Ⓥ *Closed Christmas Day.*
Location: On A525, 1 mile (1.5km) s of St Asaph. Built in 1760, Oriel
House is a mellow country house standing in lovely grounds. As might be
expected of a place designed as a private home, spaciousness is one of the
attractions here; some of the bedrooms are of really generous size.
☖ ⅋ ☐ ☑ ⚓ 〰 ⊷ ⚐

Nightlife
The **Coliseum Theatre** (*Promenade* ☎ *(0745) 51126*) presents summer
variety shows, changing nightly, and matinée children's shows. The
Gaiety Theatre (*Central Promenade* ☎ *(0745) 51251*) has a similar
program. The **Sun Centre** (*Promenade* ☎ *(0745) 31771, open
10am–11pm*) is one of Wales' prime tourist attractions offering an indoor
surfing pool, tropical pool and bar, restaurants, a rooftop monorail, a
model racing circuit and nightly cabaret. The **Little Theatre** (*Vale Road*
☎ *(0745) 2229*) presents plays for children during summer.

Shopping
High St., **Queen St.** and **Water St.** contain the main shops. The two
open-air markets at **Elwy St.** (*Wed, Sat*) and **Wellington Rd.** (*Sun*) sell
fruit, vegetables and general goods; the two covered markets in **Sussex
St.** (*open Mon–Sat*) sell only general goods.

St David's
Map 8J2. Dyfed. sw tip of Wales. Population: 1,700
i Grove Car Park ☎ *(0437) 720747, or Pembrokeshire
Coast National Park Centre, City Hall* ☎ *(0437) 720392.*
This is a straggling, bleakly situated, remote little place, an
overgrown village boasting the title of city. When the sun is
hidden, the wind searching and the all too frequent mist
creeping in, St David's can seem like the end of the world; a
promise of sun and balmy weather and it becomes not only a
charming curiosity, but also a place from which to explore
exhilarating cliff scenery and secluded sandy bays where,
whether as ancient chapel, holy well or simply legend, the spirit
of St David never seems far away.

Sights and places of interest
Bishop's Palace
Close to the cathedral (see below) ☎ *(0437) 720517.* WO 🏛 ⊷
*Open mid-Mar to mid-Oct 9.30am–6.30pm; mid-Oct to mid-Mar
Mon–Sat 9.30am–4pm, Sun 2–4pm.*
When this palace was built in the 13th–14thC, bishops were statesmen,
administrators and great landowners as well as churchmen. Like other
powerful lords they had not only to look to defense, but also to be ready
for important visitors and their retinues, not to mention the constant and
demanding flow of pilgrims who brought their diocese so much of its
wealth. Few places emphasize so strongly the dichotomy of a medieval
bishop's life; one side of the stream the serene spiritual cathedral, on
the other this large, essentially secular quadrangle with its two great halls
where the animated daily scene is not difficult to visualize.
St David's Cathedral † ☆
In the Alun valley below the village ☎ *(0437) 720202.*
St David, patron saint of Wales, may have come as a missionary priest
from Ireland (the source of Welsh Christianity in the 6thC), or his

mother, Non, may have given birth to him on the shore of nearby St
Non's Bay. The choice is open and not even confined to these
alternatives. The ground becomes a little firmer with the tradition that in
*c.*550 David moved a monastery he had founded on Whitesand Bay (to
the W) to this valley. By the 11thC David had become a saint of sufficient
importance to attract throngs of pilgrims and to justify the start in 1180 of
this cathedral.

Over the years, right up to the 19thC, there has been extensive
restoration and rebuilding, but nevertheless there remains much to
admire in this fine edifice, the largest church in Wales. The ornamented
Norman nave with its splendid Irish oak roof (probably 15thC) will
appeal to the architecturally minded who may at the same time deplore
the original inadequate foundations which have resulted in a
disconcerting slope. In the crossing they will also note that only one
Norman arch survived the collapse of the central tower. Connoisseurs of
church furnishing will appreciate an elaborate 14thC rood screen, a lofty
medieval bishop's throne and lively misericords.

St David's Shrine (13thC) is in the presbytery, but there is also a
teasing recess on the W side of Bishop Vaughan's Chapel; were the bones
found here during 19thC restoration and laid in a coffer those of St
David, hidden perhaps from Reformation despoilers?

H **Warpool Court**
St David's, Dyfed SA62 6RD ☎ *(0437) 720300* 💳 ➷ *25* 🛏 *25* ⇔
🛏 ⇌ AE ⚫ *Closed Jan.*
Location: SW quarter, on road to St Non's Bay. Warpool Court provides
conservative comfort and some large bedrooms. The restaurant enjoys
high repute for its fresh produce.
⌂ & □ ✔ 〈〈 ⇌ ⇌

Snowdonia National Park and environs

Map 9G-H5. Gwynedd. NW sector of Wales **i** *For postal
inquiries: Snowdonia National Park Office,
Penrhyndeudraeth, Gwynedd LL48 6LF* ☎ *(0766) 770274;
for personal inquiries: Snowdonia National Park and CEGB
Centre, Llanberis* ☎ *(0286) 870765.*
Eryri, Carneddau, Gwydir, Moelwyn and Siabod; Arenig,
Rhinog, the Arans and Cader Idris – musical and legendary
Celtic names borne by the mountain masses that make up the
largest and scenically grandest of Wales' national parks, a
glorious expanse of peaks, lush valleys, dark forest and
hurrying streams reaching from *Conwy* in the N to the Dovey
estuary in the S, from **Cardigan Bay** to Bala's lake.
   Snowdon (Yr Wyddfa), at 3,560ft (1,085m) the highest point
in England and Wales, and incomparably the wildest and
grandest, forms a massif of five peaks, each linked to its
neighbors by dizzying ridges. This is the sector of the National
Park that attracts the most visitors, the ultimate satisfaction
being enjoyed by those who reach the summit wilderness either
by the railway (see *Llanberis*) or on foot. For walkers there are
six standard approaches, but Snowdon, so beckoning in fine
weather, can be a fickle friend, quick to shroud with mist or
batter with storm, and these tracks are not for the inexperienced
or ill-equipped. Those with neither the time nor the will to
reach the summit are also well served, for Snowdon lies within a
triangle of scenic roads: A4085 below the SW slopes, Nant
Gwynant (A498) balanced along the SE, and the **Pass of
Llanberis** (A4086) ★ cutting low through savage black rocks
beneath the precipitous NE face. At the junction of A4086 and
A498 is **Beddgelert**, where tourists flock to the grave of
Llewellyn the Great's heroic dog Gelert.
   Snowdon, however, occupies only the NW part of the
National Park, and the fact that this happens to be the grandest

area in no way diminishes the seduction of the remainder. Other roads and places that demand mention include (from N to S) the A5, which skirts dark **Llyn Ogwen** below the Carneddau, passing haunted **Cwm Idwal** with its nature reserve before plunging down glacier-carved **Nant Ffrancon**; **Betws-y-Coed**, spider at the heart of a web of forest walks; A470 climbing SW from here to lonely **Dolwyddelan Castle** before dropping past the great slate quarry museums of **Gloddfa Ganol** and **Llechwedd**; and **Aberglaslyn** to the W on A4085, where the torrent falls below pine-clad cliffs. Then, farther S, **Coed y Brenin** straddling A470, an area of forest, waterfalls, ancient stones and gold workings; the mass of **Cader Idris**, chair of a warrior giant, piling up to 2,927ft (892m) above **Dolgellau** and generous with its many paths; and finally, away to the E, the thrilling minor road between **Dinas Mawddwy** and **Bala**, from both directions forcing its dizzy ascent to **Bwlch-y-Groes** (1,790ft/546m), the highest road pass in Wales.

Sights and places of interest
Centre for Alternative Technology
Map 9H5. Off A487, 3 miles (5km) N of Machynlleth, Powys
☎ *(0654) 2400* 🖾 🅿 �∙ *Open mid-July to mid-Sept 10am–7.30pm; mid-Sept to mid-July 10am–6pm or sunset if earlier.*
Solar collectors of many kinds produce hot water and heat an exhibition hall; weird windmills and propellors generate electricity; a stream turns turbines and a waterwheel; and household insulation is demonstrated.
Festiniog Railway
Map 8H4, 9H5. Porthmadog-Blaenau Ffestiniog ☎ *(0766) 2384*
🖾 🅿 ✳ ◁€ *Trains run Feb–Mar Sat, Sun; late Mar to early Nov, Christmas to New Year daily. Telephone for exact times.*
Opened in 1836 as a horsedrawn system serving the Blaenau Ffestiniog slate quarries, this railway with its several small stations now provides a popular tourist run (lasting just over 1hr in each direction) through some glorious wooded mountain and estuary scenery. Tan y Grisiau station is close to the *Ffestiniog Hydro-Electric Scheme* information center, so a combined railway ride and power station visit is worth considering.
In **Porthmadog**, the former slate-export harbor has been charmingly re-developed; there is a floating maritime museum; and, from the mile-long (1.5km) embankment across the Glaslyn estuary, there is a classic view of the **Snowdon** massif.
Ffestiniog Hydro-Electric Scheme
Map 9H5. Tan y Grisiau, Blaenau Ffestiniog ☎ *(076681) 465* 🖾
🚻 🅿 �∙ *Open Easter, May Day bank holiday, then late May–Oct 10am–4pm. Tours leave every ½ hr.*
In a dramatic setting of mountain and slate quarry, this power station was the Central Electricity Generating Board's first venture into hydroelectric pumped storage (1963). For visitors there are an information center, guided tours of the power station, or a bus ride 1,000ft (300m) up to the **Stwlan Dam** spectacularly perched on the mountain's rim.
Gloddfa Ganol Slate Mine (Mountain Tourist Centre)
Map 9H5. On A470, N of Blaenau Ffestiniog ☎ *(076681) 664* 🖾
🅿 �∙ *Open Easter–Oct 10am–5.30pm.*
Once the world's largest slate mine, this is an awe-inspiring great scar into the bare mountain, a place as visually daunting as it is interesting. The mine chambers, the slateworks machinery, a natural history center, quarrymen's cottages and a museum are all here, together with slate-splitting demonstrations, open-cast blasting, and a shop.
Harlech Castle
Map 8H4. Harlech ☎ *(0766) 780552. WO* 🖾 �∙ *below only* ◁€
Open mid-Mar to mid-Oct 9.30am–6.30pm; mid-Oct to mid-Mar Mon–Sat 9.30am–4pm, Sun 2–4pm. Access is from below (long, steep clamber of 143 steps) or from the upper town.
The name means 'bold rock,' and if this is still appropriate today how much more so it would have been in the 13thC when the cliff rose sheer from the estuary waters. Then, of course, Edward I's soldiers paced the walls ever alert for an approaching enemy; today these same walls

provide tourists with a famous view – across the water to the *Lleyn Peninsula*, and up the shore to the wild heart of **Snowdonia**. Visitors who enter the castle at the top do so through the lofty gatehouse; those tackling the climb from below start through the watergate, a reminder that the sea once lapped here.

Llechwedd Slate Caverns
Map 9H5. On A470, N of Blaenau Ffestiniog ☎ *(076681) 306* 📷
🎬 *of mines* ⚹ 🅿 ⬛ *Open Apr–Oct 10am–6pm.*

Although there are various surface features here such as an audio-visual show, a tramway exhibition, and craft and gift shops, it is for the two underground adventures that people come to Llechwedd. One is the **Miners' Underground Tramway** which enables something to be seen of Victorian mining conditions. The other is the **Deep Mine** descent on Britain's steepest underground passenger system. At the bottom visitors alight and walk through an imaginative series of tableaux.

Talyllyn Railway
Map 8H4. Tywyn, on coast of Cardigan Bay ☎ *(0654) 710472* 📷
🅿 ⚹ ⬛ *Trains run daily Easter–Oct, Christmas–New Year; telephone for exact times.*

Talyllyn, the oldest and one of the best known of the 'little trains' of Wales, has been carrying passengers (and in the early days slate) since 1867. In just under 1hr the train ascends the Fathew valley as far as Nant Gwernol, beautifully situated below the s slopes of the mass of **Cader Idris** and known for its forest trails beside mountain streams.

Trefriw Woollen Mills
Map 9G5. Trefriw, on B5106, between Conwy and Betws-y-Coed ☎ *(0492) 640462* 📷 ⬛ *Mill open 9am–5.30pm (closes earlier in winter); closed Sat, Sun. Shop open Mon–Fri 9am–5.30pm, Sat 10am–4pm, Sun July–Aug 2–5pm.*

This is a working woolen mill in which visitors can walk around viewing all the processes in the manufacture of tapestries and tweeds. The shop sells the mill's products as well as sheepskin goods made elsewhere.

Hotels and restaurant

Betws-y-Coed (*11 miles/17km* NE *of Blaenau Ffestiniog*).

Ⓗ **Craig-y-Dderwen**
Betws-y-Coed, Gwynedd LL24 0AS ☎ *(06902) 293* ⬜ 🐾 *21*
🛏 *16* 🚗 ⬛ 💳 💲 *VISA Closed Christmas.*
Location: Off A5, just w of Waterloo Bridge. Gloriously located in woodland beside the Conwy river, this is the kind of personally run country house hotel one dreams of but all too rarely finds; moreover its restaurant enjoys a distinguished reputation.
🍽 ⬜ ⚘ ⚔ ✓ 💈 🚭 ♨

Ⓗ **Waterloo Motor Hotel**
Betws-y-Coed, Gwynedd LL24 0AR ☎ *(06902) 411* ⬜ 🐾 *30*
🛏 *30* 🚗 ⬛ *AE* 💲 💳 *VISA*
Location: Waterloo Bridge. On the main road, but convenient, and with bedrooms restfully styled in local weaves and natural woods.
🚗 ⚘ ⚔ ✓ 💈 🚭 ♨

Dolgellau (*17 miles/27km* S *of Ffestiniog*).

Ⓗ **Royal Ship**
Queen's Sq., Dolgellau, Gwynedd LL40 1AR ☎ *(0341) 422209* ⬜
🐾 *25* 🛏 *5* 🚗 ⬛ ⬛ 💲
Location: Town center. This ivy-clad, late Georgian, one-time coaching inn looks and is a conservative and unpretentious family hotel. Children are especially catered to with several family rooms and their own menu for supper, which can be served early if requested.
⚹ ⚱ ⚔ ⤸ ✓ 💈 🚭 ♨

Ⓡ **La Petite Auberge**
2 Smithfield St. ☎ *(0341) 422870* ⬜ ⬜ *Last orders 10pm. Closed Easter–May, Oct Sun–Thurs, June–Sept Sun.*

This French-owned restaurant, in a row cottage, takes great pride in its provenance. 'We do only genuine French cuisine,' say the owners, and that claim is pretty well borne out. Fresh ingredients are used, and all prepared items like pâtés and desserts are made on the premises. There is a short but perfectly adequate wine list.

Nant Gwynant (*10 miles/16km w of Betws-y-Coed*).

🅷 Pen-y-Gwryd
Nant Gwynant, Gwynedd LL5S 4NT ☎ *(0286) 870211* ▯▯ ⌖ *21*
▭ *1* ▱ ▭ *Closed Nov–Dec.*
Location: At junction of A498 and A4086, close to the top of Llanberis Pass.
This is the place for anybody wanting the feel of the mountains, enhanced by a touch of the past; a modest but comfortable mountain inn in wild country and close to the site of a Roman route camp. The 1953 Everest expedition was planned here.
▱ ⅃ ⚓ ⋖ ≈ ◈ 🏋

Sports and activities
Tourist offices have informative booklets on fishing in general and will give advice on boating, walking and pony trekking in the park.

Swansea
Map 8K4. West Glam. On the s coast. Population: 173,500. Airport ☎ *(0792) 204063; railway station* ☎ *(0792) 467777; coach and bus station* ☎ *(0792) 55116* **i** *Singleton St.* ☎ *(0792) 468321.*

On first acquaintance Swansea, the second largest city in Wales, is likely to puzzle the stranger. To start with, its title of city derives not from being home to a cathedral, but from a declaration by Prince Charles on becoming Prince of Wales. Also, the city center, rebuilt on a largely new plan after devastation by bombing in 1941 and with **The Circus** as its hub, is not geographically the center at all but on the eastern edge: the tourist office is some 450yds (400m) away to the sw; the **Guildhall**, a distinguished, high-towered civic edifice of 1934 and worth a visit for its panels painted by Frank Brangwyn, is nearly half a mile (1km) farther w, and it is beyond this again that most of the many parks of which the city is justifiably proud are to be found. Finally, the all-important docks lie detached from the city, to the E of the river Tawe.

Nevertheless, Swansea can be a rewarding place to visit. Connoisseurs will hardly fail to enjoy the **Glyn Vivian Art Gallery and Museum** ☆ (*Alexandra Rd.* ☎ *(0792) 55006* ▣ *open 10.30am–5.30pm, closed Sun*). The collection of rare Swansea and Nantgarw pottery and porcelain is the pride of the gallery, but the paintings and sculpture, largely 19th and 20thC British, are equally distinguished and include works by, among others, Jacob Epstein and Barbara Hepworth.

Those more nautically or industrially inclined will not be disappointed by the **Maritime and Industrial Museum** (*South Dock* ☎ *(0792) 55006* ▣ ✱ *open 10.30am–5.30pm, closed Sun*), which is housed in a former warehouse. Themes include local road and rail transportation; local maritime activity, including three ships (a steam tug, a lightship and a fishing vessel); and local industry with a fully operational woolen mill.

Swansea even has a **castle**, a sad, hemmed-in remnant of a 14thC fortified bishops' residence.

Sight nearby
Neath Abbey
Neath, on w bank of the river, 5 miles (8km) NE of Swansea
☎ *(0792) 812387. WO* ▨ ⇔ *Open mid-Mar to mid-Oct Mon–Sat 9.30am–6.30pm, Sun 2–6.30pm; mid-Oct to mid-Mar Mon–Sat 9.30am–4pm, Sun 2–4pm.*

Over the centuries these smoke-blackened ruins have served three very different purposes, starting as an abbey in 1130. Of this the main but scanty survivors are the church, which was built at the turn of the 13th–14thC with the proceeds of shrewd trading in wool, and the refectory, cloister and dormitory undercroft. Soon after the Dissolution a mansion was built on the foundations of the abbot's house, while the industrial demands of the 19thC later brought a foundry here, recalled by some chimneys on the w range of buildings.

🄷 **Dragon**
39 The Kingsway, Swansea, West Glam SA1 5LS ☎ *(0792) 51074*
🆅48309 ⅢⅡ 🕮 *118* ⬛ *118* ⬛ ⬛ AE CB ⬛ ⬛ VISA
Location: City center. A solid, spacious, 1960s-style hotel with extensive public rooms and cheerful modern bedrooms.
🛏 ♿ ☐ 🖾 🐾 ⊀ ⋅/ 🖾 🠖 🎿

Nightlife
Brangwyn Hall (☎ *(0792) 468321 for ticket and program information*) is the venue for visiting orchestras and rock concerts and for the Swansea Festival every Oct. The **Grand Theatre** (*Singleton St.* ☎ *(0792) 55141*) also stages Swansea Festival productions (opera and ballet) and plays.

Shopping
The major shopping streets are **Oxford St.**, **High St.**, **Princess Way** and **The Kingsway**. At **Swansea market** (*off Oxford St.*, *Mon–Sat*), the local seaweed delicacy, laverbread, is sold.

Tenby (*Dinbych y Pysgod*)
Map 8K3. Dyfed. On w shore of Carmarthen Bay.
Population: 5,000 ℹ *Guildhall, The Norton* ☎ *(0834) 2402.*
Deliberately developed during the 19thC as a family resort, modern Tenby has bulged well inland, but the real Tenby sprawls all over its rocky promontory, a picturesque place of narrow and often steep streets huddled within the protection of the **medieval wall** that still marks the promontory's base. It is a wall worth more than a passing glance, too, because it embodies an unusual feature about halfway along its length, namely a gate defended by a semi-circular barbican known as the **Five Arches**, the cunning defensive aspects of which are not hard to work out. The promontory effectively splits the town and its beaches into two, the cheerful small harbor being on the N side, while on the short green extension known as **Castle Hill** there survive some fragments of the once-great castle.

Few people stay long in Tenby without making the 2½ mile (4km) boat trip to **Caldey Island**, sporadically since the 5thC the home of monasteries and today owned by Cistercians who make and sell perfumes. Strolling around the island, the visitor can see a Norman tower later converted to serve as a chapel, the Cistercian abbey of 1911, St David's church (in part perhaps of the 8th or 9thC), the ruins of a priory, and, in the restored Church of St Illtyd, a stone bearing an Ogham inscription of the 5thC and a Latin one of the 9thC.

Sights and places of interest
Tenby Museum
Castle Hill ☎ *(0834) 2809* 🔾 *Open Apr–May 10am–6pm (closed Fri afternoon); June–Sept 10am–6pm; Oct–Mar 10am–1pm, 2–4pm (closed Sun, Fri afternoon).*
Here the local story is told from all sorts of angles, including geology, natural history, and the shore with its caves and shells.
Tudor Merchant's House
Quay Hill ☎ *(0834) 2279. NT* 🔾 *Open Easter–Sept Mon–Fri 10am–1pm, 2.30–6pm, Sun 2–6pm. Closed Sat.*
There is some evidence that there was a house here in the 14thC, but if so

it was almost entirely rebuilt as a prosperous merchant's home a century later. It is this that survives today, complete with its Flemish chimney (many Flemish clothworkers settled here in the 12thC) and the murals which were so popular at that time.

Ⓗ **Fourcroft**
Croft Terrace, Tenby, Dyfed SA70 8AP ☎ *(0834) 2516* ☐ ☎ 39
◻ *34* ☎ ≈ 🆑 *VISA* *Closed Nov–Easter.*
Location: Above North Beach. This hotel is delightfully positioned above the sea; it lies behind a private clifftop garden, tempting enough in itself but also giving direct access to the beach.
‡ ☐ ⩐ 《 ⚏

The Valleys
Maps 9J– K6. Gwent; Mid, South and West Glam.
Running inland from s coast between Newport and Port
Talbot i Valleys Inheritance Centre, Pontypool Park,
Pontypool, Gwent ☎ *(04955) 52036, or 3 Castle St., Cardiff*
☎ *(0222) 27281.*

There is poetry in the names – Cwm Afan, Rhondda, Cynon, Taff, Rhymney, Ebbw, Sirhowy – splayed fingers probing deep into Wales' coastal mountains, once remote wild fastnesses but in the 18thC transformed by coal, iron ore and the Industrial Revolution into diseased yet, paradoxically, dynamic limbs. There were two worlds here: below the smoke pall, the seething, belching valley floors; above it, clean open moorland. The flirtation with industry was as brief as it was passionate, and already by the early years of the 20thC it was clear that for all sorts of reasons the fires were dying, leaving these valleys bewildered and unsure of their identity.

Today, however, a new identity is being fashioned. True, some mining and industry clings on, but the emphasis is now directed elsewhere; to reclamation of the landscape, coupled with a pride in the past evidenced by an enthusiasm for industrial archeology. It is a policy that is succeeding, for discerning tourists are casting off their preconceived ideas and heading for this rather special corner of Wales to enjoy the contrasts between ugly industrial patches, adjacent wooded and moorland scenery, and long, long built-up areas with equally long rows of brightly painted, stone houses.

Sights and places of interest
Afan Argoed Country Park
Map 9K5. Gynonville, on A4107, 8 miles (13km) NE of Port Talbot
☎ *(0639) 850564. Country Park* 🎦 ☛ *open daylight hours.*
Countryside Centre and Welsh Miners' Museum 🏚 ☛ *open*
Easter–Oct 10.30am–6pm; Nov–Easter Sat, Sun noon–5pm.
Here, along the pleasant **Cwm Afan Scenic Route** (A4107), will be found an information center, picnic sites, guided walks, film shows and a museum illustrating both the technical and the human aspects of Welsh mining.
Big Pit Museum of Coalmining
Map 9J6. Blaenavon, Gwent ☎ *(0495) 790311* 🏚 🛈
underground workings ☛ *Museum open 9am–5pm; underground*
tours lasting 1hr leave 9.30am–4pm (no tours Mon).
Closed in 1980, this coal mine is being developed as a museum showing the surface workings, pithead baths and workshops. The underground tour reveals the working conditions down the mines.
Blaenavon Ironworks
Map 9J6. North St., Blaenavon, Gwent ☎ *(0222) 824249. WO* 🎦
☛ *Open Mon–Fri 9.30am–4pm.*
An 18thC ironworks complex is being developed as an industrial archeological site. For the present, visitors must be content with a temporary viewing platform.

Caerphilly Castle ★
Map 3K5. Caerphilly, Mid Glam ☎ *(0222) 883143. WO* 🅿 🚻
Open mid-Mar to mid-Oct 9.30am–6.30pm; mid-Oct to mid-Mar Mon–Sat 9.30am–4pm, Sun 2–4pm.
After Windsor, this is the largest castle in England and Wales and, with its theatrically shattered SE tower (a botched demolition job by Cromwell), also one of the most visually satisfying. There were early Roman and Welsh forts here, but the ruins seen today are those of the Norman castle started in 1271, a formidable mass of concentric defiance embodying the most sophisticated water defenses in Britain.

Today's visitor, strolling into and through the castle from E to w, should reflect on how very different this route would have appeared to a medieval attacker, forced first to cross the outer moat with its twin drawbridges before assaulting the towering curtain wall protected by the great **gatehouse**. This achieved, and at the mercy now of fire from both the inner ward and any unsubdued sections of the outer curtain, he would in turn have to cross the inner moat, assault and carry a second curtain and cross the outer ward before attempting to overcome the heart of the castle, the dauntingly walled inner ward.

Castell Coch
Map 3K5. Off A470 at Tongwynlais, South Glam, 5 miles (8km) nw of Cardiff ☎ *(0222) 810101. WO* 🅿 🚻 *Open mid-Mar to mid-Oct 9.30am–6.30pm; mid-Oct to mid-Mar Mon–Sat 9.30am–4pm, Sun 2–4pm.*
Castell Coch is unashamed fairy-tale fantasy, a whim realized in 1865–85 by the 3rd Marquess of Bute and his architect William Burges at the same time that they were creating their Cardiff Castle (see *Cardiff*) extravaganza. Here, resting on medieval foundations, a pseudo-Rhineland affair of round towers capped by conical turrets shelters rooms splashed with romantic murals, of which the most notable are the scenes from *Aesop's Fables* and the figures from Greek mythology.

Cwmcarn Scenic Forest Drive
Map 3K6. Cwmcarn, Gwent. Signposted off A467, 10 miles (16km) N of Newport ☎ *(0495) 244223* 🅿 ◁🚻 *Open Easter–Aug 11am–8pm; Sept Sat, Sun 11am–6pm.*
Parking lots, picnic sites and walks along some 7 miles (11km) of scenic forested mountain affording magnificent views. There is also a **hillfort**.

Wrexham
Map 9H6. Clwyd. On A483, between Chester and Llangollen. Population: 39,000 𝒊 *Guildhall Car Park* ☎ *(0978) 578459.*
A fine feature of this industrial center is the church of **St Giles**, whose pinnacled spire is traditionally known as one of the Seven Wonders of Wales (the other six include Snowdon, St Winefride's Well and Llangollen bridge). There is also a strong American connection here, because Elihu Yale (1649–1721), benefactor of the university bearing his name, is buried in the churchyard, just w of the tower.

Sight nearby
Erddig ☆
Off A525, 2 miles (3km) s of Wrexham ☎ *(0978) 355314. NT* 🅿 🔲 🚻 *Open Apr–Sept noon–5.30pm; Oct 2–4.30pm. Closed Fri except Good Fri.*
The unusual thing about this 17th–18thC mansion is the emphasis that is placed on 'below stairs.' Many stately homes show their large kitchens; few, if any, lead their visitors through such a range of service quarters: the joiner's and blacksmith's workshops, the stable yard, the laundry yard (with some bizarre equipment), the bakehouse, the kitchen, and the servants' hall which contains a possibly unique collection of **portraits of the staff** ☆ commissioned by the 18th and 19thC owners of Erddig.

The family's part of the house has portraits (Gainsborough, Cotes, Kneller), pictures, 18thC furniture and many antiques.

Two other attractions bring visitors to Erddig. One is the **garden**, restored to its 18thC design; the other is the **Agricultural Museum**.

England and Wales for children

England and Wales offer the usual range of special arrangements for children, including reduced fares on trains (for those under 16), coaches (for those under 17) and local transportation, and lower entrance fees at most sights. Most hotels welcome children – some even make a point of this, providing highchairs, junior menus and baby sitters – and quote a variety of special rates.

In the *A–Z* the symbol ✻ has been restricted to selected places likely to appeal to most children. These places are indicated below, by categories. (W) denotes sights in the *Wales A–Z*.

Specific sights apart, England and Wales abound in places and activities of general interest for children. Beaches (not all safe) ring the coast, and if the British water temperature is rarely likely to appeal to parents it never seems to deter their offspring. Pony trekking, notably in Wales, is an increasingly popular activity, and the National Parks attract many young visitors. There are numerous nature reserves and, more modestly, nature trails are frequently an attractive and instructive adjunct to sights. Boat excursions are rarely hard to find, and all over the country exciting ruined castles await exploration.

In *London* there are many sights obviously geared to children, such as **Madame Tussaud's**, the Planetarium and **The Zoo**, but many of the major museums such as the Natural History Museum, Science Museum, **Victoria and Albert Museum** and the military museums (National Army Museum in Chelsea, the Imperial War Museum in Lambeth, the RAF Museum in Hendon and the National Maritime Museum in **Greenwich**) can provide hours of fascination and enjoyment for both adults and children. Historic and traditional attractions include **Hampton Court** with its maze, the changing of the guard at **Buckingham Palace**, the **Tower of London** and the London Transport Museum. A trip down **The Thames** or a Round London Sightseeing Tour on a double-decker bus provides an excellent introduction to the city, while London's many parks – notably Hyde Park and Kensington Gardens, and Regent's Park – provide wide-open spaces for letting off steam. For more specific information telephone ☎(01) 246–8007 for recorded information, or **Kidsline** ☎(01) 222–8070.

See also *Sports and activities* and *Calendar of events* in *Planning*, and also *The American Express Pocket Guide to London*.

Amusement and theme parks
Amazement Park   See *Blackpool*.
Blackgang Chine Theme
   Park   See *Isle of Wight*.

Battlefields
Bosworth Field.
Hastings   See *Battle*.

Caves and caverns
Cheddar Caves   See *The Mendip Hills*.
Dan-yr-Ogof and Cathedral
   Caves   See *Brecon Beacons National Park* (W).
Great Rutland Cavern and Nestus
   Mine   See *Peak District*

National Park.
Kent's Cavern   See *Torquay*.
Llechwedd Slate Cavern   See
   Snowdonia National Park (W).
Peak Cavern   See *Peak District National Park*.
Poole's Cavern   See *Peak District National Park*.
Speedwell Cavern   See *Peak District National Park*.
Wookey Hole   See *The Mendip Hills*.

Model villages
Babbacombe Model Village
   See *Torquay*.
Bekonscot   See *Beaconsfield*.

Museums

Abbey House Museum   See *Leeds*.

Beamish North of England Open Air Museum   See *Newcastle-upon-Tyne*.

Castle Museum   See *York*.

Childhood, Museum of   See *Anglesey* (W).

Dinting Railway Centre   See *Peak District National Park*.

Doll Museum   See *Llandudno* (W).

HMS Cavalier   See *Southampton*.

HM Submarine Alliance   See *Portsmouth*.

HMS Victory   See *Portsmouth*.

Imperial War Museum (Air)   See *Cambridge*.

Maritime and Industrial Museum See *Swansea* (W).

Maritime Museum   See *Exeter*.

National Railway Museum   See *York*.

National Tramway Museum   See *Peak District National Park*.

Oken's House Dolls Museum   See *Warwick*.

Redoubt Fortress and Museum See *Eastbourne*.

Royal Pump Room   See *Harrogate*.

Shuttleworth Collection   See *Bedford*.

The Smallest House   See *Conwy* (W).

SS Great Britain   See *Bristol*.

Steamtown Railway Museum See *Lancaster*.

Torbay Museum   See *Torquay*.

Windermere Steamboat Museum See *Lake District National Park*.

Yorkshire Museum of Carriages and Horse-Drawn Vehicles See *Yorkshire Dales National Park*.

Stately homes

Arreton Manor (toy and doll collections, radio museum)   See *Isle of Wight*.

Beaulieu (attractions, motor museum, special events)   See *The New Forest*.

Belvoir Castle (special events including jousting).

Gatcombe Park (play area, exhibition of bicycles and carriages)   See *Isle of Wight*.

Harewood House (adventure playground)   See *Leeds*.

Holker Hall (motor museum, ballooning, aquarium, model railway, children's farm, adventure playground, special events)   See *Lake District National Park*.

Knebworth House (attractions, special events)   See *St Albans*.

Littlecote (Wild West township) See *Marlborough*.

Longleat House and Safari Park (attractions, dollhouses, boats, lakeside train, special events).

Penshurst Place (toy museum, adventure playground)   See *Tunbridge Wells*.

Sudbury Hall (Museum of Childhood)   See *Derby*.

Sudeley Castle (collection of toys, woodland play area)   See *The Cotswolds*.

Train rides

Brecon Mountain Railway   See *Brecon Beacons National Park* (W).

Dart Valley Railway   See *Dartmoor National Park*.

Festiniog Railway   See *Snowdonia National Park* (W).

Isle of Wight Steam Railway   See *Isle of Wight*.

Lakeside and Haverthwaite Railway   See *Lake District National Park*.

Lake Steam Railway   See *Llanberis* (W).

North Yorkshire Moors Railway See *North Yorkshire Moors National Park*.

Ravenglass and Eskdale Railway See *Lake District National Park*.

Snowdon Mountain Railway   See *Llanberis* (W).

Talyllyn Railway   See *Snowdonia National Park* (W).

Vale of Rheidol Steam Railway See *Aberystwyth* (W).

West Somerset Railway   See *Exmoor National Park*.

Wildlife, domestic animals, fish, zoos

Aqualand   See *Torquay*.

Aquarium and Dolphinarium See *Brighton*.

Compton House (Worldwide Butterflies)   See *Sherborne*.

Cotswold Farm Park   See *The Cotswolds*.

Cotswold Wildlife Park   See *The Cotswolds*.

New Forest Butterfly Farm   See *The New Forest*.

Riber Castle Wildlife Park   See *Peak District National Park*.

Safari Parks   See *Longleat*, *Windsor* and *Woburn Abbey*.

Slimbridge Wildfowl Trust   See *Gloucester*.

Swannery   See *Abbotsbury*.

Whipsnade Park Zoo   See *St Albans*.

Zoological Gardens   See *Bristol*.

Sports and activities

Spectator sports
Athletics
International meets are held in London at the **Crystal Palace National Sports Centre** (*Ledrington Rd., London SE19 2BB* ☎ *(01) 778–0131*), and at the **White City Stadium** (*Wood Lane, Shepherd's Bush, London W12 7RU* ☎ *(01) 743–7220*). General inquiries to **British Amateur Athletic Board** (*Francis House, Francis St., London SW1P 1DL* ☎ *(01) 828–9326*).

Auto racing
Among the principal meets are the **Marlborough British Grand Prix** (*July*), alternating between **Brands Hatch** and **Silverstone**; the **International Tourist Trophy** (*Sept, Silverstone*); **International Formula 2 races** at **Silverstone** (*Mar*), **Thruxton** (*Easter*) and **Donington Park** (*June*); and the **World Endurance Championships** (*Sept or Oct, Brands Hatch*). The governing body is the **RAC Motor Sports Association Ltd** (*31 Belgrave Sq., London SW1X 8QH* ☎ *(01) 235–8601*).

Boxing
For information on professional boxing: **British Boxing Board of Control** (*70 Vauxhall Bridge Rd., London SW1V 2RP* ☎ *(01) 828–2133*).

Cricket
Cricket is the principal summer team game in England. The level ranges from professional international Test Matches lasting up to five days, through inter-county games, down to the village cricket which is so much a part of the English scene. Top-class professional matches can be seen in London at **Lord's** (*St John's Wood Rd., London NW8 8QN* ☎ *(01) 289–1615 for tickets, or 286–8011 for scores and prospects of play*) and **The Oval** (*Kennington, London SE11 5SS* ☎ *(01) 582–6660 for tickets, or 735–4911 for scores and prospects of play*), and, outside the capital, at county grounds. General inquiries to **National Cricket Association** (*Lord's Cricket Ground, London NW8 8QN* ☎ *(01) 289–1611*).

Equestrian events
The most important equestrian events are the **Royal International Horse Show** in July; the **Horse of the Year Show** in Oct (*held at Wembley, London*); and the **International Show Jumping Championships** (*held at Olympia, London*) in Dec. General inquiries to **British Show Jumping Association** (*35 Belgrave Sq., London SW1 8QB* ☎ *(01) 235–1066*). Major three-day events are held at **Badminton House** (*Badminton, Avon GL9 1DF* ☎ *(045421) 272*) in Apr and **Burghley House** (*Burghley, Stamford, Lincs PE9 2LH* ☎ *(0780) 52131*) in Sept.

Football (soccer)
'Football' normally means Association Football, or colloquially 'soccer.' The principal domestic professional football fixture is the Football Association Cup Final played in May at London's **Wembley Stadium** (*Empire Way, Wembley, Middlesex HA9 0DW* ☎ *(01) 902–1234*). The **Football Association** (*16 Lancaster Gate, London W2 3LW* ☎ *(01) 262–4542*) promotes the game at all levels.

Horse racing
The two principal forms are flat racing and steeplechasing (over fences), the latter often called National Hunt. The best-known flat race is the **Derby** (*Epsom, Surrey, first Wed in June*), one

event of a colorful and popular meet known for its fairs, gypsies and large crowd. The best-known National Hunt race is the **Grand National** (*Aintree, Liverpool, Sat in late Mar or early Apr*), a race world-famous for its challenging fences, but whose future may be in doubt. The most fashionable meet, attended by the Queen, is **Royal Ascot** (*Berkshire, four days in June*). Amateur, cross-country and point-to-point meets, organized by the various hunts, are another form of racing. General inquiries to **Racing Information Bureau** (*Winkfield Rd., Ascot, Berks SL5 7HX* ☎ *(0990) 25912*).

Polo
Near London, visitors can go to see the games played in the fine setting of Windsor Great Park. General inquiries to **Hurlingham Polo Association** (*Ambersham Farm, Ambersham, Midhurst, Sussex GU29 0BX* ☎ *(07985) 277*).

Rowing
Major rowing events include the **Boat Race** (*Mar or Apr*), when teams from Oxford and Cambridge Universities row up the Thames from Putney to Mortlake, and **Henley Royal Regatta** (*June or July*), international rowing championships which are a major social occasion. For further information contact the **Amateur Rowing Association** (*6 Lower Mall, London W6 9DJ* ☎ *(01) 748-3632*).

Rugby
This essentially British game comes in two forms: Rugby Union, which is amateur and has 15 players on each side, and Rugby League, a professional 13-a-side game, played mainly in the north of England. For the former, **Twickenham** (*SW London*) and **Cardiff Arms Park** (*central Cardiff*) are the principal grounds for major matches, although it is not easy to obtain tickets as these are normally allocated to clubs. General inquiries to **Rugby Football Union** (*Rugby Rd., Twickenham, Middlesex TW2 7RQ* ☎ *(01) 892-8161*); **Welsh Rugby Football Union** (*National Ground, Cardiff Arms Park, Cardiff CR1 1JL* ☎ *(0222) 390111*); **Rugby Football League** (*180 Chapeltown Rd., Leeds LS7 4HT* ☎ *(0532) 624637*).

Tennis
The world-famous Wimbledon championships are held in late June and early July. Although a few Centre Court and No.1 Court seats can be bought at the gate, the vast majority are sold by ballot months in advance. Entry to the grounds is by payment at the gate, beyond which there is free access to all the outside courts and limited standing room for the major courts. Inquiries to **All England Lawn Tennis and Croquet Club** (*Church Rd., Wimbledon, London SW19 5AE* ☎ *(01) 946-2244*). For general information on all tournaments: **Lawn Tennis Association** (*Barons Court, West Kensington, London W14 9EG* ☎ *(01) 385-2366*).

Participatory activities
The choice of activities, whether as part of a vacation or as its prime purpose, is huge and only the most popular fields can be indicated here. Two booklets, *Activity and Hobby Holidays*, published by the English Tourist Board, and *Activity and Special Interest Holidays*, published by the Wales Tourist Board, list useful addresses.

Angling
There are various options: to join a club, to buy a license for a particular stretch of water, to stay at a fishing hotel, or simply to put out to sea. Among organizations that can advise are the

Sports and activities

National Anglers' Council (*11 Cowgate, Peterborough, Cambs PE1 1LZ* (☎ *(0733) 54084*); the **National Federation of Anglers** (*Halliday House, 2 Wilson St., Derby DE1 1PG* ☎ *(0332) 362000*) for river angling; and the **National Federation of Sea Anglers** (*26 Downsview Crescent, Uckfield, Sussex TN22 1UB* ☎ *(0825) 3589*).

Camping

The rule is either to choose a recognized site or to seek out the owner of the land and ask permission. Tourist boards, local information offices and the **Forestry Commission** (*231 Corstoporphine Rd., Edinburgh EH12 7AT* (☎ *(031) 334–0303*), which has particularly attractive locations, provide lists of sites. For rental firms specializing in campers or camping equipment, see the telephone directory Yellow Pages. The **Camping Club of Great Britain** (*11 Lower Grosvenor Pl., London SW1W 0EY* ☎ *(01) 828–1012*) and the **Caravan Club** (*East Grinstead House, London Rd., East Grinstead, West Sussex RH19 1UA* ☎ *(0342) 26944*) list approved sites. Many of these sites are for club members only but temporary membership is available for the Camping Club, while those holding an international camping carnet may use Caravan Club sites.

Canoeing

A sport that is on the whole placid in England but can be more adventurous on the white waters of Wales. General inquiries to **British Canoe Union** (*Flexel House, 45–47 High St., Addlestone, Weybridge, Surrey KT15 1JV* ☎ *(0932) 41341*); **Welsh Canoeing Association** (*Pen-y-Bont, Corwen, Clwyd LL21 0RA* ☎ *(0490) 2345*).

Caving

An activity for which there are opportunities in many parts of England and Wales. Specialist center: **Whernside Cave and Fell Centre** (*Dent, Sedbergh, Cumbria LA10 5RE* ☎ *(05875) 213*).

Cycling

General inquiries to **British Cycling Federation** (*16 Upper Woburn Pl., London WC1H 0QE* ☎ *(01) 387–9320*); **Welsh Cycling Union** (*93 Wentwood View, Caldicot, Gwent NP6 4QH* ☎ *(0291) 422136*).

Field sports

This term embraces angling, hunting and shooting. General inquiries to **British Field Sports Society** (*59 Kennington Rd., London SE1 7PZ* ☎ *(01) 928–4742*).

Field studies

A term with a wide embrace including such activities as bird and animal watching, helping in conservation or archeological work, studying geology or natural history, and much else. For addresses see the tourist boards' publications referred to above.

Gardens

Several gardens open to the public are listed in the *A–Z*, but many hundreds of others are opened to benefit charity. For details contact **Gardener's Sunday Organisation** (*White Witches, 8 Mapstone Close, Glastonbury, Somerset BA6 8EY* ☎ *(0458) 33119*); **National Gardens Scheme** (*57 Lower Belgrave St., London SW1W 0LR* ☎ *(01) 730–0359*).

Gliding

Inquiries to **British Gliding Association Ltd** (*Kimberley House, Vaughan Way, Leicester LE1 4SG* ☎ *(0533) 531051*).

Golf

Many of the best courses belong to clubs which normally

require membership but sometimes allow visitors to play on payment of a fee. Several hotels offer golfing vacations using either their own or nearby courses, while there are also municipal courses at which equipment can be rented and a game enjoyed for a fee. Inquiries to **English Golf Union** (*12a Denmark St., Wokingham, Berks RG11 2BE* ☎ *(0734) 781952*); **Welsh Golfing Union** (*2 Isfryn, Burry Port, Dyfed SA16 0BY* ☎ *(05546) 2595*).

Hang gliding
Inquiries to **British Hang Gliding Association** (*167a Cheddon Rd., Taunton, Somerset TA2 7AH* ☎ *(0823) 88140*).

Inland waterways
Tourist offices provide lists of firms from which boats can be rented. General inquiries to **British Waterways Board** (*Melbury House, Melbury Terrace, London NW1 6JX* ☎ *(01) 262–6711*).

Mountaineering and rock climbing
Snowdonia, in Wales, offers the best opportunities for any sophisticated pursuit of this activity. Inquiries to **British Mountaineering Council** (*Crawford House, Precinct Centre, Booth St. East, Manchester M13 9RZ* ☎ *(061) 273–5835*); **National Centre for Mountain Activities** (*Plas-y-Brenin, Capel Curig, Betws-y-Coed, Gwynedd LL24 0ET* ☎ *(06904) 214*).

Pony trekking and riding
The opportunities are many and varied, ranging from riding instruction, available in most counties, to pony trekking in the more remote regions. Descriptive lists of approved centers are included in the tourist boards' booklets referred to above as well as in a special Wales Tourist Board publication. For further information contact **Ponies of Britain** (*Ascot Race Course, Ascot, Berks SL5 7JN* ☎ *(0990) 26925*).

Railways
Both England and Wales have plenty to offer the steam railway enthusiast. Inquiries to **Association of Railway Preservation Societies Ltd** (*Sheringham Station, Norfolk NR26 8RA* ☎ *(0263) 822045*).

Sailing
Most of the many clubs around the coast and inland welcome visitors and provide temporary membership for a reasonable fee. The tourist boards' booklets mentioned above list establishments offering sailing vacations with or without instruction. Inquiries to **Royal Yachting Association** (*Victoria Way, Woking, Surrey GU21 1EQ* ☎ *(04862) 5022*), which issues a list of recognized centers for practical courses; **Welsh Yachting Association** (*86 Sketty Rd., Swansea, West Glam SA2 0JZ* ☎ *(0792) 202699*. -

Surfing
This sport is most popular along Cornwall's N coast. Inquiries to **British Surfing Association** (*Room G5, Burrows Chambers, East Burrows Rd., Swansea SA1 1RF* ☎ *(0792) 461476*).

Tennis
Both England and Wales abound in clubs, and there are also many hotels (especially country house and resort hotels) which have their own courts. There are also municipal courts in larger towns and resorts.

Walking
Best in the National Parks and around the coast, but both England and Wales are rich in public footpaths and bridlepaths. Inquiries to **Ramblers Association** (*1–5 Wandsworth Rd., London SW8 2LJ* ☎ *(01) 582–6826*).

Excursions

The Channel Islands

How to get there Daily scheduled flights to Jersey and Guernsey (with links to Alderney) from several mainland British airports. By sea, the main routes to Guernsey and Jersey are those of the Sealink car and passenger ferries out of Portsmouth and Weymouth. Additionally there are inter-island boat and hydrofoil services connecting the larger islands and Alderney, Herm and Sark, while the islands are also linked by both air and sea with several points in France.

Getting around If you bring your own car – and remember, no cars are allowed on Sark or Herm and it is not really practicable to take one to Alderney – then you will need a driver's license, national identity sticker and registration and insurance documents. But transportation rental facilities are well developed throughout the islands, enabling visitors to choose between a car, a scooter or a bicycle, and there are also good bus networks.

Language and currency The language of the islands is English, although French is widely spoken. The currency is the same as in mainland Britain, although with the added interest of local notes and coins which are not accepted back in England.

Of several reasons for visiting these islands, about 80 miles (128km) from England's s coast, three stand out. The climate is sunnier and milder than in England and Wales; being close to France they enjoy a continental atmosphere with many French names and a tradition of French cuisine; and, blessed with low taxes, they can be a shoppers' paradise. But go easy on the shopping, because to HM Customs the islands are foreign parts. In fact the islands are a constitutional curiosity, all that survives under the English Crown of William the Conqueror's duchy of Normandy. Administratively they are divided into the Bailiwick of **Jersey** and the Bailiwick of **Guernsey**, which includes the smaller islands of **Alderney, Herm** and **Sark**. Although Britain carries some responsibilities, in all local matters these bailiwicks are self-governing.

Beyond those suggested above, the principal attractions are coastal scenery, beaches, flowers and, on Guernsey and Jersey, some interesting prehistoric sites.

Events On second Thurs in Aug in Jersey, and on third Thurs in Aug in Guernsey, Battle of Flowers. Competitors decorate their floats and parade through the streets, but no longer throw flowers at each other after the judging.

Bailiwick of Guernsey

i For written inquiries and accommodations list: States of Guernsey Tourist Committee, P.O. Box 23, States Office, St Peter Port. For personal inquiries: Crown Pier, St Peter Port ☎ (0481) 23552.

Greenhouses, walled little fields, flowers and tomato plants, sheltered winding lanes, breezy clifftops, beaches – these are just some of the landscape features of the island of Guernsey. **St Peter Port** is the capital, climbing steeply above its harbor to scatter its stone buildings and narrow, sometimes cobbled, streets around the hills. Here **Castle Cornet**, built in the 13thC to guard the harbor approach, is now home to several small museums, while in the town are the **Guernsey Museum and Art Gallery**, the **Beausejour Leisure Centre** in which to while away a rainy day, and **Hauteville House**, home of Victor Hugo between 1856–70 and filled with the antiques he collected.

There is also much to be seen around the island, notably the shell of medieval **Vale Castle**; for those interested in the German occupation during World War II, there are **fortifications**, an **Occupation Museum** and the extraordinary **Underground Hospital**; for horticulturists, a **Tomato Centre and Museum**; and, above all, a number of prehistoric sites.

Alderney (*i States Office* ☎ *(048182) 2994*) is 5 miles (8km) N of Guernsey. With low-lying land and sandy beaches to the N, and rugged cliffs to the S, this is an island under 4 miles (6.5km) in length and about 1 mile (1.5km) across. Quiet roads, lanes and beaches are lure enough here, but for those who demand sights, there are daunting coastal defenses, the **Museum of the Alderney Society**, and even a railway first opened as a quarry line in 1847.

Herm, 2 miles (3km) E of Guernsey's St Peter Port, has one hotel, one pub, one shop, one farm and one church. Stand in the center, and it will be just about half a mile (1km) to any point on the shore, the N half of which offers fine beaches, including **Shell Beach** famed for its many small shells.

Sark, some 6 miles (9.5km) E of St Peter Port (although the crossing is longer because the harbor is on the E side), is the most rugged of the Channel Islands. It stretches about 3½ miles (6km) from N to S and comprises two peninsulas running N and S from the spectacular, narrow **La Coupée** isthmus, crossed by a ribbon of road some 300ft (91m) above the sea. Visitors normally arrive at Maseline. Those who are staying overnight are taken by tractor or horse-drawn carriage to their hotels. Others can make their way up to the plateau (about 20mins' climb) to spend the day as time and inclination dictate, perhaps S to La Coupée or N to the 16th–18thC **Seigneurie**, home of the Seigneur, a lordship granted by Elizabeth I.

Bailiwick of Jersey

i For inquiries and accommodations list: States Tourism Committee, Weighbridge, St Helier ☎ (0534) 78000 ☎4192223.

Some 9 miles (14.5km) from E to W and 6 miles (9.5km) from N to S, Jersey is the largest of the Channel Islands and the one with the most to offer: splendid beaches, prehistoric monuments, medieval castles and more recent defenses, Norman churches, and museums. The capital and port is **St Helier** on the S coast, a bustling place with some pleasing 18th–19thC buildings. Perhaps the most popular attraction here is the 16th–17thC **Elizabeth Castle**, not in fact a part of the town but out in St Aubin's Bay; reached at low water by causeway, or otherwise by ferry, it houses the **Museum of the Jersey Militia** and an **exhibition center** which includes material on the German occupation. Within the town there are the **Jersey Museum** and the vast early 19thC fortifications of **Fort Regent**, which now embrace one of Europe's most modern and comprehensive leisure and sports complexes.

The island's N coast is rugged, but the other three shores consist almost entirely of great scooped bays bordered by magnificent beaches. **St Ouen's** (4 miles/6.5km long) lines virtually the entire W coast; **St Brelade's**, **St Aubin's** and **St Clement's** form the S coast, the arcs of **St Catherine's** and **Grouville** the E coast. These last two are separated by a small headland on which sits the massive pile of **Mont Orgueil**

Castle, a fortified site since at least Iron Age times although what is seen today is largely medieval.

Jersey's other castles are **St Aubin's Fort** (in origin Tudor, but rebuilt in the 18thC), offshore in western St Aubin's Bay, and 14thC **Grosnez** perched atop the precipitous cliffs of the island's NW tip. But castles are not the only links with medieval days. The churches of most of Jersey's 12 parishes are Norman or earlier in origin. Among these are **St Peter's**; **St Brelade's**, near which the little **Fisherman's Chapel** is a Celtic survival with 6thC walls; and **St Lawrence Church**, from which it is only a short distance to the grim **German Underground Hospital**. Another church of a very different kind is that of **St Matthew**, near Millbrook, known for its elegant Lalique glass.

Jersey has several prehistoric monuments but by far the most renowned is **La Hougue Bie**, a Neolithic grave complete with forecourt, chambers and cells. Two miles (3km) to the N **Jersey Zoo**, established by the author Gerald Durrell, contains many endangered species.

The Isle of Man

i *For inquiries and accommodations booklet: Isle of Man Tourist Board, 13 Victoria St., Douglas* ☎ *(0624) 4323, or Isle of Man Information Centre, 4 Bouverie St., London EC4 8AB* ☎ *(01) 353–5272.*

How to get there By air, from London and several other British airports. By sea, car ferry services from Liverpool, Fleetwood and Heysham. Some services are summer only.

Getting around Many visitors bring their own cars (driver's license, registration and insurance papers are required). For others there are several car rental firms, a good bus network, and the island's varied vintage transportation – the electric tram between Douglas and Ramsey, the electric mountain railway up Snaefell from Laxey, a Victorian steam train system between Douglas and Port Erin, and horse-drawn trams along Douglas' promenade.

Language and currency The island's language is English. The currency is the same as in mainland Britain, although the Isle of Man issues its own notes and coins which are not accepted on the mainland.

The area of the Isle of Man is 237sq. miles (614sq.km). It lies halfway between England and Northern Ireland and, following some four centuries of Norse rule, it has enjoyed constitutional independence under the English Crown since the early 14thC.

Douglas, the capital, is renowned for its entertainment; the term embraces a casino, huge dance halls, a beautifully restored theater, many restaurants and the famed **Summerland Leisure Centre**. And all this in a town which is otherwise of almost prim Victorian ambience, so ordered and neat that it has several times won awards.

Yet Douglas is in a class of its own on this island of contrasts. Around the coast charming and calmer resorts welcome the less demanding visitor; away from these the escapist can find unspoiled countryside of mountain and fell, wooded glens, cliff walks and rolling fields; and, perhaps greatest contrast of all, the ancient **Tynwald** mound, site for over 1,000yrs of the annual proclamation of the island's laws, stands close to the road along which thunder the modern world's fastest motorcycles as they take part in the TT Races in early June.

There is much to see here too, including several museums, medieval castles at **Castletown** and **Peel**, a wildlife park at **Ballaugh** and a towering water-wheel at **Laxey**. From the distant past there survive a megalithic chambered cairn, also near Laxey, and a wealth of early Christian crosses in the island's churches.

The Isles of Scilly
i *Town Hall, St Mary's* ☎ *(0720) 22536. For accommodations booklet, write to British Tourist Information Centre, 64 St James's St., London SW1A 1NF* ☎ *(01) 499–9325.*
How to get there By air, the British Airways helicopter service operates from Penzance to St Mary's. By sea, Isles of Scilly Steamship Co. ferry from Penzance to St Mary's.
Getting around The islands can be explored by bus, taxi or bicycle, or on foot, and there are motor launch services between the principal islands. In summer, motor launches go also to the seal colony on the Western Rocks and to the Bishop's Rock lighthouse.

Some 28 miles (45km) SW of Land's End, but still a part of the county of Cornwall, the low-lying Scillies archipelago of more than 100 islands, islets and rocks awaits the visitor in search of somewhere remote, different and even romantic, for tradition insists that this was King Arthur's fabled Lyonesse.

Only five of the islands – **St Mary's**, **Tresco**, **St Martin's**, **St Agnes** and **Bryher** – are inhabited. St Mary's is the largest, although it is only 2 miles (3km) across. All these islands have sandy beaches and are remarkable for their flowers. Sights include **St Mary's Museum** and **Tresco Abbey** with its sub-tropical gardens, the 13thC ruins of a Benedictine priory, and a museum of figureheads from ships wrecked on the Scillies. There are also prehistoric remains, best on St Martin's and St Agnes.

A glimpse of Scotland
i *Scottish Tourist Board, 23 Ravelston Terrace, Edinburgh EH4 3EU (no telephone inquiries), or 5 Pall Mall East, London SW1Y 5BL* ☎ *(01) 930–8661.*
Scotland is a large country of enormous interest and splendid scenery, a place worthy of more than just an excursion. Nevertheless, visitors to England's northern counties can easily slip across the border to enjoy a glimpse of the Lowlands. This is glorious countryside – wooded, pastoral and bare high moor – and within about 20 miles (32km) of the border there is much to see. Here, for instance, are the great ruined abbeys of **Dryburgh**, **Jedburgh**, **Kelso** and **Melrose**; stately homes such as **Mellerstain**, **Floors** and Sir Walter Scott's **Abbotsford**; the grim Borders stronghold of **Hermitage**; and **Gretna** of runaway marriage fame. This is tweed and knitwear country, too, with many mills offering attractive goods at often surprisingly reasonable prices.

Nor is **Edinburgh** much farther. With famous Princes St. and its gardens below the spectacular Castle Rock, this is not only one of Europe's most visually thrilling cities but also one steeped in history. Distinguished museums and art galleries, a world-famous festival (Aug-Sept), the plush and glitter of Victorian pubs and superb shops are just a few of the other attractions of Scotland's dignified yet exciting capital.

Index and gazetteer

Numerals in ordinary type indicate a mention; numerals in bold type indicate a main entry. Places of interest, towns and areas are indexed separately and under the relevant county. Map references refer to the maps at the end of the book. Page numbers in italics denote an illustration.

Index and gazetteer

Index and gazetteer

Index and gazetteer

Index and gazetteer

Michael Jackson's hotels and restaurants

The following hotels and restaurants, and all those recommended in *London*, were contributed by Michael Jackson.

ENGLAND AND WALES

1

2-16 ENGLAND AND WALES

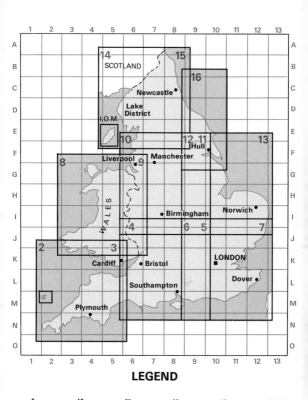

A B C D E F G H I J K L M N O

14 SCOTLAND
15
16
Newcastle
Lake District
I.O.M.
10
12 11 13
8 Liverpool 9 Manchester Hull
WALES
Birmingham Norwich
4 6 5 7
2 3
Cardiff Bristol LONDON
Southampton Dover
Plymouth

LEGEND

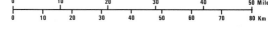

0   10   20   30   40   50 Miles
0   10   20   30   40   50   60   70   80 Km

=O= Superhighway (with
     access point)

▬ Main Through Route

▬ Other 'A' Class Roads

─ 'B' Class & Other Roads

A 60 Road Number

─ ─ ─ Ferry

▬ Inter-City Railway

✈ Major Airport

▨ National Boundary

𝒊 National Park Information
   Center

🏛 Historic House

♜ Castle

∴ Ancient Site, Ruin

⛪ Church, Abbey

♈ Seaside Resort

■ Other Place of Interest

•2928 Heights in Feet

6 ▶ Adjoining Page No.

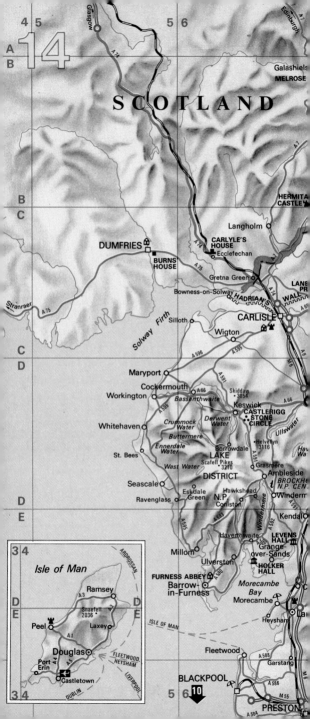

B

Glasgow

Edinburgh

Galashiels

MELROSE

S C O T L A N D

HERMITA CASTLE

B

C

Langholm

CARLYLE'S HOUSE

DUMFRIES

Ecclefechan

BURNS HOUSE

Gretna Green

LANE PR

Bowness-on-Solway

HADRIAN'S

WALL

Stranraer

Solway Firth

Silloth

CARLISLE

Wigton

C

D

Maryport

Cockermouth

Skiddaw
· 3054

Workington

Bassenthwaite

Keswick

CASTLERIGG STONE CIRCLE

Crummock Water

Derwent Water

Ullswater

Whitehaven

Buttermere

Helvellyn
3116

Hav
Wa

Ennerdale Water

Borrowdale

LAKE

St. Bees

Scafell Pikes
·3210

Wast Water

Grasmere

Ambleside

Seascale

DISTRICT

BROCKH
N.P. CEN.

Hawkshead

Eskdale
Green

N.P.

Winderm

Ravenglass

Coniston

D

Kendal

E

Haverthwaite

LEVENS HALL

Millom

Ulverston

Grange-over-Sands

HOLKER HALL

FURNESS ABBEY

Morecambe Bay

Barrow-in-Furness

Morecambe

La

Heysham

Fleetwood

ISLE OF MAN

BLACKPOOL

5 6 **10**

Garstang

PRESTON

M 55

A 584

A 586

ARDROSSAN

Isle of Man

Ramsey

Snaefell
2036

Peel

Laxey

D

E

ISLE OF MAN

Port
Erin

Douglas

FLEETWOOD,
HEYSHAM

Castletown

LIVERPOOL

DUBLIN

NORTH SEA

SUNDERLAND
C
○ Seaham

D
○ Peterlee
A 19
15

□ **HARTLEPOOL**
A 689

STOCKTON-ON-TEES ○ Redcar
A 19
MIDDLESBROUGH
A 171   A 174   ○ Staithes

A 19   *CLEVELAND HILLS* ○ Whitby
A 171
○ Danby
Grosmont

D
CLEVELAND
MOUNT GRACE PRIORY
○ Goathland
A 171

NORTH YORKS MOORS
RIEVAULX ABBEY   Fadmoor   **N.P.**
A 170   A 169   ○ Scarborough
Thirsk   Helmsley
A 170   ○ Pickering
BYLAND ABBEY
○ Filey

Ure
CASTLE HOWARD   ○ Malton
A 64

A 165

YORKSHIRE WOLDS

Ouse

BENINGBROUGH HALL
A 64   A 166   *Flamborough H.*
A 59   ○ Bridlington

E
YORK
A 166   ○ Great Driffield

F
A 64   A 163   A 164   ○ Hornsea
A 19
A 1079   Market Weighton
A 163   A 614   ○ Beverley
Selby □
A 1   A 63   M 62   A 164   A 165
A 63   **HULL**   ○ Wither

○ Goole   *R. Humber*
Pontefract ○
M 62   ○ Barton-upon-Humber

A 1   A 19   ○ Thorne
M 180   **GRIMSBY**

F
□ **DONCASTER**   Scunthorpe
A 18   ○ Cleethorpes
Don   M 180   A 18

G
CONISBROUGH   Brigg
A 1(M)   Trent   *LINCOLN*   A 46
A 15   A 16   **12**

11
A 631   Gainsborough   A 631   ○ Market Rasen
A 631